NOT A DRESS REHEARSAL

War, Military, Government Service - A 60-Year Journey

The Story of my Life

Lieutenant Colonel (Ret'd) Leonard D. Dent, OMM, CD

Thank you for your support of Cystic Fibrosis Research. I hope you enjoy this book

Len Dent

Apr 12, 2019

Book cover design by Judith Rostenne.
Cover photo by WO William (Bill) Cole

Published by LEONARD DENT
ISBN -1-387-978-86598-7

Granddaughter Stephanie was nine when I started this book just over 20 years ago. She had been battling Cystic Fibrosis since birth at which point her life expectancy was 18. As this book goes to print, she has just turned 30, is married with two beautiful twin daughters and works as a psychiatric nurse in Ft McMurray. But her fight with this horrible disease continues.

I pledged at the start to take any income that will come from the sale of this book and donate it to Cystic Fibrosis Canada. And so I will.

ACKNOWLEDGEMENTS

When first considering writing this book in the 1990s, I had lunch with a publisher at the National Press Club who gave me advice on how to proceed. He told me simply to just write the book, not to worry about any corrections and not to reread what I had written before I finished it. Just write it! And so I did . But I didn't give it the highest priority over the next 20 years.

I soon realized how important it would be to have highly qualified people to go through the book. And so I enlisted a number of colleagues with whom I had worked and others who without their help this book would not have been possible.

My cousin Paul Prechner, who had a career as a professional proof reader, provided helpful comments regarding the family and the content of the book.

Major General David Wightman, who was the Commander of the Canadian Forces in Europe during my tour there, provided insightful input for the chapter concerning my time in Lahr.

Col Ralph Coleman, with whom I had served in DND Information Services for many years, read the material on Defence and made many helpful suggestions.

The chapter on my work at the Privy Council Office needed careful scrutiny. I am so grateful that Dan Gagnier, Mary Gusella, Bob Parkins and Greg Gertz took the time to read this chapter and provide guidance.

I am particularly pleased that retired Senator Lowell Murray, who had served as the Chairman of the Cabinet Committee on Communications during my time at PCO, agreed to read this chapter and indeed did go through the entire book. His observations and suggestions, particularly concerning my work at PCO, provided great comfort that my recollections were accurate.

My neighbour Judith Rostenne who has worked as an editor, went through the book several times making valuable suggestions and corrections. Judith provided invaluable help in the design of the front and back covers.

I would also like to thank Tim Bacon, David Rostenne and Allan Nodelman for their help and suggestions for the production of the book.

Another friend and neighbour Guy Thatcher, who is a bestselling author, took the time to go through the almost final copy to find errors and omissions.

Allan Bacon has been a tremendous source of encouragement for the past number of years. Not only has he helped in my recollections of some of the events in which he and I were involved at Veterans Affairs, but he has also gone through the entire book at various stages on at least three occasions providing most helpful suggestions and necessary corrections.

Of course this book would not have been possible without the encouragement, help and sacrifice of my dear wife Shirlie. It was she who, more than 20 years ago, told me I had to write this book. It was she who was also there to help me remember some of the details. And it was she who insisted that she would take some of my responsibilities around the house so that I could spend the time to, "write my book."

FOREWORD

The genesis of this book is based on the fact that I can and like to tell stories. For years, particularly as I got older, I have taken any realistic opportunity to recount my experiences. And indeed, I have been blessed in that my life has taken me all over the world and allowed me to be in situations and to meet people that most individuals would never get to experience. An exposure to war in my early years, living and travelling in a number of countries around the world, and working with the Canadian Forces, Allied Forces, the United Nations and NATO, has provided a wealth of opportunity.

In telling these stories, often I have been encouraged to put them down in the form of a book. My wife Shirlie continually encouraged me to write this book, telling me that she never really learned anything about her father's life and that this would be an excellent record for our children, grandchildren, etc.

In 1995 I selected the title of the book and wrote the names of 21 chapters to form a framework for what I would write. Unfortunately work and many volunteer jobs always seemed to be given more priority than this. But gradually I began to realize that if I didn't write it soon, I just might not ever have the opportunity. It has now been given more priority.

Much of what I have written is based on my memory and recollections of experiences and events in my life. Where possible, I have referred to documents, papers, letters and memorabilia saved through my life, particularly when working with the military and government. I have also, when possible, spoken to those who might be able to help in this work. In the first half of the 2000s, Shirlie and I met with family members in Canada; Las Vegas and Nevada in the USA; Sydney and Melbourne in Australia; and London, Manchester, and Birmingham in the UK. They all told me stories and provided information that has helped me to put this work together.

I have tried to ensure that the writing is factually correct. When necessary, I have checked the Internet for historical background often using Wikipedia as a reference. As to my accounts, I can only state that they are written as best as I can remember them. No doubt there might be an occasion when someone, somewhere, will recall the details of events or incidents in a different manner. That might be because my sense of what happened has become coloured over time, or perhaps that someone's recollections have also been changed from what really happened.

Having said the foregoing, I have written this book with the principal aim of trying to leave a snapshot of what the world was like around me as I grew up, worked and travelled, and a little of the history which might be of interest regarding some of the areas in which I was involved.

Given that I have worked with so many people in many areas at high levels, including the military and government both in Canada and abroad, there, of course, have been incidents involving individuals that would perhaps provide some titillating stories and draw considerable interest. I have avoided including these, since it is not my intention to try to expose or embarrass anyone in any way. If for any reason I have done this anywhere in this book, I apologize in advance.

I have learned a lot in my 75+ years and have taken the liberty of ending this account with a number of the lessons that I have learned and that have helped me lead a wonderful, happy, and in my mind at least, a very successful life. If these lessons can be of any value to anyone reading them, then I am thankful that I have been able to, perhaps, contribute in some small way to someone else's happiness.

TABLE OF CONTENTS

"We make a living by what we get,
but we make a life by what we give."

Winston Churchill

"What lies behind us and what lies before us are small matters
compared to what lies within us."

Ralph Waldo Emerson

CHAPTER 1 - TOO DAMN CLOSE

LEDRA PALACE HOTEL, NICOSIA, CYPRUS – AUGUST 1974

Zing!

"Shit... that's too damn close."

I'm not exactly sure, on reflection, that's what I yelled, or thought, as I raced out of my hotel room in the Ledra Palace. But I've thought many times since, that the difference between my living and dying came down to a bullet hitting the width of a two-inch railing.

I had been on the balcony of my hotel room watching Turkish tanks rumbling across the plains towards the capital city of Nicosia. It was 5:05 am and already over 100°F in the room. My room was in a part of the hotel undergoing renovation. The air-conditioning wasn't yet installed. There was no running water in the bathroom. Someone had used the toilet before I moved in a week ago. The smell from the refuse penetrated throughout the air and into my clothes.

As I raced from the room, I could hear the sound of bullets continuing to thud into the walls of my third story room. Someone standing just outside the hotel gardens had decided that a UN officer would be a good target. To this day I don't know who was shooting at me! The hotel was on the 'Green line' dividing the Greek Cypriots and Turkish Cypriots. We were in the middle.

We were Canadian peacekeepers trying to ensure that Greek Cypriots and Turkish Cypriots led by invading Turkish troops didn't start a war, which could also involve Greece and Turkey. This was a war that could rip the island nation apart, a war that could possibly cause great harm to the North Atlantic Treaty Organization (NATO), of which both countries were members.

Why would anyone want to fight over this island? Well, first Cyprus is strategically located as the most easterly island in the Mediterranean, 40 miles from Turkey, 60 miles from Syria, 250 miles from Egypt and 300 miles from the Greek islands. It has become known in recent years as the listening post of the Middle East.

Second, copper was discovered on the island about 2,500 BC. The wealth derived from the copper mines and its location made it a much sought after prize of the great powers of the Middle East.

From the XIV century BC onwards, Cyprus was successively colonized, dominated or ruled by Greeks, Phoenicians, Assyrians, Egyptians, Persians, the Ptolemies of Egypt, Rome, Byzantium, the Frankish Kings, the Venetians, Genoese, Turks and finally until 1960, the British.

1

Cyprus came under Turkish rule in 1571 when the island was invaded and taken away from the Venetians. It remained so until 1878 when Russian encroachments on the Ottoman Empire began to alarm Britain as well as Turkey. Thus, in 1878, a defensive alliance between Britain and Turkey led to an agreement by Turkey that Britain should occupy Cyprus.

Following the entry of Turkey into the Great War in 1914 on the side of the Germans, Britain formally annexed Cyprus. In the following year, the island was offered to Greece if she would enter the war with the Allies. Greece declined. In 1925, Cyprus was given the status of a crown colony. Serious riots broke out in 1931 when Greek Cypriots demanded *enosis* or union with Greece. But suspected leaders were deported and the movement was suppressed for the time being.

After the Second World War, the *enosis* movement became more vocal. In 1954, Greece claimed self-determination for Cyprus at the United Nations. Rioting and armed insurrection broke out on the island. Finally, in February 1959, meetings in Zurich and London, between Britain, Greece and Turkey, and including both Greek Cypriot and Turkish Cypriot representatives, led to an agreement establishing an independent Republic of Cyprus.

The Republic came into being on August 16, 1960 with a Greek Cypriot President and a Turkish Cypriot Vice President, and a House of Representatives elected from the two main communities.

Of the approximately 600,000 population, 78% were Greek Cypriots and 18% Turkish Cypriots. The remainder included various minorities. Britain retained certain areas as sovereign base areas.

However, *enosis* supporters were not satisfied and unrest continued on the island. In 1963, clashes broke out between the Turkish and Greek Cypriots. The British on the island were able to achieve an uneasy truce by establishing a 'green line', which divided the two groups. But in 1964, fighting broke out and President (Archbishop) Makarios called for UN peacekeepers.

The Canadian aircraft carrier HMCS Bonaventure arrived at Famagusta in October 1964 with the first of 1,000 Canadians troops. They were part of a 7,000 UN peacekeeping force charged with the responsibility of keeping the Turkish and Greek Cypriots apart. It was to be the start of a 29-year duty for the Canadian Forces.

Many of us who served on the island saw the beauty of it, as well as the friendliness and humanness of both the Turkish and Greek Cypriots. But as the years passed, following the early 1960s, a life of peace and tranquility was being replaced by one of mistrust, misunderstanding and fear.

What could be so important that would destroy a virtual 'Garden of Eden'? To make children and former neighbours and their children hate each other? Was it all about politics, power, and control?

2

In retrospect, this inability to get along with each other is something that I have seen throughout my lifetime, whether it is in small communities, large cities or in countries around the world. How do we cope in a world where people treat each other in such a manner? What is the future for such a world?

From 1964 to 1974, there were isolated incidents on the island, which caused concern for the peacekeepers and the UN. But in July 1974, the Turkish government decided to flex its muscles and take control of more of the island, which they thought was 'rightfully theirs'. At this point, the UN force had been reduced to approximately 3,000 troops, including 575 from the Canadian Airborne Regiment.

Turkish troops landed on Cyprus, causing residents to flee. The Turkish Air Force quickly destroyed the Nicosia airport. There was no threat from the Greek air force, which was too far away. The Turks had air superiority.

The UN responded by sending in more peacekeepers. Canada dispatched 500 troops - the Second Battalion from the Canadian Airborne Regiment in Edmonton. And so here we were.

When the Turkish troops first invaded the island, I had 'volunteered' as a public information officer to bring a Canadian media pool of nine to Cyprus to cover the action. I had already served a six-month tour on the island as a Canadian Public Information Officer (PIO) and had worked with some major senior players on both sides. The media were at the Hilton and I was bedded down with the troops stationed in the Ledra Palace Hotel on the 'green line.'

Running down the wide staircase of the main lobby, I could hear the voices coming from the dining room. In this room, presidents, prime ministers, other world leaders and the cream of Cyprus society had wined and dined in years gone by. It was now filled with commissioned and non-commissioned officers in full combat gear. Drinking coffee and smoking cigarettes, they were calmly discussing the shooting that was going on outside.

"Listen to that 50 calibre machine gun, nothing as sweet as that sound," someone said nonchalantly as bullets ricocheted off the outside walls of the hotel.

I realized that the sound of live fire did not faze these army guys. They were used to such noise during training exercises. In fact, I wondered if they realized that this was not a training exercise. For me, an Air Force guy, this type of experience was limited to shooting a 9 mm handgun while qualifying on the firing range, perhaps once a year. I was scared!

The CO came in, looked at the two padres and me, and told us that he wanted all 'non essentials' out of the way. We should move out now to the relative safety of Camp Maple Leaf at the airport. "The last thing I need now is to have you guys getting shot." He didn't have to tell me twice. I trusted his judgment. The evening before, he had predicted that the fighting would break out at 5:00 this morning.

3

"The cease-fire deadline is midnight," he said while casually sipping a beer at the Ledra Palace bar. "No one will agree to the terms being proposed in Geneva. So it will take the Turks about two hours to get the message back to Ankara, and then another couple of hours to decide to give the troops orders to advance towards Nicosia, and another hour for them to actually start to move. That makes it 5:00 am so be ready." He was bang on!!

I ran out the door across the hotel parking lot towards Wolseley Barracks. The Barracks across the road housed the supply and transport depots and the Officers' Mess. As I crossed the road I could hear the sound of bullets clipping through the trees over my head.

Troops in full combat gear were crouched down in make-do trenches. A sergeant looked at me: "Major, I really think you should have a flak jacket on."

"You bet! Do you have any?"

"See that truck over there?" he said with a big grin, while pointing to a three-ton truck sitting in the middle of an open field, "the back is full of them."

Leaves were floating down on my head as bullets continued to whisk through the trees. The sergeant had and 'I dare you look' in his eye. The troops watched as this little drama unfolded wondering what this 'Air Force Major' would do.

Without much thought, I dashed across the field and dove into the back of the truck. I put on a jacket, jumped out and did a 10-second, 100-yard dash back. When I arrived the sergeant was finishing a note on the back of a cigarette package. 'Received one flak jacket.' With a big smile, he handed it to me and asked for a signature.

It was 7:00 am and in the past two hours, I had twice faced the possibility of death.

But these weren't my first such experiences. I had had a number of them. Many occurred in the first six years of my life.

I was born in the East End of London, England, six weeks before Hitler invaded Poland, in 1939.

4

CHAPTER 2 - GROWING UP IN A WAR ZONE

"Here's another little bloke to help fight Jerry," said the operating room nurse. And that's how Fay Dent learned that she had a little boy.

It was July, 1939. Most English people were aware of Adolph Hitler and his ambitions. His statements to the Reichstag, in February 1938, had clearly demonstrated his resolve to reunite all Germans in a greater Reich and to expand eastwards in Europe. That speech also publicly opened his case against Czechoslovakia.

On March 13, 1938, Hitler entered Vienna and Austria fell. His next target was Czechoslovakia. Many thought that Britain should fight rather than have this happen. But Prime Minister Chamberlain was prepared to negotiate. Hitler assured him in a September meeting in Munich that he did not want to include the Czechs inside the Third Reich. Chamberlain allowed that he was not opposed to separating Sudetenland from Czechoslovakia.

Prime Minister Chamberlain met with Hitler a second time in late September, while the British Government put pressure on the Czechs to accept the transfer of part of their country. Thus, the Prime Minister returned triumphantly in October 1938 with a signed agreement between himself and the Führer. The agreement would cause the dismemberment of the Czechoslovak state but in Chamberlain's view 'prevent a war in Europe.' From the windows of his residence at 10 Downing Street, waving a copy of the document, Chamberlain shouted, "I believe it is peace in our time."

But few in England believed that this would prevent another war. Many had lived through the "War to End all Wars" which had ended just 20 short years before. They saw the signs and could sense that Hitler's appetite was greater than what had been achieved to that point. Many members of the British Cabinet wanted to rearm as quickly as possible. The crisis in Europe had identified the vast shortages in Britain's military armaments. The German government and media were highly critical of such a move by Britain, given the terms of the recent signing of the Munich pact.

However, Hitler openly stated that he would continue to construct his country's fortifications and armaments. He justified his actions by claiming that, should Churchill or Eden replace Prime Minister Chamberlain, they would start a war against Germany.

On August 23, 1939, Hitler and Stalin signed the Soviet-German non-aggression pact. Two days later the British government proclaimed a formal treaty with Poland that provided unconditional assurance to come to the aid of Poland "regardless of the causes from which a conflict might spring."

One-week later, on September 1st, German forces attacked Poland. Two days later, on September 3, Britain formally declared war against Germany.

Fay and Bill Dent had been married in the fall of 1938. Both had come from large families. Both had difficult hurdles to overcome while growing up.

Fay was the fifth of eight children born to Phillip and Sara Stein in London. She was the youngest of the three girls and wedged between two boys, Sam and Harry, which was to have a significant impact on her as she grew up.

Phillip Leonard Stein was born in St Petersburg, Russia in approximately 1880. He was the first son of Nathaniel and Natasha Stein. Nathaniel's old friend Leon Brunavitch lived with his wife and two girls of marriageable age in London. In 1900, Nathaniel asked his friend if Phillip could come to London and stay with them. The Brunavitchs owned a bakery and saw the possibility of a worker and potential son-in-law. They were quick to agree. So Phillip came to London, but didn't care for either one of the girls. Neither did he want to be a baker. A tall, blond, blue-eyed, good-looking youth, he loved to get dressed up, play the piano, and sing. In fact, on many nights he entertained at a local pub. A few pints of beer and the few shillings he was offered helped pay the rent. But it wasn't enough.

Phillip went to work in a custom boot-making store in the East End of London. The owner Richmond, his wife and daughter Sarah had fled Poland in 1895, changed their name and arrived in the relative safety of England. Sarah was 10 when they moved.

With this outgoing, happy-go-lucky Russian close by every day, Sarah soon fell helplessly in love. They were married in 1903. A year later, Celia was born. Leah, always called Lily (1905), Jack (1908), Sam (1912), Fay (1913), and Harry (1915) were added to the family. Twins were born in 1918. Both died of colic at the age of six months.

In 1914, Imperial Russia declared war on Germany and Austro-Hungary although they were in no position to do so. It brought about the destruction of the Russian army. By 1917, almost two million Russians soldiers had died and five million more were wounded. The Russian people had had enough. In April 1917, Czar Nicholas II was forced to abdicate. The Imperial Russian Empire ceased to exist. A temporary provisional government replaced it. In November 1917, the temporary government was replaced by the Bolshevik Revolution. Under the Bolshevik doctrine, as formulated by Lenin and Stalin, there was no such thing as a national Jewish identity. Lenin stated that, "The Jews in the civilized world are not a nation; they have in the main become assimilated. They are still a caste here (in Russia)." It was a very difficult place and time for Jews from White Russia.

In 1918, just after the twins were born, Phillip decided to go back to St Petersburg to try and bring his parents and brother and sister to England. By this time, the Bolsheviks had introduced edicts, which in practice were a systematic campaign against all aspects of Judaism and Jewish life. With the help of the Red Cross, Phillip was able to send letters to Sarah for about three years outlining his continuing efforts to bring his family to England.

6

But suddenly the letters stopped. He was never heard from again, nor was there ever any correspondence from his family. There is a family suspicion that he and his family were sent to Siberia. One scenario also suggested that the family was shot on a train and thrown off en route to Siberia. But no one knows!

Sarah was left in the East End of London with six young children. She had been educated in Poland and spoke Yiddish, could not write and only barely spoke any English. But she was a very strong and domineering lady and kept a very kosher household. Out of necessity, Sarah took any job she could. She acted as a mid wife. Having just lost two babies, she could serve as a wet nurse, suckling babies of wealthier mothers who were unable to nurse their babies. She took in washing, did sewing and ironing.

Celia was now 14. She quit school. With the help of the West End Jewish Girls Club, which was created by Lily Montague, a prominent Jewish benefactor, Celia was educated in office skills and found a job as a secretary. She divided her time between her work and helping her mother look after the younger children. Lily, the second oldest, quit school a year later and through the efforts of the Club also received office skills but spent the next few years helping to raise her siblings.

Life was difficult for Sarah Stein and her children in a city and country that was suffering from the impact of a World War. London was full of men who had returned from Europe following five traumatic years in conditions that went beyond imagination. Many were suffering from the aftermath of poison gas and couldn't do any hard work. Many were amputees. Those who had not been scarred physically or emotionally were trying to reclaim their youth and their lives. There were not always jobs for them. And then in 1929, the Great Depression only added to their problems.

For the Stein family, earning enough money to buy sufficient food to feed all seven was a challenge. But like many other families living in not dissimilar circumstances, it gave the children an early education in the school of hard knocks, which would help them face life successfully in their adult years.

Jack was a natural photographer and it wasn't long before he had enough experience, contacts, and money to open up his own small business. Harry began working for an electrical firm and within several years was able to open a small business which expanded in later years with stores in Paris and Copenhagen. Sam was attracted to the General Post Office and joined as a trainee and spent the next 40 years working with that organization.

Celia and Lily were both married while quite young. Fay, a 5' 5" willowy brunette, was the apple of her mother's eye. She doted on her mother, but was often treated rather harshly by Sam and Harry. They were both self-centered and resented the attention that she received from their mother. Fay did some modeling work in London as a teenager, but her main source of income was from her job at Marks and Spencer's on Oxford St. She was popular with the boys and had lots of dates. In her early twenties, she met a charming young Jewish man and they fell head over heels in love. The romance blossomed and grew stronger and seemed to be destined to result in marriage. But the parents of this young man, a relatively well-to-do couple from the west end of London, realized that the relationship was getting too serious and stepped in. After all, they couldn't have their only son, marrying a Jewish girl from a poor family from the East End who didn't even have a father. Fay's 'love of her life' was shipped to Europe for an 'extended holiday.'

Fay was devastated. So much so, that, in 1935, her mother had to put her into a psychiatric hospital for care. Both Sam and Harry rejected her. Given the era, they might have seen the stigma attached to a sister in an 'institution.'

By chance, Bill Dent had a chum who was suffering from a nervous breakdown in the same facility. Bill and Fay met in that hospital. He was understanding and kind to her and stopped to see her on every visit. And so when she was released from hospital in 1936, they continued to see each other. Fay's family wasn't particularly pleased. Following her experience, they were unimpressed that she was already looking seriously at another man. In addition, he was a Gentile. But this good-looking, soft-spoken, kind and gentle man soon overcame any opposition from the family. Sarah was particularly enamoured of Bill.

Bill, born in December 1911, was two years old when the World War 1 started. His four brothers all joined the Royal Navy and served during the war. Two of them were gunners on Admiral Jellicoe's flagship during the Battle of Jutland. Following the war, one had died of an infection picked up while in India and two had emigrated to Australia to seek their fortune as sheep farmers.

Bill had not had a particularly normal upbringing. He was the youngest of six children, five boys, and a girl. His father, Thomas, had worked as a woodworker in a London factory. But his health was fragile. In 1912, while still in his early forties, he was given a disability pension.

Thomas's disability pension, plus a little money that could be sent home from the meager navy pay check that the boys received, helped to keep the Dent household afloat. But there was no money for any extras. In 1926, Bill quit school at the age of 14 to help support at home. He had talent as an artist and with some help could have made a career in this field. However, contributing to the family's bid for existence was more important than such a career. He began working as a delivery boy in a tailoring factory named Policoffs. Working his way through various positions he stayed with this firm for the next 20 years.

Shortly after Bill started work, his father decided that he would journey to Canada to see his sister Elizabeth who was married to a farmer and lived just north of Toronto. He thought that the change of climate would help his health. He also hoped to do some work on the farm and send some money home.

Elizabeth had left London in the 1890s as a 16-year-old. A missionary and his family who were headed for China had taken her on as a nanny. Their route would take them by sea to Halifax, across Canada to Vancouver by train and then by sea to China. When they reached Toronto, the missionary decided that they could no longer afford to take 'Eliza' with them to China. They would have to go there and send for her later when there was more money. But he found her a job as a 'house girl' through an acquaintance. She now worked for the editor of the Arthur Enterprise News, an Ontario weekly newspaper. The missionary and his family went on. She never heard from them again. She learned later that the family had reportedly been murdered in China...not an unusual fate for a missionary and his family in those days.

When her boss at Arthur died suddenly, she found another similar job with Mr. Carleton, the editor of the Beeton weekly paper. Shortly after she met Francis Gowan. Francis, a widower, worked at a planing mill in the small cattle town of Creemore, Ontario, some 80 kilometers north of Toronto. He had met and married 19-year-old Anne Meredith and moved to her hometown of Beeton. She died in childbirth during their first year of marriage. Their little girl was stillborn. Frank met Eliza in Beeton in 1898 and they were married the next year. Frank decided to move onto his own land and with a small down payment was able to purchase 100 acres of land on the outskirts of Creemore.

Dent Gowan was born in 1899 but died soon after. Albert was born in 1900, and William in 1902. Three more boys were born to the Gowan's during the next 15 years but all died shortly after their birth. Carmen, born in 1920, was the last of the seven boys in the family. Francis had dearly wanted a girl to replace the one he had lost but apparently Eliza vowed she would never give him one!

It was to this farm that Thomas Dent came in 1926. He worked on the farm. But the post-war era made money scarce. Francis and Eliza were able to give him only room and board. Thomas decided to return to England.

Three years later he returned to Canada and his sister's farm. However, this time he looked for work with pay. On October 1, 1930, a neighbouring farmer, Jack Hisey, who was able to offer him $250.00 per year, hired Thomas. But his fragile health caught up with him and in June 1931 he was hospitalized. He received $155.00 for his work.

From June 1931 until August 1932, he was in and out of hospital, helped by the Gowans when possible. Transportation back and forth from the hospital, located in Collingwood some 30 kilometers away, presented a challenge. Carmen recalled that on one occasion his dad and he took the horse and sleigh during a storm and made the journey to Collingwood. They wrapped 'Uncle Tom' in buffalo blankets and started home. But the storm was so severe and the weather so cold that they had to stop every hour or so at neighbours homes to get warm. It took almost 24 hours to make the round trip

9

With no money, and continuing bad health, Tom Dent was threatened with being put into an institution for the incurable in Toronto. But the town council, who would have been responsible for paying his hospital 'maintenance' fee of $17.50 per month, decided it would be cheaper to pay his ship fare home. And so, on August 7, 1932 he boarded the SS Asconia from Montreal bound for England. He arrived home on August 16. He was able to stay at home for only 10 days before the doctor checked him into the Hackney Hospital in the east end of London. He was in and out of hospital until 1935 when he died. Meanwhile, Sarah Ann Elizabeth, Bill's mother, died on December 31, 1933. She was 64. Tom's doctors allowed him out of hospital long enough to go to the funeral.

So, at the age of 24, Bill was without parents and basically on his own. By this time his sister Mary was married and Bill moved in for room and board and to help pay expenses.

Bill and Fay were married on Oct 1, 1938. She had been able to go back to her job at Marks and Spencer's, and Bill now worked on the cutting floor at the tailoring factory. They lived in a small rented house in Hackney in the East End of London close to Policoffs.

I was born on July 23, 1939 and christened Leonard David. I always said my mother took one look at this baby and said, "If this is the best I can do, I quit." I am an only child!!

Our lives as a family, like most in England, took a dramatic turn on September 1, 1939, when Hitler threw the disguise off his intentions and invaded Poland. Two days later we were at war. For the next year, life was not really impacted for our family. There was an influx of Allied soldiers from the Commonwealth including from Canada. Amongst those was our cousin Albert, Elizabeth and Frank Gowan's first surviving child. He was stationed at Aldershot in Surrey and spent the whole war at this army base. My father was excused military call up as a result of his rheumatic heart. Albert visited us for Sunday dinner on a regular basis and life continued pretty much as normal.

The first impact for us came in August 1940. Hitler realized that the success of the plan for the invasion of Britain, nicknamed Operation Sea Lion, depended on winning air supremacy above Britain and the Channel, and securing landing sites on the southern coast. Thus, he focused on the destruction of the Royal Air Force and the country's aircraft industry. At the same time, a prime target was the city of London and in particular the port of London with its long line of docks and potential for massive shipping of materials to the continent.

The real onslaught began on August 15, 1940. German and British aircraft fought in five separate air battles. The result: the Germans lost 76 aircraft and the RAF 34. Of course the Luftwaffe had many more aircraft. In the first week of September, serious attacks were targeted against London. On September 7th, 300 German aircraft attacked the city. The Royal Air Force's Fighter Command had lost 230 pilots killed or wounded and 466 Spitfires and Hurricanes were destroyed or damaged. For ten days after September 7, there were continuous night attacks against London docks and railways centers. Many civilians living around us were killed and wounded. On September 15, the Luftwaffe made its most concentrated effort against London and attacked in daylight. Wave after wave of bombers and fighters came across the English coastline only to be met by crippled but valiant squadrons of RAF Spitfires and Hurricanes. The ferocity of their opposition and the losses sustained by the German Air Force was such that two days later Hitler decided to postpone Operation Sea Lion.

As the battle began in August, Mom and I were evacuated, as were many youngsters and mothers with young children. We went to Kinross in Scotland, on the outskirts of Edinburgh. We were to stay there for about a year before we returned to London.

Life in England in general, and London in particular during the "blitz", was akin to being on the front lines. Bombs fell indiscriminately all over the city, but particularly in the East End near the targeted docks. They spared no one from pauper to king. But King George and Queen Elizabeth refused to leave London or send their daughters, Princesses Elizabeth and Margaret, to a safe haven.

When the war broke out, there was panic amongst the civilians. Shortly thereafter, they began to show their 'British' resolve. As the intensity of the bombing grew so did the resolve of the Londoners. During the nightly bombing raids, they crowded into underground shelters or the passageways of underground railways. Some more courageous souls slept in the small Anderson shelters that they had built in their gardens. When the all clear sounded, those that could, left the shelters, took stock of the damage, cried, buried their dead and went back to work. The pubs were the centres of their social world and many couples and their families would go there to gather strength from each other. 'Those damn Jerries are not going to beat us!'

Mom and Dad would take me to the pub with them and then if the air raid siren went off, which was often every night in the early years and sometimes several times a night, we would go to the shelter. I first remember the shelter as going down a long flight of stairs into a big long, narrow room that had benches on either side. Lots of people cried but I don't remember being scared because for me this was normal life.

It was dangerous everywhere. One day my father was walking home from work when he heard an increasingly loud noise. Suddenly, he was roughly grabbed and thrown down into an alley. For an instant he thought he was being mugged. Then he saw the Salvation Army tags on the shoulders of the man bending over him. At the same time he heard a chattering of gunfire. When they went back into the street where he had been walking seconds before, the brickwork was covered in machine gun bullet holes. A German fighter had strafed the street. Dad never turned down a request for help or a contribution to the Salvation Army after that.

11

The city was often in flames at night. Once people entered the shelter they never knew if they would come out. Sometimes shelters were hit directly with devastating results. Survivors never knew what they would find when the raid was over.

One evening Dad was visiting his sister's home when the alert sounded. After the bombing Dad went home. All that was left of our little house were the front steps.

Mom first learned about our house when Dad came to Scotland that weekend. He had routinely been able to get a ride with a trucker friend who drove to Edinburgh every Friday night with supplies and drove back on Sunday night. It was a long haul but made life a little more bearable for Mom and Dad. She was distraught, but obviously happy that Dad had not been in the house. He had been able to arrange for quarters in the basement of the tailoring factory where he worked. A number of families had been moved into makeshift rooms. It provided spartan and cramped living space. Mom and I moved back to London in 1942 and checked into our new lodgings. This time Mom was able to get a job as assistant manageress at a tobacconist shop. It was located beside a butcher shop and so we often 'received' an extra ration of meat, and the butchers got extra cigarettes.

In 1943, Mom and I were sent once again to the relative safety of Yorkshire where we spent six months. But the attacks on London continued and the casualties mounted, both against the civilian population and the homes they lived in and the factories they worked in. Heavy raids on London began again in January 1944 and continued until April 1944. There were thousands of casualties.

Policoffs was hit during one raid and the workers rushed in to help the firefighters put out the fire. It was particularly dangerous because of all the chemicals stored in the uniform-making facility. Dad was on the roof with several of his colleagues when they were given the signal that it was too late. "Get off the roof," came the order from the firefighters. But when they raced to the stairs they were met with a gulf of flames. Their only possible escape route was to jump into the nets that firemen held below. My father told me that when he looked down the six stories, it looked like, "a bunch of ants around a postage stamp." Nevertheless he jumped. Unfortunately he hurt his back when he hit the mat. I didn't learn until years later that this incident would permit a most significant change in our lives. After the war ended, Policoffs gave Dad a small check for his misfortune and it was this money that allowed him to buy the tickets to take us to Canada two years later.

When we came back from Yorkshire in 1944, Dad had found a small flat on the top of a three-storey building at 49 Lansdowne Road, in the east end of London. The apartment had a large living room window facing London Fields – a park in front of the school, which I would go to for the next three years. One late afternoon, when Dad had just got home from work we heard a whirring noise and Dad said, "Len look at this." It was a V-I 'buzz-bomb' gliding by our window. With some hidden strength, my 5'

12

5" mother grabbed both Dad and I by the collars and threw herself and us back onto the floor, just as the window imploded and shattered slivers of glass that would have hit both of us in the face.

The V-1 'buzz bomb' was a 2,000 lb liquid-fuelled pilot-less flying bomb. You could hear it droning and then the droning would stop. That's when the bomb would start to fall. No one knew where it was going to land. I remember thinking that as long as you could hear the explosion we were OK.

The V-1s, thought of by the Germans as a 'retaliation' weapon, began falling on London just six days after the Normandy landings, on June 6, 1944. In all, more than 6,500 were counted over London and the surrounding countryside. While many were shot down or destroyed by RAF fighters, more than 2,300 hit London resulting in close to 5,500 deaths and 16,000 injuries. In September 1944, the V-2s replaced the V-1s. These were much faster, travelling faster than the speed of sound. Over 500 of these rockets hit London killing more than 2,700 people and injuring many more.

My cousin Paul, nine at the time, was sleeping downstairs for safety the night before being evacuated to Bournemouth like many others his age. A V-1 exploded at the bottom of his street and the ceiling fell in just missing him. My Aunt Lily was frantic but Paul slept through the whole thing and was quite shocked when he did wake up and saw what had happened.

In the spring of 1944, my mother and I were visiting my Grandma at 55 Malvern Road about two blocks from our flat. While we were there, the sirens went off, so we all headed for the underground shelter. About an hour later the all clear sounded, and Mom and I headed for home since it was getting close to 5:00 pm when Dad would be arriving home for his tea.

Shortly after we got into the flat the siren went again. Mom decided it was too late to go back to the shelter so decided we would use our solid, heavy kitchen table as protection.

Suddenly, there was a loud explosion and it felt like the house was collapsing. In fact a bomb had hit the house next to us and the concussion caused the roof of our building to collapse on top of us. Only the table saved us. Within minutes firefighters were coming up the stairs and pulling my mother and me out from underneath the table. Covered with soot and pieces of rubble we looked like two ghosts. Dad could see the flames from where he worked and raced home. "Where are Fay and Len?" he shouted to a neighbour. "Are they all right?" "They are right over there," the neighbour replied. Dad could not recognize us wrapped in blankets with our filthy, tear-stained faces.

We were given the use of an Anderson shelter to stay in until Dad could find another place for us to live. About five feet long by five feet wide by five feet high, as I remember it, and half buried underground it provided basic accommodation for the three of us. But a week later Dad was able to arrange to move into the house where my grandmother lived. She moved upstairs and we lived downstairs. That way she could eat with us and look after me when I came home from school while Mom and Dad worked.

The bombing continued, not like during the blitz in 1940-1941, but raids were steady during a period known as the, "little-blitz". Strangely, on reflection, it didn't seem to bother me. I didn't know any different. After all, that is all I had ever known. Day by day we went to school, ate our meals, and went to the shelter when the raids came. We saw destruction and devastation and buildings on fire. We didn't miss white bread, fresh eggs and many other foods that I learned about later because I didn't know they existed. When very young, I thought milk came in a box and was a powder mixed with water. But that was normal. It obviously wasn't normal for my mother and father. My mother often had to take me to the big shelter once, twice, and sometimes three times a night. Dad usually went to the Anderson shelter in the back yard because he had to go to work earlier than Mom in the morning.

What did upset me very much, and has stuck with me ever since, was the loss of my hero and friend who lived next door to us. Gerald was 10, twice as old as me and to me everything I wanted to be when I grew up to his age. One day after school he asked his Mom if she would sign a library card for him that would allow him to take home some books from the library. Kids had to be 12 before they could take home books on their own. "Wait till your father comes home," his Mom said, "and he will sign for you. He will be coming home for tea soon." "But Mom," he argued, "it will only take me a few minutes and then I won't have to go out when Dad is home." After a few minutes of passionate pleading, Gerald's Mom agreed but with the caution, "you'd better be back by the time your Dad gets here."

Watching this take place outside our house, I pleaded with my Mom to let me go with him. "No," she said firmly, "Your Dad will be home for his tea and he won't be happy if you aren't here." Understandably, parents were very protective of their children in the war years. My burst of tears did nothing to change her mind. So Gerald said in his grown-up manner, "Never mind Lennie, I won't be gone long and we can play after supper."

Little did I know that would be the last thing he ever said to me. Shortly after he got into the library, a raid occurred and a bomb hit the library directly. At the request of his parents, my father took on the gruesome task of going through several morgues trying to identify Gerald among the dead children. He never really told me what Gerald looked like when he found him, but from what he did say, I have always had the impression that he had been slammed against the marble wall of the building and was much disfigured. Dad had nightmares for weeks.

The safety of children was a huge issue during the war years. Up to the age of six, they normally stayed with their parents. In my case, Mom and I went to several "safe" locations outside the cities. From then on, they were evacuated on their own to homes in safer locations. Thousands of kids spent several years living with temporary parents. My cousins Irene and

14

Elsa, 15 and 13, in 1939, children of Aunt Celia and Uncle Mark, were evacuated with their school mates to a small village in Norfolk where they lived in two different farmhouses. They spent 11 months there before getting back to London to their parents. They told me that they were very lonesome for their parents. But they were relatively safe and the food was good since they ate what was grown or raised on the farm. Paul went to Bournemouth, a seaside resort on the south coast which although there were lots of soldiers camped there, was relatively safe.

Some children were sent to other Commonwealth countries including Canada, Australia, New Zealand and South Africa. Approximately 2,500 children were evacuated to these countries as part of the Government's scheme to save children in areas of greater risk in England. However, the program virtually came to a halt following the sinking of the luxury Liner City of Benares. The ship set sail from Liverpool en route to Nova Scotia in Sept 1940, carrying 100 children, ninety of whom were evacuees aged from 6 to 16, plus 10 volunteer escorts. Four days later a German U-boat torpedoed the ship, 600 miles out in the Atlantic. Some died onboard the ship, others died of exposure in lifeboats. In all 77 of the young evacuees and five of their escorts died. It was the worst disaster ever in one incident involving British children. The Government stopped the program.

When we think about the World War II today and commemorate the efforts of those who fought and died to protect our freedom, the focus is most often on those men and women in uniform. Indeed the total number of dead and wounded is staggering when taking into account the casualties of both the Allies and the enemy. But we seem to have forgotten the toll on the lives of innocent men, women and children who were victims of this terrible period in our history. Sixty-four thousand civilians were killed and 87,000 seriously injured in England, most of them in London. However, to put this into perspective, in Germany the toll was much higher with more than three million civilians being killed, which was close to the 3,300,000 Axis soldiers who died.

Despite the loss of life and the devastation (more than 2 million houses, 60% of which were in London, were destroyed in England) the stiff upper lip of the Englishman prevailed. I will always remember a rather portly Prime Minister Churchill pictured smoking his cigar and holding a glass of cognac saying, "we must tighten our belts." As a youngster, it didn't look to me that he had tightened his belt much.

As news came of the Allied troops moving eastward towards Germany every day, morale continued to climb and people began to believe that the end was in sight. You had to be in London on May 6, 1945 to appreciate how Londoners felt. For more than six years they had lived with the threat of death and injury and destruction. Now it was over. At almost six, I was really too young to remember much except that my mother and father took me to Trafalgar Square and I vaguely remember being kissed and hugged by many strangers in the midst of what seemed like a sea of people all of whom were laughing, drinking and crying at the same time.

Millions dead all over the world, millions wounded, families devastated, lives ruined. And for what? Nothing but the cruel idealistic desires of a man who wanted to rule the world. True, many people aided him, but it was his ability to build followers and stir them to a passionate frenzy that made them do unthinkable things to their fellowmen; that is what made him such a demon.

Fortunately, our family, including my mother's siblings and their children, had all survived the war. All bore the emotional scars that five years of living in war creates. Uncle Jack had been wounded by flying glass and was having some trouble healing. Uncle Harry had joined the army and returned from Europe as a Captain but had psychological problems that he never got over.

Like most other people living in England, our family began looking forward optimistically to what post-war conditions could bring us. There was still rationing, but no more fear of bombs or rockets falling on our heads.

For the next 18 months life seemed good. I went to school, played and made new friends. Dad continued to work at Policoffs and Mom worked in the tobacconist shop. Then, in November 1946, our world began to fall apart.

My grandmother Sarah was taken to hospital suffering from heart problems. A week later Aunty Celia, aged 42, died of breast cancer. When Mom walked into her hospital room, Sarah looked at her with tears in her eyes and said in her broken English, "you have come to tell me that Celia is dead." A week later grandmother died. She was 61. Less than a month later Uncle Jack died as a result of complications from the wounds he had suffered during the bombing. Mom was devastated.

We had lived through six years of war and everybody had survived. Then in a month she had lost her mother, a sister and a brother. She was so distraught that Dad had to take her back to a doctor fearing that she might have to be admitted again to a psychiatric hospital. The doctor told Dad, "The best thing you can do for her is to get her away from all of this. Take her to another country."

Dad told me he had three options to consider, Australia, the United States and Canada. He had brothers, living in New South Wales, Australia, but really hadn't heard from them and didn't know how to contact them. A number of people suggested he try immigrating to the US since there seemed to be lots of opportunities in that country. But the friendliest choice for Dad seemed to be Canada. He wrote to Cousin Albert who was living in Meaford, Ontario and told him about his problem. Albert wrote back and said that his Mom and Dad had bought a second 100-acre farm adjoining their current 100 acres. It had a house and a barn. So after apparently discussing the situation with his parents, Albert proposed that we come to

Canada, move into the house on the adjoining farm and Dad could help farm with brothers Bill and Carmen.

A house to ourselves. Lots of land. It seemed hard to believe. Dad went to Canada House in Grosvenor Square and talked to immigration officials. The High Commissioner and his staff were encouraging families like ours who were given visions of, "a car in every garage and two chickens in every pot to immigrate to Canada." So Dad began making the arrangements. Mom was tentative about leaving the remaining members of her family but Dad convinced her that this move would be the best for her health and for our future.

For some reason I do not know, Dad decided to come to Canada early to get himself established on the farm and also decided to fly, a very costly method of travel in those years. Nevertheless, in mid-August 1947, Dad climbed onboard a Trans Canada Airline (now Air Canada) North Star for his 20-hour flight from London to Shannon, Gander, Montreal and finally Toronto. From there he boarded the train for a two-hour ride to Stayner, where he was met by his Aunt and Uncle, and cousins Bill, Carmen and Albert.

Six weeks later, on Oct 1, 1947, Mom and I sailed from Southampton on the SS Aquitania bound for Halifax, Nova Scotia.

Mom and me 1944.

Dad and me July 1939.

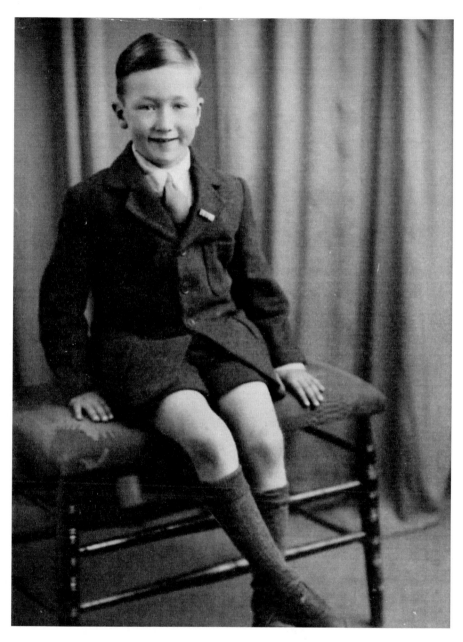

An official portrait before leaving for Canada at age 8.

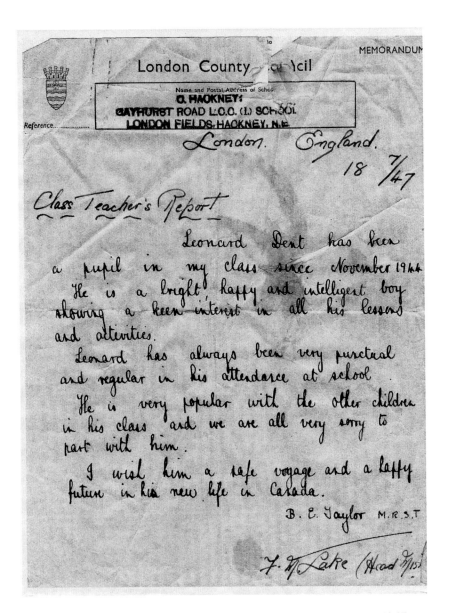

London County Council

MEMORANDUM

C. HACKNEY:
GAYHURST ROAD L.C.C. (1) SCHOOL
LONDON FIELDS, HACKNEY, N.E.

Name and Postal Address of School

Reference................

London. England.

18 7/47

Class Teacher's Report

Leonard Dent has been a pupil in my class since November 1944. He is a bright, happy and intelligent boy showing a keen interest in all his lessons and activities.

Leonard has always been very punctual and regular in his attendance at school.

He is very popular with the other children in his class and we are all very sorry to part with him.

I wish him a safe voyage and a happy future in his new life in Canada.

B. E. Taylor M.R.S.T

F. M. Lake (Head Mis)

My final class teacher's report before leaving for Canada in 1947.

CHAPTER 3 - THE PROMISED LAND

"Captain, is the boat going to sink today?"

I can still remember the look of amusement on the young officer's face as he looked down at me and said rather sternly, "Not today, sonny."

Mom and I were entering the dining room on the Aquitania to start another feast for breakfast. I was still in awe of the lifeboat drill we had on the first day before we sailed from Southampton. Putting on the life jacket and going up and standing, waiting to jump into a life boat was exciting to this eight year old. So every day, I always wanted to know if we were going to get a chance to really sail in the lifeboat, obviously not realizing how serious a situation this would have been.

I had played games like this before, practicing for what might happen, with my Mom and Dad. During the war years, we had gas masks and mine had a Mickey Mouse face on it. Once in a while Mom and Dad would show me how to put on the mask and how to breathe and then let me look in the mirror. I looked just like a big mouse.

Leaving England for me was exciting. For Mom it was a terrifying experience since she had really never been far from her family and now she was sailing to a far-off land where she knew no one and didn't even know how we would survive. We had few possessions and little money. She was the planner and Dad was more the romantic. He was happy if he had three meals a day and cigarettes to smoke. He wasn't hard to please. I had often dreamed of what it must be like far away.

In December 1946, shortly after my grandma and uncle and aunt had died, my Uncle Sam took me to see Judy Garland in the Wizard of Oz. at the London Palladium Theatre. When Dorothy sang 'Somewhere over the Rainbow,' I couldn't help but think that there was a better place for us somewhere far away. That somehow I could 'wish upon a star and wake up with all the clouds behind me.' To this day I still get tears in my eyes when I hear that song sung. I met Lorna Luft, Judy Garland's younger daughter, who was performing on a transatlantic cruise in 2006 and told her why and how much this song meant to me. We both had tears in our eyes.

After the war ended, Mom and Dad would take me once a year to stay with friends in Lancing on the south coast of England. I would stand and look out across the water, always wondering what it would be like to be where the sea and the sky came together. And so now Mom and I were sailing towards that point but for some reason, which I couldn't figure out at the time, we never seemed to reach it. Being on the Aquitania was beyond my imagination.

The ship was launched in Liverpool in April 1913 and survived service in both world wars. When built it was the largest liner in the world. Given the fate of the Titanic, care was taken to make sure that there were enough life jackets and boats for each person on board.

It served as an armed merchant cruiser patrolling the waters of the western approaches to England and later served as a hospital ship. At the end of World War I, it was used to repatriate Canadian troops back to Canada.

From 1932 to 1939, it was used as a cruise ship sailing in the Mediterranean and the Atlantic. The ship had been refurbished so that it had accommodation for 650 first class, 600 tourist class and 950 third class passengers. It was requisitioned as a troop transport in November 1939, at first transporting Canadian troops to Europe. Later it was based in Sydney and transported Australian and New Zealand troops. At the end of the war, it began repatriating Canadian and American troops home to North America and also taking the wives and children of Canadian servicemen to Canada.

So it was amongst this group that Mom and I found ourselves. More than 48,000 war brides and their 22,000 children came from Europe to Canada after the war. Most of the wives and children aboard had experienced the same hardships that we had during the war years.

And so, to enter a beautiful dining area where there were tables with items that I had never seen or tasted before was a dream come true: white bread, real milk, fresh eggs and butter, and as much as you could eat. And there was peanut butter. During the war years, I remember that Mom would bring home a small jar of peanut butter about once a year. She and Dad told me that it was all for me but it had to last until she could get another one. I think it was because sometimes the grocer next door got a bigger ration of tobacco from Mom that she got a small reward. I thought then that if someone offered me a sack of gold or a jar of peanut butter, the peanut butter would win. I still enjoy it to this day. I don't remember ever going hungry during the war. There were just lots of food items that we never got.

I enjoyed the trip and meeting and playing with other kids, but Mom didn't have any sea legs and spent several days in her bunk. We were sailing third class and so shared a cabin with several two-tier bunk beds with two other women and their children. Years later when I was in high school in Collingwood, Ontario, I met a pretty girl who was one year behind me in school. Anxious to meet her, I got talking and when I heard her English accent asked her where she was from. She came from north London and to my surprise was on the Aquitania on the same crossing. Small world!

Finally after six days of what Mom described as the "voyage from hell" we saw our new homeland - Halifax. For hundreds of thousands of Canadian servicemen seeing Halifax for the first time in up to six years brought tears to their eyes. Many of these men and women thought they would never see their homeland again. And indeed for more than 40,000 Canadian servicemen and women buried in Europe or lost at sea this was the case. But for me it seemed a disappointment. This initial glimpse of Canada did not live up to what we have been led to believe we would see when we arrived.

Grey skies met grey ground on which were built hundreds of grey buildings. A slight drizzle was falling and it was cold early on this October

Sunday morning. From the deck of the ship there didn't seem to be any life on the streets.

How different Halifax had been during the war years. For nearly six years it had been the hub of a huge military and merchant marine activity. Halifax was the headquarters of North West Atlantic Command, the only theatre of war commanded by a Canadian. Hundreds of thousands of Canadian troops had sailed away bound for Europe. Large convoys had been assembled in Bedford Basin and, escorted by Canadian Navy ships, had taken necessary food and supplies to troops and civilians in Europe. And when the war ended in Europe in May 1945, troops, as well as thousands of women and children, made their way to Canada, with the largest influx being in 1946.

Everyone seemed to be very happy to have reached Halifax, particularly my Mom who couldn't wait to get her feet onto firm ground. The landing process didn't seem to be very difficult, and before long Mom and I, along with what seemed like a thousand other moms and kids, were put into train cars that were sitting waiting for us on a track just outside of Pier 21.

Within a few hours of landing we started winding our way out of the city. For the next two days the train seemed to stop at every small depot where one or two women and their children with assorted amounts of luggage would get off to be met by what appeared to be strangers who also seemed overjoyed to see them. I have often told people that Mom, Dad and I came to Canada with a matching set of luggage… three paper bags. In fact, Mom and I had an old trunk that her mother had brought with her from Poland when she was a youngster. In it were a few precious possessions that had survived our three bombings in London and that Mom felt she needed to keep reminding her of her roots.

My most scary experience on that train ride came in Quebec City. Mom left me with another woman while she got off to go into the station to send Dad a telegram telling him that we had arrived. She seemed to have been gone a long time and then suddenly the train started to pull away from the station and there was no sign of my Mom. I was frightened. Thankfully, within a few moments Mom appeared. She had got on a car farther down the tracks and walked through the cars until she reached me. I have never forgotten that moment when she finally showed up!

We changed trains in Montreal and then continued on to Toronto. Another change and we were headed north towards Stayner where we would meet Dad. I was so excited, having not seen him for nearly two months. I didn't really know what to expect regarding my relatives.

Our train chugged into the small Stayner station and came to a jolting stop accompanied by screeching brakes. Excitedly, Mom and I gathered up our belongings and got off our car. The chilly October air hit us in the face momentarily taking our breath away. But we were too excited to see Dad, so it passed with little notice.

23

Dad, who was about 5' 7", stood with a small group of people and he was the tallest. I first saw Aunt Eliza, bent over wearing a black heavy coat with a black hat sitting on her head at a crazy angle; she looked like a little 4' 6" gnome. Standing beside her propped up on two canes was Uncle Frank. He stood about 5' 3". He wore grey pants and a suit jacket which didn't match and both were stained... I am not sure with what. He wore a dirty fedora and had an old pipe drooping from his mouth. Behind them were the three boys. Albert, at 47, was the oldest. Bald with a white ring around his crown he stood about 5' 5". Behind him stood his wife Elvie who was wearing a flowered frock and seemed anxious to meet us. Beside Albert stood Bill who looked very much like his brother including the bald-head. Carmen was slightly shorter than his brothers and was also bald although the hair around his crown had not yet turned white. Dad, grinning from ear to ear ran towards us and seemed to pick both Mom and me up in a giant hug at the same time.

Our trunk came off the train baggage car and we headed to the parking lot. Sitting there were two automobiles the likes of which I had never seen. Albert was driving a 1928 Model A Ford, which had a rumble seat. The Gowan's car was a 1926 Pontiac four-door sedan. Albert and Elvie took the Model A and Willy and the luggage went in the rumble seat. Dad, Mom and I along with Carmen, Aunty Eliza and Uncle Frank crowded into the sedan. We were off to see our new home. For me it was the first time I had ever ridden in a privately owned motor vehicle.

We drove about 10 miles along a two-lane road at about 25 miles an hour, before turning onto a dirt side road. We drove for a mile before we turned into a long lane way, which took us into the farmyard and the house.

It was big, two-storey and it was all brick. I was excited about seeing this house because we had never been in a single home like this in our lives. I soon got a cold dose of reality. When we entered the house, the first thing I noticed was the smell. I remembered sometimes when we went to the shelter and the urinals had overflowed. I learned later that Uncle Frank, who slept in the front bedroom downstairs, had a pee-pot under his bed and it was emptied once a week or when full, whichever came first. Aunty Eliza slept in another room downstairs and she had the same arrangement. I am sure that everyone was used to the smell and it wouldn't bother them.

The second thing I noticed was the flies that swarmed around the table. When we sat down to eat our dinner later they also tried to eat from the same food. Aunt Eliza tried to correct that by spraying the room with insect repellent just before we ate. That only meant that some of the flies overcome with the poison, died and did kamikaze dives into the plates of foods.

Following our first meal, I learned that there was no running water in the house, no electricity and no heat. Water was stored in a barrel outside the kitchen. Kerosene lamps provided lights and the big stove, which was kept full of wood, provided heat. Finally there were of course no inside toilets, just the little outside shed which sat at a curious angle behind the house and which had two holes and some pages from an Eaton's catalogue. I have never been able to understand why it had two holes. Did this mean that sometimes two people could sit together?

We had been poor in London, but every home we were in had electricity, heat, running water and inside toilets.

Surely this was not the 'Promised Land' that we had been told about at Canada House in London?

Our transport Oct 1 - 6, 1947 to Canada.

CHAPTER 4 - DOWN ON THE FARM

Seven days… one week. That's all it took. Then I began to realize that life down on the farm was not going to be a holiday.

In the beginning, the idea of getting up at the crack of dawn, helping to bring in the cows, feeding them, cleaning out their stalls and carrying the milk up to the separator and then heading for a breakfast, sometimes eggs, bacon and sometimes fresh baked pie, was neat. But after a few days, I began to realize that this had to be done every day, seven days a week, and the glamour began to fade.

After that first week, another dose of reality. Mom told me that I would have to start school.

In London, I had attended a large school in London Fields where everyone wore uniform; blue shorts or skirts for the girls with a gray shirt. The boys were on one side of the school and the girls on the other. We were separated by a huge wall and so only saw the girls when coming to school and going home. I had started at the age of 4, so was used to school and discipline but none of that prepared me for what I would encounter here in rural Canada.

The first day, Carmen drove Mom and me to the little schoolhouse (Cashtown - SS23) that sat by itself just off the main road in a field no doubt donated by one of the farmers from his property. It was a small rectangular building with one room, two bathrooms and a small cloakroom.

We went inside and it appeared just about big enough to hold the 23 students seated in small desks, all facing a row of blackboards that stretched across the front of the schoolroom. A pretty young gal came to meet us. She looked about 10 years older than me. In fact, I found out later that her name was Audrey Rumble and she was 18. She had finished grade 12 that past June, had gone to two months of Normal School in Toronto to be educated to be a teacher and now was in charge of SS23. She also was the only teacher for the grades 1- 8. Her responsibilities included everything involved with the school including making sure it was clean and that the pot-bellied stove was filled and lit. I was introduced and told to come back the next day.

So dutifully after helping with the chores, Carmen told me that I could walk across the fields through their property and then onto the Lageer's farm past their house until I reached the road and then walk a few hundred yards and I would be at the school. It turned out to be about two km from our house to the school.

It was now mid October and a little cool but I felt quite comfortable in my blue shorts and grey shirt walking to school. That first day I learned a big lesson I had never known in England. About half way across the fields, I had an urgent need to go pee. I had been taught to go to the bathroom and I tried my best but I just couldn't make it to the school. I peed in my pants. I was embarrassed. What would Mom and Dad say? Fortunately the pee on

27

the blue pants dried before I reached the school so nobody noticed. When I told everybody that night at home my cousin Willie laughed and said you had 200 acres around you. "When you need to go, just do it where you are." First lesson!

When I arrived at the school, Miss Rumble, as everyone called her, welcomed me and again introduced me to the class. The boys were dressed in overalls and obviously had been working in the barn before coming to school as I could tell by the look of their boots and the odd odour. The girls had dresses and looked nice.

I had brought no paper work with me from England so Miss Rumble had no idea in what grade I should be. Neither did she understand my accent very well. It was no doubt the first time she had heard anyone speak from the east end of London where the cockneys live.

She stood looking at me for a while, trying to come to a solution. Suddenly like a light going on, she said, "Bobbie and Roy stand up. Leonard you stand between them. Oh good," she said, "You are all about the same height so Leonard you can be in Grade 4." Given that I had been in school for about 4 years it probably was about the right place. I found out that there were subject areas in which I was ahead and some other areas behind. In England we were still printing in my class while here in this small school they were writing. I had to catch up by myself but to this day I believe my less than perfect writing is due to that poor start.

In general, I adjusted rather easily. The kids were friendly and laughed at my 'accent' but tried to make me feel welcome. It fact the contact with the kids at school was my only real contact with anyone my age. As soon as school was over, I would walk back across the fields to the farm and begin the evening chores.

Carmen was 27, Willie 45 and Aunt Eliza and Uncle Frank, ancient... both in their 60's. Mom and Dad had their own bedroom but I had to sleep in a room where Carmen and Willie slept. I wasn't that happy, having had my own room in England and my own bed. Here I had to share a bed with Willie, sleeping on a mattress filled with straw. At least it felt like that. The house wasn't well insulated and the only source of heat was the wood cook stove in the kitchen that went out at night and had to be lit by the first man up in the morning. So it was cold. Once during that first winter, I woke up and there was snow on the bed that had come through the cracks around the windowsills.

Except for going to school, I only got to leave the farm about once every three to four months when I was allowed to go to the metropolis of Creemore (population 500). It became something I looked forward to because on each visit Willie and I would share a 25-cent brick of Neapolitan ice cream. It was a treat.

So the animals became my friends. The young calves rollicked through the fields with me chasing them and looking back to see if I could catch them. Skip, the yellow-haired mutt that was on the farm, became my best friend. Unfortunately, about a year after we arrived, an animal killed two chickens one night and Carmen thought it was Skip. He became judge, jury and executioner. In front of me Skip was shot. I have had a hard time becoming close to any dog since.

I worked hard but learned a lot in the first few months. Although I was only eight, Carmen taught me how to drive the big Massey Ferguson tractor. One of my jobs was to hook the tractor up to a stone-boat (really a wooden sled with steel runners), which had a big wooden barrel on top, and then drive to the creek. Here I would fill it up with water and drive back to the house. This became our water supply for about a week for washing, cooking, dishes, and personal hygiene. This wasn't a big issue in the Cowan house since we only changed our underwear once a week and washing in cold water was the norm. Heating water on the stove for a small bath became a treat.

The Gowans had two horses, Prince and Beauty, which they used principally for pulling the wagon during haying season. Beauty was a smaller roan that had been badly mistreated before being acquired by the Gowans. But perhaps because I was smaller, we seemed to hit it off. And soon the boys had me up and riding Beauty bareback around the farm. It wasn't long before they taught me to shoot their 22-caliber rifle. I was given the job of riding around on Beauty looking for ground hogs to shoot. Better to have a dead ground hog than have one of the horses put their leg into a groundhog hole and break it, they told me. Wow, if the kids back in my old London school could see me riding around doing this, they wouldn't believe it.

About the end of October I was walking to school one day when it started to snow. I had really never seen snow. There had been the occasional snowflake mixed with cold icy rain in London but nothing like what I saw floating to the ground here, beautiful and white. I gathered some in my hand and was able to drink from my hand.

When I arrived at Mrs. Lageer's kitchen she was upset to see me wearing my blue shorts and grey shirt. She immediately gave me a pair of her son Donald's long bib overalls and a long sleeve shirt to wear. Donald was a grade ahead of me but we had become friends and always walked to his house from the school. The overalls were a little big but much warmer than shorts. My mother was embarrassed and the following weekend she went into Creemore and bought me a new pair of overalls and a couple of shirts. I am not sure where she found the money.

Money was very scarce for Mom and Dad. Most of what they had went to buy the tickets to come to Canada. The Gowans didn't think it was necessary to give us any money because we were being given a roof over our head and food for our bellies. "You're much better off than when you lived in England," they continually told us. So the idea of staying in our own house on the adjoining acreage that they owned, and my Dad working with the boys for some pay appeared to be only a dream. At least, in their minds. Interestingly they had treated my grandfather, Dad's Dad, the same way and he had to go to work on another farm to get some pay.

Mom wasn't very happy and so Dad started looking for a job. He had had rheumatic fever as a youngster and now suffered from a rheumatic heart condition and shouldn't have done hard labour. However, Cousin Albert, who had convinced Dad to come to Canada in the first place, found Dad a job working at a construction site in Meaford doing manual labour. He stayed with Albert and his wife Elvie. It wasn't long before Dad was working outdoors in temperatures well below zero and it was more than he could take. He lasted about three months and then in February 1948 found a job as an orderly at the Workman's Compensation Board Hospital in Malton, now the site of one of the major runways at Toronto's Pearson International Airport.

That left Mom and me on the farm alone. She worked very hard to help. She also tried hard to make sure that I was fed properly and not worked too hard. I am not sure if I ever told her but once Carmen wanted me to carry up a bag of feed to the loft in the barn. I told him it was too heavy for me and he swore at me, told me I was lazy and slapped me across the face. Years later, when I was in my early twenties and 6'2" and 200 lb I came back to the farm and thought I would make him pay for that slap. But when I looked down at this 5'4", 135 lb man, I thought, "What would be the point?" But I always remembered that.

The Gowans were not very good farmers and the boys would come in at 3:00 pm every afternoon to listen to Ma Perkins, a soap opera on the radio, and have something to eat. Dinner was often not put on the table until well after 8:00 pm and both Mom and I wanted me to be in bed by then. Mom would have to ask Aunt Eliza if she would mind making me a sandwich to eat before I went to bed. I would usually eat a fat peanut butter sandwich, which I had grown to love in England.

When I looked at the kitchen table, I thought I'd just as soon eat the sandwich anyway. There was always that smell of unemptied pee pots and many flies that came through the broken screen doors. Aunt Eliza would spray this disinfectant just before dinner and it was kind of funny and gross to see flies falling onto the table sometimes into the big pot of beans, or on their backs on the table with their legs jumping in their final death throes.

For the next year, my life became a matter of doing the chores, going to school and coming home, doing chores and going to bed. Oh, and going to Creemore once every three months or so for ice cream. Life did get a little more exciting when the crops needed to be brought in, usually in August or September. That's when farmers from various farms would come to help. One farmer had a threshing machine so he would bring that. Aunt Eliza would cook well in advance including great apple pies and we would have slabs of pork, fried eggs and potatoes and pie for breakfast. Willie would also make a big pail of eggnog and put it down in the well to keep it cool and then bring it up each time we brought in a load to the thresher. I usually drove the horses and Mom helped to pitch wheat onto the wagon. When one crop was finished then all the farmers would go to the next farm.

I think the farmer who brought the thresher got part of the crop for his trouble.

Obviously, I never went to church or Sunday school while on the farm. For that matter, I don't remember ever going in England. It just didn't seem to be a priority when we were just trying to live through the war years.

But one event occurred late in 1948 that made me realize that there must be someone or something looking after us. After all, Mom, Dad and I had escaped a number of close calls during the bombings while so many others hadn't.

One Friday evening, Willie and I were in the barn feeding the horses when I thought I heard a noise like someone crying for help. I told Willie and he said I was dreaming. But then I heard another cry and then a third. So Willie and I made our way through the rather deep snow across a four-acre field until we came to the top of the hill that led down a slope to the creek. There, lying in the snow hanging onto a suitcase and trying to struggle up the hill was my Dad. He had taken the train from Toronto to Stayner, hitchhiked to the Lageer's farm and then using the light from our kitchen window had been walking across the fields. When he got down in the gully, he couldn't see the light anymore and couldn't find the path so tried climbing up the side of the hill. He was exhausted. If we hadn't been in the barn and heard his cries, we probably would have found him the next day frozen to death. Dad was pretty scared, but other than a bit of frostbite, he was OK. Mom made him promise that in future he would call from the Lageer's farm and Willie or Carmen would drive over and pick him up.

I really enjoyed school because it was the only time I got to talk and play with anyone my own age. We played 'kick the can' and pitched a ball over the roof to see if anyone on the other side could catch it. Every Friday we brought in a nickel and Miss Rumble would buy some cans of green peas and heat them up and we would have a cup of hot green peas. At Christmas time we had a concert and I recited a poem, which Mom had brought from England. Standing very proudly, from memory I recited 'Albert and the Lion' and how he used his stick with an 'orse' 'eaded' 'andle.' Both kids and parents in the audience laughed but I think most of the laughter was because they couldn't understand a word I was saying. At the end of the school year in 1948, Miss Rumble left and went to Creemore Public School as a teacher. She was replaced by a much older, rather stern but very kind Mrs. Ida Grant.

I am not sure why but Bobbie and Roy didn't pass grade four so the next year I went in to grade five alone. Not that it made much difference because I sat in the same seat. I really don't remember getting taught very much, rather just sitting there and listening as Mrs. Grant taught the other kids. So I got lessons from grades 1 – 8. I don't even remember writing any exams for the three years I spent in Cashtown.

After about a year on the farm, Mom decided that she had enough of this life in Canada. She urged Dad to try and save as much money as possible so we could buy ship tickets to sail back to England. Given that Dad wasn't making much money it was a slow process. It wasn't helped when one payday Dad went into Toronto to buy a money order to ship home his two-week pay cheque to Mom. His 'buddy' suggested they go in to a local pub for a couple of beers. Dad had to go to the bathroom so his buddy told him no problem "I will watch your coat," which of course contained his wallet. When Dad came back his 'buddy' was gone and so was his wallet. He never came back to work at the hospital. Mom was furious. To help make money faster, she decided that she should come to the hospital and work as a female ward-aide.

Married couples weren't allowed but couples could work if one lived in the female quarters and the other in the male quarters. Children were not allowed and Mom wouldn't let me stay on the farm without her. They found a family in the west end of Toronto that agreed to look after me. I was to go to school at the nearby Humber Public School.

This arrangement didn't last long. The couple had a very large, very ugly sixteen-year-old daughter who immediately took on the role of looking after me and telling me what to do and when to do it. The last straw occurred one night only a few days after I arrived. A plate was put in front of me containing some turnips spiced with sage seasoning. I tasted it and it was awful. I said I wouldn't eat it. "Eat it or there will be nothing else," I was told by this bespectacled ogre. I didn't eat.

The next morning at breakfast the same plate of cold turnip with sage seasoning was placed in front of me. "Eat or there is nothing else," I was told by a smiling daughter. I went upstairs, packed my things in my little brown cardboard suitcase and snuck out the door. I was only nine but I didn't intend to stay there any longer. I made my way to the bus stop and got a bus that took me to Malton. Then I walked to the hospital. I found Mom and told her what happened and said I wasn't going back there. Mom had no choice. She quit her job and we moved back to the farm.

For the next year, Dad worked hard to save money and Mom and I did what we had to do on the farm. Dad couldn't always come home on weekends because it cost a lot of the little he was earning, so once Mom sent me to Malton on the bus to stay with him for few days.

It was in late August 1949 just before school started. Dad had a few days off; we could spend some time together. One evening about 5:30, we were walking to a store just outside the gate of the hospital grounds to get Dad some cigarettes when we heard a loud roaring noise above us. It was the Royal Canadian Navy aerobatic team practicing for the CNE air show in Toronto on Labour Day weekend.

Suddenly during a manoeuvre, something happened and we saw the three Seafires (Navy aircraft) split apart from their formation. One crashed close to us near the store. The second appeared to be heading for the runway to land. The third was heading straight towards the hospital dining room. The plane seemed to struggle to get its nose up, skimmed over the roof by no more than 50 feet and then crashed into a tree. There was a huge puff of smoke and dust and parts flew but no fire. Dad and I ran towards the site of this crash. When we got there I saw something that is imprinted in my brain forever. It was the open torso of a body with the stomach contents showing what the pilot had eaten for dinner probably a short time before. ...I remember undigested corn. That's all that was left of the pilot.

He was a hero. Had he hit the dining room probably several hundred patients and staff would have been killed. But I don't think anyone ever knew, except for Dad and me, the heroic gesture he had made just before he died. I found out later that he was Lt Alfred Charles 'Chuck' Elton. The other pilot killed was the team leader LCdr Clifford Watson. He was the brother of a well-known CBC broadcaster, Patrick Watson.

I didn't have nightmares that night but I decided that I never wanted to ever, ever fly in an airplane.

I went back to Cashtown School and the farm for the next year and played with the animals and had few friends. Both Mom and I were getting more excited about when we could go back home to London.

That day seemed to be much closer when Mom and Dad told me in the summer of 1950 that they had saved enough money to buy the tickets to sail home.

In early September, when school started, I told Mrs. Grant that we were leaving and the school sent me off with a little gift. Willie and Carmen took us on an overnight trip to Niagara Falls, which Mom really wanted to see before we left.

A week before we were to take the train to Toronto and on to Halifax, to catch a ship, something happened that would change my life forever.

I don't know how or why, but Dad was offered a job working on a construction project at the Camp Borden army base. How he convinced Mom, I will never know. Just as quickly as we were going back to England, we weren't. I'm not sure but I don't think Dad ever wanted to go.

Within a week we moved into Creemore away from the farm and Dad began his new job at Camp Borden. He found a little apartment above a grocery store on Creemore's main street.

After three years on the farm, we had moved into the Metropolis of Creemore. Population 500...I was back in the big city!!

The Gowan family with Mom and me

Mom and I working in the fields, I was 8

Riding Beauty

Life on the farm

CHAPTER 5 - LIFE IN A METROPOLIS

Imagine... living in a place that had inside toilets, running hot and cold water, a bathtub and electricity. That's what we had when we moved into the small apartment in Creemore. It wasn't much, perched above Bishop's Grocery store, on the main street of the village. Small and barely furnished, but it had features which we hadn't enjoyed in the past three years on the farm. More importantly, it was our home. And perhaps for the first time in my 11 years, we were a family. Just Mom, Dad and I, living together in our own place without fear that it was going to be destroyed or that we were going to have to move somewhere else for our safety.

Creemore was an interesting village. It was founded in 1845. Nestled in a valley and surrounded by hills on three sides, it is about 130 km northwest of Toronto.

Settlers began coming to the area in the 1830s and 40s. They needed a mill to grind their wheat and one to saw their lumber. In 1845, an enterprising settler named Edward Webster decided to bring them what they needed. A sailing vessel was bought, loaded with material, and the long trip was made from Brockville to the mouth of the Nottawasaga River, which is now the famous Wasaga Beach close to Collingwood, Ontario. The remainder of the trip was made with ox teams to take the material through heavy forest without even a trail to finally reach Creemore. A crude saw mill and a flourmill were built and put into operation.

Gradually more settlers came to the village. The first store, a drugstore, was opened in 1878, a hardware store in 1881 and a Bank of Toronto in 1902. A rudimentary school was opened in 1847 and a four-room brick school was built in 1881. It had the names of Creemore Public School and Creemore Continuation School, so that you could go through the junior grades and then high school at the same school.

In 1854, St Luke's Anglican Church was built, the first church in the entire district in the townships west of Barrie. In 1886, the Creemore newspaper opened its doors. And in 1885 the first shipment of hogs was made to a slaughterhouse in Collingwood. In 1887, the train came to Creemore and ran from Beeton near Toronto to Collingwood. It made the shipment of hogs much easier and, although it carried passengers, mail and goods, it became known as the Hog Special. By 1900, there were more than 800 people in the village.

When we arrived in 1950, many of the stores were still operating and were owned and operated by descendants of the original owners. The town was well established. There were also many other towns in the area that had developed. Creemore was not relied upon as it had been 100 years before and the population had decreased to about 500. Many of the village's inhabitants were either merchants or worked in Camp Borden. There was also a group of servicemen and their families, based at the Camp, which lived in the village.

Shortly after we arrived, my Mom took me to enroll in the Creemore Public School. Thankfully, I was put in grade 7, which was where I now felt comfortable, except there were 10 people in my class. Being a small town, everyone knew I was a new kid on the block. At the first recess, one grade-eight boy who I soon learned liked to show off, particularly in front of the girls, came up to me. He introduced himself shook my hand and then kneed me in the groin. Fortunately it wasn't hard enough to make me not able to retaliate.

Obviously this 'city boy' didn't realize that I had spent the past three years working on the farm and was tough. I had never had a fight before. But I guess the shock of what he did made me start throwing punches. I had heard of the Marquess of Queensberry rules that laid out how to fight in a 'gentlemanly fashion' but I didn't know what they were. The fight was short. Nursing a bloody nose he headed back into the school. I never had another problem after that with anyone trying to pick a fight. It was a tough introduction to my first day at school in Creemore.

But it didn't really compare to the blow that my mother was dealt during our first week in this village.

One day Mom went to the post office to mail a letter to England and was told there was a letter for her, the first she had received in the village. Fortunately she waited until she got home to open it. It was one single sheet of paper and a short sentence scrawled in ink. It read, "We don't need people like you in this village." Of course it was unsigned.

Why would anyone do this? Lack of knowledge, hatred, who knows. It is interesting to note that in the village, there were five churches, but no Roman Catholic Church. It was a town devoted to the Orange Lodge type of thinking.

Mom was devastated. She had given up her dream of sailing back to her home and the family in England. Now she was told she wasn't wanted here. No doubt they were referring to the fact that she was Jewish. How anyone found out is difficult to know. But in this village, like many small communities, nothing seemed to be a secret. As I grew up there, I learned more about life in this village, about affairs, people stealing from their bosses, the state of relationships and how families got along. Little seemed to be sacred or private.

It was kind of a double whammy for Mom because her family had not been very gracious to her when they learned that she was marrying a Gentile, and now she was being persecuted for being a Jew. To this day, although I have read and studied considerably on the subject, I still am not completely sure why Jewish people are vilified as they are by some. I have learned what some people believe, but none of what I have heard made any sense. Perhaps there is no answer that makes sense!

My Mom and her family, living in England had not faced the hatred that so many Jewish people did during the war. However, there was one person who would marry my first cousin Esme in Australia, whose experiences growing up were an indication of what it was like for so many Jewish people during the war years.

Fabio Cantori was born in Trieste, Italy and was eight when World War II began. His parents had emigrated from Hungary in the 1920s. He lived with his mother, father, two sisters and a brother. He was the youngest child. As a Jewish family, they were not allowed cars, or radios and some families were put out of their homes. In 1938, Fabio was kicked out of school. In 1942 fascists were throwing stones at them and burning Jewish stores.

On September 3, 1943, King Victor Emmanuel III ordered the Dictator Mussolini arrested. Chaos broke out on Sept 9 when it became known. The King fled the country. Mussolini was released by some of his followers. He was invited by the Germans to come to Berlin where Hitler asked him to set up the Italian Socialist Republic. He basically became a puppet of Hitler.

Fabio and his family decided they must get out of Italy. They boarded a train and unfortunately a US aircraft attacked it. The train stopped and everyone was kicked off the train into the fields. All their belongings remained on the train. As soon as everyone was off, the train took off. After the war the Italian government received some recompense from the US but none of it ever was given to those who suffered. The Italian government would not recognize their tickets or claims.

Returning to their apartment, they found out that some German sympathizers had already occupied it.

At this point, his Dad decided that the only way for the family to be safe was to split up. He had himself committed to a mental hospital with the help of a doctor he knew. His mother hid with a family who had a restaurant and she worked as a dishwasher. The brother and two older sisters were told to run away. At 12, Fabio was on his own. He would go to the back of the restaurant where his Mom would sneak him out some bread to eat. He often slept in a broom closet behind the restaurant using the warmth of the oven to keep warm. He wore the same pair of trousers and a blue jacket for two years, gradually growing out of them but he had nothing else to wear.

The Germans were sweeping all the abandoned homes looking for Jews and then taking all the furniture out of the homes that were abandoned. Many people, including Fabio, were scavenging in garbage cans for food. His 19-year-old brother escaped the sweep with the help of friends and went into hiding with a Hungarian woman. She made cakes, which was illegal. Fabio delivered them but couldn't eat the cakes.

Meanwhile the doctor told his father that if he stayed in the hospital he would have to be treated as a patient. That meant shock treatments every day. He wasn't there long. Spies in the hospital told the Germans who he was and so he had to escape.

Fabio moved in with a group of old men who had a little shop fixing bikes and selling eggs. The old men would leave a little lunch for Fabio and in return he would help fix and clean the bikes.

In June 1944, Fabio heard the air raid warnings go off. US aircraft attacked the German locations, but according to Fabio many Italians, were killed. He got shrapnel in his legs and back, some of which remain. He found a first aid station, didn't give his correct name, and received treatment. He then was able to stay with an old man and his wife who knew his mother. Their daughter who was 24 had a boyfriend in the SS. He saw Fabio and wanted to take him to the German camp to use his trade, fixing bikes. Fabio quickly left and met a woman who took him back to a farm about six hours from Trieste.

In April 1945 he was sleeping in the stables. It was hard to sleep in the manure and not get it all over him. He decided to go back to the area where they had lived. Miraculously he did find his father, mother, sisters and brother all of whom had survived. On the way to finding them, he met some partisans who told him that he was big enough to fight. They gave him a gun and bullets and told him to go and shoot any Germans he saw. He said that he shot in the general direction of many Germans but didn't think that he ever hit anyone. Early in May, the New Zealand troops came into the city with tanks and the Germans surrendered to them.

The Italian collaborators were still living in their apartment. A partisan woman and her sons went to the apartment and wanted to kill them. Fabio's father told them not to do it. Rather he told the family they had two days to get out.

After the war, his father was never quite the same. He learned that his father, (Fabio's grandfather), and two brothers had been killed in Hungary by the Germans. After a month, Fabio's Dad started selling pictures and materials and making porcelain plates with photos on them for head stones. There were so many dead in Trieste.

Fabio went back to high school but soon dropped out. He took up photography and worked with his father, developing and printing films, and making student photos for identity cards.

The US and British armies founded a police force for the area. In 1950, Fabio applied and in January 1951 started training at the Police Academy.

In 1955, he decided to start life anew. He emigrated with several friends to Australia. Like many immigrants, he was sent to the country to do manual labour including cane-cutting and harvesting tobacco. On his return to Sydney he had many jobs mostly in construction and some in hospitality. He worked at the Sydney Airport as a flight service labourer from 1967 to 1974 when he joined Alitalia as a catering officer in 1974. He met my cousin Esme in 1957 when she was 18 and married her a year later, shortly after her 19th birthday.

My Uncle Jack, Esme's father, had been wounded by shrapnel in the war, and he never fully recovered. In 1947 he was diagnosed with cancer and died a short time later.

After Uncle Jack's death, a salesman, who had worked with my Uncle Jack and Aunt, selling them supplies, came to their photo shop to pay his condolences to my Aunt. The salesman had moved to Sydney but by coincidence was back in London at that time to close out his affairs in England. Strangely the attraction between this salesman and my Aunt was very strong and by the time he sailed for Australia, my Aunt had agreed to go with him.

Cousin Esme and her younger sister Helene were brought to Australia by their maternal grandparents. When they finally arrived in Australia their mother, my aunt, was married and four months pregnant. Unfortunately, the salesman, their new father Henry, was not particularly kind to the two girls. When my Aunt gave birth, the girl was named Nina, after his first wife who had died along with the child while giving birth. He regarded Nina as his only daughter.

Esme and Fabio married and he went on to have a great career with Alitalia ending up as Director of Customer Relations with the company for Australia. He retired in 1994.

It took Fabio a week to tell me his story when we visited them in Sydney in 2004. Even though he is a kind, gentle, even-spoken man, you could feel the hurt that rushed forward when he thought about how he and his family had been treated so long ago.

It was the same with Mom. She cried and then never said another word about that letter but I knew she carried the words in her heart until the day she died. People just do not realize or probably don't care how much they can hurt others who suffer innocently.

Mom began to make friends in Creemore because she was very outgoing. Dad liked his job although it was hard on him physically. I began to make friends in school. Mom found us another place to live in a house, which we would share with an elderly spinster, Miss Hopper. We had one side of the house, which consisted of a living room and kitchen downstairs, and two bedrooms and a bathroom upstairs. Miss Hopper had the other side of the house. Mom made friends with Miss Hopper who enjoyed the occasional meal with us. We had more space than the apartment and the rent was less. Life started to look good for the Dent family.

One day Dad came home and told us that the building under construction was about to be finished. The company had no more contracts so he was being laid off.

In 1952 there was no unemployment insurance. Dad was too proud to take welfare. Mom fortunately, quickly found a job looking after Price's hardware store. Mr. Price was a very nice man but had little head for business. Mom's experience in London paid off. She soon had the business running well. Dad was not particularly happy staying at home. In early 1953, he was told that the Camp Borden was looking for cleaners. Dad applied and was given a job with the federal government working at the Joint Nuclear Biological Chemical Warfare School as a cleaner. A number of men in Creemore worked at similar jobs on the base so it seemed a good move for him. Dad was meticulous in his cleaning and soon was receiving accolades from his military bosses at the base.

Later in life I realized the lesson that Dad had taught me. Regardless of what you do in life do your best and try to be the best at what you do. It really was a great job for Dad. He was inside, the work was not too physical and he was basically his own boss just having to finish his cleaning each day. He also had good conversations with the many military men who were training at the school. He came home each night happy and content.

Dad was a great guy but also very proud. So as soon as he got a job, he told Mom she had to quit hers. He was the breadwinner and she was to look after the house. Mom was devastated. She really enjoyed working and she knew we really needed the extra money. But Dad would have none of it. So she quit.

Mom and Dad also began to get involved in the community. Mom joined the Royal Canadian Legion Woman's Auxiliary based on the fact that her brother had served in the British Army during the war, and became involved in many activities. Dad joined the Orange Lodge.

The Orange Order has existed in Canada since at least the 1830s. The Order organized community and benevolent activities and helped Protestant immigrants to settle. It was a central facet of life in Ontario and very important in Creemore. Members were required to be Protestant. Parades formed a large part of the Orange culture particularly those leading up to the Twelfth of July. This date recognized the date of the decisive Battle of the Boyne in July 1690, when William of Orange defeated James II.

Encouraged by Dad, I joined the Loyal Orange Young Briton Association, which was a junior branch of the Orange Order of Canada. It was open to Protestant (Christian) young men between the ages of 12 and 25, and was involved in social, sporting and community activities. I became a proud member and even was involved in helping to organize events and take part in parades.

It was during one of these parades that one of the men from the Orange Lodge, with whom we marched to the church, died. He carried the banner into the church, put it into a stand at the front and came back to sit beside me. He suddenly grasped his chest, made some horrible noises and then died. I was 14 and it was the first time I had experienced death in front of me.

I enjoyed going to the Young Britons and being privy to the little secret signs and codes one needed to get into the Orange Lodge Hall and wearing the sashes and badges on parades and going to different towns to take part in events. But I soon began to realize, at least in my mind, that this organization was all about a lack of tolerance for anything Catholic. That, I

42

couldn't handle, so I quit. I told Dad what I thought and, bless him, he quit as well.

Although the OYB provided some social life for me, I soon found a much better organization, which I think, shaped me for the years ahead.

I had gone to St Luke's Anglican Church occasionally with Mom. She had been invited by some of the ladies in the Legion. But there wasn't really much that interested me. That all changed in May 1954. Rev Walter Dyer, with his wife Ina and children Alan and Pat arrived to become the church minister. Walter Dyer was 34 and this was his first church since being ordained. He was also responsible for two small community Anglican churches in Banda and Avening. He had left a promising career with Peterborough Carpet Company, where he was involved in public relations, because he felt the call of God. During his studies, the Archbishop of Toronto told him that he had been assigned this parish even before he had completed his studies at Trinity College in Toronto, in recognition of his abilities. "They need you in Creemore now," the Archbishop told him.

Rev Walter Dyer was honest, committed to his faith and led his life in the same manner inside and outside the pulpit every day in the community. During his days in Creemore, he was gentle but firm; good to his family, and to everyone he met.

Even though I was only 14 when I met him, he soon set the benchmark for me as to what a minister should be.

It didn't take the Dyers long to start organizing activities in the church. They soon had a number of clubs established including, most importantly for us teenagers, a young people's group. In Creemore, there were basically two groups of young people. Those who hung around the downtown restaurant and those who wanted to be more involved in groups that did positive, constructive activities.

The St Luke's Anglican Young Peoples Association was established in Creemore with an initial group of about eight teenagers. As the group began to evolve, more teenagers became aware and wanted to join, even some who were not Anglicans.

What bothered some of us teens was the fact that we had no church hall in which to meet. Every meeting for every church group was held in the Rectory, the house in which Rev Dyer, Ina and the children lived. Every day, often morning, afternoon and evening, their privacy and peace and quiet was disturbed. Ina, a wonderful wife and mother, was always making pastries and serving tea. To us youngsters, it didn't seem fair.

Having discussed this at one of our AYPA meetings, we approached the church board and asked them if they would consider building a church hall. Too expensive was the immediate reply. Well, what if we could raise $1,000 in the next six months to get the building fund started. You could almost see the board trying not to laugh. Sure, if you can raise that much we will start a building they said, obviously not believing for a minute that a group of young teenagers (in 1955) could do this.

43

We set out on this daunting task. First we decided to have a play. We picked out a script, assigned parts and began practicing. We convinced the town council to let us use the town hall for free to put on the play. To our surprise, we had a full house and made money. We were asked to put it on in other areas and that added to our fund. At the same time we decided to have an auction and began asking storeowners and farmers for donations. We got a lot of stuff including a small piglet. The auction was held in the local arena. We made more money. Six months later, we turned just over $1,500 to the board. Can you imagine the look on those board members' faces? It was a good start on the approximately $10,000 needed to build the hall.

In addition to the money, many of us came after school and our summer jobs to help carry bricks and mix mortar. Finally the church hall was built. The Dyers had their home to themselves. This hall is where we took our daughter Susan from Newfoundland as part of her christening ceremony in 1963.

In the spring of 1954, just before the Dyers arrived, the Creemore Continuation School was closed. We high school students, along with many others in the region, were moved to the Collingwood District Collegiate Institute, 17 miles from Creemore. That meant being bused everyday through the country for about an hour in order to pick up the kids who lived on the farms.

CDCI was another broadening of my social life. I met more kids and became involved in more activities. I played on the football team, which meant practicing after school and missing the school bus. Each day after practice, I would hitch- hike 17 miles home. People were more likely to pick up young teenagers and it was much safer in the 50s. I was involved in boys' athletics and was eventually elected head of boys' athletics on the student council. I helped to organize a winter carnival in the Collingwood arena. Because many of the boys weren't good enough to make the school basketball team, I invented several activities that allowed them to compete and win ribbons they could wear on their jackets. One such was called "foul shot". Each person was given points for each basket scored from the foul line and when a certain number of points were attained, given a ribbon of recognition.

For some reason, in Grade 13, I was given the responsibility for introducing Robert Service when he came to address our school. Robert Service was called the bard of the Yukon and was best known for his poems. Among the most notable were 'The Shooting of Dan McGraw' and 'The Cremation of Sam McGee.' He was 83 when he came to our school and died a year later.

It was a memorable experience. After his address, he gave me a signed copy of his latest book. Unfortunately, it disappeared when Mom and Dad left their house some years later.

I enjoyed school and was particularly good in math. It didn't endear me to my classmates, however. One day when no one else could give a correct answer, our old teacher Miss Clark said, with some exasperation, "Oh, for heaven's sake Leonard tell us the right answer." Knowing that would only get me in more trouble with my peers, I said, "I am sorry Miss Clark but I don't know." She knew I knew. She was so angry she took her false eye out of its socket and began cleaning it with her rather soiled handkerchief. We were unkind; we did have a saying for her, when she wasn't around. "Here comes Ma Clark, walking down the hall, one eye upon the ceiling and one upon the wall."

In Creemore, I joined the baseball team and we played against many small towns in the surrounding area. We didn't have enough money to buy uniforms and one day we decided to approach merchants to get them to buy each of us a uniform. Because I was one of the organizers and had broad shoulders, I guess, I had to approach the local funeral home. So when we trotted out onto the field with our new white uniforms, in big black letters, stretched across my back were the words, 'Decker and Mumford Funeral Home.'

I became more interested in going to dances in Creemore and surrounding communities. Although I had never had a lesson I seemed to have good rhythm. That made girls want to dance with me. Sylvia Swan who was older than me and now working and driving her own car, would take me to dances but with a proviso. "Leonard," she would say almost every time we went to a dance, "If I meet anyone really interesting, you will have to find your own way home."

In addition to Sylvia, I went out or chummed around with a number of girls including many of those in our AYPA group. I went out on occasion with girls from high school in Collingwood, but I never really had a girlfriend. Sylvia, Robyn and I went to several church camps together and enjoyed each other's company. At 16, I was 6'2" and 200 pounds. A little chubby and maybe that is why I was tagged with the nick name 'Spud' Maybe the girls didn't think I had as much appeal or potential as some of the other boys in town.

We went as a group from Creemore to the Anglican Young People Association's National Convention held in Ottawa in 1955. I remember opening my envelope at the registration desk and reading that my host was Miss Anne Massey. "Probably some little old lady with a house full of cats," one of the guys said as he announced he was staying with Mr. and Mrs. Bert Smith. So off I went to a rather attractive older home on Churchill Avenue in what was then the western end of Ottawa.

Imagine my surprise when I met my hosts Dr. and Mrs. Massey. Dr. Massey was a scientist who worked at the National Research Council in Ottawa. He was related to Vincent Massey a former Governor General of Canada and Raymond Massey who was then a well-known Hollywood actor. Then I met Miss Massey. Anne was 16, blonde, and gorgeous. At some point I asked her if she was going to the dinner and dance being held at the Chateau Laurier and she said yes. I said I guess you have a date and

45

she said no. "Would you like to come with me?" I asked and much to my surprise she said, "Yes."

We walked into the banquet hall at the Chateau that Saturday night, Anne looking radiant in a beautiful full length gown and I in my only blue suit. We got stares, particularly from my Creemore friends. "Where did you find her?" one guy whispered to me. "That's the lady with the cats," I smirked.

The AYPA group also got us involved in some cultural activities. Some of us went to St Michael's in Toronto to hear the Messiah at Christmas time. We also went to see plays at the recently opened Stratford Festival.

The world was also opened a little wider when television came to Creemore in 1955. We didn't have a set at home but my good friend Bobbie Corbett's Mom and Dad bought one, so I would go there on many evenings after ball practice to watch shows. Bob and I played together on the baseball team and hung around together after school.

Television was not new to me because in 1943 in England the local barbershop had a huge piece of furniture in the middle of which was a 9 inch round screen. Almost every Saturday morning Dad would drop me off there while he and Mom went shopping. I would sit mesmerized in front of a snowy screen watching little match sticks chasing a ball in what I learned was a soccer game. The problem was that there was so much snow on the screen that it was hard to determine where the ball was. But it kept me busy for a couple of hours while Mom and Dad did their necessary weekend chores.

In 1956, I entered Grade 13 when many of my friends, for a variety of reasons, had already quit high school. Many of them got jobs at Base Borden or in some of the local businesses, or they worked on their parent's farms. I palled around a lot with David Palmer who was older than me. He had finished Grade 13 and now was working as a teller at the Bank of Toronto in Creemore. He suffered from ulcerative colitis and consequently was very small and weighed very little. Give him a couple of beers though on a Friday night and he wanted to take on the biggest guys in the dance hall. On several occasions, I had to convince his would-be assailants that I needed to take him home right now.

At 17, I wasn't sure what I wanted to do with my life. For some reason, which I can't explain even now, I knew I had to get out of Creemore. My Mom who managed the finances asked me at 16, if I was going to stay in school all my life. I guess she saw that many of my friends, including Bob Corbett, were already out making money and in some cases contributing to the family income.

Mom was a financial wizard and managed all of the money that Dad brought home. In 1955, she had managed to save $500 to make a down payment on a house on Caroline Street. It wasn't very big, a family room, kitchen, two small bedrooms, one bathroom, a scullery and a one car garage, albeit it was on a nice big piece of property on a corner lot close to the Creemore jail. The jail is still billed as the smallest jail in North America, holding only one cell and just enough room to walk through the door and into the cell. I don't remember anyone ever being in the jail. Indeed, I don't think we even had a policeman in Creemore. Occasionally the OPP would drive through, particularly if there was a dance on a Saturday night at the town hall.

The house cost Mom and Dad $4,500. It was the first time that we had ever had our own home. Dad only made about $200 a month so Mom really had to do magic with those dollars.

Discussing my dilemma with David one night, he said he would join the Air Force if he could, but knew with his medical problems he never could. "So why don't you join?" he quipped. "Hell no," I immediately replied. "You are never going to get me up in one of those things," remembering all too vividly the crash that I had seen in Malton eight years earlier.

There was a guidance and career counselor at the school, so one day I met with her. "Well," she said, "Canada Packers in Toronto has a personnel recruiter coming to the school next month. Would you like to talk to him?" "Sure why not," I said.

So in May of 1957, I met with a very nice recruiter who told me about the benefits and potential for a career in his company in Toronto. He had read the CV that I had provided to the counselor along with a copy of my marks and achievements at the school. At the end of the interview, he offered me a starting position with the company at a salary of $60 a week. Good heavens I thought, that's more than my Dad makes.

I graduated from CDCI in June 1957. I had won a $500 scholarship to the University of Toronto. That wasn't enough to tempt me to apply to University since I didn't have any other financial support and certainly couldn't get any from Mom and Dad.

The job didn't start until early September so in the meantime I got a job in Barrie as a teller at the Sterling Trust Corporation. I worked there for two months giving Mom about half of the $35 a week that I earned and saving most of the rest to get me ready for my move to Toronto.

On Labour Day weekend, David drove me to Stayner and I got on the bus for Toronto. I carried a small suitcase with my clothes, wore a new grey suit that I bought with money I had saved and had $17 in my pocket.

Mom cried as I left. I was her only child and her real love. I was confident and ready to face the world.

Mom, me, my best friend David and Dad.

Mom and I before I left home to work in Toronto, 1957.

CHAPTER 6 - LEAVING THE NEST, SPREADING MY WINGS

As the Grey Line coach arrived at the downtown bus terminal on Bay Street in Toronto that Sunday afternoon, I was excited and optimistic.

It hadn't hit me yet that I had left home. All that security, the meals cooked to my liking that magically appeared on the table three times a day, school packed lunches, along with going to bed snacks. All were gone.

I just saw the magic of this huge city-well, huge to me, and the opportunities it presented. Toronto, with its population of 250,000, was not nearly as big as London but certainly much larger than Creemore where I had spent the past six years of my life. I didn't even have a plan. But I had a job.

I got off the bus asked directions to the YMCA on Gerrard Street. Fortunately they had a room that I could rent for $4 a night. It didn't even dawn on me then that $17 wouldn't go very far.

The next day I got on a street car and made my way to the Canada Packers Headquarters at Keele and St Clair in the west end of the city.

Art Evans, the Head of Personnel who briefed us on our training program welcomed me, along with two other men. We would be started in the mailroom where we would work for three months. At the same time we would take evening seminars twice a week that would orientate us to the Canada Packers organization. Most importantly, from my perspective, we would be fed dinner for free at the wonderful cafeteria each night while we received our classroom instructions.

Working in the mailroom for me, as I am sure it was intended to be, was an excellent way to learn about Canada Packers. We had to sort the mail, put it in a mailbag and then walk to every corner of the office and plant in this huge complex. It took us from the president's office to the killing floor. We were well prepared to be sent to different assignments within the company by the time the three months were up. I am not sure how my two colleagues felt about this seemingly menial task. One was a recent graduate of the University of Toronto who was now playing for the CFL's Toronto Argonauts. Art Evans, who had also played for the team at one time, had recruited him. The other was a 27-year-old German who I soon learned had a PhD in economics from the University of Munich. When I asked him why he wasn't doing something better like teaching at U of T, he told me that he had just arrived in Canada with his new wife and was trying to learn to speak better English. I actually think we all started off at the same salary. Not that it mattered to my football-playing colleague because his contract with the Argos paid him $14,000 a season or $1,000 a game, equivalent to four months of our Canada Packers salary.

I confess I had some problems working alongside the German who did seem to be a quiet, soft -spoken man. Thoughts of what had happened to my family and our fellow citizens in England during the war made it hard for me to feel any kindness. Then one day shortly after we started, perhaps sensing my discomfort with him, he told me the story of his family. His father had owned a large factory in a small town in Bavaria until one day the Nazis walked in and told him he had 24 hours to get out with his family and anything they could carry. So from a very comfortable life with a big home, the family suddenly had to flee and had nothing. They had to rely on relatives and friends to help them with accommodation and money. My colleague was 'recruited' as a boy soldier at the end of the war to go and fight the western allies. The alternative was to be shot. Suddenly I realized that the Nazis had also ruined the lives of many German people. It made it easier to work together.

I was excited about starting my new job but I had a big problem. The second day of work was the last day that I could afford to stay in the YMCA. The nightly rate, plus the cost of eating and streetcar fare had depleted my $17. I asked my new boss if there was a way I could get an advance on my salary. He said he would ask the finance people.

The next day after work, I walked about four miles to the home of Scotty and Anne Morton who lived on Eglinton Avenue because I no longer had the fare for a streetcar or any money to buy any food.

I had met the Mortons at their beach home on Wasaga Beach the previous summer. Actually I first met Donna, their very attractive daughter, who was four years younger than me. She had introduced me to her Mom and Dad. Donna was in Grade 10 at Havergal College, a private school for girls, which was situated on Avenue Road in Toronto. Her Mom approved of me, even though I was older and I had shared several meals with them at the beach during the summer.

Scotty was smaller and much older than Anne. He was born in Scotland and as a youth worked in the coal mines which played havoc with his lungs. In his early thirties he immigrated to Canada and settled in Toronto where his first job was sweeping floors at the Timothy Eaton Company on Yonge St. Ambition and a glib tongue landed him a job working for O'Donnell-Mackie, a new and used car dealership on Bay Street. They specialized in Studebaker cars but also held the license to sell Rolls Royce in the Toronto area.

When the war broke out in 1939, Scotty's medical condition would not allow him to enlist. So he remained in the company while all the other salesmen went off to fight the war. When cars stopped being produced in the early 1940s, he lived on a meager salary without any commission. But many customers would visit the dealership hoping that someday soon cars would start to be built. Scotty wisely took their names and promised them that as soon as cars started to come off the assembly line, they would be first on the list. By the time cars did start to roll in, Scotty had an extensive list of customers and made a fortune in commissions.

He married Anne during the war years and Donna was born in 1943. He bought a small building on Eglinton Avenue, which held a shop on the first floor and a large apartment on the second floor. Anne turned the shop into a beauty parlour and had a good business going with the help of several assistants.

When I arrived at their apartment I was a mess. Tired, hungry and my clothes were dirty. Anne made me take a bath, wrapped me in a housecoat while she washed my clothes and fed me dinner. Meanwhile she started looking through the ads for a place for me to stay. I spent that night in a spare bedroom and they gave me enough money to get me to work and back. At work, my boss told me they would give me a $10 advance on my weekly salary to last me until payday at the end of the week.

The next evening, Anne drove me to a house in west Toronto owned by a woman whose husband had recently deserted her and her two children. To help pay the mortgage she was taking in some boarders. She already had two young brothers from Ireland sleeping in the downstairs bedroom. She and her two young daughters, both preschoolers, slept upstairs. The room she showed me was not really much more than the porch made into a small bedroom with a single bed. I had to walk through the bedroom occupied by the two Irishmen to get to it. But she only wanted $15 a week including breakfast. I had nowhere else to go, so I took it.

The Irishmen, as I found out, were nuts. They loved to drink and fight. Every Friday night they would be off to the pub to see how much they could drink and how many fights they could get into. They would come rolling in usually after midnight singing at the top of their lungs. Waking up, I could smell the beer and had to listen to them laughing about how much fun they had had.

Meanwhile every Friday night, my landlady, who was a rather attractive, slim, middle-30s, would put the girls to bed and start drinking from a six-pack of beer she bought every Friday night after working at a local grocery store. After a few beers she would start making toasted tomato sandwiches. I was allowed to watch her TV in the living room. Armed with a beer and a toasted tomato sandwich, which she also offered me, she would sit on the couch beside me and start to cry about how lonesome she was. When she started to get too close, I excused myself and went back to my little rented nest somewhat scared of what this older, deserted mother of two children had in mind. After four weekends I left.

Fortunately, by searching the ads, I had been able to find what sounded like the ideal solution to my housing problem. A family, with a daughter, in Forest Hill Village, an upscale Jewish area in mid-west Toronto, was offering a room, and meals along with an opportunity to share the living room with the family.

On a Saturday I visited the house, which was on a well-developed street and in excellent shape. The bedroom was far superior to the one I was living in and the landlady was very pleasant. The daughter was younger than me and would prove no threat, unlike the time I had lived in Toronto 10 years earlier. The family had recently emigrated from Scotland, where the husband was an engineer,

Unfortunately, the company that he had come to work for had closed and so now he was looking for another job while receiving some benefits from the government.

Twenty dollars a week seemed quite reasonable and so I gave my notice to 'Miss Friday Night Blues' and moved to my new lodgings.

It didn't take long to realize that my new accommodation was less than ideal. My bedroom was fine but that was about all. First, I realized that they hadn't ever fed a strapping 18-year-old who walked for eight hours a day carrying a mailbag.

Breakfast was some toast; my lunch packed in a small paper bag was usually two slices of white bread with one slice of ham or cheese and sometimes a piece of fruit. Dinner came on one plate with a potato, a small piece of meat and a few vegetables. I was always hungry.

But that wasn't the worst part of my new digs. On about my third night of sitting in the living room and watching TV, I heard a voice coming from the kitchen saying, "Who does he think he is sitting in our living room and watching our TV? We need our privacy. He should be in his room. He should be in his room." His wife obviously hadn't told her husband that our agreement was that I could share. He was a bitter and arrogant man.

One night I came home and he was furious because he went to pick up his government welfare check and they called him by a number rather than by name. He swore at everything about this country and about me living in his house.

After hearing those remarks, I walked out into the pouring rain and walked up and down the street. I was in a big city, basically all alone, away from home, and no decent place to live. I started to cry. Something I don't know if I had ever done before, certainly not since I hit my teens. Thoughts ran through my head of giving up and going back to Creemore. But my instant reaction to that thought was, "Hell, no!" I went back inside, went to my room got out of my soaking clothes and went to bed. The next day I started looking through the ads again for a new place to live.

It took about two weeks for me to find a new place. The ad read, "Quiet, middle-aged couple with no children has room to rent. One other person renting who is a professional. In quiet neighbourhood. Spacious room on third floor of single dwelling. Rent $15 a week."

I went to 460 Brunswick Ave, near Bloor and Bathurst, the first opportunity that I had. A very gracious 30-something lady and her husband, who turned out to be an inspector for the Canadian Restaurant Association, met me. They showed me a spacious and comfortable looking room on the third floor and introduced me to Bruce. Bruce had recently graduated from the University of Toronto as an accountant and now worked for a small accounting firm nearby. He was to become my soul mate for the next year. The next weekend, I moved into my new digs!

Unless we had dates, or I went home for the weekend, Bruce and I spent a lot of our free time together, mostly just in the evening. With no TV to watch we simply talked about our lives and what we thought might lie ahead. Bruce was 22, four years older than me, so a good mentor.

We developed an interesting routine regarding our supper meal, which we usually ate together. We decided shortly after meeting that we would take turns buying groceries for supper. We would eat in one or the other's bedrooms, sitting at a rather comfortable small table that our landlady had placed in each room. Neither of us had much time to shop on the way home. I began buying tins of corned beef and a loaf of bread and some pickles when needed at a nearby grocery store. Corned beef sandwiches every other night actually are quite good. Bruce liked meat pies so we had cold meat pies on alternate nights, sometimes with a little salad.

Looking back it is funny that usually on Friday nights we would head for a nearby pub or small restaurant for a few beers and a good meal, the cost of which would have bought us some much better fare during the week. The pies came in packets of two so there was no problem sharing. But soon we were measuring the length of the corned beef to make sure that we got an equal share.

Our landlord was able to give us good advice about what restaurants to frequent and which ones to avoid. He gave me a tip, which I have never forgotten and over the years have put to good use. "When I am inspecting a restaurant," he said, "I always go to the washroom first. The state and cleanliness of the washroom will normally always be the same as that of the kitchen. If you don't like the look or smell of the washroom, don't eat in that restaurant."

I didn't really have many dates. Donna was too young to go out and was busy with her schoolwork. I went to dances at the YMCA and danced but didn't connect with anyone in particular. It wasn't until Canada Packers held their annual Christmas party for workers and families that I met a rather interesting girl named Julia Spivak. Julia lived with her widowed father who was a meat cutter at the plant. He had come from Poland shortly after the war. I never found out what happened to Julia's mother and never asked. She had recently graduated from high school in the west end of Toronto and was working as a steno in an office. She was attractive, a good dancer and my age. We went out to dances, to the movies and to eat once in a while.

After a couple of dates, I decided to play a trick on her to learn more about her background. J M Dent and Sons was a large publishing house started in England in 1888. My father once told me that we had been part of that family many years ago but my great grandfather had run away to sea and had been disowned. "That's how we became the poor side of the family." At least that's the story my father told me. The company expanded and had branches all over the world including in Toronto.

One day at the office, from my mailroom, I called the high school where Julia had attended and asked for the principal's office. I identified myself to the principal's assistant and told her that I was Leonard Dent from the J M Dent and Sons Publishing house and had an application for a job on my desk from a Miss Julia Spivak. "Could you give me some background on her," I asked. "What were her grades like and was she involved in sports activities?" "Certainly," the assistant replied. Shortly she returned to the phone presumably with Julia's file. "She was very good in school, and in particular excelled in math," she told me. "She was very athletic and liked all sports; she was captain of the volleyball team. A good all around student," she gushed, presumably think she was helping to clinch the job for Julia. "Thank you so much," I replied, "this is so helpful."

Several nights later Julia and I went out for a small supper after work. I looked at her and said, "You know I bet you were a very good student in school." "Yes I was," she replied. "You probably excelled in math." I volunteered. "In fact that was my favourite subject, but how would you know?" "I am kind of psychic," I said rather shyly. "I look at people and can guess what they are like. For example I bet you like sports and probably most of all volleyball considering your height." "That's amazing," she replied. "You were probably good enough at volleyball to be the captain of the team." She was very impressed with my insight; I never told her how I found out.

We enjoyed each other's company but I never really thought of her as a girlfriend in the sense that we were going steady. Transportation became a problem because she lived so far west of where I lived. I started looking at purchasing a second-hand car. I found a 1955 Dodge sedan, which looked in good shape. I had attended a six-week driver mechanics course at an Army Cadet Summer camp in Camp Borden in 1955. We had been required to learn everything about how a four-cycle engine worked including partially stripping the engine and putting it back together again. So I knew something about cars.

The cost was about $500, which was roughly two months' salary. After my inspection and considering my finances, I bought it. The car helped immeasurably in getting to work, going out on dates and going home to see Mom and Dad, usually a couple of weekends a month.

On one of those visits home to Creemore, I met my Aunt Lily from Australia and Cousin Elsa from Las Vegas who were visiting Mom and Dad.

This was an opportunity to meet family whom I hadn't really known. Frankly, I never really thought of any of the Gowans as family even though we lived with them on the farm for more than three years.

Aunt Lily, one of Mom's two older sisters, was a diminutive, attractive 50- something woman who loved life and men, particularly older men. She married in her 20s in London to a man almost 30 years her senior. Paul, my cousin, was born in 1934 and he was the only child she ever had. When her husband died, she eventually found two more husbands, both much older. Perhaps she was looking for that father figure that she remembered since she was about 13 when her father, my grandfather, left for Russia and never came back.

She had tried to immigrate to Canada but during a medical, a spot was found on her lung and she was denied entry. Strange that at the time Canada was accepting refugees from Africa regardless of their status or medical condition. So she and Paul had emigrated to Australia. She came to Canada in the late 50s and spent a year here enjoying the country, before heading back to the land of OZ. Paul came to Toronto in 1960 and stayed. He and Elsa, my first cousins, were really the only relatives I had in North America.

Perhaps love of life and men ran in our family. Elsa was about 5 foot tall, a size 2 waist and very buxom. She was also gorgeous. When her mother, my Aunt Celia and mom's oldest sister died in 1946, her father remarried shortly thereafter. Elsa and her older sister Irene were part of the marriage arrangement. But their new mom apparently didn't relish the reality of two lively young women in her home.

In 1946 when her mother died, 19-year old Elsa was already being wooed by 32 year-old Stanley Black who was conductor of the BBC Dance Orchestra. In addition to his achievements as an orchestra leader, over the years, he conducted, arranged, performed and produced a large number of albums and arranged and directed music for about 200 films. A recipient of the OBE, he was popular worldwide and conducted many of Britain's major orchestras until the 1990s. He died in London in 2002, aged 89.

Stanley Black was born Solomon Schwartz, by Polish and Romanian Jewish parents. He was crazy about this vivacious, young Jewish girl. Elsa had been dancing since she was three. At 18 she was offered a job in the Paris Follies. Stanley Black sent a chauffeured car over to pick her up and take her to Paris. Her father refused to let her go because her mother was ill.

When her new step-mom arrived on the scene, arrangements were soon made to ship her to the USA. 'Mom' had friends in Boston who told them about a religious 38 year-old man that would make a perfect match for Elsa. Elsa came to Boston but quickly negated any thought of marriage and moved in with an old girlfriend who was a look alike. They partied, had many boyfriends, but couldn't stand the cold climate in Massachusetts.

In 1950, the two girls moved to California with $40 each in their pockets. Here they stayed with a movie-extra in Malibu who only could afford to feed them ham to eat. They were Jewish, but hungry, so they ate ham. They got jobs as models, worked in department stores, and joined a dance team working in the local area. Elsa dated movie stars and producers including Victor Mature and Al Siegel. At one point she tried out for a movie role but lost out to a young dancer in her early 20s named Mitzi Gaynor.

In 1953, she went back to London but didn't feel that there was any love for her at her parents' house so returned to the US, this time choosing Miami. Here she lived a good high life, mixing with some of 'the' people in Miami with whom one should be seen or perhaps shouldn't be seen. In 1954, she met a 6'5" handsome Armenian who lived next door. He loved to party, go to the races and gamble. They spent a wonderful summer together and then Paul, her beau, was offered an opportunity to open a restaurant in Colorado so Elsa went with him.

They both worked in the restaurant but it was hard and the owner didn't pay them much for their 16-hour days. They decided to head back to California. Driving through Las Vegas, they stopped to have dinner with a friend of Paul's. He offered Paul a job as a headwaiter in one of his restaurants. Elsa started working in a shop and was soon running three shops including one in the Riviera Hotel.

In1962, Paul and Elsa were married. They began buying and running their own restaurants. The first was the Hof Brau House from which they opened up two more of the same name. Their only daughter Lisa was adopted in 1964 and she became the apple of her father's eye. He spoiled her rotten.

In 1968, they went into partnership with a well-to-do businessman and opened a five star restaurant. Unfortunately, the agreement was 51% ownership to the businessman and 49% for Paul and Elsa. They poured all their money into this new venture. But as Elsa told me years later, it was the beginning of the end for them. Many celebrities who came to play or lived in Las Vegas frequented the restaurant. Caroline Onassis had her wedding dinner hosted by the restaurant. Paul and Elsa became part of the 'in' crowd. They lived only for the day, she told me, although most often the long days stretched into the early morning. Their business partner was the front man and Paul did all the work. Finally Paul had had enough and tried to get out. He was told that there was no money left. They took their partner to court and won, but the defendant simply claimed he had no money. Elsa said she believed the money had all gone to a Swiss bank account. They were left with nothing.

But in 1958, walking down the main street of Creemore with Mom and these two gorgeous women, we drew stares from everyone, particularly the men, regardless of their age. Many of the people in Creemore could trace relatives back more than100 years in the area. For us, these were the first relatives that we could ever show-off and show-off we did.

By the beginning of January 1958, at 18-1/2 my life was looking very good.

Shortly before Christmas I had finished my three months indoctrination period and was moved into Canada Packer's traffic department as a shipping clerk responsible for making sure that the correct amount of ice and salt was loaded in the freight cars destined for the Maritimes depending on what each car carried.

Obviously, 38,000 lb of meat and poultry required much more attention than cases of canned processed meats. A wrong instruction to those responsible for actioning my orders and the contents of a whole car could be spoiled. With my new job, I had been given a five percent raise and was now making $63 a week. I had a great place to live, a car, and a girl with whom I enjoyed going out.

For the next few months, I just enjoyed life. In addition to going out with Julia, I also continued to go to the occasional dance. I enjoyed the dancing but didn't really meet any interesting girls that I wanted to date. But, I did meet Jerry Harris.

Jerry Harris was a slightly shorter than average guy, good looking with a tremendous ego. He and his family including his father George Sr, his mother Mary, and older brother George Jr., had all emigrated from Yorkshire England in 1957. Both George Jr and Jerry now worked at AV Roe on the AVRO Arrow project.

Gerry and his parents lived in an apartment building at the corner of Yonge St and Highway 401, where George Sr and Mary were the superintendents. In that building, as I found out, lived many engineers, some that had worked on the V1 and V2 projects in Germany, and some on the Spitfire and other fighters in Great Britain. After the war they had been recruited to come and work on the Arrow. There must have been some interesting conversations in the cafeteria as these former adversaries now worked on a common project.

The Arrow was a delta-winged interceptor, which began as a project in 1953 and flew for the first time in 1958. It was to have been the primary interceptor for the Royal Canadian Air Force. Some say it would have been a formidable fighter today with its promised speed of Mach 2 and altitudes above 50,000 feet.

But at 11 am on Friday, February 20, 1959, the project was unceremoniously cancelled. An unexpected announcement by Prime Minister John Diefenbaker immediately put more than 14,000 Avro employees out of work as well as close to another 15,000 others who were employees of outside suppliers for the aircraft.

Although reportedly the cancellation came as a surprise to Avro management, within hours George Jr. had a call from an aircraft builder inviting him and his wife for the weekend to go to Detroit. When he came back he told us that the company had offered him a job and apologized because in accordance with company policy his salary for the first six months would have to be a basic amount; then he would be starting at his real salary. He smiled when he told us that the temporary salary was much more than he was being paid at AVRO.

Prime Minister Diefenbaker bore the brunt of the criticism for the cancellation and some say that this contributed to his minority government's defeat in the 1963 election. Indeed the controversy still swirls around why the project was really cancelled. But, at the time, I was led to believe that the Military Industrial Complex in the USA was bound and determined that the US Forces would fly no foreign-built aircraft, and as such, considerable pressure was put on the US Administration not to buy the Arrow. There were many factors at play at the time. Many Canadians, who have an interest in the subject, have made up their own minds why it happened and are convinced they are correct.

Aside from losing an incredible aircraft, Canada lost perhaps a unique team of engineers, designers and aircraft builders. Like George, many were offered jobs in the USA and UK. One group went to work with NASA and others to help design and build the Concorde. I am not sure if Canada's aviation industry has ever completely recovered from that loss of expertise.

The Harrises had invited me to move in with them in the fall of 1958. I had told Jerry that I was being a bit smothered by my landlady. One evening when I was out with Julia, I had a nosebleed and it wouldn't stop. I dropped her off at her home and then went back to my digs. My nose was still bleeding, I had blood all over my clothes; I was a mess. When I went in the front door, my landlady was still up and she almost went into hysterics. She had once gone through a car windshield and thought the same had happened to me. From then on she tried to be more of a mother than a landlady. I appreciated what she was trying to do but felt that I had left home to get away from this type of nurturing.

In October I moved in with the Harrises. George and Mary treated me like one of their own. I was spoiled rotten with too much food for dinner each night and too big a lunch each day to take to work. Gerry and I worked hard during the week and toured the countryside on the weekends. He was one of the few kept employed by AVRO.

He was into guns and owned a small arsenal. Often we would drive up to Creemore, stay with Mom and Dad and go to a local gun range to shoot. One Sunday he drove me out to Wasaga Beach and dropped me off at the Morton's cottage to visit with Donna and her family. He took off in his new 1958 Ford telling me he would be back to pick me up in a couple of hours. Four hours went by and he hadn't arrived. I borrowed Anne's car and Donna and I went off to downtown Wasaga Beach to see if we might find him. It didn't take long.

There was the Ford parked in front of the Ontario Provincial Police station. We went in and found a rather sheepish Jerry sitting in a small office. Apparently he had been stopped for speeding on the main street and the policeman had opened the trunk and found the arsenal. He had a shotgun, several hand guns, including a 357 and a 44 magnum, as well as a couple of 22 rifles and loads of ammunition. They were now calling all over Ontario to see if there had been any recent robberies. It took about another hour before they let him go.

Jerry was a great guy but a little off the wall. One Saturday morning, we got up about 9 am after probably drinking too much beer the night before. He said, "Len, we are going to Buffalo to join the Marine Corps." Too weak to argue, I said "ok" and off we went. We got to Buffalo, found the Recruiting Centre, parked the car and then went in. Fortunately, it was 12:05 and the office closed at noon on Saturdays. If not, we probably would have been recruited and ended up in Vietnam. There is no official figure but it is thought that as many as 12,000 Canadians fought with the US over the years in Vietnam, and that between 500 and 1,000 died in the fighting.

I thought at the time that this brush with joining the US Marine Corps would be the closest that I would ever get to being in the military. I had no desire to join any armed force. Little did I know that within a few weeks an event would occur that would begin to push me towards a lifelong career in the Canadian Armed Forces.

One evening in the fall of 1958, I received a call from Marilyn Melville, with whom I had gone to school in Collingwood and who also had been an active member of the St Luke's Anglican Young People's Association. She was in nursing training at the Toronto Wellesley Hospital. She told me that our friend David was in hospital and had just had an operation as a result of his suffering with Ulcerative Colitis. It had taken her a while to find me, because I had recently moved. David was eight days post-op and was doing fine she told me.

The next evening I went from work straight to the hospital to see him. He was in fine spirits and told me that this was the first day that he had been able to get up and walk around. After a 30-minute visit and a promise to come and see him again tomorrow, I left for the 30-minute drive back to North York.

I was still a little upset that I hadn't heard about his being in hospital sooner. After all David was the closest person I had to being a brother. We had spent a lot of time together before I left Creemore. Since I had moved to Toronto and he still worked at the Toronto Dominion bank in Creemore, we didn't see each other as much anymore. But we had had some great times together. When I graduated from school in June 1957, he had borrowed his Dad's car and off we went on a 10-day trip. We drove to Sault Ste Marie, Ontario, across the border and down through Michigan, Wisconsin and Illinois before coming back home. We even took in a football game and saw the Green Bay Packers play. Wonderful memories, that I cherish to this day.

The phone was ringing as I walked into the empty apartment at about 7 pm. The Harrises were out doing their evening walkabout the grounds, so I answered it. I could hardly recognize Marilyn's voice. I had difficulty understanding what she was trying to tell me as she sobbed on the phone. Finally, she gained some composure and said, "Len, David is dead. David is dead." "What you mean he's dead, I shouted, "I just left him." "I know," she said "but after you left he had an embolism and there was nothing they could do for him."

I was devastated, crushed. I told her I would come down to see her tomorrow at the hospital and hung up. I was 19; Dave was 21. It was the first time as an adult that I had lost anyone close to me. I walked around in a stupor for several days. Unrealistically, after thinking about it for a while, I came to the conclusion that I would live to 21, then I would die.

I went to work every day and came home at night in a daze. Jerry and his parents tried to console me but it didn't really help.

One evening, George Harris announced at supper that they had been offered a better superintendent's job at a brand new apartment block named

59

Newtonbrook Court, which was being built between Finch and Steeles on Yonge St. He said we would all be moving there on January 1, 1959. It wouldn't make much difference for Jerry and me because we still shared a bedroom. It just meant I had a lot further to drive to work. It also meant a lot farther drive to visit Julia.

With David's death still clouding my thoughts, I don't think I was much fun anyway, so gradually I saw less and less of Julia and shortly after we moved to the new apartment, I told her I couldn't see her any more.

Just before Christmas, I had received my annual pay raise envelope at Canada Packers. When I opened it was empty. I spoke to my boss who called the pay office and was told that there would be no raise for me. When I questioned why, I was told that for my age and education level I was being adequately paid. While that might have been true, I wasn't happy. "I should be paid for what I am doing," I told my boss. There was nothing he could do about it he told me. So without much thought I handed in my resignation.

Thinking back, if they had given me a $3 a week pay raise I might have ended up with a career at the plant. I would have missed a lot in my life if I had taken that path. I was now out of a job. That didn't last long. After searching the newspapers I found an opening. The head office of the Canadian Commercial Credit Corporation on Eglinton Avenue close to Yonge St, in downtown Toronto, was looking for an executive assistant to the Chief Financial Officer. I called and was invited in for an in interview; I got the job. The pay was $55 a week, $8 less than I made at Canada Packers but it was a much nicer environment and much closer to where I lived. Looking back I think the title they gave me was in lieu of money because I really was a 'gofer' for the CFO.

The Harrises and I moved into our new digs on New Year's Day and quickly settled in to a much larger, brand new apartment.

Jerry and I went to a few dances mostly at the YMCA/YWCA in North York and it was there one evening that I met Caroline. She was a rather attractive, tall, 5'10 1/2" brunette who had danced with the National Ballet of Canada. Now she taught would-be ballet dancers at a dance school. Her father was a captain on a merchant marine vessel and was seldom home. In fact in the six months I knew Caroline, I never met her father.

Her mother was something else. Every time I would pick Caroline up to go to a movie or a dance, her mother would invite us back afterwards for tea and sandwiches. So, on one occasion, we went back. She was very pleasant but soon began to ask me questions about my career at Canada Packers. What were my chances of promotion; how far could I go in the company. I felt like I was being interviewed for a job, as a husband for Caroline. I don't think she knew I was only 19 or I doubt she would have approved of me going out with Caroline who was 24.

But I still wasn't happy. One day at lunch hour I was walking down a Toronto street and it began to rain. Not having an umbrella I rushed into a nearby building. I soon discovered it was a Royal Canadian Air Force Recruiting Centre. A young NCO asked me if he could help me. I told him honestly I was just trying to escape the rain. "Well, how about writing a little test," he said, obviously smartly taking advantage of the fact that he had a potential enrollee. "Why not," I replied, not really thinking about what I was doing or that this was a military building.

I wrote the test and he asked me to have a seat for a few moments. Shortly after a young officer appeared with my test in his hand and said "How would you like to write a test for the ROTP?" "What's that?" I said. He replied, "It's the Regular Officer Training Plan. If you are accepted we send you to university or military college for free and you serve for five years." I was a little bit dubious but then it struck me that David had always said he wanted to join the RCAF. It was eerie, as if he somehow had led me to this place. Now I was being encouraged to try and get in. I looked out the window and it was still raining. "Can I call my boss and tell him I will be a little late getting back from lunch?" I asked the young officer. "Of course," he replied. So I wrote the test and was told as I left that I would be hearing from them.

About two weeks later, I received a letter saying that I had been selected to attend a two-week selection centre at Centralia, Ontario, to determine if I would be acceptable under the ROTP plan. I spoke to my boss who was a former fighter pilot during WWII. He said, "Go for it. I will grant you some vacation time."

In early April 1959, I boarded a train for London, Ontario. There were a number of us on the train and we were met by a bus and taken to RCAF Station Centralia. Centralia had been a training base during the war years. It now provided basic primary training for cadets who would go on to a flying career.

The next two weeks were a blur as a couple of hundred of us would-be officers and flyers were introduced to military life. Marching to the mess hall for our meals; to the gym for exercise; and, to the drill hall for parade instruction, as well as interviews with 'shrinks' filled our days.

Most memorable was the time we each spent in a link trainer, a small box-like structure that simulated the cockpit of a single engine aircraft. Each one of us, guided by two instructors, had to try and fly this simulator, keeping it straight and level, or turning, or whatever else instruction was given. There was a good instructor who tried to soothe you and encourage you, only to be interrupted by one who screamed obscenities and questioned your birth as he tried to make you fly under pressure.

Finally, there was the prisoner-of-war exercise where each of us in small groups of eight-ten was given an opportunity to use our ingenuity to try and escape from an enclosure. The top wire around the enclosure, we were told, had enough voltage running through it to kill us if we touched it. An experience I have never forgotten and not necessarily a comfortable time; then we were on our way home. Most of us were not sure if we really wanted to "make it" into this RCAF organization.

61

In early June, I received a telegram telling me that I had indeed been selected to attend a university of my choice for a period of four years and would be trained as an aviator. My veteran fighter pilot boss was very pleased. He told me he would make it easy for me to leave my appointment with Commercial Credit at the end of July so I could enjoy some vacation time. Everyone I knew, perhaps except for Caroline, was elated and very happy for me. My cousin Paul thought it might be a mistake because the RCAF would be very tough, but I told him I could take it. I told my parents who told the Creemore Star, and in the next weekly edition of the paper the story ran on the front page.

My first priority was to get accepted to a university so out went the applications. It didn't seem to take very long until I had acceptance letters from Acadia University in Wolfville, NS, and Carleton University in Ottawa. I decided to go with Carleton because it was in Ontario and Nova Scotia was far away.

Jerry offered to take me on a week's vacation so off we went into the US, driving like mad south until we hit Knoxville, Tennessee, and then turned around and came back. I spent lots of money, but then I was going to be looked after by the RCAF in the future, so what did it matter.

Next, I had to go to Ottawa to check in with the RCAF and find a place to live. Mom, Dad and I piled into my car, picked up my Aunt Lily in Toronto and off we went to the capital. We stayed way out of town (in those days) at the Bel Air Motel in a little village called Bells Corners because it was much cheaper than staying downtown. Today Bells Corners is very much part of the city and the Bel Air Motel is still there.

The next morning, I headed for the RCAF headquarters on Carling Avenue. An old, rather grumpy flight lieutenant, whose ribbons stated he was a veteran of WWII, met me. I gave him my paper work and he went and got my file. He read for a while and then destroyed my life! "There's a problem here," he muttered. "Doesn't look like you can join up as part of the ROTP." "What do you mean there's a problem," I gasped. `"Well, Carleton says you can start in second year except you have to take first year French. That just won't work."

My mind tried to come to grips with what he was telling me. Yes, I had quit French at the end of Grade 12. But when I had applied I had told everyone this. They had my records. "Just won't work, just won't work," he said looking at me with absolutely no sense of sympathy. "Isn't there anything I can do?" I pleaded. "Well, you can write your Grade 13 French when you are ready and reapply but that won't get you in this year but probably next year". "But I've quit my job, spent most of my money and I just sold my car at the end of the month." "Well we could look at perhaps getting you into a military college but time is very short, or we might be able to have you start on the next direct entry officer training course in September."

He explained that I wouldn't go to university but would go through officer and aviation training and on successful completion would be given a five-year short service commission.

I was shattered. All my dreams and hopes seemed to disappear as this, what appeared to me, unfeeling, bureaucratic, zombie gave me my options. "But you will have to let us know very soon if you want to start this year," he added.

I told him I would get back to him tomorrow and stumbled out of the building. What had been a beautiful, sunny day in this capital city now seemed to be as dark as the end of time. I drove straight back to the motel and dumped the whole problem on my parents and aunt.

At the time I really didn't seem to have much of an option. I was turning 20 years old. I had heard that life could be very difficult for new cadets at a military college. Most would be much younger than I; most would not have had the opportunity of living on their own and doing as they pleased.

After some discussion with my family and a night of tossing and turning, I decided I would take the option of trying to start the next direct entry course in September.

Interestingly, many years later, I related this story to Wally Downer who was a former MPP and lieutenant governor of Ontario who came from the Creemore area. He told me that he wished I had told him when it happened. "That was nonsense," he said "I have connections in Ottawa and I am sure I could have got that turned around."

But it was a giant lesson for me. Many times since, I seemed to have run into roadblocks and had to take the rougher road, only to find out that it was to my advantage in the long run. Indeed, God does move in mysterious ways!

Three weeks later, orders in my pocket, I was driven by my cousin Carmen from Creemore to RCAF Station Centralia where I would begin my career. It was almost exactly two years since I had left Creemore to go to Toronto and now I was starting on a new chapter in my life.

63

CHAPTER 7 - SEEKING MY WINGS

We came from all walks of life and all parts of Canada.

Some, like Fred, came from a farm in northern Saskatchewan. He was amazed to see so many toilets and wash basins all lined up in one room with as much hot water as one wanted. Mike came from a small fishing community on the east coast of Newfoundland. He had problems because apparently no one explained to him that the chits they handed him in an envelope allowed him to eat every meal in the train's dining car. He bought 10 chocolate bars with the $2 his mom gave him when he left and that's all he had to eat during the three-day journey from St John's to London. His mother complained about how he was treated to her member of parliament.

Hank's father was an Argentine diplomat. Hank had come to live with his parents when his father served at the embassy in Ottawa. Hank was 24 and quite sophisticated. He spoke five languages and dressed in the best of clothes. Mark had just served five years with the RCMP, had his private pilot's licence, and passionately wanted to be a fighter pilot.

There were more than a hundred of us, each with our own reasons for joining up and each with our own life experiences. The objective for the RCAF trainers was to mould us so that each of us would react in the same way. It was more difficult for some of us who had lived away from home and had had the freedom to do what we wanted when we wanted. But the RCAF wanted us to reach the stage that when asked to jump, our only question on the way up, would be "how high?"

In the first few days, we were issued with air force blue uniforms, work clothes, boots, underwear, socks, shaving gear and toiletries. Then, we were told to go and get a haircut.

Pete, a tall handsome teenager, with long curly hair who no doubt had girls swarming all over him, at least that's what he told us, was one of the first in line. Just a little trim he told the old barber who must have cut thousands of heads over the years. "Yes sir," he said without a smile and he took his razor and started to work. Soon large clumps of curly hair began tumbling to the floor and out walked a rather dazed Pete with only short stubble remaining.

The rest of us all received the same treatment. To add insult to injury the barber charged us 45 cents for the haircut. We had to get it cut three times a week to make sure that it didn't grow.

When we lined up to go on the parade square for the first time, except for varying heights we looked the same; dressed alike in blue and all bald.

I started working on my boots as they had instructed, using the spit and polish method. I worked 17 hours on those boots before they ever went on my feet. You could see your face in them. The first time we marched to the parade square for inspection, the sergeant walked around looking me up and down and yelled in my ear, "Cadet, charge card." I was taken aback. "What for," I mumbled. "No talking," he replied as he wrote something down and handed back the card. When I looked at it later, it said 'dirty boots.' I was mad. I took off my boots and inspected them. On the back heel of my right boot, there was a smudge of dirt probably picked up when marching to the parade square. I walked straight to my course director's office and asked permission to see him.

"Sir," I asked, "what do you think of my boots?" "They look great," he said. "So why this?" I said not too graciously throwing my charge card on his desk. He looked at it and smiled and said, "Oh, that's Sergeant Christie, he's just trying to test you. Don't worry about it," he said as he signed it off. There were no repercussions and I didn't get any further marks on my card while I was at Centralia. I still have that card.

Each of our days was full. We started very early at 0600 and went to lights out at 2200. In addition to marching drills, gym instruction and volleyball, we had classroom instruction. General Service Knowledge, RCAF history, English writing and Basic Navigation were among the daily classes.

I was a little miffed that they taught us how to use a knife, fork and spoon properly, but then realized as I looked around the class at some of the other cadets, that perhaps as a group we needed it. At night we made sure the space around our bunks in the big barrack room was clean, our clothes washed and pressed and our boots sparkling. We had to learn to make our beds so that any inspector could bounce a quarter on it.

Discipline was harsh. On one occasion, a group of us were told to wax and polish the floor in a large classroom using only razor blades, wax and a toothbrush. We were just completing the job about three hours later when an instructor came in with muddy boots and walked the length of the room. Then he turned, saw the scuffed floor and dirt that he had just caused and said, "This floor is filthy, do it again." I am not sure if that would be allowed today.

To be a good officer, a number of characteristics, including honesty and integrity were emphasized throughout our training. The instructors were serious. On one occasion during a test, a cadet was caught cheating. The instructor knew he was cheating. A question on the test asked what file number would you use if you were writing a memo or letter about your own career. The answer was C for confidential plus your serial number, e.g. in my case C64256. This cadet didn't know the answer so looked over the shoulder of the person in front of him and copied what he had written. When confronted with this, he adamantly stated that he knew the answer, couldn't remember his own number but knew that of the guy in front of him. If he had admitted he had cheated he might have been given a reprimand and allowed to stay. Because he would not admit it, the next day he was on his way home.

My test of honesty came about three weeks after the course started. I received a letter from Caroline telling me how much she missed me, how lonesome she was and that she was prepared to wait as long as it took for me to come back to her in Toronto. I guess I hadn't realized how serious she was and frankly I wasn't prepared for that kind of relationship. So I decided I should tell her the truth. Having never had to write such a letter before, I was stumped. So I enlisted the help of my ex-RCMP colleague who apparently had gone through the same experience. With his guidance, I carefully crafted a letter which talked of my admiration for her, but noted that with a long training period in front of me I didn't want to stand in the way of her happiness, neither was I ready for a permanent relationship. I sent the letter and never heard from her again.

It was tough going through the basic training. But we were all in the same boat so we worked together, helping each other when we could, be it in studying or in making beds or in learning gym skills. We couldn't leave the station for the first three weeks. Then one Friday afternoon, we were told that that evening we could go off the base and that there was a dance in nearby Exeter if we wanted to go.

They also told us we needed to have a number of vaccinations against a variety of diseases. They knew what they were doing, obviously. The shots made our arms sore and made us feel horrible. Those of us who did venture to the dance were met by a group of lovely, primarily farm girls who loved to dance particularly square dance. They seemed always to grab the arm that we had had punctured. They laughed and we soon went back to the base muttering about those sadistic instructors. We also wondered if this hadn't been arranged between the ladies and the instructors.

Weeks flew by and soon we were approaching the end of our course. Strangely, one day a cadet, who told me what my course test average was to that point, approached me. He said that I was standing first on the course, he was second and that he was going to beat me. He probably shouldn't have done that. I had no idea where I stood on the course, nor did I care. But when he suggested he was going to beat me, it just gave me some extra incentive to do well.

Finally, the tests were all written and we were told to report to the base theatre one morning for our results. It was brutal.

"The following cadets have failed and will report here tomorrow morning at 0900 for instructions re going home." Then the officer began to read out the names. My name was not on the list. I felt relieved.

"The following cadets have passed. You will report here tomorrow morning at 1000 for instructions about your next posting." Then he read the list. As he went past the 'D's I didn't hear my name. He ended and I still hadn't heard my name.

Then he continued, "At this point I would normally tell you who the honour cadet is for Class 5913. But I can't now." He smiled and said, "If Flight Cadet Dent passes his rewrite navigation exam tomorrow morning he will be your honour cadet. If not he will be on his way home." I was shocked.

It was hard to get any sleep that night. With the help of one of my buddies, I figured out what I was doing wrong. Basically, whenever I got an answer to the wind direction, I was getting it backwards. I had where the wind was going to, rather than where it was coming from, e.g., 090 instead of 270 degrees.

There was a party throughout the barracks. The crying was coming from those who had failed and the laughing from those who had passed. Finally about 3:00 am I drifted off to sleep. Five hours later, I reported to the classroom to write the exam. I felt confident. There was one other cadet writing and after we finished, we starting comparing answers. Much to my dismay my answers were just about all 180 degrees different from his.

A few minutes later I was called into the course director's office. "Have a seat Flight Cadet Dent," he said. Flight Lieutenant Slade was a kind man who had always treated me with respect and I liked him. He was a veteran of World War II and not one of those who tried to make cadets feel inferior. He looked at my test in his hand shook his head and said rather grimly, "I have gone through your test twice and there is nothing else I can do." My heart sank. I got a knot in my stomach. Flashing through my mind was the fact that I had no job, no money, and no car and would have to go back to Creemore as a failure. And then with a big grin he said, "I have to give you 100% on the test." Was I hearing correctly?

"Congratulations," he said, "you are off to Winnipeg to start your training as a navigator." I had passed both written aptitude tests as a pilot and as a navigator but really wasn't as passionate about being a pilot as some of my colleagues. They had asked me if I would take navigation early on in the course and I had agreed. As I walked out of the classroom, I saw the other cadet anxiously waiting his turn and tried not to look happy as I quickly walked by him saying softly, "good luck" although I already knew he was on his way home that day.

That afternoon, we were bussed to the London train station and I caught a train for Toronto and Stayner, and then back to Creemore where I spent most of the Christmas holidays with Mom and Dad. They were happy to see me and proud of what I had accomplished, although Mom was not happy that I was going so far away to Winnipeg.

Donna's parents had invited me to come and stay with them for New Year's Eve mainly because they wanted me to take Donna to a dance. Donna had a girlfriend and so I coerced Bob Stewart, with whom I had developed a friendship during the course, to be a blind date. We both stayed at Donna's house. Her friend was petite, good-looking and bubbly, and we had a great time at the dance. Donna and I had a great relationship. It was more like being really good friends than anything serious, but we did enjoy being together.

On New Year's Day, 1960, Anne made us a wonderful breakfast and drove us to the airport where we met Hank Morris. That afternoon we climbed onto a Trans Canada Airlines (now Air Canada) aircraft for my first flight ever. We arrived in Winnipeg about 4:00 pm. I will never forget standing on the tarmac outside the terminal and seeing a thermometer, which read -30°F. It had been + 40°F when we left Toronto. Were we nuts? We were met by an Air Force bus and driven to our barracks at RCAF

Station Winnipeg, which was on the other side of the runways. This would be our home for the next 12 months. If we had known something about what we faced in the next year, we might just have got on the next TCA aircraft and flown home.

RCAF Station Winnipeg was opened as an aerodrome in 1925; a year after the Royal Canadian Air Force was formed. During WWII, it played an important role in the British Commonwealth Air Training Plan (BCATP).

The BCATP was one of Canada's great contributions to the war effort, training more than 131,500 people in a variety of aircrew categories at more than 220 sites across Canada. There were students from many Commonwealth countries and some from outside the Commonwealth who would graduate and serve with the British or Canadian Air Forces. Some of these came from the United States before the US entered the war. President Roosevelt called the effort as transforming Canada into the, "aerodrome of democracy" although someone told me that the phrase was actually thought up by Lester B. Pearson, who was serving as a Canadian Foreign Affairs officer in Washington at the time. After the war, the station continued providing training for pilots and navigators from Canada as well as some from allied countries.

Our basic navigation course didn't start immediately. We were told that there weren't enough of us to make up a course so we would have to wait until the next batch of cadets arrived from Centralia. In the meantime, they made sure we were kept busy. We spent lots of hours learning to drill and clean our rooms. We were also given classroom instruction, which included subjects that would leave an impact.

First we were shown British-made films that explicitly talked about syphilis and venereal disease. They were very graphic and showed the potential results of indiscretions. It was enough to make most of us consider becoming celibate for the rest of our lives.

The British had also made an excellent series on maintenance and servicing of aircraft by disgruntled ground crews, and the results it could have on the flying capability of the aircraft. I remember specifically seeing one leading aircraftsman having a terrible fight with his wife and going to work where he spent more time rehashing the fight than he did paying attention to his maintenance check. They showed an engine bolt not tightened up enough and a tool left in the engine, and shortly after takeoff the aircraft going into a dive and crashing.

This stuck with me all throughout my flying days. I always took the opportunity, whenever I saw a mechanic working around our aircraft, to ask him how he was and how were the wife and kids today. If all was bright and cheery, I felt we were ok. If not, I would suggest to the captain that we all be a little more vigilant in our safety checks.

They also taught us Morse Code and encouraged us to become proficient at sending and receiving messages using the key. Apparently the RCAF was short of radio officers. They hoped that some of us who were proficient enough would volunteer to become radio officers. Hank, Bob and I found this out and made sure that we never did reach the required level, which upset the instructors because they knew we could do it.

The other cadets arrived from Centralia and we started our course. Prominent in our basic navigation course were astronomy, navigation, basics of flight, and learning how to take sun and star shots with a sextant. Of course there was the usual drill instruction, gym each day, early morning room inspections and 2200 lights out.

My first flight came on January 20, 1960. A number of us boarded a C47 Dakota aircraft for a 3hr. 15-minute familiarization flight. The C47 was the militarized version of the Douglas DC3 that first flew in December 1935. More than 16,000 DC3s were built with more than 10,000 military versions. It was used extensively during World War II and some are still flying in many parts of the world. The weather was clear and crisp and most of us quite enjoyed flying straight and level on this introductory flight.

Our life at Winnipeg was not all work, studies and drill. We also had some fun. The flight cadets had their own mess. It was a large building with a huge dining room, a recreation room with pool tables, and an area for receptions and dancing which also held a bar. It was here that we could go and buy a beer for 10 cents and a mixed drink for a quarter. Our cadet pay was approximately $200 per month and we had food, clothes and accommodation provided. The pay was basically spending money so we could have a lot of fun. In retrospect, I think allowing us to drink as much as we wanted was part of the test for becoming an officer. They didn't question your drinking, but expected that every morning you could show up on time and be able to do your duty, whether it be in the classroom or in an aircraft. A number of cadets could not handle this test and were sent home during the training period.

Shortly after arrival, I was elected as Postal Officer for the course which meant I had to look after making sure that the mail was delivered properly to the cadets, and more importantly, handling complaints. It wasn't much of a job and I think some of my colleagues actually thought they were giving me a 'Joe' job as a joke. But they didn't realize that I got to wear two bars on my shoulder and was called a Cadet Flight Lieutenant. More importantly, along with the other cadets who had been elected into various positions, I got to sit at cloth-covered tables where we were served by waitresses. The other cadets had to line up and go through the cafeteria-style line up. Every day for lunch and dinner, there was a large buffet table covered with salads and cold roasts of beef, pork, ham, and desserts. Then there was a daily menu from which we could order hot dishes. Many of us had never eaten so well.

Shortly after the course started, I met Joan who eventually would become my steady girlfriend for the duration of my stay in Winnipeg. Joan had been married to an RAF officer whom she had met while he was training in Winnipeg. They got married and were posted to a base in Northern Ireland. At the end of his five-year short service commission, they returned to Canada and he joined the RCAF. He was attending a basic training course in Centralia. One Friday afternoon, he called Joan to tell her he was going to London to catch a flight home for the weekend. Unfortunately, he and a friend were killed in a traffic accident on the way to the airport. Joan was devastated. She was a 24-year old widow with a 10-month old baby girl to look after. She found some comfort in drinking, but her friends were worried that she was drinking too much.

One of my buddies had a date with one of her friends and I was asked if I would like to double date. Even though Joan was a few years older, we enjoyed each other's company and I guess I had a good shoulder that she could cry on when she needed to, and when I first met her she needed to a lot. I continued to emphasize that drinking was not the answer and that she had to get on with her life and think of her daughter. We went to a lot of functions on the weekends at the mess and I spent time with her when I could during the week. Ours wasn't an intimate relationship as some of my colleagues thought, but it became a very caring one. I was supporting her in her struggle to overcome the loss and to provide needed affection for her baby, Cathy. She was there to support me when I had difficult times in the training. I had someone to complain to about what sometimes seemed like unjust treatment. And this happened often.

One morning we were lined up for cadet inspection in front of our barracks at 0600 for inspection. The instructor announced that there would be a room inspection in five minutes. "Break off and go to your rooms," he said. So everyone dashed for their rooms. "Cadet, halt," I heard behind me. I turned to face one of our officers. "Charge card," he said. "What for?" I replied while digging out my card, which had to be carried at all times. "Running on the grass," he snorted. "But everyone is running on the grass," I said. "Insubordination," he said and marked down a second charge. My punishment was reporting to the Guard House at the Base gates every hour on the hour for the next 48 hours beginning on Saturday morning. I didn't get much sleep and I was understandably upset. But Joan tried to soothe me by saying that this was just a test to make sure that you could take discipline and obey rules without question. It wasn't until a couple of years later, flying on a Lancaster out of Iceland, that I realized how important it was to do what you are told when you are told without questioning or it could be fatal for everyone involved. But that story comes later.

My next military flight came in early March when some of us were asked to fly a search and rescue mission as observers, looking for a missing aircraft. I had no idea that this rather bumpy five-hour flight was a precursor of what my flying career would be all about.

In late March, we began our basic navigation flying training and over the next three months I flew about 75 hours in navigation training.

Our basic training course ended, and about half of the cadets that started the course graduated and were posted to the advanced navigation course which would begin in September. Those who didn't graduate either didn't pass the academic course, had no airborne navigation capability, or simply couldn't take the strict discipline and quit.

The advanced navigation course differed primarily in that we were doing much more flying. In the four and one half month course I flew 30 flights and 150 hours, with each flight being a little harder as the basic requirements necessary to pass each flight were increased.

As the months passed, we were becoming much more aware of how to handle the discipline and how to best enjoy our time in training, both on and off duty. I went to the occasional dance at the mess without Joan, when we invited a busload of student nurses from one of the local nursing schools to come out for a Saturday night dance. I enjoyed the dancing but didn't meet anyone that made me want to stop going out with Joan.

One Saturday evening, as we were nearing the end of our training, an event occurred that would change my life forever. Joan and I were at a dance at the cadet's mess to which instructors had been invited. One of my flight instructors cornered me at the bar while I was buying drinks for us and said, "That girlfriend of yours is quite something. I think she is too much for you to handle so I want you to give me her phone number." I knew the instructor was married and thought he was kidding. "Bugger off," I told him in what I thought was a rather friendly tone. "I am serious Flight Cadet Dent," he said. "Give me her number."

"No," I told him a little more firmly. "This is not a suggestion." His voice started to rise and his face started to get red. Obviously he had had a few drinks. "This is an order from a senior officer."

"This has nothing to do with the military." I began to get mad. "This is man to man."

"Do you know that I can fail you on every flight you take and if you don't give me her number I will."

"Then do it," I said. I walked away leaving him fuming at the bar as others began to watch.

I took Joan home and told her to be careful of this guy and not to worry, he wouldn't hurt her. I couldn't say the same for myself.

Within a week I began to feel the impact. One day I completed a flight trip where I had flown as second navigator. It only counted for 10 points out of a total of 1000 for my final mark. Often instructors would ask students, "How do you think you did?" They would usually reply 95%. "How about I give you 90 %," instructors would suggest." "OK," and 90% was marked on the envelope containing their navigation charts; it was never opened. That day mine was given to an instructor who had obviously been briefed. I got the results the next day. He had gone through it with exacting detail. My mark was below zero. And so it went on every trip that I did. I would mostly get below zero or just above.

One day I was told to report to the officer commanding the Flight Training School. As I stood at attention in front of him, he looked at me very seriously and said, "Flight Cadet Dent, when you went through basic you had the highest flying marks that we have had here in 10 years. Now in the Advanced School, with your marks you should not even be allowed on the tarmac. What's going on?"

"I am not prepared to talk about it," I said with a sinking feeling. "Do you realize that at this point you are failing the course and this means that you will probably be CT'd (ceased training) and sent home? Your career will be over." "Yes," I murmured. "Well," he said, "I think I know what is happening. So Flight Cadet Dent, I am going to take a big risk. I am going to erase your marks and make you pass every trip. And you will graduate." Of course, I had a high average in all my written classroom exams. "But you have to promise me that when you go to the OTU (Operational Training Unit) you won't disappoint me." "I promise," I said, with a feeling that a huge weight had been lifted off my shoulders.

But it didn't end there. On my final night check ride, one of my colleagues, the cadet who had always tried to beat me, was flying at the same time in a different aircraft. He was in the lead aircraft and had onboard the instructor who had engineered my failures. The sky was heavily overcast that night which made it very difficult and mostly impossible to shoot the mandatory three-star fixes, which were so necessary to pass the check ride. When we landed, I spoke to my instructor and asked that, since the weather had made it impossible to get all our mandatory requirements, would he change the mandatory requirements.

"What's your problem Dent, Flight Cadet 'A' got 100% on his star fixes. I guess you just couldn't hack it."

I found out later from my friend Jamie who had been flying as second navigator on the aircraft with Flight Cadet 'A' that every time he took a star fix he asked Jamie where they were. Jamie, who was manning the radar, obliged by giving him a radar fix. The cadet was simply able to 'cook' his star fix readings to make it look like he had taken them all. So 24-hours later, I and three other cadets, who had also failed during that night flight, had to take a re-ride.

The next afternoon, the eight of us who were scheduled to graduate were on the drill hall parade ground practicing for our graduation ceremony, even though four of us didn't know if we would graduate. Finally, during the practice and about three hours before the ceremony, we were called in and told we had all passed.

My mark was just over 90% on a re-ride of a flight I had failed 24 hours earlier. It took 25 years before I had a chance to pay back that cadet for the hell he had put my colleagues and me through.

And so, on January 20, 1961 after 16 months of training, which included many great and some not so great memories, eight of us were formally commissioned as flying officers into the Royal Canadian Air Force and as long-range navigators.

We had an incredible graduation party in the mess with the eight of us buying drinks for all until no one was left, sometime in the early morning. Some parents had made their way from far away to see their son graduate. Unfortunately, good looking confident Pete, who had girls swarming all over him during the training even without his long hair, didn't. It was sad to see his parent's disappointment. Joan was there for me; it was just too far and too expensive for my parents to come.

Interestingly, the following Monday night, 72 hours after graduation, I was tasked by my former instructor, who had almost scuttled my career to accompany a junior navigation training exercise as the Navigation Instructor on the mission.

Almost immediately after graduation, we were given our next posting and it was then that I realized the full, ongoing implications of my problem with my instructor.

Historically, cadets were allowed to request what careers they wished to follow. Many navigators asked to be transferred to Transport Command. Here crews flew in large aircraft similar to a commercial airliner and often flew to exotic lands taking various groups, including the Prime Minister, on missions around the world. At least that is what we had been told.

Crews got to sleep in good hotels and have great meals. The alternative was Maritime Command where you flew in aircraft for many hours low and slow over the Atlantic or Pacific looking for submarines on antisubmarine warfare missions. Crews slept in barracks on bases, a far cry from beds and meals they would have got in a hotel.

The cadet achieving the highest standing in the class would normally get his wishes. My wish was to go to Transport Command. Until I began to get the failing marks in my navigation flights, I stood number one in my class. By the time I finished, I stood number eight of eight. I was posted to the Operational Training Unit at Summerside, PEI, where I would learn how to fly on antisubmarine warfare missions.

Little did I know the impact that this posting would have on my career and on my future.

Being presented my commission and wings by Wing Commander Evans

CHAPTER 8 - BEING RESCUED -BECOMING A RESCUER

"Congratulations, gentlemen," our ex-instructor and now fellow officer chuckled as he came into a classroom where we had been asked to gather a few days after graduation.

"As a small reward for graduating you have been selected to attend the Winter Bush and Arctic Survival Training Courses. That will keep you busy for the next three weeks, and then you will be off to your new postings." I don't think any of us had ever heard of this survival training course let alone considered we might be 'selected' to go on it.

Three days later we boarded a train and chugged our way out to Edmonton. Once there, we were met and taken to RCAF Station Namao and introduced to some Survival School instructors. The Americans had built this facility 11 kilometers north of the city during the war and ran it until the Canadian Government took it over at the end of the war. The US had used it as a staging point for the US defense of Alaska and also to ferry in supplies for the construction of the Alaska Highway. RCAF squadrons and units were transferred from the old facility downtown, and the RCAF Station Namao opened on October 1, 1955.

It was the middle of January and very cold in Alberta, even colder than Winnipeg. "Wait for it," one instructor said, "this will feel like paradise compared to what you are going to get when you get to the bush outside Hinton."

One day of classroom instruction on survival techniques and then we were sent to the clothing stores to get our issue of clothing for the Winter Bush course. The aim of the course was to teach us how to survive should we crash in the north or the Arctic during winter conditions. I wasn't sure how we would get from the Atlantic where most of us would be flying anti-submarine warfare missions to either of these areas, but none of us questioned the rationale for giving us the course.

Basically we would wear the same clothing as if we were flying over the bush or Arctic. We would take into the bush a small survival pack that fighter pilots would carry which contained a piece of Christmas cake, a package of 'Smarties' (like M and Ms), several tea bags and matches. We were also issued with personal hunting knives.

We were loaded into a bus, along with a number of other lucky candidates who had been selected for the course and off we went to Hinton, about an hour drive north-west of the station.

It was minus 30°F when we got to Hinton and never got any warmer during our 10 days in the area. We were issued with parachutes and sleeping bags and then marched to a spot and told to start setting up our lean-tos. The group had been divided into teams of two. Each team had to work together to build their shelter.

Carl Crymble, whom I had known since day one of our days in Centralia, and I were teamed together. First, using our knives, we hacked down limbs and prepared them to be the poles of our lean-to. Then we took the nylon string out of the parachutes and tied the poles to two trees so that we had a framework forming a top, back and two sides. Using the silk parachute material we then covered the frame. We put boughs on top of the shelter as well as inside to form a floor, which would keep us and our sleeping bags off the cold snow. In the front of the shelter we hollowed out a pit, which would be our fireplace. Once we were finished, we lit our fire using one of our few precious matches. We gathered enough firewood so that we could go to bed at night and basically keep the fire going continually. That process took about three hours. We only had nine days and 21 hours to go.

It is amazing how quickly one's morale can lower when you are 'living' in such conditions, even when you are with a group of people you know and who are in the same situation. You just want to survive. You don't want to do anything but stay by the fire and use as little energy as possible. We had one US marine warrant officer who arrived from the US base in Guantanamo Bay, Cuba. He didn't make it through the night. In fairness, he was just finishing four years in a hot climate and it had been 80°F when he left the day before. It was a change of more than 100 degrees. He went to the instructors and told then he couldn't hack it. Imagine reporting back to your CO in Guantanamo and telling him you didn't last 12 hours on a foreign course.

My friend Jamie sighted a 'fool's hen' and decided it would make a great dinner so he started chasing it. The bird is like a small hen and thus can't fly. It took Jamie about three hours of chasing and he finally trapped and killed it. He plucked it and cooked it over the fire. It netted him perhaps two-three ounces of meat. No wonder they call it a 'fools' hen. We would have trapped rabbits but apparently once every seven years rabbits get a disease and die. They cannot be eaten. At least that's what our instructors told us. So we basically lived on the few rations that we were given. We were cutting 'Smarties' in two and eating a small piece every hour or two.

About Day four we were told that a Dakota from RCAF Station Edmonton would be over the next day to drop some emergency rations. We had to build a big SOS symbol in the snow to mark the drop spot for the aircraft. This energized us and we spent a great deal of effort putting together a sign in the snow. The next day came and we eagerly awaited an aircraft that never came. Finally the instructors told us that the aircraft had mechanical problems and wouldn't be coming. Whether that was a ploy to further test us, we didn't know. We drank lots of hot tea reusing and reusing the tea bags we had been issued. Our cups became filthy and there were bits of leaves and other foreign material in the cups but we drank anyway.

Finally Day 10 and we were walked out to an awaiting bus. The only 'casualty' had been our American friend. The first stop was at a big hotel in Hinton. We were taken in and told we could order whatever we wanted for breakfast. The waitress told our table that on the menu were eggs, pancakes, waffles, bacon, sausage, ham, potatoes, and toast. Jamie quickly replied, "Yes, please." Most of us, on the advice of our instructors, had a very small breakfast even though we were starving. Jamie tried to eat all of his, which came on two plates. He didn't finish. On the bus ride back to the station, the driver had to stop. Jamie lost all his breakfast on the side of the road. He ate too much, too fast for a stomach that had shriveled over 10 days.

Meanwhile most of the people sitting in the restaurant, which was quite full when we came in, began to leave. Many of them had not finished their meal. We couldn't figure this out until we got back to Edmonton. On arrival we rushed to the shower stalls. After 15 or 20 minutes we began to walk back to our rooms and the smell hit us. It reminded me of the killing floor at Canada Packers; that sickening smell in a room where day after day pigs that had been slaughtered were processed. It was like an invisible shield. Immediately we realized it was our clothes. The instructors had issued us with clean clothes on arrival and told us that we could get rid of our old ones if we wished. Ten days of being over an open fire without washing. This was the result.

The next day was filled with lectures about our next adventure, survival in the Arctic in the middle of winter.

The following morning, equipped with arctic clothing, we boarded a C119 flying boxcar in Edmonton and headed for Resolute Bay. Resolute, (pop in 2006 was 229) is a small Inuit hamlet on Cornwallis Island and one of Canada's most northern communities. It is reportedly one of the coldest inhabited places in the world with an annual average temperature of -16°C.

When we arrived on a clear, sunny late January afternoon it was close to -50°C. We had never heard of wind chill in those days, and probably wouldn't want to know what it was anyway.

We were taken into a warm building and fed a hot meal, the last real meal we would have for a week. Here some Inuit women offered the opportunity to make some seal skin slippers for us. For four dollars they traced your foot on a piece of paper and presented you with the slippers at the end of the course.

Then we were taken out across the ice to the village of igloos. The Eskimos (now Inuit) had built several ice structures for us and we were assigned in groups of four to one for the night. Before leaving the main building we had been taught how to build a "kudilik", a pound of shortening melted and put into a small container with a long wick, which would provide light, and some heat for us during the week.

Four of us cuddled up in sleeping blankets. We had also been provided with a bearskin rug to help keep us warm. The next day each team had to start building its own igloo. Carl and I, using a snow knife provided, started cutting snow blocks and building our structure. In order to make a small domed structure we were supposed to start angling each block so it would be just big enough to house the two of us. We didn't do it soon enough, and when we finished the Igloo could have held the whole group for a meeting.

Eating in our Igloo at - 20 F; it was -45 F outside.

This is where Carl and I would spend the next six days. We had more and better emergency rations than had been given to us in the bush. We needed to keep warm and preserve our energy as much as possible. We were both over 6' tall and filled an individual sleeping bag. We thought we could sleep better if we shared our body heat, so we zippered our sleeping bags together. We agreed that at this temperature we would have slept with a polar bear to keep warm.

During the few daylight hours, we would get out of our igloos for exercise and play with a soccer ball donated by the staff. Unfortunately, my feet sweated and then once we stopped playing, began to freeze. It took some months before they got back to normal. Peeing was not a problem, but when one needed a bowel movement it was more problematic. A small enclosure had been placed about ¼ mile away from the igloo village. So about Day 4, I couldn't wait any longer and headed for the privy. When I got there and took off my mitts, my hands were so cold that I couldn't pull down any of my zippers. So I put on my mitts and trekked back down to the igloo, crawled in and asked Carl if he would pull down all my zippers. Then I walked back up and by the time I got to the 'house' all my parts were so chilled that nothing would happen. It took another day before I could perform that function.

Finally, our week was over. There was a draw for who would be able to ride back with the staff on their snow vehicle. I won while the others had to walk the roughly two miles back to the main camp. Given the state of my feet, I felt like I had won a major lottery.

They fed us another hot meal, not too big; we got our slippers and boarded the aircraft to fly back to Edmonton.

Our survival course was over and we had survived. But what bothered me was the fact that even though we knew we were relatively safe, how long the stay would be, and that there were instructors close by if we really needed them, it was still a very difficult time and one's morale sank. So what if one really did crash and didn't know if he would ever be rescued? Since that course, I thought that it might be easier to just take your Very pistol (which most aircraft carry to fire emergency signal flares) and shoot oneself.

When we got back to Edmonton we were given a day of debriefings and then allowed to make our way back to Winnipeg. The night before we left I called a cousin that I had never met on the Cowan's side, but that Carmen had given me the name. She invited me over for dinner that evening. She was a 30-something pretty lady with two young children about one and three years old. I didn't see any sign of a husband. I didn't ask and she didn't volunteer.

I had taken my new slippers to wear since my feet were so sore and wearing ordinary street shoes for long was agony. After dinner we sat in the living room and had coffee and the girls played around. At one point I noticed my cousin sniffing the girls. I also noticed an odour that was unmistakably that of pee. I bent over and smelt my slippers and they were rank. I learned later that the Eskimo (Inuit) women cured their sealskin used for the slippers with urine. It worked fine in the very cold temperatures up north, but in a 72°F house the smell was just too much. I told my cousin that it wasn't one of the girls but my slippers, and related the story of where I got them. We both had a laugh and she fetched a bottle of hair spray and used the whole bottle to hide the smell.

The next day I took the train back to Winnipeg and had a few days to pack up my gear, put it in the car, and get ready to head for Summerside, Prince Edward Island.

Joan and I had a tearful parting and I assured her I would write. I knew I would miss her and Cathy, but I had to get on with my career.

I stopped in Toronto to say hello to Donna and her family and then drove home to Creemore to spend a couple of nights with Mom and Dad. Once again they were very proud of me but Mom was upset that my next posting was so far away.

I drove back to Toronto and picked up Jamie who had been visiting his parents in Hamilton. We headed off for the island. It took us two days to reach Moncton, NB, and there we learned that the island was snowed in and that the ferry SS Abeweight was having trouble making the crossing across

81

the Northumberland Strait because of the ice. We drove onto the ferry where we remained for 20 hours making the crossing.

When we arrived in Borden, the roads were all closed so we slept on the floor of the Borden Legion Hall. The Legion ladies were great and fed us sandwiches and coffee. One joked to me that I should enjoy my freedom while I could because no young RCAF officer ever came to the island and got off without being married. "Not me," I exclaimed. "I'm 21 and finally have some money. I have no intention of getting hooked up with anyone."

The next morning we followed a snowplough into Charlottetown and got there in the early evening. We found a room in the old Queen Hotel, which was very basic but did have a room free with two beds. Just as I was drifting off to sleep Jamie came racing back from the bathroom as white as a sheet. "There is a dead body in the bathroom," he yelled. I got up and we went back together. The body was that of a street person who had taken refuge in the common bathroom. He wasn't dead, just out cold.

We called RCAF Station Summerside and told them where we were. They said to make our way out to the airport and they would send a DC-3 to fetch us. So, the next morning, we parked my car at the Charlottetown airport and caught the ride back to our new base. We were two days late starting the course. It had taken four days to drive from Winnipeg to Moncton and four days to get from Moncton to Summerside. It was late February but because of the roads and our schedule I didn't get back to the airport to pick up my car until Easter Sunday in early April.

RCAF Station Summerside opened in April 1941. It was established to train aviators under the British Commonwealth Air Training Program. As such, thousands of individuals from Commonwealth countries around the world, plus others from European countries and the USA came to earn their wings before joining either the RCAF or RAF.

While, in Barbados, as part of a Canadian contingent helping to celebrate the independence of Barbados on November 30, 1966, I met Bajan Prime Minister Errol Barrow at a cocktail party. When he noticed my RCAF uniform with my navigator wings, he told me that he was one of the young men who had taken his training at Summerside. After his training, as a member of the RAF, he flew 45 operational bombing missions over the European Theatre.

The Station was closed after the war in 1946 but reopened in 1948 and became the home of No. 1 Air Navigation School as a NATO training facility. The school was moved to RCAF Station Winnipeg in 1953. But Summerside became the home of several other units over the years including #2 (Maritime) Operational Training Unit.

Jamie and I joined several of our former classmates at #2 (M) OTU for our operational navigation-training course. The first thing we were told was, "forget what you learned at Winnipeg. This is where the real training begins."There was much more emphasis on the flying side of the training here, and we were taught the tactics involved in anti-submarine warfare which would prepare us for postings to ASW squadrons.

I didn't find the course particularly difficult and did well. I never tried to tell my former officer commanding the Flying Training School back in Winnipeg who had made it possible for me to pass. I assumed if he were interested he would find out.

Life was good in Summerside. The $300 + paid us each month was more than I had ever earned before. Our rooms, food and uniforms were provided for free.

Since we were young, for the most part single officers, we were also targets for the local girls as well as those on the base. Most of the servicewomen on the base were enlisted with only a few female officers. The young enlisted gals went out of their way to meet us and try to entice us to take them out.

Although fraternization between the officers and the enlisted women was not officially allowed, most of our instructors turned a blind eye to any liaisons that might occur. Stevie was one of the young airwomen who caught my eye and we did go out several times. She had a beautiful voice and sang in the church choir in Summerside. She was originally from Vancouver.

I asked her why she hadn't tried to have a singing career. She confided that she had been approached by a couple of agents from Hollywood who told her that they would take her to that city and make her a star. The fly in the ointment was that she had to sleep with them. So she joined the RCAF instead. Jamie also met a beautiful, petite girl from Summerside and he soon fell head-over-heels in love with her.

Much of our flying was out over the water, often at low level and usually very bumpy. Jamie had always had trouble with airsickness. I had seen him come back from flights with blood vessels burst in his eyes because he had fought nausea that hard.

One day we were flying on our PV3 Neptune on a particularly bumpy day. The crew had bet Jamie that he couldn't fly the flight without getting sick. As the flight progressed the weather deteriorated and the bumpiness increased. The radio officer thought that if he ate something he would feel better. So he grabbed a box lunch, had a bite of a cold greasy meat sandwich and immediately threw up in the box. In his distress he put the remains of the sandwich back in the box closed the lid and put it back on the pile.

A short time later, Jamie feeling much the same as his colleague reached down for a box lunch and as luck would have it, grabbed the same box lunch. He opened the lid, saw and smelt the contents and immediately, threw up all over the box and himself. Unfortunately, it was this problem that finally led to Jamie leaving the RCAF.

In fact Jamie needed to have an extra ride to pass the course and so one day he asked me if I could come with him as a second 'nav' on his flight to give him support and help. I had a bad cold but couldn't turn down my buddy. We flew out to our training area over the Gulf of St Lawrence at

83

about 6,000 feet and then descended rather rapidly to about 500 feet. My eardrums wouldn't clear and didn't.

Several days later I went to see the doctor and found out that I had a throat infection, which worsened. He told me I would have to have my tonsils out and that meant I would be grounded. We were only about two weeks from graduation. I was told that I would have the operation at the Naval Hospital HMCS Stadacona in Halifax and, when ready, would be re-coursed. I was devastated. Until the infection could be brought under control and the operation could be scheduled, the order was that I work in the Station Administration office. Nothing could be more boring as far as I was concerned.

I was grumbling to anyone that would listen in the bar about getting this lousy break and my new assignment. One of the officers, Flight Lieutenant Ted Patterson, overheard me and said, "I need someone to help me as an assistant public relations officer. Would you be interested?" His PRO role was a secondary duty since his prime responsibility was as the station's Nuclear Biological Chemical Warfare Officer. Without even asking him what the job entailed, I said "You bet," thinking it must be more interesting than shuffling papers in an office.

The next day Ted had spoken to Group Captain Creeper, the station commander, and I was officially designated the assistant station PRO until I restarted the OTU.

1961 marked the 25th anniversary of women being allowed to join the RCAF. My first assignment was to take each of the approximately 25 women on the station and do short photo stories which would be sent to their hometown newspapers. I always joked that I took the good-looking ones to the beach and the others to the museum. It was a pleasant way to spend the next three weeks before I had to report to Stadacona for my operation.

I arrived in Stadacona in mid-June and was told my operation would be in the morning. I joked with the nurses that this was nothing and I would be up and about the next day. I even asked one of the pretty Navy nurses if she was free the next night for a date on the town. Little did I realize that removing tonsils from an adult could be a serious surgery.

When I woke up a few hours later after my surgery, back in my room, I couldn't even talk. I was in terrible pain and tried calling for the nurses. They thought I was just looking for attention and didn't respond. Finally I started throwing up and painted the room with blood. Almost immediately I was back in the operation room and was being treated with silver nitrate to repair damage I had done when retching.

I felt horrible. To make matters worse later that day a nurse brought in a letter for me that Joan had written. When I opened and read it, I was destroyed. "I miss you and think so much of you," she said, "But I just can't have a permanent relationship with another flyer." Basically she ended up by saying, "I hope you have a good life." All the months we have been going together, we had never mentioned getting married. But she had never suggested that she could never be serious, that she couldn't bear the thought of losing another husband in the Air Force, even though her husband did not die in a flying accident.

The pretty navy nurse came in and saw my distress. She asked me what was the problem and I told her. Then she related that she had had a similar letter from her fiancé in Montreal a few days before. So we could commiserate.

I stayed in the hospital for 10 days. The doctor told me I could leave after seven, but I felt so weak, I didn't want to. I was going to go home to Creemore for a couple of weeks to recover.

When I finally left, I caught a TCA flight to Toronto and a train to Stayner and then hitchhiked to Creemore. I knocked on Mom and Dad's door. Mom opened the door and her face went white. "What's happened to you," she cried. I guess I looked awful. I had lost 14 pounds during my hospital stay and was pretty unsteady on my feet. Mom took the next two weeks to fatten me up and in mid-July I flew back to Halifax to pick up my car for the drive back to Summerside.

En route I passed through Pugwash, NS, a small fishing village on the Northumberland Strait. In 1957 Pugwash was the site of an International Conference of Scholars organized by Bertrand Russell and hosted by Pugwash's native son Cyrus Eaton. The conference was designed to focus on the opposition to nuclear weapons and was attended by high-level scientists from both sides of the Iron Curtain.

It was a Sunday, and as I came into the town the roads were full of cars and there was a huge gathering in the local park. Curiosity got the better of me so I stopped and made my way to the edge of the crowd. "What's going on?" I asked one observer. "It's Cyrus Eaton and Yuri Gagarin on the stage." he gushed.

On April 12, 1961, Yuri Gagarin became the first man to travel in space. After the flight he became a worldwide celebrity and toured many countries. Cyrus Eaton was no doubt the reason Gagarin was here. Eaton became an ardent critic of the US foreign and military policies during the Cold War. He became personally involved in the 1950s trying to promote friendlier relations and more trade between the Soviet Union and the United States. In 1960 he was awarded the Lenin Peace Prize.

I raced back to my car and got my camera, ran back to the crowd and tried to get closer to the front. I aimed my camera and much to my chagrin realized I was out of film. I had been thinking what a great opportunity to get a shot for the local paper, the Summerside Journal Pioneer that probably didn't have a reporter here. I had started to develop a relationship with them because of my public relations duties at the base.

In desperation, I looked around and saw a man holding a funny looking camera, which I recognized as one of the new Polaroids. I quickly explained the situation to him and asked if he would take a picture for me. "If you can get me closer to the stage, I will, " he said. So using my 6'2" height and a rather official tone, I pushed my way through the crowd, shouting, "excuse me, excuse me," until we reached the front of the stage. My new friend took two pictures and passed me the almost instant results. I thanked him profusely and ran back through the crowd to my car.

When I got to Caribou, NS, I found a phone and called the editor of the paper. He said, "We won't put the paper to bed until you get here."

The next day the photo was on the front page of the paper. I don't know if Canadian Press picked it up, or not. But from then on the editor told his staff that anytime I called and wanted something in the paper they were to cooperate to the fullest.

Shortly after getting back to the station, my boss F/L Patterson called me in and told me that he had an assignment for me if I was interested. He wanted me to take a Maritime Air Command display to three exhibitions. The first would be at the week-long Charlottetown Old Home Week, followed by two weeks at the St John, NB, Annual Fair and finally one week in Fredericton at their week-long exhibition. He told me he would try to visit when he could but basically he wanted me to put a team together and take off for the month.

I started immediately looking for some clean-cut people who could represent the Air Force at a display and didn't mind working hard and long hours for a month. The word spread quickly and in a few days I had four enlisted men plus an officer -a fellow navigator on 415 Squadron. Flying Officer Pat Torrens had been in the RAF, and at the end of his short service commission had come to Canada and joined the RCAF. He was well spoken and 'well turned out.'

Old Home Week started in early August so we only had about a week to put everything together. The focal point of our show was a large-scale model of the new Argus ASW aircraft that had recently come into service with the RCAF. It had been donated by Canadair and reportedly was worth about $10,000, a huge amount in 1961. We had to guard it carefully.

The Argus built by Canadair was first delivered to the RCAF in September 1957. It was capable of carrying 28,000 pounds of fuel and thus could fly for 22 hours at normal power settings. It was the most effective anti-submarine warfare aircraft of its day and was the mainstay for the RCAF in maritime roles.

Pat and I headed for Charlottetown to look at our site and to find a place to live for a week. The enlisted guys decided they would travel the 45 miles back and forth from Summerside to Charlottetown each day. F/L Patterson told me that we were late registering and so would have to put our display in a tent outside the main show building. But it was in a good spot close to the entrance.

We found a bed and breakfast owned by Mrs. Bumstead, not far from the grounds. We would share a room with two beds and get a "good breakfast" she told us for a total of $10 a night. Since our travel allowance was $9 a day each, we figured we could afford this, and this close to the fair-opening day there probably weren't any rooms left anyway.

So the tent was erected, the display mounted and we were all ready for opening the next day when Pat told me that his wife Barb had complained about him being away for seven days in Charlottetown. He told me that he would be driving home each evening. I told Mrs. Bumstead and she quite graciously told me that I could still have the room, but it would still be $10 a night. That meant I would have to subsidize the cost of the room and not be able to eat on my allowance.

I went back to the fair, to the Women's Institute booth and told them my plight. "Do you know anywhere else that I might get a room, preferable with a cheap rate and a good looking daughter, but not necessarily in that order?" I pleaded.

"No way," they said, "Too late." I pleaded some more. "I just can't afford Mrs. Bumstead's room." One lady spoke up and said, "I doubt she has any room, but why don't you try Flo Clay up on St Peter's Road. She might be able to help."

So off I went. I was in my work clothes, having just finished helping putting the tent up and assembling the display, unshaven and rather dirty. I arrived at 46 St Peters Road and a nicely dressed woman came to the door and I told her my plight. Her immediate reaction was, "I'm full." I told her my problem.

We started to talk and she asked me where I was from. I told her Toronto, before I joined the Air Force. She said, "I have a daughter in Toronto who is a special education teacher." Finally she said, "Well, I could give you this small room at the front of the house but it isn't much more than a cot." "I'll take it," I exclaimed.

"How much?"

"Well, how about $2 a night and I'll give you a good breakfast."

"Done."

I drove back to the WI to thank them. "How did you make out?" they asked as I walked in." "Well 50/50," I said. "I got a cheap room, but the daughter works in Toronto."

We were all set for the fair opening the next day. I drove my car back to the Clay's B and B. Little did I know that this would be a major turning point in my life.

When I got to the house, I met Mr. Clay in the yard, a small man, well-dressed in a three-piece suit and fedora, and smoking a pipe. I introduced myself and thanked him for letting me stay. "That's the wife's business, nothing to do with me," he said. "But I am glad she could help you."

I looked at my filthy car covered in PEI red clay and asked if he knew where I might find a car wash. A good Scot, he replied, "Don't be wasting your money on them car washes. I have a hose here you can use. Besides my daughter is in the house and she can help you."

Mrs. Clay hadn't told me her daughter was home from Toronto. So he went in and yelled for 'Shirlie' to come out and help me. Out came this little bouncy, redhead wearing short shorts and her hair in Toni curlers. She was cute but only looked about 16. How could she be a teacher in Toronto? I mused.

We washed the car and she was good at it, even cleaning the inside. She smiled when she found an earring between the seats. She didn't say anything and neither did I but I couldn't think whom it might belong to. I had bought the car from the car dealership in Winnipeg where Joan worked as secretary to the boss, so it might have been hers because she had driven my car sometimes.

We finished and the car shone. I thought, well it is about suppertime and I need to eat. Perhaps I should invite Shirlie out but I couldn't take her to a place where they serve drinks because she wasn't old enough. So I asked her and she said, "ok, but I will have to clean up and change, give me about 20 minutes."

I also got into some clean clothes in my little room and 20 minutes later she walked down the stairs. "Holy cow," I thought. A tight fitting white dress accentuated her buxom figure and with her hair swept back in a beehive, she sure looked older than 16. I found out later that she was 26, had graduated from Dalhousie University in Halifax, had a nursing degree and was now teaching nursing at the Prince County Nursing School in Summerside.

We went out to a local restaurant and had a nice dinner together. Although I had had a few dates with girls in Summerside in the past few weeks, it was the first time that I had really enjoyed being out with a girl since leaving Joan. We just seemed to click.

On the way home I decided to check the display because I was worried about that expensive model sitting in a tent. So worried in fact that I had hired a young fellow to guard it during the night. When we got there a portion of the tent had come down probably because the pegs weren't tight enough. What really got my dander up was that the guard was sitting in a chair asleep. I was furious and on our first date Shirlie saw that I did have a temper. Fortunately the model wasn't harmed and the guard promised to stay awake.

At the end of the week, after the fair was closed, I invited Shirlie, along with her younger sister Myrna and her girlfriend who were visiting from London, ON, to go to the local Legion. We could have a dance and I could have a beer. At the door, Myrna, who was six years younger, and her 19-year-old friend walked in, but Shirlie was stopped and asked for ID. I thought it was hilarious.

Sunday, the team packed up and moved to Saint John, NB, where we set up the display in a nice location at the end of a display building. Pat had come with me and we needed lodgings. I had met Joe Zed who had a display at the Charlottetown show. He was from Saint John, and when I mentioned our problem, he suggested staying at the Admiral Beatty Hotel, the best in the city. "We can't afford that," I said. "Let me see what I can do, I know the manager," he replied.

Later that day he came to see me and said, "How about a dollar a day each for a room?" I couldn't believe it. Joe was a mover and a shaker.

The show went well and that week Ted Patterson came to visit us and help for a couple of days manning the display. I wasn't scheduled to work until Friday evening, so I took my uniform to the dry cleaner who promised that it would be ready before their 6 pm closing time. I went back at about 5:45 only to discover that they had closed early and that they wouldn't open again until Monday morning.

When Ted came to the hotel I told him my problem and he said, "Well, I'm off so just borrow mine." And I did. I don't know what either of us was thinking. Ted was a flight lieutenant and had an observer wing and two rows of medals to show for his WWII service. That evening I received lots of curious stares. "Where were you during the war?" one grizzled veteran asked. "In London," I honestly replied. If any senior military officer had come along I probably would have gone to the military hoosegow.

We finished the show in Saint John and moved to Fredericton where there was great interest in our display. I had written a letter to Shirlie and called her once or twice. I told her I would be home on Monday evening and she told me to come and see her.

On Sunday morning we were packing up the display and one of the guys said to me, "Sir, we know you are anxious to get back to Summerside. We can finish up and drive the truck back tomorrow, so why don't you leave now." Pat and Ted had gone home and I felt quite comfortable that the four junior NCOs could handle what was left. So I said ok, jumped into my car and headed for Summerside.

I got there just about suppertime. I had to find Shirlie's apartment and bounced up the stairs to the second story where she was living. I knocked on the door and felt excited about seeing her. I don't think I had felt this way with many girls, even with Joan. Shirlie opened the door to her small apartment and I said enthusiastically, "Hi, I'm here early." Over her shoulder I saw a man sitting at the small dining table eating dinner. I recognized him as one of my instructors from the base. I was mad. Without any thought I said to Shirlie pointing at this guy, "I'm coming back in 10 minutes and if that SOB is still here I am going to throw him down the stairs."

I raced down the stairs and marched along the sidewalk, checking my watch. It didn't even occur to me then, but it has since, that I had only been out with Shirlie twice and had spoken to her on the phone twice and now I was telling her what she had to do. She would have had every right to tell me to get lost. But it didn't happen that way. Ten minutes later, by my watch, I climbed the stairs knocked on the door and her visitor was gone. I learned later that he had said to her, "Well I guess I had better go," and she hadn't tried to stop him so he left.

From then on Shirlie and I saw a lot of each other. She was busy with her teaching nursing duties and I started my OTU course again but we saw each other when we could, usually on weekends.

89

One Saturday night after we had had something to eat at a local restaurant, I complained about a pain in my abdomen. Shirlie said, "You do that a lot. I hate to tell you this but I think you have an ulcer." "A what?" I said. "How can I have an ulcer at 21?" "Well, you should go see the doctor and have it checked out." She insisted.

On Monday morning, primarily to keep her happy and prove she was wrong, I went to the station hospital. When I met the doctor he asked me what was wrong and I told him what Shirlie had said. His reaction was much the same as mine.

"But," he said, "if it makes you happy we will do the test." Ten days later I got called into the hospital. The doctor said, "Your girlfriend was right. You have a duodenal ulcer." So once more I was removed from the course and put immediately into the Station hospital for a month. Only this time the school commandant decided not to re-course me again. I would just miss a month of the course.

My treatment began with lots of cream and a bland diet. Once the pain went away I felt fine. But I had to wait for everything to heal. It was perhaps one of the most boring 30 days of my life. I had lots of time to think.

My life over the past two years had included lots of beer, pizzas and spicy food, coupled with lots of pressure, particularly during the training period to get my wings. I told myself that I just had to change my attitude, not to get so upset and watch my diet. Shirlie came to see me just about every night, although it was a strain on her because she had taught all day and dealt with student nursing problems, and when she left me after an hour's visit she had to go home, make her supper and prepare for the next day of classes.

She was very helpful and encouraged me to change my habits and my outlook on life. I believe that the Len Dent who walked out of that hospital was a very different man than the one who had walked into it thirty days previously.

Shortly after getting out of hospital in early October, Mr. Clay asked me if I could help him out. "My wife and I are going to Florida for the winter," he said. "I have never driven that far. Do you think you could come with us to help me drive and I would buy your ticket to fly you back as soon as we get there?" I thought, well it would only mean missing a couple of days of classes if we did it over a weekend so, why not. "Sure," I said, "but I will have to get cleared by my instructor."

The next day I went to see an instructor and as luck would have it, it was the same guy that I had threatened to throw down the stairs at Shirlie's apartment. When I explained the situation and asked for permission to miss two days of classes his immediate response was NO. "Dent, you have missed enough classes already," he said. "But I have already written the exams and won't miss any training flights," I exclaimed." The answer is, "No."

Reluctantly I called Mr. Clay and told him the bad news. "Well, you tried," he said and thanks you for that. I will just try and take it easy."

They made it to Savannah, Georgia and checked into a small motel besides the highway. It was very hot. When they had checked into their room, Harold Clay told his wife that his left arm was very sore. "Let me go to the bathroom," she said, "and I will come and rub it for you." A few minutes later she came out and he was sprawled on his back on the bed, dead.

It was Friday, October 13, 1961. Harold Waldorf Clay was 68 years old. He had suffered a massive heart attack. He had had an overall physical before he left and his GP had pronounced him, 'fit as a fiddle.'

One can only imagine what it must have been like for Flo Clay. An inexperienced traveler, in a strange motel, in a foreign country, far from home. The motel staff helped and the city authorities came. She called her elder son Keith in Welland, Ontario and he agreed to fly to Savannah as soon as possible to pick up the car and drive it home. Arrangements were made and Flo made the long slow train ride back to Prince Edward Island with her husband in a coffin in the baggage car. She must have cried all her tears because at the funeral a week later, she never shed a tear.

Her house in Charlottetown had been rented for the winter so she had no place to stay. Shirlie invited her to come and stay with her in Summerside. Her apartment was too small, so Shirlie found a two bedroom in Inman Apartments, a new small building close to the hospital. Coincidentally, Pat Torrens, his wife Barb and their son lived across the hall.

I was devastated when I heard the news of Mr. Clay's death. You can image my guilt feelings which I still carry to this day. What if I could have driven them, I thought. But Shirlie correctly suggested that if his heart were in that poor condition, it would have only been a matter of time before he had such an attack even if he had made it to Florida.

I never confronted the instructor who had denied me permission; what would have been the point? But the story became known on the station and I suspect he found out about it.

Shirlie was very close to her father and it affected her greatly. So once again I had to try and support someone who had suffered a great loss. In a way it seemed to bring us closer together.

A few weeks later tragedy struck again. My pal Jamie, who had completed the OTU and been posted to RCAF Station Greenwood, NS, became engaged to his gal Irma Casey in Summerside. They had set a date to be married in early December. Jamie had visited her and left his dream car, a Porsche convertible, and had flown back on a military flight to Nova Scotia. The idea was that his fiancée could drive over in a week's time and then they would be married.

The day before the rehearsal she set out for the ferry. Driving around a steep curve on the icy road just outside of Borden she lost control of this muscle car and hit the side of the road. The car rolled and Irma was killed instantly. Jamie was inconsolable. She was buried a few days later in her wedding dress.

Our OTU course finished and our class graduated just before Christmas. I was told I would get my posting shortly. I had asked to stay in Summerside at 415 Maritime Patrol Squadron and was told there was a good chance that would happen. Shirlie and I decided we should invite my Mom and Dad down for Christmas so that she could meet them.

I sent them a letter and they were overjoyed at the thought of seeing me and what they began to suspect might be my long-time partner. Unbeknownst to Shirlie, I began looking for a ring and finally found what I thought would be perfect. It cost more than two month's salary but I knew this is what I wanted her to have. I even took Flo Clay to the store to show her and she was very impressed.

Mom and Dad arrived on Christmas Eve. They had driven down with Shirlie's older sister Mona, the teacher in Toronto. They immediately took to Shirlie. The next day we had breakfast and then began opening our presents. It was a happy time and even Flo seemed to forget her great loss for a short time. She had tic douloureux, causing the nerves on one side of her face to give her severe pain. This had been exacerbated by Harold's death. The only remedy then was surgery which would have left her partially paralyzed on one side of her face and which would have caused her to drool. She was too proud for that.

When all the presents were opened, everyone sat back and thanked each other for their generosity.

"Oh," I said, "I forgot something." So I went into a bedroom and into the closet where I had hidden a big box. "This is for you Shirlie," I announced with a big smile. "Just something I forgot to give you." She said, "But you've already bought me a present," as she began to unwrap.

Imagine her surprise when she opened it up only to find another wrapped gift box inside. This happened five more times and each time the gift got more smaller until finally she held in her hand a gift about the size of a ring box. She looked at the box, tears welled in her eyes and she ran from the room.

A few minutes later having composed herself, she returned and opened it. Inside was the ½-carat diamond engagement ring. She cried, I cried, and then everybody cried as we hugged each other.

To this day she always says, "You never even proposed, you just gave me a ring." The rest of the day we talked about wedding plans and all agreed a date in the late spring would be an ideal time. Mom and Dad probably could get back for the wedding but I knew I would have to help them with the airfare.

In early January, I got my posting and much to my relief it was to 415 Squadron.

About a week later I was visiting Shirlie one evening when the phone rang, about 8:30. It was my squadron leader. "I've got news for you,"

92

he said. "You have been posted." "Posted where to?" I said incredulously. "To Torbay," he replied.

"Where in the hell is Torbay?" I was almost shouting.

"It's in St John's, Newfoundland. 107 Search and Rescue Unit is there and they want you to come and be a navigator on the squadron," he said.

"When?" I uttered in disbelief.

"There is an aircraft coming in tomorrow at 11 am and leaving at noon. They want you to be on it."

I was dumfounded. I found out later that Flying Officer Hal Smith's wife had had a baby prematurely and he had requested that his posting from Greenwood to Torbay be delayed until she and the baby were well enough to travel. So the career manager in Halifax had agreed to that and looked for a single, trained navigator who could be moved instantly. That was me.

The next morning I requested a meeting with the station commander. I told him that Shirlie and I were engaged and that we planned to get married in the spring. He was understanding and said he would talk to Maritime Air Command Headquarters about delaying my posting. The word came back shortly. I could have two weeks and had to report to Torbay by February 8.

Shirlie's Mom had already ordered the invitations for a wedding in late May. But a quick decision had to be made. A new date was set for February 3. Shirlie had classes to teach and couldn't get time off to help plan the wedding. She went over to Moncton, NB, on a Saturday to find a dress, which they mailed to her just in time for the wedding.

Shirlie's Mom had to plan the wedding. To make matters worse, her father died in mid-January, so in the space of three months she had lost her husband and her father and now had to plan her daughter's wedding in less than two weeks, all the time coping with the debilitating facial pain.

The wedding went well. Held in Park Royal United Church in Charlottetown, about 400 people showed up, although only 80 were invited guests. Many came as a tribute to Harold and Flo Clay. He had been the Federal Agricultural Representative on the island and was well known.

Flo was very active in church groups. I only knew Shirlie, her mom, her sister Myrna and the six RCAF officers who formed a guard of honour for us as we left the church. Jamie was my best man. Shirlie's Uncle Ira, who came from Boston for his father's funeral, walked her down the aisle. Unfortunately, there just hadn't been enough time to arrange for my Mom and Dad to come.

The wedding reception and dinner was held in the posh Charlottetown Hotel. After a great dinner and a few speeches, Shirlie and I changed and we left in our car to the roar of well wishes from the guests. Most thought we were headed for a honeymoon off the island. Only a few knew that I had to leave on Monday morning to drive to Torbay, Newfoundland.

So we circled the block and came back to a small motel adjacent to the hotel. We dumped our luggage in the room and then headed for the furniture store located close to the Clay's homestead on St Peter's Road.

We had told as many as we could, "Don't give or send gifts, send money." So armed with almost a $1,000 we started negotiating with the store manager who knew the Clay family well. By store closing time that Saturday night, we had enough furniture to furnish a small apartment.

Sunday was a day by ourselves and early Monday morning, I headed for the ferry well aware that a ferocious storm was forecast to be headed to the Atlantic Provinces. In fact, I was only a few hours ahead of it as it came in and closed roads and pulled down hydro and phone lines.

The ferry crossing from North Sydney to Port aux Basques was rough but uneventful. Once there, my car was loaded on the 'Newfie bullet' and I relaxed in a passenger car for the 12-hour trip to St John's. There were no paved roads at the time connecting the west and east coasts of the Province.

On Tuesday night the train puffed into downtown St John's. I got my car and headed for RCAF Station Torbay. It had been almost 30 months since I had joined the RCAF and now I was ready for my first operational role as a search and rescue navigator.

Shirlie and I on our wedding day, Feb 3, 1962

CHAPTER 9 - LIFE AS A RESCUER

Search and Rescue. Truthfully, my move here had all been so sudden and with getting married so quickly, I hadn't had much time to really think about what my job as part of 107 Rescue Unit would be like.

There were basically four crews at the unit each consisting of two pilots, a navigator, radio officer, engineer and a para-rescue specialist. I was introduced to the duty crew and those I met seemed friendly and willing to fill me in regarding what our job was.

They told me that Torbay had been established in December 1941 as the home of a Bomber Reconnaissance Squadron. Both the Royal Air Force and the United States Army Air Corps had also used the station during the war years. It was disbanded in April 1946 and reopened in April 1953. 107 Rescue Unit was established in 1954. It had four Lancaster bombers, which had been converted to a search and rescue role.

Our principal role was to find and provide assistance to passengers and crew of downed aircraft, and to come to the aid of vessels at sea or persons lost or in distress. The area of responsibility covered out to 30 degrees West Longitude or about half way across the Atlantic towards the UK and also covered all of the Atlantic Provinces, the eastern half of the province of Quebec and the southern half of Baffin Island. In all it was an area of approximately 4.7 million square kilometers. Eighty percent of the region was covered by water. Some job, I thought, for four Lancasters and four crews.

The Lancaster, one of the main heavy bombers of the RAF and RCAF, came into service in 1942. In all, 7,377 were built primarily by AVRO in the UK, with 430 being built by Victory Aircraft in Malton, Ontario, now home of the Pearson International Airport, Toronto. The Lancaster had a 33-foot bomb bay, which allowed it to deliver the heaviest bomb built, a 22,000 lb 'grand slam.' The aircraft we used had been converted for our role, which primarily included being able to use the bomb bay to carry a MA1 kit. It consisted of two large inflatable dinghies and three large bundles of food and supplies all held together with heavy rope.

I had been given a room in the officer's quarters on the station and settled in. I tried to call Shirlie to tell her I had arrived safely, but the phone lines from Newfoundland to PEI were down. In fact it was nearly six weeks before we would communicate. I had got a letter out on an aircraft that was flying to RCAF Station Summerside, but it was put into the mailbox at the officers' mess and returned.

Her students and her colleagues often asked if she had heard from her new husband and at first she smiled and said, "No, but I will soon." She never admitted it to me, but I think she did get a little nervous as weeks went by without hearing from me.

Finally, close to Easter, one of the senior officers on the station who needed some flying time took me in a C45 Expeditor and we flew to Summerside for a day.

'Unfortunately,' when we got there, a storm came in and we couldn't leave for almost a week, so I did get some time to spend with my new bride. It was during this visit that she told me she had just discovered that she was pregnant. I was even more anxious to get her moved to Newfoundland. Finally, a month later, she finished her contract, and I found an upstairs apartment in St John's, which was really three bedrooms with a hallway serving as a kitchen. It wasn't much and it cost almost half my salary each month, but we would be together which was most important. She arrived in early May.

By this time, I had started my duties as a Squadron Navigator. We were required to have one crew on duty 24 hours a day, seven days a week. The crew slept in the hangar beside the aircraft because under International Civil Aviation Organization (ICAO) rules, we had to be airborne within 30 minutes from being told there was an emergency. There was always a second crew on standby that could stay at home and only come in if the first crew was called out. The third and fourth crews had a day off.

So basically, every third and fourth day I had a day off albeit, if there was a rescue mission or a search, that free time would be wiped out. All too often that was the case. I also was soon given some secondary duties, which usually meant I had to come into work on one of those days off.

It was tough for me as a new operational navigator. The Lancaster navigation equipment consisted primarily of an APS 22 Radar, a B2 Drift meter and a sextant to take star and sun shots. The equipment was the same as when the Lancaster had been flown on bombing missions over Germany during WWII. The aircraft was also equipped with a LORAN (long range navigation) system but over the ocean as you got farther from shore, its reliability was often in question.

I once gave a search and rescue lecture to an RCAF Association in Sydney, NS. The 'old' vets were kidding me that, "I should have been flying missions during the war with the equipment they had." They were surprised when I told them that nothing had changed in the past 17-20 years.

It made me realize the importance of the navigator on a search and rescue mission over the ocean. People usually think of a pilot when you mention that you are an aviator. Certainly the pilot's role was and is very important to launch the aircraft, fly the aircraft safely and land it. But in our role, it was the navigator who had to find the search area where a ship or fishing boat was missing and conduct a very rigid search pattern over a period sometimes of 12 -14 hours and then get back to base.

All too often these searches took place in bad weather with high winds and rough seas with the aircraft 100 - 500 feet off the water. If the navigator failed to find the correct area or stay in the proper search pattern, it could mean that crews of ships or boats might never be found. This was always in the back of my mind.

I soon discovered that everyone on the squadron really loved what they were doing. Crews really worked as a team to try and carry out a successful mission. I think that no one regarded our work as a job because we were helping people, and that brought a great deal of satisfaction. That came home loud and clear one day when in the space of less than 12 hours we were involved in two successful missions.

Early one morning we were awakened and told that there was a requirement to drop some blood to the Cunard Line's Empress of Britain which was sailing towards Halifax and was about a 90 minute flight east of Newfoundland. The Canadian Red Cross personnel in St John's were bundling up the correct blood type in a canister and bringing it to the base where it was loaded in the bomb bay.

At about 6:00 am we took off and headed eastward. Although the ship had sent us its position, there was no guarantee that it was exactly at that spot. Ships' navigators didn't have any better navigation tools than we did. To compound the problem, morning fog covered the Atlantic area we were flying over and there were also many smaller vessels sailing, so the radar was picking up a lot of contacts. With the help of a radio signal from the ship we were able to locate it but couldn't see it. We were told that a woman was in the operating room and needed this blood desperately.

The fact that contacts picked up by the APS 22 radar disappeared in a hole in the centre of the screen when about two nautical miles from the target, didn't help. I asked the Captain to turn on to what I thought was the correct heading and told him once the contact disappeared I would count the seconds I thought it would take to be over the ship.

Just as the image disappeared on the screen, the fog rolled back and showed the ship about 10 degrees to our left. It was like someone had taken a knife and split the fog. The captain made the heading alteration and we dropped the blood package to a small lifeboat from the ship that was in the water. We made a 360 degree turn and less than two minutes later came back and the fog had rolled back in; we couldn't see the ship. My belief in God having a hand in things took a major leap that day.

We returned to Torbay just after 10:00 am and since our 24-hour shift was over, the crew went home. I related to Shirlie our successful mission and went to bed.

About two hours later there was a loud knock on our apartment door. Shirlie was surprised to see a military policeman at the door asking to speak to me. I am not sure why the unit didn't call but he told me that another mission had come up, the other crews were already tasked and another crew was needed immediately.

I found out when we got to the briefing room that a man was scheduled for an emergency operation in a cottage hospital in Springdale, a small community in northern Newfoundland. Roads into the community were not passable because of a snowstorm and they needed some blood for this operation.

Once again the Red Cross came, the canister full of blood was loaded into the bomb bay, and we took off and headed north. We reached the area in a little over an hour and saw that we had a challenge.

The community was along the shoreline with a large cliff behind it. Flying northeast along the shoreline was the only way we could fly at an altitude of about 200 feet and the winds were blowing at 90 degrees to our heading. There were lots of houses, all with TV antennas sticking up. The area of open lawn in front of the small hospital looked like a postage stamp. Time was of the essence so the captain flew the heading I gave him and we prepared to release the life-giving package from the bomb bay. Taking the aircraft speed and wind direction and speed into consideration I gave the command to drop. As we turned the aircraft around and came back over the town, our flight engineer yelled that he thought he saw a parachute hung up on a TV antenna.

Well, I got razzed for the rest of the flight back to the station. "So much for saving that guy's life," said one crewmember. I was distraught. Later I thought that no one on the crew really meant what they had said to me. In fact every crewmember always wanted every mission to be a success. They were probably frustrated at thinking that we weren't successful and it might mean that someone would die. But that experience stayed with me on every mission that we flew after that.

When we landed and walked into the operations room, the ops officer said, "Nice job you guys." "Don't you start," I said. "I have had it from these guys all the way home." "What do you mean?" the officer said. "The hospital called and said if they had had a window open they could have caught the package."

It took several weeks before the unit received a letter from Cunard thanking us and telling us that the woman had survived a successful operation and that the blood we dropped had made it possible. About the same time the cottage hospital advised us that they had had a successful operation and that the man was recovering well.

That's two lives saved in less than 12 hours I thought. OK God, I think I have paid my dues.

Unfortunately not all our missions were successful. Newfoundland relied heavily on the fishing industry, and a large percentage of the men in small out-ports around the island owned small boats and made their livelihood venturing out every day into the unforgiving North Atlantic looking for a big catch.

All too often, one of these small craft would be swamped by huge swells and the crew consisting usually of only a few men was hurled into the icy waters. Most Newfoundland fishermen had never learned to swim I was told. I am not sure why. Perhaps they thought that knowing how to swim and having to contend with the huge swells they would encounter miles from their home shores would make little difference to their chances of survival. Nevertheless we would be called out to search.

Another mission that called us out on occasion was to intercept commercial airliners that had problems and been diverted to the Gander airport. Several airlines were using the Super Constellation on transatlantic routes between North America and Europe. Lockheed built 856 of various

100

versions of the aircraft between 1943 and 1958. It was used as a civilian airliner as well as a military transport and saw service in the Berlin airlift. Unfortunately, this four-engine aircraft was prone to engine failures and in some circles earned the nickname of, "the world's finest trimotor aircraft."

We would be called out usually late at night to intercept and escort the aircraft back to the eastern Newfoundland field. Fortunately, we never ever had to deal with a crash.

Three months after arriving at the unit, I was involved in my first Royal Flight escort. Aircraft carrying members of the Royal family flying to Canada were normally shadowed by search and rescue aircraft which would be in the area should the aircraft have to ditch in the Atlantic.

On May 12, 1962, we spent 6 hours and 45 minutes along the track of the Royal Flight, which was en route from London to Montreal. Of course, it was flying at 30,000 feet plus and we were below 10,000 feet. Prince Phillip was actually flying the aircraft and while in contact with F/L Owen, our captain, suggested we come up and join them so he could see the venerable old Lancaster. Our captain told him that if we could have climbed to that altitude, they would be safely on the ground in Montreal before we got there.

Shortly thereafter we flew the first of a number of escort missions, which would take us from Torbay to Goose Bay to Sondrestrom, Greenland to Keflavik, Iceland and then on to Scotland and to England. Canada had reached an agreement to give a total of 60 single-engine T-33 jets and C-45 two-engine aircraft to Turkey and Greece. Our RCAF pilots would be flying them from Canada, and our unit was tasked with the responsibility of providing navigation assistance as they flew across the ocean and also to be there in the event of a ditching. Giving these aircraft, which were used primarily for training purposes in the RCAF, was part of Canada's involvement in NATO's Mutual Aid Program

The first mission, as part of what was named Operation Western Weal, is one that I will never forget. On May 21 we left Torbay in Lancaster 104 and flew to RCAF Station Summerside to meet up with the aircraft and escort them to RCAF Station Goose Bay. The following day we left Goose Bay and flew out across the North Atlantic about half way to Keflavik, Iceland, where we circled for more than an hour until all the aircraft had passed us. They were using our radio signals as a beacon. Once past us, and when our signal would begin to weaken, they would find the radio signal coming from the base at Keflavik and use it to home in on. With the entire aircraft safe in Keflavik we landed at the US base.

The next morning we discovered we had a flat tire. Where do you find a tire for a Lancaster in 1962? The answer was at RCAF Station Trenton close to Toronto. It would have to be flown up to Keflavik. The escorted aircraft commander decided that they would continue on their own from Iceland to Scotland using radio signals and without our escort. The tire arrived on May 25, so our captain, F/L McLennan, with the Unit commander's approval, decided to continue our flight to the UK for training purposes since we would be doing a number of these missions over the next few months.

Our flight plan took us from Iceland to Prestwick Scotland and south, to arrive at RCAF Station Langar, Canada's only base in the UK. It was provided to us by the British after the Second World War and remained operational until 1963.

Once past Prestwick, the skipper contacted Langar tower on the radio to confirm our ETA, which was just before 1800 hrs. on Friday, May 25. The tower told him rather abruptly that the station closed at 1700 hrs. and would be closed for the weekend. "But what about us?" the captain asked. "Guess you will have to find somewhere else to land," was the curt reply.

Today, it sounds difficult to believe but I have related that story for years and can't imagine that I dreamed it. "What other base is close?" asked the captain. I told him that RAF Cottesmore was very near and so we contacted this base. When hearing that we needed a place to land and stay for a few days, also that we were a Lancaster crew, the station couldn't have been more co-operative.

The Station was opened in March 1938 as an RAF training facility. The US took over the facilities in September 1943. On June 5, 1944, the hangar at Cottesmore served as a temporary barracks for the men of the 82nd Airborne Division. That night 1,256 paratroopers left Cottesmore in 72 aircraft for a drop near Sainte Mère Église, France, as part of the Normandy Invasion.

Cottesmore was turned back to the RAF in July 1945 and became a training station. A number of the officers and men who served at the station were WWII vets and were familiar with the Lancaster. The Lancaster had been retired from the RAF for some years so during our stay we took several of them for a ride.

We were fed a British steak for dinner that first evening, which by Canadian standards was thin and overcooked, but they did their best to show us how welcome we were. In fact, for the remainder of the operation we never filed a flight plan to Langar again since we were told we would always be welcome at Cottesmore.

Our skipper told us we could have a couple of days off and so I decided to head to London to see my Uncle Sam and Aunt Bella. Just before we left the next morning, we were told that there was a problem with one engine and that we would need parts to be flown in from Canada. So we were told we could have four days off in London.

The co-pilot and radio officer, neither of who had been in London, and I, boarded the train and headed for Victoria Station. The guys stayed at the Cumberland Hotel on the edge of Hyde Park while I went to stay with Uncle Sam. I did come to the hotel to find them one morning. I was told they had turned in their key and had gone 'sightseeing.' Knowing these guys, I thought perhaps they might be looking at some of the sights in Soho. So I went to Soho and headed for a place called Raymond's Revue

Bar, which they had talked about earlier. Sure enough there were my two single friends walking up and down outside this burlesque theatre waiting for it to open at noon. The bar opened in 1958 and billed itself as the, 'World Centre of Erotic Entertainment.'

Our little vacation over, we headed back to Cottesmore. The aircraft had been repaired and the following morning we did the mandatory air test before heading out, on June 2, for Keflavik. It was an uneventful six-hour flight to the US station in Keflavik.

At 1000 hours on June 3 we took off for a scheduled routine eight-hour flight to Torbay. About 30 minutes out at about 8,000 feet all hell broke loose. Suddenly there was a great deal of activity in the cockpit. I looked out and could see flames gushing out of the far engine on the starboard side. I heard the whoosh as the fire bottle was activated and repellant hit the flames. There was a cloud of smoke and then a few seconds later the flames came bursting from the engine again.

"Nav – heading to Keflavik!" yelled the skipper. As he did I could feel the old aircraft creaking as it turned to starboard and began to descend rapidly. Doing a quick calculation in my head I shouted back, "Turn onto 010."

We could feel the airplane shudder as we thundered down through the sky. I thought the wings were going to fall off. I wasn't sure exactly what the skipper was trying to do but I trusted him. F/L McClellan had been a fighter pilot during World War II. I figured with his experience and the fact that he survived the war; we couldn't be in better hands. I later learned that by diving he was trying to starve the fire from getting any oxygen thereby blowing it out. Both he and the young co-pilot were pulling on their respective controls and suddenly we were leveling off at about 500 feet which seemed to be all too close to the water. I quickly did some calculations and gave him a corrected heading for Keflavik. Smoke still billowed from the engine but there was no fire.

About 30 minutes later we were cleared for an emergency landing at the base. US fire trucks and ambulances were there to greet us. The landing was uneventful and we were taken by some American colleagues to the mess for hot rum toddies, which we needed.

Once safely on the ground I realized why we had been trained to do what we were told to and not to start asking questions when orders were given. That became even more relevant when the engine was taken off. The maintenance crew told us that the fire had burnt through the cylinder walls. They told us that 30 to 45 seconds more of burning and the fire would have hit the gas tank. Obviously we wouldn't have made it back. The skipper had also had the option of having us bail out but the chances of survival in those North Atlantic waters would have been very slim over any period of time.

An engine was flown in from Canada the following day and replaced. Two days later on June 5 at 1800 hours we once again headed for Torbay…this time successfully. We had been away 12 days and flown 38 hours on what should have been a five – six day trip. To my knowledge we never had another engine problem with Lancaster 104 before the aircraft was retired in November 1963. The aircraft now is on display at the Canadian Aviation and Space Museum in Ottawa.

A week later F/L McClellan and the crew, including myself, flew another phase of the Operation Western Weal, flying from Torbay to Goose Bay to Sondrestrom and back to Torbay. This time everything worked well and we were gone only three days.

Because I was new on the unit and also a new operational navigator, the unit commander assigned me to every escort mission. I was assigned to two more missions to Cottesmore in July and August. The older pilots, who mostly were WW II veterans, just loved to fly these long missions; it was hard to stop them.

On my third mission we had trouble starting out. The airfield was completely fogged in and the tower couldn't see us as the captain asked for takeoff clearance. We were told to wait until the fog lifted. The skipper kept asking the tower for clearance, telling them we needed to go in order to make our rendezvous with the aircraft to be escorted. Finally the air traffic controller asked if we could see 25 runway lights. The captain asked the young flying officer co-pilot how many lights he could see. He replied 12. The captain said, "OK, I can see 13, which makes 25 so let's go." I don't think that is what the controller meant. But we did launch without a problem!

On the fourth mission I ran into trouble with the co-pilot of the aircraft. We had arrived in Cottesmore, had a couple of days off and were heading back to Torbay via Iceland. At the 6:00 am briefing, the meteorological officer told us to expect severe clear icing on our route over the Atlantic between Scotland and Iceland.

Knowing that the aircraft had limited de-icing equipment to combat this type of icing, I stood up and declared that, well, I guess we can go back to the barracks. "No flying today," I said. The co-pilot, a brusque Englishman who had also been in the RAF during WWII said, "What the hell do you mean?" I said, "I am not going to fly in those weather conditions." He looked at me and said, "You fly or I will have you court-martialed." I spat back, "Fine, just let me take a copy of that weather forecast into the court." Before he could answer, the skipper who was of the same vintage as the co-pilot said, "Len look, I understand your concern. Tell you what; let's fly to Prestwick and if it's getting bad we'll land there, or if we start running into these conditions over the Atlantic we will turn back to Prestwick." "That sounds fair," I said and off we went. Interestingly, we did not run into any bad weather. By my calculations, the weather was well to the north of our track.

When we arrived in Keflavik, I made a point of going to the Met office and telling the duty forecaster. He told me that he had the same forecast as the one we had been given in England, so I must be wrong. I realized that perhaps I had been just a little too cocky back in Cottesmore and that these experienced pilots weren't about to get any of us killed by doing something stupid. So I wasn't about to argue with this Met officer. I just left.

In early September, the unit received an invitation from RAF Cottesmore to come over and do a fly-past as part of the Battle of Britain ceremonies on September 15. Once again I was told I would be part of the crew. A few days later Shirlie told me that it felt like our new baby was "not happy with the cramped conditions it was living in" and there were signs that the birth would happen sooner than scheduled. I went to the unit commander and pleaded with him to take me off this mission. He wasn't particularly understanding, but finally relented. So, coincidentally, on the morning of Sept 15, 1962 at about the time the fly-past was taking place, Shirlie and I became the parents of a beautiful baby girl we named Susan Faye.

Walking up the stairs on the outside of the building that we lived in to reach our apartment was going to be difficult and a little dangerous with a new baby. So I found a small basement apartment in the west end of the city owned by a young lawyer who had just moved in. His name was Clyde Wells, and 27 years later he would become premier of Newfoundland. We stayed there only a few months and then were offered an attached house on the former US military base at Fort Pepperell. It was great, with three bedrooms, and our first real home as a married couple.

In addition to my flying duties I had been assigned to be the Unit Public Relations Officer and the Liaison Officer to the local Royal Canadian Air Force Association. Both of these were great jobs, and I also had the opportunity to meet with some wonderful local Newfoundlanders in the media as well as in the Association whose members came from all walks of life.

Newfoundlanders are perhaps the friendliest people we have ever encountered. It was during the several social evenings that we shared with these couples that we tasted our first seal flipper pie...and were introduced to Newfoundland Screech. When Shirlie was in the hospital for six days, the women from the Association came to visit her every day, often bringing presents. Most of them we didn't even know.

With a new baby, moving, and my secondary duties added to my already full schedule of flying and being on standby, I was a very busy man. In addition, the unit commander believed that when we spend 24 hours living beside the aircraft we should fly a five-hour training mission every day, just to give us practice. The only problem was that sometimes we would fly that five hours and then be called out on a search, and we were already tired.

When I had free time I wanted to spend it with Shirlie and Susan. One new young pilot who told me that I should be going to the mess on Friday nights and drink and play poker with the guys chastised me. "You never will make it as a career officer if you don't," he told me. "Fine," I told him, " but my family is more important to me than losing money I can't afford to lose." Eight years later I had been promoted to major, and he spent the remainder of his career as a captain.

One night about midnight when we were flying our compulsory five-hour training mission, we were returning from flying out over the Atlantic. Our heading was taking us directly over Signal Hill where Marconi sent forth his first radio signals across the Atlantic. Signal Hill was renowned as a spot for watching 'submarine races,' where gals and guys parked to have 'private time.'

Our skipper said, "Watch this." We were going to pass at about 200 feet over the Hill and just before we got there he turned on the 70 million-candle-power lamp that was on our wing. The whole sky lit up like it was daytime. I can only imagine what was going on in some of the dozen parked cars in the parking lot!

Our busy lives continued, and when Susan was old enough, Shirlie went back to work as a nurse at the St John's General Hospital. Part of it was the fact that we could use the money and part of it was because she had trained for a career and did not want to become stale.

Our neighbour Jane Ann Clarkson, who lived on the other side of our duplex, and had two older children, agreed that she would look after Susan while Shirlie was at work. Just about everyone at this small station was very friendly and because the men were often away for periods of time, the wives were there for each other as needed.

Thirty-five years later, Jane Ann, now living in Thunder Bay Ontario, discovered that she had cancer. One day while visiting her general practitioner she learned that he had been born and received his medical training in Newfoundland. She told him that she had lived in Newfoundland many years ago when her husband Ron served at Torbay. "Oh," the GP said, "I think your cancer specialist's dad was in the military at Torbay and that's where she was born." "Do you mean Len Dent?" she asked. "I think that was his name." So the next time Jane Ann visited Dr. Susan Dent, her cancer specialist, she said, "Dr. Dent, you don't remember me but many years ago I used to change your diapers and look after you. Now it's your turn to look after me." Small world!

The cost of food was very high in Newfoundland because many items were imported. Milk cost us about a $1 a quart and eggs were $1 a dozen. We would feed Susan whole milk and us drink milk made from powder.

One day we flew to RCAF Station Greenwood on a training mission. While there, one of our crew negotiated with a local poultry farmer and bought 1,200 dozen eggs for 35 cents a dozen. The eggs were loaded on the aircraft and we flew back to Torbay. Over the Atlantic, just as we were passing the islands of St Pierre et Miquelon, we lost an engine. "We have to lose some weight," the captain told us, "or we won't make it back". Well, we agreed that none of the eggs were going to be thrown out. So other pieces of equipment were unplugged and thrown out. They will have to be replaced, was our thought, but nobody would replace our eggs.

In mid-1963 we learned that the old Lancaster was finally going to be retired. The replacement would be an old North Star.

The aircraft, built by Canadair was a Canadian version of the American Douglas DC4. It first flew in July 1946 and was used by the RCAF as a general transport aircraft. This was the aircraft flown by the Air Force to ferry supplies to Korea from 1950–1952. I assume those we were given to fly search and rescue were from that squadron. They were noisy and not built to fly low-level search missions. But that's what we were given, so that's what we had to use.

My first flight on the North Star was in June, 1963 on a training mission, and over the next month we flew more and more in the North Star as the Lancaster was being phased out.

At the end of October, I flew my first long mission in the North Star from Torbay to St Mawgans, an RAF Station on the west coast of England. From there we flew to the Azores and back to Torbay. When we arrived at the Azores the weather was very bad, with the wind blowing at almost 60 nautical miles an hour at 90 degrees to the runway - the only one at this USAF base. When the skipper asked for landing clearance, he was told that the runway had been closed because of the winds. "Well," he said calmly "you have two choices. Either you clear us to land or you pick us up out of the ocean. We don't have fuel to go anywhere else." There was a long silence, probably while the control officer conferred with higher authority. Finally a rather short sharp reply, "Cleared to land. But at your own risk."

It was an interesting landing with our nose pointed into the wind at right angle to the runway, and just as we were about to touch down, the skipper made his correction and we landed safely. Each one of the crew treated him to his favourite drink that evening at the mess.

On Nov 27, 1963 our crew flew a 'Lanc' from Torbay to Halifax and on to RCAF Station Downsview in Toronto - the last operational flight of a Lancaster. I had logged 650 hours in this venerable aircraft since arriving at the station.

Shortly after we started flying the North Star, we learned that the decision had been made to close RCAF Station Torbay. It didn't make sense to us since our location was ideal, given the search and rescue area of responsibility. The nearest base, which would assume our responsibility, was RCAF Station Greenwood, which was about a three-hour flight west of our station. At that point in my career, I didn't try to make any sense of what was happening, but the older guys told me it was all politics and which provinces needed more from the federal government.

On February 11, 1964, I flew my last operational flight at Torbay. My total flying since arriving two years earlier was 741 hours. Perhaps not a lot but we had had many successful missions and some scary flights in aircraft which should have been retired long ago.

For Shirlie and me this first posting in Newfoundland formed the foundation of our marriage. In two years, we had welcomed Susan into our lives and lived in three different places in St John's. I had spent a great deal of time away from home. So we made the most of the time that we did have together and treasured every precious moment.

We had made many friends in Newfoundland. We had also come to realize and appreciate the importance of our military family and how many people in similar positions were there for support when needed. To this day, we look back with fond memories of our time in Newfoundland.

My posting was to RCAF Station Greenwood as a navigator on the 404 Anti- Submarine Squadron, not something to which I looked forward. Flying 12-14 hours over the Atlantic on anti-submarine patrols didn't strike me as very appealing.

A couple of days in advance of our departure from St John's we dropped our car off at the train station. It was to go on ahead and be there for us when we reached Sydney, NS. We boarded the 'Newfie' bullet for our overnight trip to Port aux Basques where we would take the ferry to Sydney. Imagine our surprise when we woke up in Corner Brook and saw our car with many others sitting on a rail car in a siding. We made it to Sydney and had to stay in a hotel for two nights before the car finally arrived. Our pretty white Austin was now a dull gray and washing didn't help. With financial help from the railway company the car was repainted.

Two weeks of leave in Charlottetown visiting with Shirlie's mom and we were off to our new station.

RCAF Station Greenwood, located in the Annapolis valley in Nova Scotia, was originally selected to be the site of a RAF Station in 1940 to train aviators for WWII. It became the RCAF Station in 1944. 404 Squadron, to which I was posted, had originated as a Coastal Fighter Squadron in April 1941 at RAF Thorney in southeast England and disbanded in May 1945. It was reformed at Greenwood in 1950 with a maritime reconnaissance role.

When we arrived in Greenwood, Shirlie, Susan and I ended up staying at Dick's Cabins close to the nearby town of Kingston. It was very small and rustic. To provide heat, there was a pot-bellied stove that I had to feed with firewood given to us by the owners. The bathroom was so small that a recently added bathtub extended beyond the room, and a small box-like addition had been built to cover that portion of the tub.

There were no permanent married quarters (PMQs) available. I searched in the nearby towns, and about two weeks after arriving in the area we found a small upstairs apartment in Middleton. We left our palatial digs at Dicks Cabins.

Meanwhile there was no advance for our claims for lodging and meals, so I had to borrow money from a bank to be able to pay our expenses.

Shortly after arriving I reported in to my new squadron. The next day I was sent on an eight-hour training (for me familiarization) mission in the Argus. I wasn't impressed. The next day I made an appointment with Wing Commander Hy Carswell, the Squadron Commander.

"Sir," I began, "I am a fully-trained, experienced search and rescue navigator. I understand that 103 Rescue Squadron here is short a navigator. Wouldn't it make sense to have me transferred here?" "Yes," he said, without hesitation. I was surprised. I thought he would have told me to get back to what I had been told to do but as I found out he was a very reasonable officer. "Let me call Maritime Air Command Headquarters and see what they say."

The next day I had a call from his office and was told that my posting had been changed and I was to report the following day to the SAR Squadron, which was located on the other side of the runways at the base.

103 Rescue Unit

"Good Morning, Flying Officer Dent." Squadron Leader Russ Janzen, the unit commander, shook my hand firmly and invited me into his office. He told me he wanted to personally brief me on the unit. His enthusiasm made me quickly realize that he loved flying and his role in search and rescue.

The Unit had been formed on April 1, 1947 as 103 Search and Rescue Flight at RCAF Station Shearwater in Dartmouth, NS. Later that year it was moved to Greenwood and in 1950 was renamed 103 Rescue Unit.

He explained that our role and responsibilities were much the same as those that I had had at my previous unit. He then told me that he had learned that I had experience as a Public Relations Officer (PRO) at Summerside and Torbay and asked me if I would I like to take on these same responsibilities at 103 Rescue Unit.

At this point in my career, and since I was meeting the commander for the first time, I did not think I should say no. Indeed, I had enjoyed my experiences to date in the public relations field. But I couldn't appreciate then how involved I would become in public relations or the impact it would have on my career and the future of my family.

The commander gave me a few days to become familiar with the unit, including flying a couple of familiarization trips; then I was put into the regular roster.

On April 10, 1964, I flew my first search mission in an Albatross aircraft for five hours looking for a small light aircraft that had gone missing. We located the aircraft but unfortunately the pilot did not survive the crash.

What a difference between the aircraft I used to fly in and the Albatross. The Grumman Albatross replaced the RCAF Canso aircraft in 1960. The first, Alb 9307, arrived at 103 Rescue Unit in late 1961 and six months later, on May 24, 1962, set an endurance record for flying non-stop from Comox , BC, on Vancouver Island to Greenwood, a distance of 6,115 km, in 16 hours 32 minutes.

The fact that the aircraft could be landed on land, water or ice added greatly to the unit's capability, particularly since many incidents involved ships and fishing vessels. In fact, it allowed the unit to make open sea landings when sea-state and winds would permit. The capability was enhanced by being able to use the Jet Assisted Taking Off (JATO) bottle, which provided much needed extra thrust to launch off the sea surface.

In addition to the Albatross, we also had two DC3 Dakota aircraft, which were excellent for air evacuations. Two helicopters added greatly to our flexibility.

Shortly after arriving at the Unit, I was introduced to Albert who had arrived on Feb 21, 1964, two months before me. On arrival, he was a 120 lb, 9-month-old St Bernard pup who had been named Albert and made our unit mascot. He was given the honorary rank of AD2, (Air Dog 2nd Class). He would prove to be a PRO's dream to help get recognition for the rescue unit and its activities.

And there were lots of activities on the unit. Since the population of the three Maritime Provinces was much larger than that of Newfoundland, the call for our services seemed to come much more frequently, particularly for air evacuations. These often were the result of car accidents and we were needed to take victims to a much larger hospital than what was available locally.

Sometimes we flew two airevacs on the same day and sometimes I flew three days in a row. These were often emotionally difficult especially when they involved young children who had been involved in car accidents and whose chances of survival were slim.

One late afternoon, we picked up an eighteen-month old baby boy in Sydney, NS, who had been involved in a car accident and flew him to Halifax. He had a serious head injury and the onboard medical staff was fighting to keep him alive. I couldn't help but think about our daughter Susan who was the same age.

One air evacuation that has stuck with me involved one of our own RCAF officers. We were called out at about 3:00 am in the middle of winter to fly to RCAF Station Chatham. The weather was terrible with strong winds, heavy snow and some freezing rain. We learned on the flight up to Chatham that a Flight Lieutenant had been in the Officer's Mess watching a Stanley Cup playoff game and had been drinking rather heavily. Apparently this happened on a regular basis and on this occasion, when he finally got back to his permanent married quarter residence on the base, about 2:00 am, his wife and children were gone. She had left a note telling him that she had taken the children and was moving back to Montreal. We learned later that he had stumbled around the house smashing furniture and found a gun he had hidden away. He put it in this mouth and pulled the trigger. The bullet went into his brain but did not exit the skull. I am not sure how he was found but he was still alive.

Our Search and Rescue crew with mascot Albert

When we arrived and landed at the base, the hospital staff immediately loaded him into the aircraft. The freezing rain had already formed a solid coat over the entire aircraft so that we had to be de-iced. By the time we taxied out to the end of the runway we had another layer. We were able to take off but the landing gear came halfway up and froze. The flight engineer lifted the floorboards on the aircraft and started banging on the gear structure with a hammer to break the ice. Finally the gear came into place.

Meanwhile, the patient who was over 6 feet tall and more than 200 pounds was writhing in the straps we had used to keep him safely on a stretcher. The flight nurse who was about 4'10 " and weighed about 100 lb was trying to force-feed him oxygen. She asked me if I could start doing compressions on his chest. Every time I pumped his chest a spew of blood came out his mouth and generally all over me. I worked on him for about forty minutes. My hands felt like hunks of lead. But I didn't want to quit because I was afraid he might die. Finally it appeared that there was little reaction from him and I turned to the nurse who had been watching me for some time and said, "I think he died." She said, "He died about 10 minutes ago but I couldn't get you to stop."

At the same time, the skipper was trying to find a place to land. Apparently, all airfields in the Maritimes were closed and we were told the closest airport with safe landing conditions was Montreal. But luckily we

111

got a call from Greenwood air traffic control, at our home base, which told the skipper that the ceiling had lifted somewhat and the visibility was such that we could probably land safely. We did so, arriving about 7:00 am.

We were met by a civilian provincial medical examiner. While the body was being taken off he asked me, "Where did he die?" I said, "What difference does it make." "Well if he died over New Brunswick it isn't my responsibility. There's a lot of paper work, you know."

I was really upset. We had risked our lives trying to save this man. I was covered in blood, physically and emotionally exhausted, and all this bureaucratic examiner could think of was the paper work involved. I wasn't 100% sure but I told him emphatically that this man had died while we were flying over Nova Scotia.

Many of our searches were flown in bad weather conditions, at low altitude over terrible seas or unforgiving terrain. Search and rescue crews risked their lives all too often to fly air evacuations or search for people who sometimes were creators of their own predicament.

One such search stays in my mind. One late night in mid-August, 1965 we were told that a light aircraft that had been en route from Scotland by way of Prince Christian, Greenland with a final destination of Blanc Sablon, PQ, was missing.

The pilot, named Binderman, was an ex-flight engineer with the RAF and had recently acquired his pilot's license. He apparently only had about 45 hours flying as a pilot and this was his first long flight in this particular type of aircraft. He had called the tower at Goose Bay, Labrador, and then contact was lost.

We headed for Goose Bay at 8:15 pm and once we were over Labrador, we ran into severe thunderstorms. They were the worst I had ever encountered. The skipper told me to keep us out of these CBs (cumulonimbus). The up and down drafts in these types of clouds could tear an aircraft apart and fling it to the ground in tiny pieces.

I saw such a case in April 1966, when a Dakota aircraft flown by Robert Shaw Jr, the son of Robert Shaw, deputy commissioner general of EXPO 1967, had got caught in such a storm north of Quebec City. We searched for three days using the Albatross and helicopters. On the third day, the helicopter found the remains of the aircraft and brought back what they could find. It filled two gunnysacks!

It took us two hours to make our way back to the coastline in what was a scary and very turbulent ride. The dark furious balls were very distinctive on my old radar set and I just kept telling the skipper to turn left or right to avoid them. Finally we reached the Gulf of St Lawrence and entered clear stable weather. We made our way to Sept Isles, PQ, at 4:15 am. We checked into a motel. Six hours later we headed again for Goose Bay and started the search.

Four days later we spotted the remains of an aircraft down in a clearing east of Goose Bay. Two of our SAR Para technicians onboard jumped into the site. They reported back that the aircraft was in good condition and the pilot had made a good emergency landing. Judging from the remains of a campfire, cigarette butts and some empty soup cans, it appeared that he had set up camp for a few days but his fresh footprints lead to a river and disappeared. Black flies were extremely bad at that time of year and one thought was that he had gone into the water to try and escape the flies. Searches were conducted on both sides of the river and no sign of his ever coming out of the river were found. The captain reported back that it appeared that any more air search would be of no value.

We had flown over 38 hours in four days and had risked out own lives just getting to Goose Bay. But before we could leave the base, Binderman's wife contacted the Defence Minister's office and told them that her husband would have survived and that, "He was always one step ahead of the air force."

The Minister's office ordered us back into the search area. So for the next three days we re-covered the ground flying more than 10 hours back and forth with no sign of Binderman. Finally we were authorized to cancel the search and return to Greenwood. No trace of Binderman has ever been found.

What is intriguing though is why he would have chosen Blanc Sablon for an entry point into Canada where there are no customs officials. We also learned that he had had engine problems when leaving Prince Christian, located at the bottom of Greenland, and returned, landed and fixed the problem before continuing on his route. Inexplicably, even with his flight engineer's background, he did not take on more fuel so it appears he ran out of gas about 100 nm short of Goose Bay. In seven days we had flown 53 hours and were a tired crew.

All these searches and air evacuations gave the unit a considerable degree of media exposure and public interest. The provincial media particularly in Halifax provided regular coverage of our searches and our air evacuations. The reporting was extensive and fair. There was never any negative comment when we were unsuccessful as if the journalists and reporters realized that we were doing our best and that not every search would be successful.

Air Dog 1st Class Albert was now fully grown and weighed about 185 lbs. He lived during the warmer months in a doghouse outside the hangar and he would meet many visiting crews on arrival. This big affectionate slobbering St Bernard became a favourite to everyone.

One Friday evening, some visiting crewmembers took Albert to the mess and fed him lots and lots of beer, which he greedily slurped up. Can you imagine a rather happy huge dog staggering around the officers' mess? Albert must have had a heck of a hangover the next day.

We were invited to take him to various fairs in the Annapolis Valley and he became an attraction, particularly with the kids. The unit was looking for a new badge; we used a photo of Albert as the centrepiece, since the St Bernard is a symbol of rescue. The words 'Seek and Save' were placed underneath his picture. It was submitted to RCAF headquarters in

Ottawa and was approved. It was later submitted to the Queen for approval and her crown was added to the top of the Badge.

I once took him to Halifax in one of our helicopters for a CBC television interview and to attend a fair in the city. The press and the president of the Chief and Warrant Officers' mess, who arrived at the helicopter-landing pad with a huge, juicy, raw T-bone steak, met us. The Chief was rather miffed when Albert turned away and showed no interest. "What's wrong?" he asked me. "He likes his steak medium rare," I told him with a grin. Later that day Albert was taken to the mess and offered the steak cooked to medium rare. He devoured it in short order.

As a result of our increasing notoriety we received many requests from different types of groups to tour the unit. These included Boy Scout troops, Girl Guides, school classes, local service clubs and on one occasion a group of visiting professors from across Canada, who were attending a conference at Acadia University in Wolfville. This gave me lots of work since I was tasked to brief each group on the role and responsibilities of the unit and then show them the various aircraft and equipment we used.

RCAF Station Greenwood was big, with two large Argus anti-submarine warfare squadrons, 404 and 405, as well as the Search and Rescue Unit, and many support services. It was a town in itself, with a large number of military personnel and dependent wives and children.

We were a natural audience, attracting the attention of various entertainers and groups who came to perform at the station. One such group was 'Sing-along Jubilee' which played on CBC television in Halifax from 1962 to 1974. Hosted by Bill Langstroth, it featured local talent, playing folk, country and gospel music, and offered a number of would-be stars an opportunity for exposure.

The stage was set up in a large station drill hall and I was assigned to help with the promotion for the show. When I met Bill Langstroth, he briefed me on the show and told me he had a bright new talent who would 'wow' everyone. I had heard about his reputation as a ladies' man and said rather rudely, "Right, I bet you do have your eyes on this new talent." "Seriously," he told me, "she is something else." Later that afternoon I was introduced to this new 'star'. Bill said, "Len, meet Anne Murray."

That night the drill hall was full and Sing-along Jubilee including Anne Murray put on a memorable performance leaving everyone on a high.

I have loved Anne Murray's singing and her songs ever since. In fact, years later in 1970 when doing peacekeeping duties in Nicosia, Cyprus, I would set my radio alarm for 6:00 am and every morning would be woken up to Anne Murray singing "Snowbird" on the BBC Overseas Services radio. Apparently the disc jockey loved her as well.

This was the same drill hall which a year earlier had been full of a very somber group of military personnel, wives and children, who were gathered at a memorial service to say goodbye to 17 members of a crew who died while on a night training mission, 60 miles north of Puerto Rico.

On March 23, 1965, the Argus with 15 military and two civilian scientists onboard disappeared. The cause of the accident was never determined but some have theorized that the aircraft might have caught a wing tip in the unforgiving Atlantic Ocean, during a low-level anti-submarine warfare manoeuvre.

The station and the whole Maritime community were shaken. It was the first such loss of this type of aircraft and the impact on Greenwood and surrounding area was huge.

A response centre was set up to contact the next-of-kin of the victims as well as to issue media releases or respond to queries, which were coming in from all over the world. I was asked to help. It was a difficult time for me since only days before the crew left I had given the squadron a lecture on survival-techniques and what we as a rescue squadron would do in the event of a crashed aircraft.

There were many calls during the next three days but two stick out in my memory.

One morning just after 9, I answered a call from a gentleman in Toronto. He identified himself and then said curtly, "I have just heard on CFRB radio that my son died in a crash of an Argus. I thought that the RCAF could have had the courtesy to have called me before releasing his name to the media." I apologized profusely and told him I would investigate and get back to him to find out why he had not been informed.

I checked with those responsible for approving the names for release and found out that the individual's parents were divorced and that he had only listed his mother as next-of-kin. Once she had been notified, we had been given his name for release to the media. I briefed one of the padres and suggested it was more his role to tell a father that his son didn't think enough of him to list him as a next-of-kin.

Following the crash, the rules were changed and everyone had to fill out a form listing a secondary as well as primary next-of-kin.

The same day I had a call from what sounded like a rather frail, older lady who very nervously told me that she lived in Saskatchewan and that she had heard about the crash of an Argus. She told me that her son was flying on an Argus crew and she wanted me to tell her that he was ok. "What's his name," I asked. She told me his name. I went down the list of the deceased and there it was. I immediately told her to hold for a moment and quickly handed the phone to a padre, briefing him and telling him that this was his call to handle.

In addition to my flying duties and PRO duties, I had also volunteered to help at the Protestant Sunday School. F/L Bill Penfold, who lived across the street in the Married Quarters, had asked me if I would serve as his assistant superintendent of the Sunday school.

Because of the large population on the base we had more than 300 young people attending each week. That required considerable administration and a constant search for Sunday school teachers. In the fall of 1965, Bill decided to step aside and I was asked to assume responsibilities as the superintendent. Two of my teachers were teenagers, the children of Flight-Sergeant Major, who lived just up the street from us. They, like their mom and dad, were clean-cut and good living people. It was thus very strange when an incident occurred that resulted in the unexplained disappearance of Flight-Sergeant Major.

One day around noon, an Argus was conducting routine low flying exercises over the Bay of Fundy just to the west of the base. Suddenly while flying at about 100 feet, the captain received a red light on his instrument panel indicating that a door or entry point on the aircraft was not secure.

He immediately called for a check-in by all onboard and everyone replied except for F-S Major who had been sitting at a location in the back of the aircraft. When someone went back to check, the hatch on the floor of the aircraft was unlocked and was ever so slightly ajar. F-S Major was nowhere to be seen. The aircraft did several circuits over the area that they had just flown over and nothing was sighted.

Immediately 103 Rescue unit was alerted and aircraft and helicopters were sent out. About an hour later the elder of the two teens showed up in our ready room, stopped at my desk and asked, "Do you think they will ever find the body?" I thought at the time and still think that it was strange that he didn't ask, "Do you think they will find my Dad?"

Nevertheless, we never did find any sign of F-S Major and not long after this, his wife and two children left Greenwood, and I have never heard of them since.

An investigation was conducted. F-S Major was over 6 feet tall and 200lbs +. A man about his size was strapped in and then stood on the unbolted trap door while the aircraft was flown at the same height and speed over the same route on the Bay of Fundy. The door due to the updraft pressure would not move.

How could he have fallen out? It remains a mystery to this day.

Despite my being completely involved in my work and volunteer activities, 1965 was a wonderful year for Shirlie and me. On May 7, our son David was born at the nearby Middleton Hospital. Both Shirlie and I were so thrilled that we now had a girl and a boy to make up our family. Then shortly thereafter, I was offered a permanent commission in the RCAF. As direct entry officers, we had joined with a five-year short service commission, which meant after that most would have to look for a new career. Not a pleasant thought for someone with a wife and two children.

That year two officers on the base were offered this career opportunity. It now meant that I could serve to retirement age, which, dependent on rank, would be at least 45. I would have 25 years of service and a pension for life.

So, life looked good for us. We continued with our lives although it was harder for Shirlie now with two children and my being away so often on extended searches.

Searches conducted usually at very low altitudes over the Atlantic Ocean and in the mountain areas of the Atlantic Provinces and Labrador were dangerous. Fortunately we never had an accident on our unit during my tour of duty. However, we did have a crash one day in mid-January 1966 on a routine training flight.

I had been asked to give a lecture on search and rescue to the Newfoundland Fisheries College in St John's. The unit commander had authorized a training trip on one of our Boeing Labrador helicopters to fly me there. We left Greenwood and flew to Stephenville, NF, refueled and the next morning headed for St John's on what was a clear sunny day.

Just south of Deer Lake our captain F/L Hamel told us that one of our two engines had malfunctioned and that he was shutting it down. Unfortunately having just refueled we were too heavy to fly on one so he began to auto-rotate looking for a safe spot to land... soon. He spotted a clearing amongst the heavily wooded area, which appeared to be covered with freshly fallen snow and offered a safe place to land.

We descended rapidly into the clearing and suddenly all hell broke loose. The snow covered a huge rock and the helicopter hit it, rolled on one side and started sliding downwards. Rotor blades began hitting the ground, breaking off and slapping into the side of the fuselage. Thankfully, they hit flat against the side rather than at 90 degrees, which would have meant that they would have sliced through the thin fuselage, and probably caused some serious if not fatal injuries to the five of us on board. In a few seconds it was all over. The helicopter slid to a stop and miraculously none of us had a scratch. But the helicopter was a total loss.

We had managed to get a message out to Gander Airport tower that we were making an emergency landing so we took some comfort that our downed position was known; we hoped that help would soon be on the way. Once making sure that everyone was ok, we spotted what appeared to be a hunting cabin on the edge of the trees. We headed for it. Inside we found a rather comfortable and cozy room, which contained a big pot, bellied stove and some cans of food including some Irish stew. We got a fire going and opened the cans of stew and within minutes were eating what I remember as perhaps the finest meal I have ever eaten. We had narrowly escaped a fatal crash, were warm and eating hot food.

About an hour later we heard the sound of a helicopter and soon saw it approaching. An army helicopter, the twin of what we were flying, landed and a very happy Captain Dave Guy greeted us warmly with a hug for each. Then he started kidding us that it was his honour to come to the rescue of a rescue crew. We climbed aboard and headed for Deer Lake, about 25 minutes away. As we were coming in for a landing, the helicopter suddenly lost an engine. Moments later, we thumped onto the runway rather heavily but safely.

We were met by a civilian airport official who drove us to a Deer Lake hotel. As we walked into the combination reception desk and bar room, we couldn't help but notice that a movie playing on the TV was showing the Dakotas flying over 'the hump' in the Far East during WWII. Quickly the scene shifted to a Dakota being hit by ground fire and crashing into the side of a mountain. We looked at each other, looked at the bartender and ordered triples of whatever he had behind the bar. It was enough excitement for one day.

Shortly after getting back to the unit, I received a call from Lieutenant Commander Stu Murray who was the head of a newly formed Atlantic Regional Information Office in Halifax. He told me that under the new system of integration that was being established for the Canadian Forces, the staff would consist of an officer from each of the three services. He had an army captain already but needed an air force officer who would be interested in being a public relations officer for the Atlantic Region.

"Do you know anyone on the station that might be interested," he asked. "Not really," I told him," but I will ask a few of the people I know who are involved in PR or associated functions and see what they say."

For the next few weeks, I asked squadron PROs, and members of the station newspaper staff if they were interested, with no takers. LCdr Murray called me once a week to see how I was doing. Finally after about a month, he asked me a question that would change my life forever. "What about you?" he questioned. "How about you coming to take this position in Halifax. You have about seven year's experience working at the base level and I know that you enjoy this work."

Frankly, I had never even considered myself as a candidate for such a job. I felt like I would burst. "Let me think it over and discuss this offer with my wife, and I'll get back to you." "OK," he said, "but I would really like to have you. I don't know why you didn't suggest yourself." Neither did I!

I could hardly wait to get home to tell Shirlie about our conversation. Here I was a 26 year-old flying officer married with a wonderful wife and two children. I now had a permanent commission and was being offered what I considered to be a new career. I had very much enjoyed flying, up to this point. But I admit I was often scared while flying out over the Atlantic, particularly during stormy weather looking for lost fishing vessels, when I knew that if I didn't do my job correctly, people could very well die. Besides, flying search and rescue missions meant that I was often away from home for days and sometimes weeks at a time, flying from an airport closer to the search area.

In one such instance, I had been away in Newfoundland for almost a month and arrived home on Friday evening. On Sunday afternoon Shirlie suggested dressing up and going out for a nice Sunday dinner with the kids at a hotel in Kentville, a larger town nearby. We were all dressed and getting in the car when I heard the phone ring. "Don't answer it," said Shirlie fearfully. "I have to," I said.

"There's an aircraft missing out of Frobisher Bay," my Captain told me. "We're taking off in 90 minutes. Be prepared to stay for a couple of weeks."

With tears in her eyes, Shirlie never said a word. She just unloaded the kids from the car and went back into the house while I rushed around getting my gear ready. I thought to myself, I have to stop doing this to my family. So here was my chance.

That evening we discussed the pros and the cons. It would give me an opportunity to start a new career in the Air Force doing something that I really liked to do and which I could pursue when I got out. It would also mean, or so I thought, that I wouldn't be away from home as much. At the same time we probably wouldn't be able to live in military married quarters in Halifax and I would lose my flying pay. That, as I would find out later, would mean about $300 a month.

Shirlie said, "Len, if you really want to do this, let's do it. I will go back to work and what I make will make up for what we lose in your salary." It was a true demonstration of her love.

The next day I told my Squadron Commander who was not particularly enthusiastic about the idea. At this point, I was the deputy unit navigation leader and the Public Relations Officer. He was enjoying all the attention that my work in PR was giving to the unit. But he didn't discourage me and helped me talk to my career officer. He was even less enthusiastic. When it seemed I couldn't be dissuaded from taking the job, he suggested that he could get me a ground-tour posting into a recruiting office in Saint John, New Brunswick. I was unimpressed. I had been stationed in PEI, Newfoundland, and Nova Scotia for the past five years and didn't fancy moving to New Brunswick. His final plea was that I would, "Never be Chief of Defence Staff if I went into public relations." I told him I didn't want to be CDS. I just wanted a job that I loved to do and that I thought I could do well.

So on May 12, 1966, I flew my last search mission when we located a missing fishing boat in the Gulf of St Lawrence. And so ended my flying career. During the past four years I had flown more than 1,500 hours on countless search and rescue missions. Many had been successful. Some had not. But I was satisfied that I had made a contribution and had helped in saving a number of lives.

Now I was headed for Halifax, Nova Scotia, and a new career.

CHAPTER 10 - A NEW LIFE

Integration – Unification. I had heard these words on occasion while serving for the past two years at RCAF Station Greenwood. But they really didn't come sharply into focus until I arrived in Halifax in mid-June of 1966.

Members of the Royal Canadian Navy (RCN) were incensed at the thought of unification.

Integration, which was introduced in the 1964 Liberal government White Paper on Defence, called for a common administrative structure for the Canadian Armed Forces under a single Chief of Defence Staff. There was some support for integration within the three services because it did serve to eliminate duplication, streamline the command structure and thereby create more capital which could be used for purchase of much needed equipment.

Although not entirely happy, the RCN generally accepted the new structure. This is the reason that I was being asked to serve in an integrated Regional Information Office in Halifax that would provide information services, advice and guidance to all of the Canadian Armed Forces throughout the Atlantic Provinces. We would work with all commanders but report to a director in Ottawa.

The next step, Unification, which would abolish the three services and put all members of the three services into a common uniform using army ranks, was introduced in 1966. All three services were strongly opposed but none more so than the Royal Canadian Navy. The act was to come into effect on February 1, 1968.

The announcement in Ottawa regarding unification, and the impact it would have on the services was devastating, particularly for the morale of the troops. Since being formed in 1910, Canadian sailors had gone ashore in their round-rig uniform and had been recognized as sailors around the world. Now they would be going ashore looking like, in one sailor's words, "a mailman" even though at that point no one had seen the final design for the common uniform.

In November 1964, Rear Admiral Bill Landymore replaced Rear Admiral Jeffery Brock who had been forced to retire over his opposition to unification. Landymore became commander of the post-integration Maritime Command.

But Admiral Landymore was also strongly opposed to unification and championed the Navy opposition towards Defence Minister Paul Hellyer's unification plan.

Reportedly, Minister Hellyer considered firing him but that would have meant replacing a second top senior officer in less than a year.

In July 16, 1966, it came to a head when Paul Hellyer asked Admiral Landymore to resign and he would not. The Minister fired him and appointed Rear Admiral JC O'Brien as his successor. It would be a difficult task for the Admiral.

The dismissal became public and caused an uproar and controversy concerning unification across the country. On July 19, a retirement parade was held in Halifax where thousands of naval personnel and civilian personnel turned out to pay tribute to their former commander.

It was into this atmosphere that I arrived on June 14 as a young Flying Officer (Sub Lieutenant-Navy rank) but dressed in an Air Force uniform.

My posting message stated that I was to be, "temporarily posted for Information Officer duties with the Atlantic Region Information Office in Halifax for a period of six months after which I would be list/branch transferred if I so desired and found to be acceptable." Decision was to be made by December 12, 1966.

Because it was only a temporary posting, Shirlie and the kids couldn't come with me, so my new boss LCdr Murray made arrangements for me to stay in the Stadacona Wardroom (Officer quarters) where I would also take my meals. Of course there were a large number of young single naval officers and a few air force officers staying in the Wardroom. Every day at every breakfast and after work, and particularly on Fridays at our weekly 'happy hour' or TGIF (Thank God It's Friday) at the bar, conversations were dominated by the subject of unification.

There were very few kind words uttered towards the government and particularly Defence Minister Hellyer regarding the move to integrate and unify the three services. Many who had just acquired the dark blue naval uniform were adamant that they would never wear anything else. Of course, their objections became more intense as the unification date got closer. Interestingly, some of the senior naval officers did refuse to remain in the Canadian Forces after unification and took their retirement package or simply resigned. But many of the younger officers did not follow that path. They stayed in and went on to have good careers with a number reaching general officer rank.

I spent much of my first month in Halifax meeting and getting to know the media. My first impression was that they were keen, enthusiastic reporters anxious to get good stories and get them first. At the same time, they were generally sympathetic and supportive of the military, and particularly the RCN. Of course, the navy in Halifax was the prime industry with more than 20,000 personnel, their spouses and children, plus another 10,000 civilians, who worked in support services.

A few weeks after Admiral Landymore left the Navy, Defence Minister Hellyer decided to visit Halifax to brief officers on the benefits of integration and unification. Shortly before he arrived, I found out that LCdr Murray had been posted to Ottawa and would be leaving just before the Minister arrived. His replacement LCdr John Bonneau would not arrive for a week and my army counterpart Capt Al King was on leave. I was asked to accompany the Minister during his visit. Although the Minister didn't want to speak to the media, my boss in Ottawa, Colonel Lou Bourgeois, wanted me there just in case media intercepted the Minister. I was to," handle them."

It was to be a short visit with the Minister arriving around noon for lunch with a few senior officers, then the briefing, and then back to Ottawa.

The Minister arrived as scheduled; however, the lunch did drag on, perhaps because of the questions that the senior officers had for him. Meanwhile, the remainder officers were having a long lunch in the mess. Some were having a 'liquid' lunch.

When the Minister finally arrived in the briefing theatre, a number of the officers were not intimidated by his presence and were willing to voice their opposition to his comments. There were a few supporters. At one point in the briefing someone stood up and said rather bravely, "We're with you all the way Paul." Many others stood and some just sat and booed. At that point it wasn't clear whether they were booing the officer supporting the Minister or the Minister. A rather shaken Admiral O'Brien, who was seated on the stage beside the Minister, stood up and said firmly and loudly, "Enough, sit down and shut up," or words to that effect. Everyone did obey the new commander.

What no one realized was that someone in the crowd had a hidden tape recorder and was taping the whole session.

On leaving the Stadacona facility, representatives of all the Halifax/Dartmouth media had gathered to try and get comments from the Minister or anyone else who had been in the briefing. This was a huge story.

The tape of the briefing was handed to a CJCH radio reporter and rushed to the station in time to a make the 6 o'clock news. There was no time to edit and the portion where the Admiral had to intervene was run verbatim. It was damning for both the Minister and for the Navy.

I called the news editor Errol Weaver the next day and suggested it was not great journalism when he had not even given us an opportunity to put the comments in context. He apologized and said it wouldn't happen again. Of course that was 1966 and the media was a very different group than one finds today in a generation of 24-hour instant news station full of breaking stories.

The next morning the Halifax Chronicle Herald, the principal daily paper in the area ran a front-page headline, which if I remember correctly stated "Admiral Quells Riot at Officer's Briefing."

The stories in the media did little to improve the Minister's image or the feelings of most people in the Halifax-Dartmouth area towards the government for its integration and unification policies. The military were not happy with the portrait the media painted of their behaviour; it drove more of a wedge between the Navy and the media. The fact that a Navy person had given the tape to the radio station didn't seem to count as far as the Navy was concerned.

In fact, having stories leaked to the media was a usual and daily occurrence, as I was to find out all too often. It was encouraged by CJCH-radio who offered a cash reward for the best news tip of the day, and while it was not aimed directly at the military; this was where the best stories seemed to generate. Indeed, HMCS Dockyard was like a leaky sieve when it came to stories getting out of the base. But it also demonstrated how the media in general wanted to co-operate.

One morning when I had just arrived at work before 0800, my phone rang and it was a senior reporter from CJCH. They had just had an 'anonymous' call from the Dockyard to tell them that there had been a report of a 'sub-smash' –the military code for a submarine in distress. When asked to comment on the story, I told them I would check with Maritime Command operations and get back to them.

True enough, a young seaman onboard one of our destroyers, which was engaged in an anti-submarine warfare exercise in the Atlantic, had reported that just after daybreak he had seen what he thought was a red flare, a distress signal, coming out of the sea. There were several of our submarines involved in the exercise so it had to be taken seriously. The submarines did not have to report in until 1200. A call had gone out to all the boats, and all but one had responded. So there was concern, although experienced sailors knew that the boat could be in water layers where possibly the message had not got through to them. I suggested to the Commodore Chief of Staff Operations that we needed to confirm the story and try to convince the station not to air it until we heard from the boat, or until noon, whichever came first. He agreed.

There are dozens of submarine families who know that their husbands are on this exercise and this story will send them into a panic, I argued with the station. "When we know what has happened, I promise, you will be the first to know," I told them. Rather reluctantly they agreed but did call me every 30 minutes for updates.

At 11:00 the reporter started calling every 10 minutes and finally, after their 11:30 news update, they told me that they would have to carry the story on their noon news. My calls to Maritime Command operations were no less frequent. At 11:50, the news director called and told me they were preparing to air the story on the noon broadcast. Imagine my relief when five minutes later I received a call from the Ops staff saying that the submarine had reported in and that the boat and crew were all safe and well. Apparently the sighting by the sailor had been an error.

I immediately called CJCH. To their credit they did carry the story at noon but it was headed by, "Rumors that a Naval submarine on exercise in the Atlantic was believed to be in trouble are false. A spokesman for Maritime Command has just confirmed that the boat has reported in on schedule and that all is well with the boat and crew." It was just one example of the relationship that we in the newly formed Atlantic Regional Information Office were developing with the media and how they wanted to cooperate with the military.

In another such incident, our office was called from Maritime Command operations to tell us that they had a report of a bomb being placed onboard HMCS Bonaventure, which along with a squadron of destroyers, was due to sail that afternoon on a three-month exercise.

With the senior officer's at Maritime Command Headquarters agreement, I called all the media in the area and told them that we had this report. I also suggested to them that this was probably someone looking for publicity and that it might be better to hold the story until we had searched the ship. I called what I considered to be the most dependable stations first, and when they agreed, told the other stations that their competitors were not going to run the story. Surprisingly they all agreed. At about 3:00 pm we got the all clear from Maritime Command and I called each of the stations and told them that all was ok, and the ships were sailing as scheduled at 4:00 pm. Only then did some stations report a false bomb scare.

My dealings with the media in the area to-date had shown them to be aggressive, but fair and responsible. How things have changed in the 21st century!

While I was learning a lot and working hard, Shirlie was back in Greenwood, looking after Susan and David, and anxiously awaiting news of when she could move to Halifax to be with me.

In mid-September my boss received a message that our big boss wanted me to report to Ottawa for four weeks of orientation. I think it was also so he could have a look at me.

On October 3, I arrived in Ottawa and reported to the Director of Information Services. The new Directorate of Information Services had been formed from individuals in the three services (Army, Navy, and Air Force), which had totaled roughly 100 information officers and a number of photographers. The new organization was reduced to 33 officers and the photographers we used were on loan from photographers' section.

Our boss, Colonel Lou Bourgeois reported directly to the Chief of Defence Staff and the Deputy Minister and also to the Minister of National Defence. Regional offices across the country, although co-located with Army, Navy or Air Force commanders, were responsible for providing information support and advice, but reported directly to Ottawa. Commanders who wanted their own information officers could appoint them on a secondary duty basis.

Many of the public affairs or information officers that remained in the service were older. A few had actually served in the Second World War and a few in Korea. Most of these had come back to join or rejoin newspaper organizations. They were a rowdy lot, very good at their job but loved to party. I was told that occasionally some of the reporters who were friends of our information officers would drop into the Headquarters at the corner of Laurier and Elgin and play poker for a couple of hours.

I was introduced to the National Press Club, located above the Connaught Restaurant, on Elgin Street, where we mingled with many of the reporters. At that time there was an unwritten rule that what was done or said inside the Press Club remained inside the Press Club. That didn't last.

I soon learned that there were only two spots available in the establishment for new information officers and there were six of us vying for these two spots. To make matters worse, most of those competing for the positions had university degrees, and two of them were RMC graduates. I felt a little discouraged. But Col Bourgeois had the ability to make everyone feel that they were the best, and when I left his office I considered I had no problem. The thing is, as I found out later, each of us felt the same way.

I came back to Halifax in early November and was told by my boss that I had been assigned, along with two dockyard photographers, to HMCS St Laurent for a four-week squadron exercise in the Caribbean. It would be my first exposure to being at sea and also being with the Navy alone 24-hours a day. It was an interesting experience.

Since I wore an air force uniform, some of the younger officers seemed to think I was to blame for integration and unification. I could feel the hostility in the air and nobody would talk to me except for the squadron commander Commodore Noel Cogdon who was onboard with his chief of staff, LCdr Dutch Holland. Even in the wardroom, where the officers ate their meals, at dinnertime, there was hostility. I would ask for the salt and it would be slid down the table without a word. I am still not sure what the reason was, except that they might have also seen me as a public information officer, a cross between someone who wasn't operational and someone who gave all their secrets to the media.

My first opportunity to break the ice came early one morning as we were approaching two islands from the north. I overheard two young officers on the bridge trying to decide which of the two islands ahead on the horizon was Puerto Rico. I slipped down into the ops room and took a fix on the LORAN (long range navigation) equipment. I walked back up to the bridge and said to them, "Here, this might help," handing them the latitude and longitude of our position. "What's that," one said rather haughtily. "It's our position two minutes ago," I told him. "How did you get this?" "From the LORAN," I told him and pointing at the wings on my chest, I said, "These didn't come in a box of Cracker Jack" and walked off the bridge. It was probably the first time that anyone had recognized that I was more than just a public information officer.

We arrived in Barbados on Nov 29, which was a joyous day for the inhabitants of the island. They were celebrating their independence from Great Britain. That evening thousands of Bajans gathered as troops from a variety of nations, primarily from the Commonwealth, marched into the Garrison Savannah Stadium. At the stroke of midnight the Union Jack was lowered for the last time and the blue and gold Barbadian flag with its Neptune's broken Trident, symbolic of the island's seas, sand and sky, was raised to the top of the flagpole.

I had already written a story on the event, highlighting the Royal Canadian Navy's presence at the ceremony and sent it back through our ship's communication system so that it could be given to Canadian Press for

126

release on November 30. I was shocked to learn later that there were no other Canadian journalists present and so my story was carried by CP and used by the media across the country.

The next day, Commodore Cogdon hosted a cocktail party onboard HMCS St Laurent and among the invited guests were the Duke and Duchess of Kent who were representing Queen Elizabeth II at the celebrations. The Duke is a cousin to both The Queen and The Duke of Edinburgh.

They were a very kind and gentle couple and went out of their way to meet as many of the ships' company as they could. The ship's executive officer, second in command, asked me to make sure that my photographers got as many photos as possible but he warned, "Make sure that they stay out of the way." Unless they were invisible, I am not sure how we could have obeyed that order, but both my photographers were used to being with high-ranking individuals and were very professional in carrying out their duties.

Later that evening I was invited with the other ships' officers to a cocktail party hosted by Prime Minister Errol Barrow. Spotting my air force blue uniform, he made a point of coming over and asking me if I knew of the RCAF base at Summerside. It was then that he related to me about his training days at Summerside as a young officer under the British Commonwealth Air Training Plan (BCATP) during World War II.

Errol Barrow as First Prime Minister of the Barbados was also recognized as the Father of Independence. Recognition of how the citizens felt about him is his statue that still stands in Independence Square in downtown Bridgetown.

It was in this square that a celebration concert was held on the evening of November 30, headlined by Diana Ross and The Supremes. That evening some of the US sailors were celebrating perhaps a little too much and soon scuffles broke out between them and some of the locals. Reportedly, since I wasn't nearby, some of the Canadian sailors seeing the fighting went into the midst of it, as they stated later, "to help break it up."

Unfortunately the locals thought it was more sailors coming to help sailors and so more locals became involved. Outnumbered, the local police tried to put a halt to the fighting but it took some time, and probably ended because everyone just got tired. To my knowledge no reporting of this appeared in any media either in Barbados or off the island.

We sailed away the next day to begin our joint exercises with the US and several NATO countries. One morning I got up early and looked out, and on the horizon saw a magnificent sight that I had never seen before or since. It made me think of the stories and photos I had seen of the D-Day landings. I could count more than 90 ships of various shapes and sizes primarily from the US Navy. With the sun just coming up and shining on the sea it made for an inspiring sight.

During the next few days of exercises, my photographers and I, basically shot 'hometowners' photos with cut-lines that went back to the hometown newspapers of the sailors. These photos were mostly sent to small weekly newspapers that would almost always use them. It provided recognition for the sailors and also kept Canadians aware of what their Navy was doing. It was great for the morale of the crew on board.

We stopped in St Lucia to meet up with another one of the squadron ships and stayed there overnight. It had been an exciting experience for some of the ship's sailors. Rex Harrison and the cast of Dr. Dolittle were filming on the island and some of the crew were invited to watch the filming and meet the cast.

We sailed out of St Lucia and made our way home. For me and for some of the junior officers who were beginning to be friendlier, it had been an interesting experience.

I once again proved that I was more than just a public information officer when we ran into a storm and very high seas in the Atlantic on the way back to Halifax.

The 2,000-ton vessel bobbed like a cork in the high seas, and sitting in the wardroom trying to eat our meal meant watching your plate go back and forth along the dining-room table. Having experienced some very rough weather and turbulence during my search and rescue flying days over the Atlantic, my stomach seemed to be able to adjust. However, a number of the younger Naval officers had to head for the comfort of their beds or the "heads". I think I gained some grudging admiration from being able to sit and continue to eat my dinner.

We arrived back in Halifax on December 17 and I made plans to go back to Greenwood to see Shirlie and the kids.

Just before I left on December 22, I received a wonderful Christmas present. I had been promoted to Flight Lieutenant, effective Nov 16, 1966. This promotion, a Navy lieutenant equivalent, would help me in my day-to-day dealings with the Navy, and just as importantly, it meant a pay increase which would help make up for the loss of flying pay. It would also help to rent an apartment in Halifax when the family moved.

December 12, the date set for the decision to be made on whether or not I was acceptable and would be moved to Halifax had now passed. No word from Headquarters in Ottawa, and when my boss asked Headquarters, he was told that word would come soon.

When I got home to Greenwood and told Shirlie, she was understandably not happy with the news. I tried to placate her but her patience, after more than six months, was coming to an end.

Back in Halifax, I called the Directorate administration officer in Ottawa several times and was told to be patient.

Finally after talking to Shirlie one day in early February I decided enough was enough. So I rolled the dice. I called Colonel Bourgeois, the director, and said, "Sir with all due respect I cannot put my family through this any longer. If I do not hear by tomorrow morning, I am going to put in my release." It was a gamble because I didn't know what we would do if I did get out of the Air Force.

But Col Bourgeois had promised that a decision would come within four months, even though my temporary posting was for six months, and now it had been eight months with no word. In fairness, I am not sure if Col Bourgeois was aware that nothing had happened. After all he was a very busy person who was dealing with the Chief of Defence Staff, the Deputy Minister and the Minister everyday on a variety of difficult issues. My plight wasn't likely on his radar screen.

To my astonishment, early next morning I had a personal call from Col Bourgeois telling me to, "move my family." What a relief! And so, in late February of 1967, Shirlie, Susan and David moved to Halifax. We rented an apartment in The Park Victoria on South Park Street, which was very close to my office and to the Halifax Victoria General Hospital. This was a blessing because shortly after arriving in Halifax, Shirlie applied and was offered a position teaching as a nursing clinical and classroom instructor at the Victoria General School of Nursing.

Shirlie, Susan, David and I in Halifax 1968

With my family around me, I felt much more at ease and began to seriously cultivate a more solid relationship with the media in the Halifax-Dartmouth area. I considered this to be so important because reporters were

129

continually getting stories fed to them every day from military and civilian insiders. We needed to ensure that the media felt comfortable in coming to us to discuss these before going to print or airing them on radio or television. And so I made my rounds of the various newspaper offices and radio and television stations meeting with as many of those I thought I would deal with on a regular basis. I also joined the Halifax Press Club since this was a place many gathered at lunchtime or after work for a beer. I also had to establish my credibility with the media so that they would trust me. It paid off.

One day, I had a call from Bill Curtis who was the national CBC-TV correspondent for the Atlantic Region. He had heard a rumour about some Russian vessels off the coast of Halifax. My boss had given me a copy of a classified message just a couple of hours before outlining the details of this sensitive situation.

Bill didn't know much, just enough to ask a question. I told him I couldn't answer his question. He pressed me for more details and I finally asked him if he could come to my office, which was very nearby to the CBC Halifax building. He said yes and about 10 minutes later he arrived. I liked and respected Bill as a straight shooter and felt we had developed a good relationship. But I also knew that he was a very good reporter and that if I didn't satisfy him, he would go elsewhere to try and get to the bottom of this story, particularly if I stonewalled him.

So I took a gamble. I showed him the message. When he read it I said, "Now you know why I can't answer any questions." "I sure do," he said. "Bill," I said rather emphatically, "you have my career in your hands. If anyone ever found out that I showed you this message, I would probably be court-martialed and go to jail." His reply: "What message?" More than 50 years later, I can't recall the exact details of the situation. But I do remember that reporting it in the media would have caused difficult questions for the military and the politicians in Ottawa.

Bill never ran the story and no other media found out about it. However, relating this incident to others did get me in trouble some years later. As the director of information services, I was lecturing to a classroom of officers attending Junior Canadian Forces Staff School in Toronto and used this story to emphasize the importance of having a good trusting relationship with the media.

The next day I got a call from the Commanding Officer of the School. He said, "Colonel Dent, we have a problem. I know you were on a privileged platform yesterday and felt you could say anything you wanted to the military students. However, there was a military intelligence captain in the audience and he thinks you should be charged for what you did." "Well, Colonel," I said, "you tell the Captain that I took a considered gamble 15 years ago to save the country from what would have been an embarrassing story and it worked. So, if he wants to put me on charge for that, tell him to go ahead." I never heard another word.

I don't think that I would dare take that chance with any reporter today. It is just a different world where everything seems to get reported instantly, sometimes without even checks being done on the validity or truthfulness of a story.

The early months of 1967 were busy as we prepared for celebrations commemorating the 100th birthday of Canada. A major event was the Naval Assembly, which was to be held in Halifax from June 21 - 26. Ships would be coming from Great Britain, Colombia, France, Denmark, Finland, Germany, India, Japan, Netherlands, Norway, Portugal, Sweden and the United States. Many of the Royal Canadian Navy's 36 ships were lined up in two lines in Halifax harbour with an open space between them. Each ship would be dressed overall with flags and pennants.

With many activities being planned for the thousands of sailors, VIPs, Haligonians, and visitors from across Canada and abroad, it meant a lot of planning. Local media and representatives from many of the countries represented by their naval vessels would be there. Plans for each of these events meant considerable work for the three information officers in our office.

When the ships sailed into the harbour and took up their positions, the festivities began. Thousands of visitors took the opportunity to visit the open ships and take part in many parties and fun-filled events that had been planned.

Once again Halifax took on the appearance of a military city with thousands of sailors roaming the streets, shopping, and making use of the restaurants and bars. It was reminiscent of the six years of World War II when more than 50,000 sailors and many army troops getting ready to sail overseas, or just returning, made for a busy vibrant city. During the festivities, I think that most people both military and civilian forgot for these short few days the fact that in seven months the Canadian sailors would no longer be wearing their beloved navy uniforms.

The last ship sailed away on June 27. All events had gone well and there had been no incidents, at least none that we were aware of or that had been reported.

One week later, I left Halifax to drive to Indianapolis, Indiana. I had been told in May that I had been selected to attend the Basic Information Officers Course at the Department of Defense, Defense Information School (DINFOS) at Ft Benjamin Harrison, located on the outskirts of Indianapolis.

The school was set up in 1965 to train military and civilian members of the US Department of Defense in journalism, and radio and television arts. Notable alumni would include Al Gore, print journalist in Vietnam (Jan -May 1971); Dan Quayle; and Pat Sajak, (Vietnam- disk jockey, Armed Forces radio 1968-69).

More than 2,500 personnel attended the courses in 1967. I was the first Canadian to be selected for this DINFOS course.

131

I arrived on Thursday, July 6, and checked in at the school administration office only to be told that they had no accommodation for me but could recommend a good motel nearby; they would try to find me a room in officers' quarters. I was told to report to the school theatre for briefing at 0745 the next morning. Being a Friday, I suspected that this would be an easy day where we would be introduced, briefed and then given the weekend off to get acclimatized. Classes would start Monday morning. Was I ever wrong! The Americans were serious about this course.

At the briefing we were introduced, and I soon learned that each of the 44 US military officers and civilian equivalents had degrees in radio and television arts, journalism or political Science. Twelve had Masters Degrees. Some had worked as TV news directors or newspaper reporters and information officers. The remaining two officers, myself, and a captain from the South Vietnamese army, did not have degrees. I felt a little intimidated. Interestingly, that day I was invited in to see Col Christy, the School Commandant. He welcomed me to the course. Then, in a rather fatherly manner, he said, "Don't worry about the course, you are a foreign student so you will pass". Being a little taken back, I quickly replied, "Thank you sir, but I am a Canadian and if I am going to take this course I want to compete with everyone else." With a wry smile he said, "OK." Perhaps I had told him what he wanted to hear.

Following the introductory briefing our classes started. That day we had an introduction to each of the five subjects that we would cover: International Relations and Government; Applied Journalism; Radio-Television; Research and Oral Communications; and, Policy and Plans. By the end of the day, we had several assignments due on Monday morning. In fact, during the first International Relations and Government class, we were given a test, which would give our instructor an idea of our knowledge of world affairs and geography

I had never spent much time with Americans and particularly US military personnel. I was to learn a lot during the next eight weeks. As a result of that test, I realized that, although they were college graduates, many of the younger officers were lacking an understanding of what was happening beyond the borders of the USA. Certainly, few knew much about Canada.

There were 33 lieutenants, four captains (including myself), four majors, and five civilians. The lieutenants were mostly new university graduates. They were proud and ambitious. Most had already been assigned to units in Vietnam following the course. To hear them talk they couldn't wait to get there. They were completely convinced that what their country was doing was necessary to fight the evils of communism spreading throughout the world.

Two of the majors had already served several tours in Vietnam. They were less enthusiastic and certainly did not want to talk much about their experiences. They seldom became involved in such discussions about, "our role in Vietnam."

Both were Green Berets and Special Forces. Undoubtedly if they did talk about some of what they had witnessed, it might have dampened the enthusiasm of these young warriors. I suspect they would learn soon enough about what was happening in that faraway land.

As I was driving through the small towns and villages en route to Indianapolis, I couldn't help but think about the number of teenagers who had suddenly received an 'Uncle Sam needs you' letter telling them that they had been drafted. Many of these boys probably hadn't been far away from the farm they grew up on or the small town they lived in. Most probably many didn't even know where Vietnam was and yet soon they would be in this very difficult and deadly war.

William Calley, born in Miami in 1943, was older than most when he joined the US Army. He graduated from Officer's Candidate School, at Fort Benning, Georgia, one week after our course ended. He had dropped out of college before joining the army and did not place high amongst his peers at OCS, standing 51st. He was commissioned a second lieutenant and assigned to Company C, 1st battalion, 20th Infantry Regiment, 11 Infantry Brigade and was sent to Schofield Barracks in Hawaii for training before being transferred to Vietnam.

In the first month, his company had no encounters with the enemy. But in the next weeks there were 26 incidents during which five of his men were killed and many more injured.

On the evening of March 15, 1968, Charlie Company was briefed about a mission the following day involving finding and killing members of the National Liberation Front, better known as the Vietcong, who were hiding in a village called My Lai. There were apparently different accounts from those who were present at the briefing, with some testifying later that their orders were to kill all guerrilla and North Vietnamese combatants and suspects, including women and children and animals. If they were innocent, it was said, they would not still be in the village.

Charlie Company was the first to enter the village the next morning. They found no fighters but soldiers suspected the enemy soldiers were hiding in homes among their wives and elderly parents. The soldiers led by Calley went in firing into what they considered to be an enemy position. And a massacre occurred. Reports vary, but it was thought that somewhere between 340 to nearly 500 civilians were killed that day. Each day, in Saigon, a media briefing was held to brief primarily the US media on the day's activities. That day they were told that during a fierce firefight 128 Vietcong and 22 civilians had been killed. The Stars and Stripes, the US Army official newspaper, carried the story.

The true story of the massacre did not become known to the public until late in 1969, nearly 18 months later. US citizens were horrified, and there was an international outcry. Lt Calley was court-martialed, along with 26 others. But he was the only one convicted. He was sentenced to life imprisonment.

Some Americans were outraged that he had been tried for his actions and there was overwhelming support for the idea that his sentence was too harsh and that he had been made a scapegoat. The day after his sentence, President Nixon ordered his transfer to Fort Benning from Fort Leavenworth and he was placed under house arrest pending his appeal. He served only three and a half years at Fort Benning and then was freed.

The whole situation provided much ammunition for the growing number of US citizens, particularly the youth, who were voicing their opposition to the US's involvement in Vietnam.

As former US General Colin Powell stated years later to CNN's Larry King, "In war, these things happen every now and again, but they are still to be deplored."

Unless you have lived under these circumstances, one cannot really appreciate what it would be like to face a foe that was fighting in their own environment, using unconventional methods such as spike pits. Vietcong were hard to identify, as most did not wear uniforms and looked like villagers with guns. The US soldiers were mainly unprepared and untrained in jungle warfare. They were constantly on the alert for attacks from anywhere and anyone. Basically, everyone could be considered the enemy whether young or old, male or female. When one considers that many of these soldiers were still teenagers or barely out of their teens and unseasoned, it is no wonder that they came home with psychological problems.

A not dissimilar situation has been taking place in Afghanistan for years. Many soldiers returning home are now being diagnosed with PTSD - post-traumatic stress disorder, and being treated, although probably many such cases are going undetected.

The senior major of the two, because of his rank and seniority, was our class president. He already had his post-course posting which would send him, his wife and two children, to an army post in Oahu, Hawaii, where he would serve as a senior information officer. In retrospect, training a special forces Green Beret, fresh back from the jungles of Vietnam, to be a media handler and distributor of news releases seemed to be an odd career choice.

It was very hot in the summer of 1967, with temperatures reaching high in the mid- 90s most days. To my recall there was no air conditioning in the buildings at that time.

There was a small friendly pub just outside the gates of Fort Benjamin Harrison where many of us would go after classes for a cool, refreshing beer. One of the waitresses was a young buxom, good-looking blonde who must have been 18 or she wouldn't have been allowed to work there. Our class president seemed to like talking to her and was more at home just relaxing in the pub than discussing how to solve a media problem. Most of us didn't realize until later that he gradually began to spend more and more time at the pub.

One Monday morning he did not show up for class. Our class president was AWOL. We soon learned that the young waitress had not shown up that day for work at the pub. It was concluded that they had left together.

By the time the course was finished, I had not heard whether they had been located. Likely, his career was over. Today, would he be diagnosed as someone suffering from PTSD? It is really impossible to imagine what the impact had been on him during his time in Vietnam. No one knew how many of the men under his command had been killed, and in what circumstances, or how many Vietcong his unit had killed, and what methods they had used.

Years later when I was attending Canadian Forces Staff College in Toronto, our class director, a Lieutenant Colonel in the US Marine Corps, told me about an incident involving some of his men during one of his tours in Vietnam. One night he had sent a six-man patrol out into the jungle with the routine strict orders that they should not have anything to do with any villagers they might encounter. "After all, who is the enemy?" he said. In wars gone by, the majority of the soldiers wore uniforms so it was possible to distinguish who were the 'good guys' and who were the 'bad guys.' In Vietnam, when a Vietcong soldier was caught, he would often be dressed as a farmer and then tell those taking him prisoner that he was just a simple, poor farmer.

The patrol spent the night slogging through the steamy, thick jungle and just after dawn arrived at a small village. A small girl, about 6 years old wearing a faded cotton dress, approached them shyly carrying a wooden bucket full of water and a wooden spoon. Certainly she was no threat. Tired and thirsty, the soldiers apparently forgot the strict orders not to have anything to do with villagers. They dropped their guard and surrounded her and began drinking some much-needed nourishment. With them distracted, she reached under her dress, took out a grenade and pulled the pin. All were killed. The patrol didn't return, but an American 'friendly' in the village later told him what had happened.

He wasn't trying to excuse what happened in My Lai, he told me. But it is all too easy to pass judgments when one is sitting comfortably in front of a television, thousands of miles away, watching the nightly news and not having any appreciation of what these soldiers faced in Vietnam.

The course itself was very broad and required a great deal of work with many assignments. I did find that what was being taught was basic and somewhat idealistic. Based on my experience as a public information officer, I thought it would be difficult to use some of these techniques, as taught, in a real situation when dealing with media. This opinion did get me into trouble with my radio and television arts instructor. He was a captain who had taken the course and had then been posted to the same school as an instructor. He did not have any field experience. He was arrogant to the point of making officers junior to him, even if the same rank, call him 'sir' and salute him if outdoors.

One day I couldn't let him get away with what I thought was a rather inane media approach. I challenged him and told him it would work in the classroom, but most editors would laugh him out of their newsroom. It was a silly thing for me to do, particularly because I was embarrassing this officer in front of the class. He asked, "What is a flight lieutenant equivalent to in the US army?" I naughtily replied, "captain," and asked him, "What is your seniority date?" I don't know if I was senior to him but he didn't reply.

From then on my tests and assignments marks began to fall. Writing radio and TV news items is very subjective, so he was able to use his judgment as to what mark I should have. At the end of the course, my marks in the other four subjects were all in the 90s, and in radio and TV arts I scored in the 80s. Nevertheless, I did finish with an average of 93.3% and stood 5th out of 46 in the class... or 45 since our class president was gone. There was less than 1% difference between the top five.

The person who came first was the civilian lady with whom I had worked on several assignments. She had a master's degree in political science. After the course, she was assigned as the public information officer at Dugway Proving Ground in Utah. She was a quiet, reserved lady who really knew the public information field and I am sure was destined for a very successful career.

Dugway is a test site located approximately 140 kilometers south west of Salt Lake City. Here they conducted open-air tests of chemical and biological weapons in defense systems, in a secure and isolated environment. In March 1968, seven months after she arrived, an incident occurred that would reverberate around the world.

One day, according to local farmers, more than 6,000 sheep died in an area approximately 30 miles from the Dugway site where the Army was conducting open-air tests of a nerve agent. The army denied any responsibility, probably in a statement put out by my friend, but closely edited by her superiors. The army said the cause was most likely from local use of a pesticide on crops. Nevertheless, the Army did pay the ranchers for the loss of their sheep. But the damage had been done.

The incident received national and international attention. This was just after the Tet Offensive, and the anti-war organizations, as well as environmental supporters were becoming more organized.

The Tet Offensive, a major surprise attack by the Vietcong on the US forces and their Allies, occurred in late January 1968. The US media had for the most part strongly supported the US position in Vietnam. They, and the public, had been led to believe that because of previous defeats, the Vietcong were not capable of launching a major offensive. Although the US Allied Forces did beat back the attack and killed many communist soldiers, the media focused on what they considered to be a major setback. Public support was swayed. The Tet Offensive marked the beginning of the end of the US involvement in Vietnam.

I left Indianapolis on Sept 1, 1967 and drove back to Halifax. When I got back to my office, my boss, LCdr Bonneau, congratulated me on my course results. He then said with a smile, "Now that you know how to work with Americans, I am sending you for two weeks at the end of the month to Washington. One of our destroyers is going there to demonstrate the Bear Trap Haul-Down system and I want you to go work in the Embassy and help arrange for the media coverage."

The Bear Trap or helicopter haul-down system was invented in order that helicopters could operate from smaller warships in bad weather. The RCN Experimental Squadron 10 at Shearwater, outside Dartmouth, NS, developed the system in collaboration with Fairey Aviation (Dartmouth). The Sea King was the first RCN helicopter to be equipped with such a device. Canada was the leading nation in developing this system which was adopted by navies around the world, including the US, Australia and Japan.

The destroyer would spend a week in Washington, hosting and demonstrating to senior US Naval personnel and their staff, as well as ambassadors and their attachés from a variety of countries.

I flew into Washington, rented a car and drove to the Canadian Embassy located on Massachusetts Avenue. Our Naval Attaché, a captain who was very gracious, and during the course of my stay was very helpful, met me. He told me I had been booked into the Fairfax Hotel, which was on Massachusetts Avenue, near DuPont Circle. This was the heart of Embassy Row.

It was an elegant hotel, opened in 1927. In the early years it became the permanent residence for a number of congressmen, senators and ambassadors. Included were a young George H. Bush and his parents when they were in town. The first inaugural breakfast for President Dwight Eisenhower was held there in 1952.

In 1961, a very sophisticated restaurant opened, which hosted the elite of Washington. In fact, I am told that this is where Jackie Kennedy and her friends would regularly lunch. Consequently, it was virtually impossible to get a reservation less than a year ahead. I assume everyone wanted to have the opportunity to have lunch while Jackie was there.

Like many high-style hotels, the public areas were immaculate and designed to impress. But the room in which I stayed was small and old fashioned. Because I was going to be there for two weeks, I did a check and made a list of 17 items that needed attention. Nothing serious, but I needed those fixed and within an hour a maintenance man arrived. The Canadian Embassy, a good client no doubt, had booked the room and was paying for my bill, so that probably had an influence on their reaction time.

The Naval Attaché provided me with a list of media contacts who he believed would be interested in seeing the Bear Trap system work.

During my course at the Defense Information School (DINFOS), LCol Donald Williams, the school secretary who was responsible for the administration, helped me. He had solved a few administration problems and had also hosted me to dinner at his home on two occasions during the course. When I learned of my trip to Washington I contacted him and he provided me with a name in the Department of Defense (DoD) information office in the Pentagon who might be able to help during my stay. He told me he would also call him to pave the way for my visit.

Over the course of my career, I discovered that it was not unusual for a foreign student to be treated well. Thirty-nine years later, Shirlie and I were standing at a pier in New York City waiting to board the Holland America Noordam for an 18-day cruise to Rome. We began talking to the couple behind us who were from outside Seattle. We met them several times on the ship and enjoyed drinks and dinner together.

During one of our chats, the wife told me that she had travelled a lot because her dad had been in the US Army for many years, and her family had moved many times in the US and Europe. I told her that I had been in the military for over 30 years. She asked if I had ever served in the US and I told her that I had taken several courses at US Schools, including at Fort Benjamin Harrison in Indianapolis. She said, "That's funny, we were there for a three-year posting". "When?" I asked, and she replied, "From 1966 to 1969." "I was there at DINFOS in 1967." "My Dad was head of administration at that school," she said and then added, "I bet we have met before because my dad was always bringing home foreign students for dinner."

I actually did remember being invited to his house for dinner, but I did not remember his daughter who would have been a teenager at the time. Small world!

I called the Navy Captain who was an information officer in the Secretary of the Navy Information Bureau. We met and he provided me with a few more contacts to add to my list.

Preparing for the arrival of the ship, I travelled a lot around Washington visiting media offices. I was also invited to a number of social functions, courtesy of our Embassy, the Navy attaché, and my newfound friend at the Pentagon. I was living in something of a dream world, mixing with high ranking embassy officials and US and foreign military personnel.

I gave little thought to any physical danger that might be present in Washington. But 1967 was a turbulent year in the US. In fact, I was to have been taken for a weekend visit to Detroit, courtesy of the US government, by my course director while at DINFOS. It was cancelled because of a riot that occurred that same weekend. On July 23, coincidentally my birthday, an altercation between Detroit police and patrons at an unlicensed after-hours bar developed into what would become one of the worst riots in US history. The riots lasted for five days. National Guard and army troops were called in to help the police. At the end, more than 40 were dead and more than 450 injured. Police had made over 7,000 arrests and over 2,000 buildings in the city had been destroyed.

From June to August 1967, there also were riots in Detroit, Boston, Tampa, Buffalo, Newark and Plainfield, NJ; Cairo, IL; Durham, NC; Memphis, TN; Cambridge, NY; Milwaukee, WI; and, Minneapolis, MN.

138

Parking my rented car at the hotel garage cost $5 per day. Even though the military would pay the bill, I considered that to be too much. Throughout my military career, I tried to spend public money as if it were my own. So I would find a parking spot along a side street usually two or three blocks from the hotel and walk, even though it might be late at night.

One morning while driving to a meeting, a radio commentator reported that last evening a male walking alone on a Washington street had been assaulted and found lying on the street with what later was determined to be a concussion. The reporter added that the $2 in his wallet was gone. He concluded by stating that this type of incident occurs on average 75 times a night in the city. I made an immediate decision. I would park at the hotel and the Canadian public could pay for my parking!

The ship arrived and the next day the demonstration of the Bear Trap began, followed by a reception. Chief of Naval Operations Admiral Thomas Moorer, a four star admiral accompanied by a large group of senior naval officers, was the first to visit, and the group appeared to be impressed. Admiral Moorer was a distinguished officer who had served in the navy since 1933, and in 1970 would go on to be the Chairman of the Joint Chiefs of Staff.

Towards the end of the visit, the CO of the destroyer had agreed to take a media group for a sail down the Potomac and carry out a demonstration of the Bear Trap system while the ship was underway. I didn't have any difficulty getting journalists and cameramen to join the tour, even though it meant that they had to be on board before 0700.

We sailed on a damp, foggy and somewhat windy morning. I presume the media thought this would make the demonstration even more interesting. Somewhere during the next two hours the CO had a change of heart and decided that it was not safe to carry out the demonstration in the narrow river with the weather conditions. I had the rather difficult task of explaining to the media that their trip had been for nothing. They demanded that the CO pull this ship over at the first possible opportunity and let them off. I'm glad that this came at the end of the visit.

Regardless, we did get some 'good press' and all the visitors seemed 'impressed' with what they had seen. I don't know if this visit had any impact on other countries buying this Canadian system. I do know that a number of other countries did develop a similar system but whether or not that was a benefit to Canada, the RCN or Fairley Aviation, I am not aware. I know that there is a Military Industrial Complex in the US, which is a strong 'buy-American' lobby group and was negative towards their government buying military equipment outside of the US. I suspect that had some influence in the 1950s when the AVRO Arrow had such potential and yet Canada couldn't sell it to the Americans.

But the Ambassador was happy. In fact, he planned a reception at his residence, just before the ship sailed, for a number of the ship's officers and some of the Canadian media working in Washington. Among the group were James M. Minifie, Knowlton Nash and Arch Mackenzie. These were

139

three outstanding journalists. I had heard of them but never met them. To do so was a privilege.

James Minifie was a Brit who came with his family to western Canada in 1909. He managed to join the army at 16 and served with the Canadian Expeditionary Force in Europe. After the war, he attended university in Saskatchewan, was a Rhodes Scholar and finished his education at the Sorbonne in Paris. He worked for the New York Herald Tribune as a Paris correspondent and reported from Spain during the Spanish Civil War. After this war he joined the CBC as their Washington correspondent. He was a courageous and internationally respected journalist.

Knowlton Nash started his career selling newspapers on the streets of Toronto during the Second World War. He became a journalist for the British United Press before he was 20. He worked as a foreign correspondent for many years working for agencies as well as a free-lancer. The CBC hired him in 1961 as the Washington correspondent for CBC Newsmagazine.

Arch Mackenzie, a well-respected journalist, was born in Regina, Saskatchewan, and served 18 months in the army at the end of the Second World War. After attending the University of Saskatchewan, he joined the Canadian Press news agency in the early 1950s and worked in Montreal, Ottawa and Washington.

Ambassador Albert E. Ritchie was born in New Brunswick in 1916 and joined the Department of External Affairs in Washington, in 1944. He was also a Rhodes Scholar and held several positions, both within and outside the government, until he became Canada's ambassador to the US in July 1966.

The reception was probably smaller than the ones that were normally held at this residence, but all the invitees were Canadian. I am not sure how long it was planned to last but I am sure it went longer. As the evening progressed everyone, including the ambassador, appeared to be enjoying the event more. At one point, the ambassador's wife confided to a small group of us that she was so happy. "Edgar was enjoying himself so much. He feels like he is among family." She told us that this was one of the few times since they arrived in Washington that he had been able to relax and be himself. Normally, she said, he has to be so careful because regardless of where he is and when, he is always the ambassador from Canada, and what he says and how he acts and reacts reflects on his country.

I was impressed. I thought this was a tribute not only to those of us in the military but even more so to the group of media representatives. It obviously was a reflection of the relationship between those media in attendance and the Ambassador.

I know that he was not alone in his concern about being able to relax. Earlier during my stay, I had been invited to a club primarily for US Senators, Congressmen and Congresswomen, as well as some diplomatic staff. Here they could relax have a drink and eat without being subjected to close scrutiny of the media. Media representatives were not invited.

Wow, I thought, this is a long way from being the PIO at CFB Greenwood. I was well beyond my depth.

The ship sailed and I flew back to Halifax.

The idea of taking off the naval uniform and putting on a green one was not getting any better reception as D-Day- Feb 1, 1968 approached. In fact there was more angst and more threats from Naval personnel saying they would never put on that ******* green uniform.

I would soon get some up-close taste of how they would react.

In early January, LCdr Bonneau told me that five of our ships, including the carrier HMCS Bonaventure, the supply ship HMCS Provider, and three destroyers, were scheduled to make a visit to New Orleans in February. They would be a major part of Canada's contribution to the 250th anniversary of the founding of New Orleans.

He told me that he wanted me to go down a couple of weeks in advance to do publicity for the ships' visit, and to handle the PR surrounding the week of the events in which the ships would be involved.

A few days later, he called me into his office and told me that our boss, Col Bourgeois, in Ottawa, had called and said that External Affairs wanted me to work out of the Consul General's office and handle all of Canada's participation in the celebrations. I'm not sure if Col Bourgeois offered me, or whether External Affairs saw it as an opportunity not to have to send one of their officers to New Orleans. Regardless, I had been selected and before I left I really had no idea what to expect.

New Orleans had been founded by Jean Baptiste Le Moyne in 1718. It was to be used as a port city for materials coming into America because he thought the area would be safe from tidal surges and hurricanes. Le Moyne was a Canadian, born in Montreal, Quebec, in 1680. He served as Governor of French Louisiana for four terms during the period of 1701-1743. Some say that he and his brother Pierre Le Moyne introduced the Mardi Gras to Louisiana.

There was another close connection between Canada and Louisiana. The original French settlers in what are now New Brunswick, Nova Scotia and PEI, along with some Métis, became known as Acadians. When the Acadians refused to sign an unconditional oath of allegiance to Great Britain in the 1700s, many were expelled. Although they were later allowed to return, some sought other places to live, and in 1764 a number settled in Louisiana. They later became known as Cajuns.

When I arrived the festivities surrounding the Mardi Gras were already in progress. The annual celebrations begin on the 12th night of Epiphany, in early January (Jan 6), and continue to Fat Tuesday (Mardi Gras in French), the day before Ash Wednesday, the beginning of Lent. There are parties, debutante coming-out balls, and at least one parade every day. One can only describe it as a city gone mad. Streets are filled with

141

people in various states of dress and undress, and parties go on day and night. Events conclude on Shrove Tuesday with a big Ball, before the beginning of Lent, on Ash Wednesday.

Hotel accommodation at this time is virtually impossible to get, unless it is booked months, or for some places, years in advance. External Affairs had found me a hotel room probably through the local Consul General's office. It was in an older part of the city, some distance from downtown.

When I arrived at the hotel, it looked like something out of a, "Gone with the Wind" movie, but not very highbrow. I checked in. The elevator was like an old steel cage with a door that was manually drawn across by the elevator 'boy' who looked like he might have been around as long as the hotel. He was wearing a moth-eaten uniform that must have been issued when he got the job.

"What floor, sonny," he wheezed. "Three," I told him, which was the top floor. I'm in room 328". "Oh," he said. Then paused for a minute and said without a smile, "That's the room where they found the body of the young girl last week".

No wonder the room was available. It had the basics: a single bed with a steel frame, one dresser, and a small bathroom with a cracked stained tub. Great, I thought, and I had to live here for a month.

The next day I took a cab to the Consul General's office in downtown New Orleans. The Consul General welcomed me and showed me to an office he said I could use for my stay. It had a beautiful view of the Mississippi. He was polite but I got the immediate impression that he and his staff had other things to do and that I could do 'my thing' with regard to this naval visit. I started settling in. He came back into the office and told me that he had some tickets for various parades and that I was welcome to use them. Little did I know what these innocent looking tickets would mean for me.

With the help of the office staff I put together a list of New Orleans media to call that day. That evening I headed for my first parade and discovered that my seat was in an enclosed area saved for the mayor and guests. There were about fifty people in a box, many of whom were dressed in costumes, and all very friendly, obviously out to have a good time.

One who caught my eye was a lady dressed as Jeannie, who could have been an identical twin of Barbara Eden. The TV show "I Dream of Jeannie" first aired in 1965 and ran for five seasons. In the show, Eden is a 2,000 year-old genie trapped in a bottle and released by an astronaut, played by Larry Hagman. He went on to star in Dallas for 20 seasons.

'Jeannie' asked me who I was, and what was I doing there. I told her and she said, "My name is Deirdre and I am a special assistant to the mayor. I think he would like to meet you." She gave me her office number and told me to call her.

The parade was unbelievable with so many floats loaded with men and women dressed in often grotesque costumes and masks. People on the floats were throwing beads, stuffed animals, and aluminum or wooden coins to the crowd. And there were some incredible statuesque women with gorgeous figures wearing fashionable gowns on many of the floats. Probably seeing how taken I was, one gentleman leaned over and said, "Beautiful, aren't they?" "You bet!" I shouted, above the parade noise. "Too bad they aren't really women," he yelled back. This was my first introduction to cross-dressers.

It didn't take long to get my next lesson in what New Orleans was like. After the parade I wandered into a crowded bar on the famed Bourbon Street and took a seat at the bar. I ordered a drink. Sitting next to me was a young, handsome, blond man. We started chatting and he asked me if I was from out of town and if I was here on business. I told him the basics of what I was doing. He then asked me if I liked white rum. I told him that I drank it on occasion. "Well I have a bottle of great rum in my hotel room if you want to come back with me," he said with a wink, and briefly touched my knee. "Got an early start tomorrow," I said, and quickly headed out of the bar into a crowded street and caught a cab back to the safety of my old hotel.

After contacting a few media the next day, I decided to spend the afternoon back in the mayor's box watching another parade. The parades usually went on for several hours. Beside me was a group of five attractive women and a small four or five year-old girl, obviously the daughter of a pretty tall woman in the group. It was difficult for the little girl because when people stood up to see the floats or to catch trinkets being thrown to them she couldn't see anything. So I asked her mother if she would mind if I put the little girl on my shoulders. She agreed. Up went this little girl, and for the next three hours she watched the parade while the ladies fed me sips of pop and bites of hot dogs. I found out that three of the women were members of the King Sisters, and they were currently playing at the Roosevelt Hotel, one of, if not, the premiere hotels, in New Orleans. Another lady was the PR representative for the hotel. The whole group was very appreciative and insisted that I come to the hotel that evening to have a drink on them and watch the show.

So I found the beautiful Roosevelt Hotel, which was originally opened in 1893, just outside the French Quarter. Not knowing how to find the mother, I asked at the desk for her by name. The receptionist politely replied, "Oh she is the manager's wife. You will find her in the Blue Room." The Blue Room, as I found out later, was famous in the US and for many years featured national touring musical acts.

Many famous entertainers from across the US and the world have played there, including Sonny and Cher, Jimmy Durante, Sophie Tucker, Judy Garland, Marilyn Monroe and Ethel Merman, etc. There was even a radio show that came nightly on WWL Radio and broadcast across the US.

"Just ask the person at the door to take you to her table." Which I did, and there were the five ladies, including the King Sisters who were now adorned in beautiful full-length gowns and made up to look like the stars they were. There were four sisters in the group who were born just south of Salt Lake City, Utah. They were regarded as one of the big-band era's most popular and enduring vocal groups. Their careers included Hollywood films, tours across the country and their own ABC TV network series called the King Family Show.

When I got to the table, the manager's wife welcomed me and ordered me a drink. Shortly afterwards her husband appeared, and I was introduced. "Where are you staying?" he asked. I told him the name of the hotel and he said, "You can't stay in that place, you have to move here.""I can't afford to stay here, I told him." "Yes, you can," he said, "I am the manager. So call me tomorrow morning and we will move you into a room in the hotel." I am not sure now what I paid for the room, or if indeed I did pay, but I know that if it would have had to fit into my meager military travel budget; it would have been considerably less than the regular rate.

Meeting the manager and the group began a series of nightly invitations to Mardi Gras parties throughout the city. Each night I would dress in my tuxedo, which I had bought just after arriving in Halifax. Taking my 'tux' was one good piece of advice that External Affairs did give me before I left home.

I would head for the Sazerac Bar for a drink before leaving with the manager or one of the PR ladies for a round of evening parties. The bar is known world-wide and even has a drink named 'the Sazerac', which is the official drink of New Orleans, and which some say was the world's first cocktail. The first couple of nights we would only stay at a party for one or two drinks. When my host said, "let's go," I would quickly finish my drink and we would be off.

After a few parties, I began to feel the effects, but couldn't understand how my companions were able to cope so well. Then I realized that they were taking their drink with them. The manager would be driving down Canal Street grasping the steering wheel in his left hand and his drink in the right. No one bothered us; after all, this was Mardi Gras in New Orleans. I quickly learned to take my drink from party to party.

A couple of days after meeting Deirdre, I called her at the mayor's office. She told me that she had spoken with Mayor Victor Schiro and that he had agreed to see me. She told me to be at the office the next day at about three o'clock.

Victor Schiro became mayor in 1961, and served until 1970. The son of Italian immigrants, he had worked as a movie extra, co-managed a Nevada gold mine, and had been an assistant cameraman for Frank Capra. He was a colorful character but, I was told, an avowed segregationist. That might have rubbed off on Deirdre.

She told me once that she had gone to Chicago for a visit and one day a black man got on the bus and had the audacity to sit beside her on a seat near the front of the bus. She was so shocked, that she got up and got off the bus. This was a well-educated articulate woman. But in 1968 I guess it reflected what many people in the South still felt.

144

He welcomed me into his office and asked me to tell him what I was doing and when I had briefed him he said, "Len, whatever help you need, I will give you. If anyone gives you any trouble just call me and I will fix it." I had no doubt that he would do exactly as he said. In fact over the next number of days I met him at several of the parties and, I guess, he had taken a liking to me because he invited me to join him to go in his big stretch limousine to several parties. Wow, was I ever out of my league.

One evening at the Roosevelt Hotel, the King Sisters told me that they would be leaving the next day and introduced me to the gentleman who would be succeeding them as the next act. He looked awfully familiar and when I was introduced I knew that I had seen him on television. He was Frank Gorshin, who had played the Riddler in the TV Batman series. In fact his portrayal of the Riddler in Batman, which began in 1966, was responsible for turning a character in the comics from a minor villain into one of Batman's major recurring enemies. He was nominated for an Emmy (Outstanding Performance by an Actor in a Supporting Role in a Comedy) for his role as the Riddler.

When I met him he was 34 years old but had already starred in several movies including 'Run Silent Run Deep,' made in 1958. Before each show he and I would normally get together and have a drink. He told me he spent more than 250 days a year on the road and how lonesome it was to be away from his wife to whom he had been married for about 10 years. That may have been a reason while he later separated from his wife but remained married until his death in 2005.

By the time that Mardi Gras came to an end on Fat Tuesday, I had spoken to most of the media in New Orleans who would be interested in the visit of the ships. There was a great deal of anticipation for the visit because after Mardi Gras there wasn't much activity in the city and this would give another reason for a round of parties.

The day the ships arrived I was sitting in the office and could see them coming up the mighty Mississippi. One of the radio stations had called and asked me to do a commentary on their arrival as they made their way to the foot of Canal Street where they would be berthed. And so, I sat there and described the ships, the size and makeup of the company, and what they had been doing before arriving in New Orleans.

As a result, a number of merchants and owners of businesses began to call the radio station. The host of the show put me on the air with them. They offered many opportunities for the sailors to have a good time in New Orleans. One gentleman said that he owned a paddlewheel steamer on the Mississippi and that he would offer free admittance to the first 500 sailors who wanted to come aboard a couple of nights after their arrival. He then invited 500 girls from New Orleans who perhaps wanted to come down and meet the sailors. Another gentleman called and offered free tickets for the first 500 sailors who wanted to come to see the New Orleans basketball team play that week. Others called to offer free admission to their clubs and

145

a welcome drink for the sailors who were coming ashore. It would make for a wonderful stay for the 3,500 Canadian sailors.

Meanwhile the ships themselves were hosting several parties, particularly on board the Bonaventure. On the second night in port the Bonaventure had a grand cocktail party for the elite of New Orleans. The mayor was invited and so was Deirdre. Although I didn't meet him among the large group onboard that evening, I was told that Jim Garrison, New Orleans District Attorney at the time, was on board. He became well known for his investigation in 1966 into the assassination of President Kennedy.

Deirdre told me that she felt a little intimidated by going to this party and asked me if I would escort her. I had just changed my rank from flight lieutenant to captain, in line with the February 1st deadline for changing into all army ranks. I explained to Deirdre that I was now a captain, albeit not a naval captain who would wear four stripes. When we went on board she caught the eye of more than a few of the young officers on board. There was a dance on the back end of the ship and one of the officers came up and asked her if she would dance with him. She looked at him, looked at me and said, "I would be glad to, but perhaps you should ask my escort Captain Dent first." He looked at her, looked at me with a frown, and said, quote, "He's no Captain" and walked away. She knew what had happened. I was not so sure that the Navy could ever come to grips with using Army ranks.

A number of parties were held ashore for the officers and men on board. There was one older lady in New Orleans who was famed for the parties she would host at her elegant home. She was the owner of a very famous restaurant in downtown New Orleans, on Bourbon Street.

This party was arranged in honor of the Canadian Commodore, the senior Canadian officer on the trip and Joan Sutherland, an operatic star who was in New Orleans at the time. Ms. Sutherland, who was born in Australia, was considered to be one of the most remarkable female opera singers of the 20th century.

A photo of the Canadian Commodore, Joan Sutherland, and this famed hostess from New Orleans, would make a wonderful picture to send back to Canadian newspapers, I thought. So once again, I donned my tuxedo, borrowed a photographer from the Bonaventure, and headed for the hostess mansion. We arrived early and waited on the porch for the arrival of the two guests of honour.

After about 30 minutes had passed beyond their estimated arrival time, I decided to go into the party. It was a magnificent room filled with gorgeous old paintings and opulent furniture. There were two maids taking around beautiful platters of hors d'oeuvres and two butlers handing out glasses of champagne on silver trays. I was offered a glass of champagne and thought to myself, why not. Another hour passed and the guests had still not arrived. For that matter, neither had the hostess. It was not unusual, I was told, for the hostess often gave parties she didn't show up for. I continued to indulge with the hors d'oeuvres and champagne and meet some of the guests who were mingling.

At one point a beautiful woman who looked like the twin of Scarlett O'Hara, approached me with her big-hooped dress and long dangling ringlets. In a beautiful southern accent she said, "I don't think I've met you." I told her I was Capt. Dent to which she gushed: "I have been so anxious to meet somebody from the Canadian Navy. You must come and meet my friends"

Perhaps being bolstered by several glasses of champagne I really didn't see the necessity of telling her that although I was a Captain I was not a Naval captain. And so she took me around and introduced me to some of the elite of New Orleans. Gushing and bubbling she said to me: "I must have a dinner party and invite you so that you can meet some of my closest friends." I then became a little embarrassed and told her that I would be leaving within the next couple of days. She replied, "Never mind, we will find the time to have you." And so the party came to an end; the hostess did not show up and neither did the honoured guests, but I had had a good time.

There was a great deal of media coverage given to our visit. Newspapers, television stations and radio stations, all provided daily updates on the activities for the next few days, and always were very positive.

But without a doubt, the one to give us the most publicity was the actual live shooting of a one-hour segment of the NBC Today show, which went nationally. I had contacted the producer of the show shortly after my arrival in New Orleans on the advice of the mayor's office. After some negotiations, and with the agreement of the senior officers on board the Bonaventure, and my bosses in Ottawa, the show was scheduled to be filmed and aired live from the flight deck a few days after the ship arrived.

I'm not sure now who suggested it, but I ended up taking the producer and about six of his staff to the famed Brennan's Restaurant, located in the French Quarter, for 'Breakfast at Brennan's. And somehow I ended up paying. The bill came to just under $200. This represented approximately 20 days, or three weeks, of my meal allowance for travel. It would take me about four months after my return to Halifax, and a trip to Ottawa, to get the finance authorities to agree to reimburse me.

Nevertheless the show from the Bonaventure was an incredible success and seen by millions across the United States. As I try to tell the financial authorities, my $200 breakfast was infinitesimal, compared to the amount of publicity that we received.

The day that the ships sailed, I went back to the Roosevelt Hotel and found an invitation from 'Scarlett O'Hara'. It told me that she had invited six couples for dinner at her house the next evening to meet this Canadian captain. I felt trapped. I didn't want to embarrass her and I didn't know how to get out of this invitation. So the next evening, dressed in my tuxedo, I took a cab to the address that she had given me.

The cab stopped in front of what to me was a very large mansion. I knocked on the door and was greeted by a butler in full uniform. I was ushered into a hallway and then a room that was probably larger than anything I had ever seen. There were a group of middle-aged men and incredible looking women, who I presumed were their wives, all drinking champagne. I was introduced as Captain Dent and immediately the questions began. The questions continued throughout the dinner. We ate in a very large dining room decorated with unbelievable paintings and two beautiful glass chandeliers. The dishes were like something I had never seen. I soon learned that my host was a shipping magnate and one of the top businessmen in New Orleans, if not Louisiana.

After dinner, the men retired to a smoking room where we smoked incredible cigars and drank what, I considered to be the best cognac I had ever tasted.

Fortunately the questions were all ones which I was able to answer truthfully. I was able to name the type of aircraft I had flown on, ships I sailed on, and that I was currently serving in the Department of Defence's Atlantic Region Information Office, looking after public relations for Canada's Atlantic Provinces.

I did my best not to embarrass my host's wife. I knew the men were quizzing me because I looked so young to be a captain. If they were suspicious, which I suspect they might have been, being southern gentlemen, they did not want to embarrass me or to embarrass the hosts. It was an incredible experience, and one which I will never forget. A great opportunity to meet, eat and drink with this level of society, to which I had never before been exposed.

The next day I received a call from Deirdre, who said that Mayor Schiro wanted to see me. I showed up at the appointed time and was ushered into his office. There was a photographer present and I was curious as to what was going to happen. It didn't take long to find out. The Mayor made a short speech about the contribution and value of the visit of the ships to New Orleans during the past week and then presented me with a certificate, which made me an honorary citizen of New Orleans, after which, he opened a small box and gave me a key to the city. I was completely floored. Yes, the visit had been very successful; yes, the officers and men of the ships had had a good time; yes, there had been basically no problems that I was aware of, not even one arrest. But I wasn't sure that I deserved such an honor. In any event I thanked the Mayor on behalf of all the Canadians who had been present in New Orleans for the celebrations.

That evening, I had my final drink with the manager of the Roosevelt Hotel and Frank Gorshin, who was still playing at the hotel. The next morning I flew back to Halifax.

On the way home, I did some calculations and realized that during the 21 months since I had left RCAF Station Greenwood and come to be an information officer in Halifax, I had been separated from Shirlie and the kids for 12 months. This didn't seem to fit with my promise to her that by

148

leaving the flying business I would spend more time at home. I realized that I was being given some wonderful opportunities in a very short period of time, but I was hoping that I could now spend a little more time with Shirlie and the family.

Mayor Schiro presents me with honorary citizen certificate and key to the city of New Orleans.

I got back to Halifax in mid-March and at the first opportunity I discussed my future with LCdr Bonneau. He told me to submit a memo to him requesting transfer to the Public Information Branch, if this is what I wanted. On April 8, I sent him a letter. On April 9, he discussed it with Col. Bourgeois in Ottawa and forwarded my request and his recommendation. Much to my surprise, a few days later, I received a message from Ottawa transferring me from the aircrew branch to the Personnel Public Information Branch, effective May 2, 1968.

Shirlie and I were both finally happy; now she could get on with her life and her career.

Although the Atlantic Regional Information Office was responsible for providing information, advice and assistance to all the military units

149

throughout the Atlantic Provinces, it was in the Halifax area where a major part of the military was located.

There were many activities in the Halifax area to keep us busy, including maritime ship and aircraft exercises, visiting ships from different countries, and VIP visits, including the Prime Minister. As one would expect some sailors and airmen, on occasion, got into trouble, which meant trying to get out a balanced story in order to minimize the damage to the Canadian Force's reputation with the media and the public.

Although I had been in Halifax for nearly six months, I continued to work on establishing my credibility with the media, other major public affairs organizations in the city, and of course, with senior military personnel.

Being a public information officer was not always easy. Perhaps naturally the media see you as a representative of the military who will only provide information when he has to. The military sees you as an open line to the media and often times did not want you to be aware of what was really happening.

I recall being in that situation several years later in Winnipeg where I was the Senior Regional Information Officer. I was called to a meeting with Admiral St George Stephens, the Commander of Training Command, to discuss a very difficult situation in downtown Winnipeg involving an unexploded bomb, which had been planted in a building. The commander of the bomb disposal unit came into the room and was asked by the Admiral to brief him on what was happening. He said, "I can't tell you while this information officer is in the room." The Admiral replied, "Major Dent probably has a higher clearance than you do, so trust me, brief us both."

In 1967, LCdr John Bonneau, Capt. Al King and I had joined the Atlantic Public Relations Society, which was the Eastern Chapter of the Canadian Public Relations Society. Its members were a broad cross-section of individuals who worked in government and industry public relations organizations, and provided us with some excellent contacts.

In the summer of 1968, our office was honoured by the CPRS at the 20th Annual Conference. The office was given the Award of Excellence for PR in Print for the best public relations material in support of the Canadian Centennial. It was a real honour for our office.

I did my best to establish and keep my credibility with the senior officers in Maritime Command, but it wasn't always easy. In one particular case I almost lost access to Maritime Command headquarters.

The incident involved the USS Pueblo, a US intelligence ship, which had been captured by the North Koreans, off their coast, on January 23, 1968. North Koreans stated that the Pueblo had been inside their territorial waters, something that the US denied. The crew was held for 11 months in captivity before being released but the ship remains in a North Korean port.

Coming in the middle of the Cold War, the capture was extremely sensitive. Much negotiation took place over the next few months in order to secure the release of the crew. One morning, I was asked to come down to Maritime Command headquarters where the senior operations officer, a Commodore, told me that they had a photo of a Soviet Elint (electronics intelligence) trawler similar to the Pueblo. The picture had been taken off the Nova Scotia coast. They directed me to write a caption and then release it to the Canadian Press.

I wrote the cutline; the Commodore discussed it with the Admiral. I was told to release it immediately. On the way back to my office I had a queasy sensation in my stomach. Something just didn't seem right. And this was the difficulty. I was there to support the Commander of Maritime Command and his staff, but our office really reported to Colonel Bourgeois in Ottawa. Lieutenant Commander Bonneau was out of town. So I called the boss in Ottawa and told him that I had been ordered to release a photo, but I felt uneasy about doing so. Col. Bourgeois told me to sit tight and not do anything until he called me back.

About 30 minutes later, he called me and told me that he had spoken to the Department of Foreign Affairs and to General Allard, the Chief of Defence Staff. I was not to release that photo under any circumstances. "What about my orders from the Commodore and the Admiral?" I said. Colonel Bourgeois told me, "Don't worry, the CDS will talk to Admiral O'Brien."

An hour later I was called back to Maritime Command Headquarters. The Commodore was livid. "Lieutenant Dent," he shouted, "what the hell do you not understand about a direct order? Who the hell do you think you are, calling Ottawa when you have been given a direct order from the Admiral?" "But," I tried to explain. "Get the hell out of my office and never come back." he screamed. Great, I thought, I guess this is the end of my public information career.

What I didn't know at that time was that apparently Canadian foreign-policy officials were engaged with the US in helping the US to negotiate a release of the prisoners. Releasing this photo and caption would have been very detrimental to those negotiations. I later learned that the CDS had laid that out in no uncertain terms for Admiral O'Brien. And so, although the staff were furious with me, probably Admiral O'Brien realized that I had likely saved him from a great deal of trouble. He never mentioned the issue, but I noticed that in my dealings with him from then on, he was much more receptive to my advice on public information issues.

But an opportunity arose a little while later to get some great, positive publicity for both the Navy and the Air Force. LCdr Bonneau came back from a morning briefing and told me that one of our naval destroyers was shadowing three guided missile Soviet destroyers off the coast of Canada, which were heading south, presumably towards Cuba. An Argus aircraft from Canadian Forces Base Greenwood was going out to do aerial surveillance. He asked to me to call my "friends" at Greenwood and see if we could get a photographer onboard one of the patrol aircraft.

The aircraft assigned was from 404 Squadron. I called Wing Commander Hy Carswell, the squadron commander who had helped me move to 103 Rescue Unit in 1964. He was a great officer and very understanding of what we were trying to accomplish. He had a great career in the Air Force, ending up as a three-star general and Associate Deputy Minister of Personnel.

He told me that an aircraft would be leaving shortly and that he would task the pilot to land in Shearwater to pick up our photographer. I spoke to the photographer assigned to the mission; he was one of the best that we had. I told him that I wanted him to get a photo of the three Russian destroyers and the Canadian destroyer that was shadowing this force as well as the wing of the Air Force aircraft he was in.

About four hours later, we received a message that the photographer had his photo and that the aircraft would be back in Shearwater late that evening. I knew that by the time we got the photograph processed and delivered to the media, the Russian vessels would probably be outside of Canadian territory. I called Wing Commander Carswell, thanked him for his help and told him that we really needed the photograph as soon as possible. He said, "What do you want me to do? Recall the aircraft and send another aircraft and crew out to replace it so that you can get your photograph?" "Yes," I replied. There was silence on the phone for probably a minute and then he said, "Okay."

About mid-afternoon, the Argus landed in Shearwater and dropped off my photographer. He was grinning from ear to ear running towards the awaiting staff car, holding onto his camera as if it was a huge treasure. We drove immediately to the photo lab and went into the darkroom to process his film. No wonder he was grinning, I thought. He had taken a fantastic photo of the four ships in the form of a diamond, with the Canadian destroyer at the base of the diamond. Easily identifiable was the wing of the aircraft in the bottom of the photo. My first stop, before delivering it to the media in Halifax, was to Canadian Press. I had alerted them to the fact that we would be delivering a photo.

The media were very happy, particularly in Halifax. They had a great story and this was proof of their Canadian Forces carrying out surveillance work over the Atlantic. A few days later Jack Brayley, head of Canadian Press in Halifax, sent us a letter to thank us for the photo. He told us that he had been advised that 139 newspapers had used the photo worldwide, including a four column-wide display on the front page of the New York Times. Needless to say, the Admiral and his staff at Maritime Command Headquarters were also elated. It certainly raised the stock of our office in the eyes of the officers with whom we had to work.

Shirlie and I were very happy in Halifax. Susan had started school; we had a great housekeeper to come in and look after David, and Shirlie was enjoying her teaching job at the Victoria General School of Nursing.

We had joined St. Paul's Anglican Church and I had been made a member of the executive of the men's club. I had also been appointed to the executive committee of the Atlantic Public Relations Society. In September, I signed up for a one-year journalism course at the University of King's College in Halifax.

In late December, LCdr Bonneau told me that he was sending me off in January with a CBC television crew on board the aircraft carrier HMCS Bonaventure that, along with several other ships, would be sailing to Puerto Rico for the annual winter exercises. We would be gone about three weeks during which time the crew would be making a documentary on the Armed Forces.

The producer was Charlie Reynolds, a professional and very talented but slightly mad Irishman. Charlie loved to party. He was well known amongst the media in the Halifax-Dartmouth area. He had a drinking buddy named Charlie Chamberlain, who was a star of the CBCs Sing-Along Jubilee. It wasn't uncommon to see the two Charlie's drinking whiskey and telling jokes and keeping everybody in hysterics.

In the 1960s, the journalists worked hard and played hard. It wasn't unusual to see many of them at the Halifax Press Club enjoying themselves after a hard day's work. One evening, Charlie Reynolds was there and probably had a little bit more than he could handle. The gang decided to buy a one-way airline ticket for Charlie to Montreal. So they took up a collection in the club, somebody drove him to the airport and he actually got on the plane. A stewardess recognized him and realized that he probably didn't understand where he was going. She had him escorted back into the terminal. It seemed funny at the time, but probably would not be tolerated today.

Well aware of Charlie's antics, one of his bosses decided to come along on the trip with us to Puerto Rico. I was told that before we left, he had made a bet with Charlie that he could not go on the Bonaventure to Puerto Rico without having a drink. That was $50, not an inconsequential amount in 1969. So we sailed. The film crew began to work on board Bonaventure capturing some of the activity.

After two days Charlie was obviously getting antsy. On day three, the film crew asked to be helicoptered over to one of the destroyers to do some filming. Charlie said he wanted to go with them. This was unusual since he normally did not get in the way of what the film crew was doing. About three hours later, a helicopter brought everyone back to the Bonaventure. A very happy Charlie Reynolds got off the helicopter. Obviously he had had several of his Irish whiskeys. When his boss saw him, he said, "You owe me $50. You were drinking." Charlie slurred, "Nope, I still haven't had a drink on the Bonaventure."

We arrived in San Juan and checked into a very nice hotel on the beach. Charlie and I met the manager of the El Conquistador hotel, one of the finest in Puerto Rico, on the first night. When he found out that Charlie was producing a documentary for CBC, he offered the crew a free weekend of lodging and meals, in return for which he wanted a mention of the hotel and its facilities in the documentary. Charlie was very excited. However the crew, which was all unionized, stated that they had already been working for eight straight days and now were entitled to three days off. The crew consisted of six union members. So there was nothing Charlie could do. Interestingly, a year later, ATV Halifax sent a two-person crew from Halifax to Puerto Rico to make a similar production.

So I had a few days off. I visited the local USO office and they gave me two tickets to see Jimmy Durante and Annette Funicello. Durante was an American singer, pianist, comedian and actor. His large nose and entertaining-style made him a familiar and popular personality for 50 years, way into the 1970s. His show was one I will never forget.

Funicello was a mouseketeer on the Mickey Mouse Club in the 1950s, and then became a teenage singer. She starred in several teenage movies, before going on tours such as the one I saw her play.

Following one of the shows, I walked into my hotel and stopped by the casino. There was a woman playing at one of the tables. She was using hundred dollar chips and I would estimate that she had approximately $10,000 worth in front of her. Looking very bored she was tossing chips onto numbered spaces. Her demeanor suggested to me that if she could lose all her chips she could go home. I was staggered. The money in front of her represented about two years of my salary. I was obviously experiencing a world which I had never seen before.

The following morning, I left the hotel and its beautiful beaches, crossed the highway and went for a walk. Soon I came upon a series of ramshackle shacks that really looked more like a place where one would store garbage than where anyone would live. I later learned that a number of Puerto Ricans lived in accommodation like this. One gentleman told me it was not uncommon, in some cases, for rats and the children to be fighting over the same food.

That is an experience that I have never forgotten. On one side of the road, the height of luxury, on the other side of the road, poverty and devastation. I certainly knew what it was like to be poor. My recent experiences had given me a taste of how the rich people live. To this day, it has made me grateful for what I have.

Once the weekend was over, we got back to work and spent the next few days conducting interviews and filming in order to round out the documentary. Then Charlie, the crew and I, climbed on board an RCAF aircraft and made our way back to Halifax. Meanwhile, the ships continued their exercises. Little did Charlie Reynolds know that there would be an incident that would be front and centre in his documentary concerning the dangers of what our troops are doing, even in exercises.

On February 16, a couple of weeks after we had returned, HMCS Bonaventure was launching Tracker aircraft for routine submarine warfare exercises, when the worst possible incident occurred.

154

Navy Lieutenant Jack Flanagan and his crew of four were ready for launch. The aircraft eased forward with the 'bridle' attaching the aircraft to the catapult. The 'dog bone', an attachment to hold the aircraft in place until the catapult was fired, restrained the aircraft. Full power was applied to the engines and the co-pilot saluted, indicating to the Catapult Officer on the flight deck that the aircraft was ready to be launched.

The catapult was fired. The 'dog bone' broke normally, allowing the catapult to pull the aircraft forward starting its takeoff roll forward on the flight deck.

Suddenly the bridle, attaching the aircraft to the catapult snapped. Later it was determined it was a manufacturing defect. The aircraft now with only the power of the engines driving it forward had far too much speed to stop, but not nearly enough to fly!

Without sufficient airspeed, the aircraft fell over the bow and pancaked into the water ahead of the ship.

Captain Robert Falls, Captain of the Bonaventure, seeing the developing problem from the bridge, ordered, "stop engines" and an immediate alteration of course to avoid running over the aircraft. Despite these efforts to avoid the downed aircraft, the 20,000 ton carrier's momentum moving at 25 knots was too great to prevent the ship from running over the aircraft and the four crew members in the water.

All four crewmembers were able to get out of the aircraft as it sank. Three were able to swim clear of the ship's path as it bore down on them. Flanagan, the aircraft captain and last one out, was caught underneath the ship and was literally 'keelhauled' 900 feet, bouncing off the bottom of the ship. He went through the giant propeller. The fact that the captain had ordered, "stop engines" probably saved his life. The propeller struck his leg just below the knee. Later, the doctors would say it was a perfect amputation.

All four crewmembers bobbed to the surface. They were spotted immediately by the crew in "Angel", the rescue helicopter that during daylight hours was airborne on station for all launches and recoveries of aircraft in case of an event like this.

The rescue pilot quickly determined that Flanagan's state was the worst. There was considerable blood in the water around him. Sharks were known to be in the area. The helicopter hovered over Flanagan. A rescue crewman leaped into the water. He swam to the injured pilot placed him in a double-lift sling "horse collar." The two were quickly hoisted aboard the helicopter. The other crewmembers were floating in life jackets without apparent injury. So the helicopter immediately flew back to the carrier.

Within minutes they were back on the deck and the wounded flier was in the operating room of the Bonaventure where doctors were able to cauterize the wound. Meanwhile the Bonaventure steamed back towards Puerto Rico. While on route, Flanagan was loaded into a Sea King helicopter and flown to the American Army hospital in San Juan, and a further operation done to finalize his care.

155

A week later he was transferred from Puerto Rico back to the military hospital at HMCS Stadacona in Halifax.

This had been a big story and of course Charlie Reynolds wanted to include it as part of his documentary. He asked for an interview with Jack Flanagan so I spoke to Flanagan by phone. He reluctantly agreed to the interview. I will never forget his words as we walked into his room. He looked at us and said, "I don't know what the big deal is, I just have one leg that's a little shorter than the other!"

As soon as he said that, I knew that Lt 'Goose ' McClellan, another naval pilot had been to see him. Goose was an amazing individual. He had lost a leg in an automobile accident about five years previous. The Navy had been sympathetic and he received excellent care, but their bottom line was that he could never fly again.

'Goose' a helicopter pilot, loved to fly. He simply said, "You can't tell me that I will not fly again." So with much determination he mastered the use of his prosthesis and took private flying lessons. He re-qualified as a pilot and then triumphantly presented his newly acquired MOT pilot license back to the Navy. They agreed that he could take a test to determine his suitability. He did, passed with flying colours and was reinstated as an anti-submarine warfare (ASW) helicopter pilot. He was reassigned to his former squadron.

Jack admitted that Goose had paid him a visit and had told him he expected to see him fly again. Lt Flanagan returned to flying Trackers about a year later and subsequently converted to helicopters, flying Sea Kings in the ASW role.

CBC did the interview. It was very positive and formed a good part of the overall documentary of the Canadian Forces activities in Maritime Command.

Interestingly, one morning, almost 50 years later, I was talking to a friend, Jim Cantlie, at our church in Kanata . I had known Jim from our days in Halifax where he had served as a Tracker pilot. I asked him if he knew of Jack Flanagan and his incident. "Know him?" he replied, "I was next in line to launch. If he hadn't gone in the drink, I probably would have." Since Jim was on the ship, he was able to confirm and fill in some details for me on what happened that day and beyond.

The next few months were busy for me, including working with Maritime Command, visiting other bases within the Atlantic region and also working on my contacts within the community.

I finished my course at University of King's College. Shortly thereafter at a meeting of the alumni at King's College Public Relations Association, I was elected president, which for me was quite an honour. I'd also been named as the Atlantic Regional Director for the Canadian Public Relations Society. I was certainly getting a great network set up in the public relations field.

I also had to become accustomed to a new boss, as LCdr Don Lory replaced LCdr John Bonneau in the summer when the latter was posted to Ottawa.

A real test of my public relations capability, and the benefit of having developed some excellent contacts with the media, came about in October 1969. On October 23, 1969, HMCS Kootenay was westbound out of the English Channel as part of a task group with HMCS Bonaventure and seven other destroyers. Approximately 200 miles west of Plymouth, England, the crew was conducting engine trials when there was an explosion in the engine room. A fireball burst through the engine room and smoke filled below decks. The ship was hurt badly. The crew fought the fire for the next three hours. Helicopters came to bring firefighting supplies and help evacuate the injured.

The disabled vessel was towed back to Plymouth. Nine crew had been killed and eight seriously wounded. It was called one of the worst peacetime disasters in the history of the Canadian Armed Forces.

Our office had been notified almost immediately that this accident had occurred. We knew that the news of the accident would soon be circulating throughout the Halifax-Dartmouth community. With nine ships and more than 2,500 personnel in the task force, we knew that there would be much concern for so many family members and friends.

Our immediate aim became to get as much information out to everyone through the media about the accident, without causing any undue concern or hardship for the families and their friends. It became a dilemma for us. If we simply went out and said that there had been an accident on board one of the ships without naming the ship, as some of the senior Maritime Command staff wanted us to do, there would be a great deal of concern for just about anyone who had family onboard one of the ships. After much agonizing, Lieutenant Commander Lory and I met with the Maritime Command senior operations officers. They finally acknowledged that the best solution was to be specific. So we released the fact that there had been an accident in the engine room of HMCS Kootenay.

We knew that it would be of great interest when the ship arrived in Plymouth. So Commander Lory decided that one of us had to go to Plymouth to be there to handle the media and all the questions that would be forthcoming. We literally tossed a coin to see who would go. Heads, he would go; tails, he would stay in the office and handle the media queries at home. Commander Lory tossed a coin and it came up heads. He immediately left to pack a bag and head for the airport. I called Air Canada at the airport and spoke to the manager. I explained the situation to him, telling him that LCdr Lory needed to get to Plymouth as soon as possible but had no money for the ticket. There were no charge cards to use. Fully aware of the situation, the manager said, "Just get him here, we will get him to London and we will sort out paying for the ticket later."

In retrospect, I'm not sure which was the better job, to be in Plymouth facing the international press, or being in the Halifax office taking calls from all over the world. But certainly here my relationship with the local media was a great benefit. To those I fully trusted, I could tell them the truth, but then ask them not to use certain parts of the story before we were sure that all of the next-of-kin were aware. To those few I didn't trust as much, I told them what we were prepared to see in print or on the air. No one ever betrayed that trust!

This was an international story and queries were coming in from media all over the world, regardless of the time of day. Except for a secretary, I was alone in the office and had to resign myself to the fact that this would be an almost 24/7 assignment. Col. Bourgeois, our boss in Ottawa, stayed in touch and, realizing the pressure on me, offered to send another officer to come down to help me with the media queries. I declined. I felt that I knew the media in the local area and in the Atlantic Provinces. I knew whom I could trust. I knew what I could tell to which media and when. It would be difficult and unfair, and perhaps even detrimental, to have a public affairs officer from Ottawa coming in to help when he didn't really have the flavour or the background of the situation with which we were dealing.

So for the next three days I worked virtually nonstop from our office. LCdr Lory would call me at least twice a day from Plymouth to update me on the situation and to give me a synopsis of what the media were asking and had been told in Plymouth.

HMCS Kootenay arrived in Plymouth. There was a great deal of international media attention. However, as with most stories, the spotlight soon turned to other world events. The ship was towed back to Halifax by a Dutch tug and arrived on November 27.

As one would expect, the media coverage had been very sympathetic. There were no attempts to find fault. Indeed after many months, when the results of the investigation were made public, the media factually reported that there had been an incorrect procedure in constructing a gearbox. The media laid no blame.

LCdr Lory returned to Halifax after a week. In retrospect, I don't even remember Air Canada sending us a bill for his ticket.

Not everyone was happy with our efforts. For months after the event, our office was criticized by some members of the Navy for identifying the engine room of the Kootenay specifically as the place where the accident had occurred. There were also those who felt we shouldn't have released the names of those killed or injured until sometime later when all family members beyond the next-of-kin and secondary next-of-kin had been notified. Our arguments that this would have caused more unnecessary pain and anxiety for those who didn't have relatives on the Kootenay did not sway those who saw us as, "pawns of the press."

The Black Watch Battalion, from CFB Gagetown, New Brunswick, was now serving a six-month tour of duty in Cyprus. Naturally, the media in that province were very interested in the battalion's activities. LCdr Lory asked me to put together a group of senior media from the area that would be interested in visiting Cyprus and told me that I would be their escort.

On December 1st, five senior newsmen and I headed out on the long flight to Cyprus. It was an extremely interesting, educational, seven-day visit to this troubled island. Certainly the media came away with a better understanding and enthusiasm for the professional ability of the Canadian soldier and the importance of the Canadian Armed Forces in their peacekeeping role. Our public information officer on the ground was Capt. Denny Ryan. As a result of several conversations with him, I became quite interested in being posted at some point to Cyprus for a six-month tour of duty. Little did I know at the time how quickly I would get my wish.

On February 4, 1970 the Liberian tanker Arrow ran aground on Cerberus Rock, in Chedabucto Bay, Nova Scotia. The ship, under charter to Imperial Oil Limited, had been en route to Nova Scotia Pulp and Paper Limited with a cargo of 108,000 barrels of bunker C fuel. The Arrow was badly damaged and some of her cargo was transferred to the shore during a bad storm. However, over the next week, more than half of the ship's cargo of oil escaped, and more than 100 miles of shoreline had varying degrees of contamination. It appeared to be as disaster.

Under an international agreement, Imperial Oil was deemed responsible. They immediately assembled a team of top engineers, scientists and staff from their own company, plus specialists from provincial and federal governments and universities. Included in the team was Glenn Hancock, the senior public relations officer for the company in Atlantic Canada. Interestingly, he had been my professor at University of King's College and we had worked on drafting plans for potential disasters that might involve Imperial Oil and the Canadian Forces.

It was a very difficult problem, particularly from a public relations point of view. Hundreds of people were pouring into this town, population 500, including those working on the project, media from all over the world, interested observers and sightseers. At that point, no one knew the extent of the problem, or its future ramifications.

There was little coordination. Experts arriving on the scene quickly assessed the situation and expressed their views to the eager media. In one case a wildlife officer apparently had searched one mile of beach and found 200 dead birds. When asked by the media how many birds he thought might be dead in total, he simply multiplied the 100 miles of beach by 200 and gave them a figure of 20,000. It became an international front-page story! A Memorial University biologist, hired by Imperial Oil, told the media that this was the worst ecological disaster in Canadian history. He chastised the company and said that it would be a graveyard for marine and birdlife for the next hundred years.

With little information being communicated to them by Imperial Oil officials, plus the rumours that were spreading quickly about the severity of the disaster and media reports, local people were confused and angry. And more important, no one was telling them what was going to be done to rectify the situation.

After five days, the federal government realized that Imperial Oil could not handle the problem. Prime Minister Trudeau tasked the Department of Transport to assume control. DOT named a regional marine supervisor in Halifax to take on the responsibility for cleanup operations. Unfortunately, it soon became evident that he had neither the experience nor the authority to handle such a disaster.

Ten days later, the federal government appointed a government task force. It was headed by Dr. Patrick McTaggart Cowan, the Executive Director of the Scientific Council of Canada. Dr. Harry Schaeffer, Vice-Chief of the Defence Research Board, and Navy Captain Mike Martin, Deputy Chief of Staff Operations at Maritime Command Headquarters in Halifax, were named as his deputies.

The Task Force had been given carte blanche by Prime Minister Trudeau. Dr. McTaggart Cowan was able to pick whatever resources he needed and had unlimited financial resources. Top scientists and researchers from government quickly became part of the task force.

Provision was also made for a public relations officer from the Department of Transport and one from the Department of National Defence. Ray Stone, from DOT, who had served as a public relations assistant with DND at one time, and I, were assigned as the two PR officers.

Within 24 hours, the nucleus of the task force was on site. A military group set up a command operations centre which was manned 24-hours a day. A military signals company set up a new phone system, since the limited system in the motel which was used as a headquarters, would not be able to keep up. Each person on the team was registered and signed in, so that his whereabouts was known at all times. The days were long and hard. Each night at midnight everybody attended a 'wash-up' to report the progress and take part in planning the next day's activities.

From a public relations point of view, it was evident that there were two principal areas of concern. One was to handle the media onsite and their multitude of queries, as well as to issue updates on a daily basis to media around the world. The second was to address the concerns of the local citizens. We decided that Ray Stone would 'man' the small media centre in the motel and I would take on the task of trying to placate the local citizens in communities and hamlets around the 100-mile bay.

I first put together quickly a list of the names of influentials in each of the communities around Chedabucto Bay. I visited each town to brief them and identify their specific problems.

The credibility of the Task Force was a big problem amongst the local citizens. Many felt that the government would bring in a lot of resources and make a show of trying to solve the disaster. Then, in the not too distant future, the Task Force would leave saying that they had done

160

their best. The communities would be left with a, "hundred year mess." Their fishing industry would be dead!

Dr. McTaggart Cowan was not about to let that happen. When it was evident that the oil would probably go through the Lennox passage and subsequently into a fish factory, which would basically have to shut down, he called for a solution. I had spoken to a number of local leaders who suggested that the passage could be damned, but it would probably take up to three months because it was a mile wide. When the subject was brought up at the midnight debrief, engineers stated that it could probably be done in one month. McTaggart Cowan told them that they had 10 days.

He told me to go out and tell leaders, and everyone I could meet, what we were doing and emphasize that we would do it in 10 days. Dump trucks were located and brought in from everywhere across Nova Scotia and New Brunswick. The project required 90,000 tons of fill to be hauled to the site. Ten days later the mission was completed.

The local communities now began to believe that the government was serious. The Task Force offered to debrief the locals on what was being done but most would not come. During my rounds into the communities each day, I would brief them on the problems the Task Force faced and ask them for their suggestions on how to solve some of these issues. I would emphasize that we didn't have the answers and any suggestions would be helpful.

Some suggestions were given and a few seemed silly. But I would bring them back to the Task Force and they would be tried. Then I would go back and give the results to the community. It continued to show them that we were serious about solving this disaster.

Since most of the parents wouldn't come to the briefings, I approached schools in the area. Teachers agreed to bus some of the older students to the Task Force headquarters where they would be briefed and shown what we were trying to do, including the successes and failures. At the end of each briefing we would ask them to go home and tell their parents what they had learned.

Necessity was indeed the mother of invention in this case. Scientists invented several machines to help with the cleanup, including a slick licker that would take the oil off the top of the water, and a drycleaner to clean the oil off the equipment. More than 100 scientists on the site and in universities across the country were involved.

After several weeks, it appeared that we were beating the problem. The cleanup continued. The last members of the Task Force did not leave until virtually all the beaches were cleaned up and fishing restarted. My understanding is that except for the one mile of beach there was virtually no birdlife lost.

Towards the end of the mission, the Task Force organized a lobster dinner and invited many of the community. Lobsters came out of the bay where the Memorial University biologist had said there would be no more fishing for at least 100 years!

161

Hundreds, if not thousands, of people had been involved in this effort. Much ingenuity had been used. Certainly this disaster had brought into sharp focus the need for the federal and provincial governments to ensure that controls be exercised over shipping all along Canada's thousands of miles of coastline.

My one regret was that much of what we had learned did not appear to be of value and has been forgotten. Twenty years later when a major oil spill occurred on the West Coast, individuals involved were scrambling to look for possible solutions, many of which now lay in records gathering dust in the Archives.

Towards the end of the task, LCdr Lory called me and told me that I had been posted that summer to National Defence Headquarters in Ottawa. A few days later he called me and told me that before going to Ottawa I would be attending the 14- week course at the Canadian Forces Junior Staff College in Toronto. Apparently, I would be the first public information officer to attend Staff School.

Aware of my situation, Dr. McTaggart gave me the green light to leave the Task Force. I went back to Halifax. I had a week with Shirlie and the kids, jumped into my car, and drove to Toronto to start the course.

I was finishing four years in Halifax as a public information officer. My training and experiences had taken me to many places I had never been before. Interestingly, in retrospect, I think I was actually away from home more during those four years than I would have been if I had remained in the aviation field.

I was looking forward to a posting at NDHQ where I thought I would be involved in a fairly routine 9-to-5 job. Little did I know what my public affairs future had in store for me.

CHAPTER 11 - A MID-EAST EXPERIENCE

"Come in Len, have a seat," my boss said with a big grin. Brigadier General Lou Bourgeois was the first Director General of Information Services under the new unified Canadian Forces, and the person who had hired me. I thought he was a fair shooter. He had been promoted to that position with the encouragement of Leo Cadieux, Minister of National Defence, who put great faith in his guidance. I was told that the Minister wanted to be sure that Bourgeois would have sufficient clout at the morning meetings of the senior generals to be able to support his wishes. Thus a new position of Director General Information Services was created.

"I have a problem I want to discuss with you," he confided. I was taken aback. Here was my boss, a senior officer who spent his time providing advice to senior generals, including the Chief of Defence Staff, the Deputy Minister, and who was close to and respected by the Minister Leo Cadieux, wanting to discuss a problem with me.

I had only been in National Defence Headquarters for about three hours when he asked me to come to his office. I had just been introduced to my fellow information officers and been shown my desk in the news section. Four desks were crowded into a small room which obviously needed a lot of TLC. NDHQ was housed primarily in an old temporary building at the corner of Elgin and Laurier Ave., in downtown Ottawa. It had been built during the Second World War. But as I had been told, there was nothing as permanent as a temporary building.

Time at the Staff School Course had passed quickly. Designed for captains who had been earmarked as potential majors, it was crammed with subjects such as military law, history, English writing, administration matters, and such subjects that would prepare us for duties at a more senior level. The classes were interspersed with guest lecturers who came to provide their expertise and experience in various subject areas. Classes ran from 8:00 am to 3:00 pm each day. From 3:00 to 4:00 we went to the gym where we played compulsory volleyball, which is why the School had the nickname Volleyball U. The instructors thought it would be a change of pace for us. After the game we had time to shower, eat in the mess and then face 3-4 hours of homework each night to finish assignments usually due the following day.

Towards the end of the course we were given a four-day weekend. I flew home to Halifax to collect Shirlie and the kids. She had already made the arrangements to have our furniture packed and loaded on a moving van that would meet us in Ottawa when we arrived. We drove back to Toronto over the weekend and she dropped me off at the school. She and the kids then drove north to Creemore to spend the next 10 days with my Mom and Dad, until the end of the course.

As soon as the course finished, I went to Creemore to spend some much needed time with my family. We took a few days to 'get reacquainted' after so much time apart.

In early August we drove to Ottawa and saw for the first time the duplex that my former boss, now Commander Stu Murray had suggested we rent. It was only three doors from where he lived, just off St Laurent Blvd, in the east end of the city. The following day, a Friday, our furniture was unloaded in boxes and 'dumped' in the house. The job of unpacking and moving in was just beginning.

On Monday morning, I hopped on a bus and made my way down to NDHQ.

"Len, Captain XXX has been posted to Cyprus for six months," Gen. Bourgeois looked seriously concerned and continued. "He told me this morning that if he goes, his wife thinks she will have a nervous breakdown."

"That's too bad," I added when he stopped talking. "But what has that got to do with me?"

"Well that's my problem I wanted to discuss with you. I have to send someone and I would like to send you."

"When?" I gasped.

"Well there is a Yukon leaving from Trenton tomorrow afternoon at 4:30 and I would like you to be on it."

"What?" I exclaimed. "But I just arrived. My house is full of boxes. And I haven't really been home for the past six months," I gasped.

He thought for a moment and then said gravely, "Well, OK. I think I can find someone to go for a month while you get settled in. So you can leave a month from tomorrow. Thanks Len, for helping me solve my problem."

I stumbled out of his office. What was I going to tell Shirlie? I had spent most of the past six months away, either helping to deal with an oil spill or attending Staff School. For the four years while based in Halifax, I had spent so much time away from home. Ottawa was supposed to be a posting where I wouldn't travel. Now I had to tell her I was dumping her and the kids in a strange city, where she didn't really know anyone, and leaving for another six months.

As I left my boss's office, I heard him call out after me, "Take the rest of the day off Len. Go home and tell the wife the good news."

I did go home. Shirlie was happily unpacking the boxes and getting her new home organized. The kids were helping by tearing piles of paper off various items and handing them to her.

"What are you doing home so early, did they fire you already?" she said with a big grin. Not waiting for an answer she continued unwrapping dishes. She said, "By the way, I got a call from my sister Myrna this morning. She says now that we are living in Ontario, it would be nice if we could come to London and visit them for a few days. We haven't had any time together as a family since last Christmas. Maybe your boss would give you a week's holiday in a couple of weeks and we could go."

I stared at her, not sure how to break the 'good news'. Perhaps my boss thought the good news was that I didn't have to leave the next day.

"Shirlie," I said slowly, "I'm home because I had a talk with my boss and there has been a change in plans about my job."

"What do you mean, a change of plans?" she said with a rather startled look in her eyes.

"Let's go to the kitchen so we can talk without the kids hearing," I said. Now she did look worried, her usual big smile gone.

In the kitchen, I broke the news. At first she didn't say anything, trying to digest what I had told her. Then very calmly she said, "Well I guess the kids and I will just have to live without you for another six months. We will manage."

I hugged her tightly for a long time. How could I have been so blessed to marry such a wonderful woman?

"What can we tell the kids?" I said. "Well, they are getting used to you leaving. But I did tell them that the next time you had to go away, we would get a dog for them to play with," she whispered.

We went back into the living room. We gathered Susan and David around us and held them tight. I told them that daddy had to go away again to a faraway place to help people who were not as fortunate as we were. I told them that before I left in a month we would get a dog that they could play with so that it would help them forget daddy was gone. Surprisingly, like their mother, they accepted what I had to do. They also asked if they could get a big dog.

The next four weeks flew by. We did get unpacked. I got all my shots for travel to the Middle East. And we found a dog. Fortunately, on the next street in our neighbourhood, lived a woman who bred standard poodles. The kids picked out a cute cuddly white puppy that happened to be her pick of the litter. Her name was Park Up, Up and Away. The owner told us we could have it but she would like to train it and use it as a show dog when it grew up. At that point we would have agreed to anything.

So, this little ball of white fur came home with us. The kids were elated. What can we name her was their next challenge. They threw names out but none seemed to fit. Meanwhile, I was sitting in the kitchen 'spit and polishing' my big boots. "Hey," I said, "Why don't you call her 'Boots'?" "Oh Daddy, that's a stupid name!"the kids shouted.

A few days before I left, Stu Murray came by. He told us that he knew of a 19-year-old girl who was coming to work at the Rockcliffe base, which was just around the corner from where we lived. She wasn't making much money and needed a place to stay. "Maybe she could come and stay with you while Len is away," he said. "That would be company for you, Shirlie, and she could help with the kids and looking after the house."

Nicosia International Airport, Cyprus, September 1970

The big Yukon aircraft bounced once and then settled gently on the rain-soaked runway like some huge, ungainly bird grateful to be back on earth.

As we slowed down and taxied toward the terminal, the tires sent rain in sheets up against the aircraft windows. On each side of the runway, the driving rain disappeared into the parched sand-like earth that seemed to stretch as far as the eye could see.

The aircraft was filled with soldiers, many of whom were arriving here for the first time and probably nervously anticipating what the next six months of peacekeeping duties on this island would mean for them.

There were also a number of wives who were eagerly looking forward to seeing their husbands for the first time in several months. Most would have two weeks to spend with their husbands before heading back to Canada to assume their role as mother, father and head of the family.

Having spent a week with a group of newsmen in Cyprus less than a year ago, I considered I knew what my job would be.

A large, jovial soldier who looked like a teenager approached me in the terminal. In fact I soon found out he was 19. He introduced himself as Private Ron Cullen. He told me he would be my driver during the next six months. I didn't know at that point, but Pte Cullen would turn out to be a god-send to me during my tour. He loved his job and if I had let him he would have worked 24 hours a day. I never saw him when he didn't have a smile on his face.

He picked up my duffle bag off the luggage belt like it was a newspaper and led me out to the parking lot. We stopped behind an old but immaculate blue Mercedes-Benz four-door sedan. This would be my transportation for the next six months. Pte Cullen insisted I get in the back and off we drove to the Wolseley Barracks Compound in downtown Nicosia. The Barracks compound was the base for a number of Canadian soldiers, and also Wolseley House, which served as the home of the Canadian Officers' Mess.

Just outside the airport I saw rows of rusty old huts, which were surrounded completely by barbed wire fences. Cullen told me that this was one of the internment camps where the British troops had brought the Jews who were trying to make their way to Israel after the Second World War. The British Government had only allowed a certain number of Jews to immigrate and issued a limited number of certificates each month. Without a certificate, would-be immigrants were considered illegal. Many were caught trying to sneak into Israel by sea; the British would then take them to camps in Cyprus. The camps operated from 1946-1949 and in total held more than 50,000 people.

On this hot, humid day with the temperature in the 100 F degree range, I could only imagine what it must have been like for these people. Most of them had survived the Holocaust, the majority of them teenagers to mid-30s. They had almost made it to the "promised land"; now they faced another internment in what were said to be appalling conditions. Reportedly more than 2,000 children were born in the camps. The last detainees left in February 1949, nine months after Israel gained its Statehood.

166

Cullen stopped the Mercedes in front of Wolseley House, a stone mansion named after Viscount Garnet Joseph Wolseley who served as British High Commissioner to Cyprus in 1879. The Barracks were situated on the Green Line that divided the Turkish and Greek Cypriot sectors of the island.

Cyprus had become independent in 1960 under the Treaty of Zurich, which also protected the right of the Turkish Cypriot population. Tensions heightened between the Greek Cypriot and Turkish Cypriot communities. In late 1963, fighting broke out between the two sides and subsequently a buffer zone, manned by British troops, was set up between the two sides. United Nations troops came in March 1964.

A commander of the British Peace Force drew the Green Line in 1964. Using a dark green crayon, he drew a line on a map of the island to designate the cease-fire line separating the two sides. It divided the island in two. In Nicosia it ran down the middle of city streets so that on one side there were Greek Cypriot stores and on the other Turkish Cypriot stores. Greek and Turkish Cypriot soldiers manned positions on each side of the street. The job of the Canadians was to be between them to prevent any incident that might escalate into fighting, possibly bringing Greece and Turkey into a war against each other.

This was crucial since both countries were members of NATO. NATO was founded on the principle that an attack against one member state would be considered an attack against all NATO members. So imagine the dilemma if two member States went to war against each other. It was something that the USSR would have relished.

Making the task even more difficult for the Canadian peacekeepers was that many of the opposing soldiers stationed on the Green Line were teenagers. Likewise, many of the Canadian peacekeepers were also very young. It would not be unusual for a Canadian teenage private to be standing between two opposing teenagers facing each other 30 feet apart. Some seemed to take great delight in hurling insults towards their adversary, particularly against members of their families. Most of these teenagers had limited military training and had little understanding of what their actions could provoke.

Cullen handed me my duffle bag and I entered the Mess. The rain had stopped and the sun was now shining brightly. I could feel the intense heat. The rain we had experienced was rare. In fact, for the remainder of my tour, I can only remember it raining once. It had taken me 27 hours to get from Ottawa to Cyprus. All I wanted was a shower and a bed.

An NCO met me inside the door and told me arrangements had been made for me to have the room at the top of the stairs for a couple of days, following which I could move out to Camp Maple Leaf, close to the airport, where my office building was located. Many of the support staff lived at the base.

Following my shower, I crawled into bed and the next thing I knew, someone was banging on my door. The NCO who had welcomed me told me that if I wanted dinner, it would start in 30 minutes.

Refreshed and dressed I went downstairs and into a small bar and ordered a beer. Standing at the bar was a tall, rather stern officer sipping on a ginger ale. He introduced himself as LCol 'Boom' Marsaw, Commanding Officer of the 3rd Battalion, Princess Patricia's Canadian Light Infantry (PPCLI). The Regiment was formed in August 1914 in Ottawa. Captain Andrew Hamilton Gault provided $100,000 to form and equip a battalion for overseas service in World War I.

It didn't take me long to learn that LCol Marsaw was a deeply religious person. In fact, when he retired from the Canadian Forces in 1977, he began his service, for 25 years, as a Baptist pastor. He understood and tolerated his officers drinking alcohol beverages although he himself didn't drink. But he was dead set against any fraternization between his officers and men and any of the locals, particularly women, be they Cypriot or otherwise, including those working at various embassies and high commissions in Nicosia. He also let me know that he preferred to not see any media person in the officers' mess unless absolutely necessary.

After dinner, I met Maj Derek Bamford who introduced himself as the Deputy Commanding Officer. At 43, he had served with the British Army during the Korean War, following which he joined the Queen's Own Rifles in Canada, which had just been renamed as the PPCLI. He was immaculately dressed and stood tall with a twinkle in his eye and a snifter of Cypriot brandy in his hand. His whole approach to life seemed different than that of the CO and I wondered how these two got along.

Maj Bamford told me that he lived in a two-bedroom suite in the Ledra Palace across the street. The other bedroom was empty so he suggested that I move to the Ledra Palace and share the suite with him. Since generally the media will be staying there when they visit, it will be easier for you he suggested.

The Ledra Palace was built in 1949 and at the time was one of the largest hotels and perhaps the most prestigious on the island. Many important meetings were held there, leading up to the independence of Cyprus in 1960. It had hosted many glamourous functions for the cream of Cypriot society and prominent international guests, including stars and diplomats. Its main ballroom had fireplaces, beautiful chandeliers and featured a six-man live dance band that played every night.

The suite that Maj Bamford occupied was actually the UN presence in the hotel and was paid for by the Cypriot government. In fact, it was a kind of checkpoint. My guess was the government thought that neither side would fire at the Ledra Palace, since UN soldiers lived in the hotel. But in case of an outbreak of fighting, I am not sure how safe we would be. In fact when I did check in and opened my bathroom window, I was staring into a Turkish Cypriot 50-calibre machine gun poking out from a window directly across a lane, about 10 meters away.

168

The DCO told me that this would be the best place to have the newsmen stay when they visited. During my tour, groups of media, numbering from two to ten, would arrive on the Yukon and leave a week later. I had a week to expose them to what the UN was doing on the island and specifically the Canadian contingent. I also decided to introduce them to senior officials from both sides so the media would have a better understanding of the problem between the Turkish and Greek Cypriots.

We would work until about noon, when it became very hot. The remainder of the day I would take them sight-seeing to introduce them to the history of Cyprus; then show them the sights and sounds of the nightlife, while trying to keep them safe and out of harm's way. Most of my workdays were about 18 hours long when media were visiting.

There was another advantage to moving into the Ledra. The suite had a third large room that could easily accommodate a group of 10-12 and would hold a small bar. My thought was that I could keep the media happy by buying a drink(s) in the suite and using it as a daily briefing room. This would keep them out of the Officers' Mess and keep the CO happy.

The next day, I went to the CO's office and suggested to him that I move into the Ledra, providing him with the benefits, particularly that the media wouldn't need to frequent the mess. He was immediately in favor. He even offered to stock the bar. "Just give the barman a list of what you need," he told me, "and tell him I have authorized. Put it on my tab."

I met Andreas, the manager of the hotel, later that day and told him my plans. Andreas, a tall handsome, 30-something man, was very pleased to hear my proposal. I am sure to him it meant more business in his hotel. He told me that he would set up a portable bar in the suite and would be willing to help with any other requests I had regarding the media or other VIP visitors that might come to the island. The following day I moved into the hotel. While not quite as glamourous as some of the other hotel rooms, I am sure it was better than what I would have had at the base.

The base was an old British camp near the Nicosia airport. The PIO (Public Information Office) was one of the smaller buildings, but had all I needed to conduct my business, including a well-equipped photographic darkroom.

On my first visit, I met the two corporal photographers assigned to work with me. It was obvious that not much had happened in the office while my temporary replacement had been in Cyprus. My big wooden desk was covered with dust. The photographers were sitting drinking coffee and were bored silly. That is going to change, I told them. They seemed to be pleased.

My next stop on the base was to visit the senior Canadian in Cyprus, Brigadier General EMD (Teddy) Leslie who was the Chief of Staff of the United Nations Force in Cyprus, the first Canadian officer to hold that position.

When I first walked into his office, I immediately thought of photos I had seen of Field Marshall Montgomery commanding troops in the

Western Desert in 1942. The general was resplendent in his uniform and had a commanding presence. In his tan uniform and clipped British accent, he looked and sounded like he could be commanding with Montgomery in the desert. Indeed, as I was to quickly learn, his no nonsense, professional, energetic approach to his position was respected by the national contingents on the island as well as by the opposing forces.

General Leslie had a good background to be this kind of officer. His father, General Andrew McNaughton was a veteran of Vimy Ridge in the First World War and an army commander in WWII. In 1944, he was named Minister of National Defence.

Following in his father's footsteps, he joined the military in 1938, went overseas in 1939, and distinguished himself throughout the war. Gen Leslie had changed his name to Leslie while serving in Korea, to comply with the terms of an inheritance issue.

It wasn't long after I arrived that one day I met his son, who I thought to be about 12. After I left Cyprus, I forgot about him for many years until one day I learned that LGen Andrew Leslie had been appointed as Chief of the Land Staff and head of the Canadian Army. What a distinguished military family!

Gen Leslie seemed to be enthusiastic about my being there on the island as a Canadian PIO and indicated his support. Anything he could do to make my job easier, and anytime I wanted him to talk to the media, he was ready, he told me.

I took advantage of his offer and brought most of the media visitors to see him. He was an excellent spokesman for the UN Forces and for the Canadian contribution. The media that were briefed by him listened to him with a great deal of respect.

This was a welcome change. I had met several senior officers in my public information career who were not as understanding or supportive of my role or the importance of the media. In fact, even in Cyprus, I had one officer tell me that if he could use the money that went to pay my salary to buy boots for his troops, he considered that the latter would be more beneficial to him.

My next task was to meet with the Greek and Turkish Cypriot senior public information officers. Frankly I didn't know what to expect. Fortunately, both sides welcomed me and offered 100% support for anything that I wanted to do regarding my media visitors understanding more about their problems on the island. Obviously each side thought that they were right and wanted to convey this to the foreign media so that the world would know.

The Public Information Offices were the conduit to meeting with two of the most important senior officials in Cyprus, Glafcos Clerides and Rauf Denktash.

Glafcos Clerides was born in Nicosia, Cyprus, and served in the Royal Air Force during the Second World War. He was shot down and spent several years as a German prisoner of war. After his release, he studied law at King's College London and then practiced in Cyprus. He became a member of the EOKA organization that sought the liberation of Cyprus from British rule and often defended fighters arrested by the British. From 1968-1976, as Chairman of the House of Representatives of Cyprus, he represented the Greek Cypriot community in talks with Mr. Denktash trying to solve the Cyprus problem.

Rauf Denktash was born in Paphos, Cyprus and went to London to train as a lawyer at Lincoln's Inn. Following graduation in 1947 he returned home to Cyprus to practice law. As a member of the Turkish Affairs Committee he served as a member of the Assembly in search of self-government for Cyprus. He was a crown prosecutor from 1947 until 1958. In the late 50's he helped to found the Turkish Resistance Organization, which was a counter to EOKA. He became a leading figure in the Turkish Cypriot community and the representative who met with Clerides in their talks.

Both were anxious to tell their story to the foreign media. Through the PIO office I was able to arrange meetings with them usually together before they would go into their negotiating sessions. Sometimes, the meetings were with them individually but the encounters with the media were usually more interesting when they were together. Both would always appear to be friendly to each other and open with the media.

The two knew each other from the 1950s when Clerides would be in court defending EOKA fighters and Denktash was prosecuting them. When I met them, almost on a weekly basis, they often joked with each other. But apparently once they went into their 'in-camera' sessions, they were not able to come to any agreement to settle their differences.

Basically, Clerides wanted to have a single federated state with a power-sharing agreement between Cypriots of Greek and Turkish origin. Denktash argued for a two-state solution. It was a position that he never altered and one that some Turkish Cypriots began to resent as the years went by. Some felt that there would be more advantage to accepting what Clerides was offering.

I recall on one occasion meeting Denktash in his office alone with a group of media. Quite a large man, he seemed to be timid and almost shaking as he pleaded with the few Canadian newsmen to recognize the injustices suffered by the Turkish Cypriots at the hands of the Greeks Cypriots during the fighting in 1964.

Later we were taken by the PIO to where Turkish Cypriots had been "massacred" at the hands of Greek Cypriots during the 1964 fighting. Bullet holes in buildings and what we were told were old dried bloodstains on the walls made the argument for his case.

A few years later, in 1974 after the Turkish forces invaded Cyprus, I took a group of newsmen to his office. With Turkish troops on the island, Denktash was much more self assured, a little arrogant, and even demanding about what the Turkish community would accept.

My last visit was to the Cyprus Mail. The paper is the oldest daily on the island and was started in 1945. It is non-political. I introduced myself to the news editor and he in turn introduced me to Judy. Until recently she had worked as a reporter at the prestigious Manchester Guardian and now was the military beat reporter for the newspaper. We traded stories about our backgrounds and when she learned that I had been born in London and had family in Manchester she became friendly and told me she would be happy to cover events of Canadian activities in Cyprus.

Maybe it was just because she was new to the island and peacekeeping activities and I provided her an opportunity to get stories. Perhaps no one from the other battalions had approached her. Regardless of the reason, we Canadians were often on the front page of the Mail with stories that covered VIP visitors to our Battalion, battalion accomplishments in Nicosia as well as interviews with our soldiers on their duties as peacekeepers.

Well into my tour, I got a call from the UNPIO who told me that some of the other battalions were upset with how much coverage we were getting and asked me to stop encouraging these stories. I told him that when the Canadian battalion stopped doing anything that was newsworthy, we would stop getting coverage. I hung up and never heard from him again.

A couple of weeks after meeting Judy, I invited her to the Officers' Mess for dinner. Obviously I had forgotten about the CO's caution about bringing females into the mess. The next day I received a call from his office. I was to prepare a briefing note explaining who this woman was, why I had invited her to dinner and what we discussed. I did my bidding. It wasn't difficult. I never heard another word nor was I admonished for taking this reporter to the mess for dinner.

Seven days after I arrived in Nicosia, the Yukon landed at the Nicosia International airport carrying my first group of visiting newsmen. They were 10 editors from weekly newspapers across western Canada. Many of the editors were also owners of their papers. They were generally older than the aggressive daily reporters with whom I usually dealt. But they were also experienced journalists.

Each morning was filled with briefings by UN, Canadian, Greek Cypriot and Turkish Cypriot senior officials. Each afternoon, we went on trips around the island to visit not only the beauty but also to meet some of the locals and to hear their stories. It gave the newsmen a much more balanced account of what was happening in Cyprus and how the general population felt about the situation.

In the evenings, I would take them to some restaurants that I had discovered during my first week. My favourite was Charlie's Bar. Here one could eat meza, a large selection of small Greek dishes, and drink wonderful wine and ouzo. Charlie was in his 80s and loved to party. His son was trying to run the restaurant and make a profit. Charlie, although retired, was always there.

Apparently he consumed a bottle of scotch every day and was always happy. He would encourage patrons to throw plates, not plates designed for that purpose but real plates. His son would run around trying to stop him but he was just having too much fun. So the first night that each group arrived we would go there. Another was the Cosmopolitan restaurant, much more sophisticated and elegant but excellent food and very reasonable prices.

One night at dinner, the group asked me if I could take them to a local club that was a hangout for whiskey dollies. I told them that these girls were basically there to get them to buy watered-down drinks at outrageous prices. Nevertheless they wanted to go. So I agreed to take them for 'one' drink. Then we would have to leave.

Within seconds of entering the club and being seated there were girls all over us like flies over a honey-pot. Buy us a drink mister was their plea. Almost instantly a waiter arrived with glasses of champagne for the girls, which I am sure was coloured water sold at an outrageous price. Just as quickly the champagne was gone and they were asking for another. I told the guys that they had seen the club and we should leave. Most agreed but a couple decided to stay. They are big boys I thought. I didn't think they were in any trouble. The idea was for them to spend money on drinks. Nothing beyond that, as far as I knew.

The next morning I learned that Pte Cullen had gone back after dropping us off at the Ledra Palace and dragged the two out of the club and brought them back to the hotel. One of the editors came to me complaining bitterly that he had spent over $200 Canadian in the bar and wondered if I could help him get some of it back. I laughed and told him chalk it up to a lesson learned. I didn't say that I had told him what to expect and that he should have known better.

Except for that small incident the visit had gone well. When they were getting ready to leave Cyprus, one senior editor came to me and told me that he didn't think that he could write enough stories to justify what they had seen or done, plus the hospitality of the Canadian troops. I told him that we were not measuring the success of his visit by how much he wrote. Rather we wanted him to have a better understanding of what was happening here. If, in the future, some journalist, or politician made a case for withdrawing our troops from Cyprus, he would be in a much better position to agree with or challenge that assertion.

As they climbed wearily on the aircraft after a full week of work and play, two senior radio reporters came off eagerly looking forward to a week of, as I was to find out, a lot of fun.

I had been advised in advance that they really wanted to interview Archbishop Makarios during their visit. He had been voted Archbishop of Cyprus in 1950 and became involved in the 'enosis' movement but later leaned more towards an independent Cyprus. He ran for president and was elected in August 1960. His mandate was expanded from 1965 to 1968 and then he was re-elected.

173

I was able to arrange the interview for them a couple of days after their arrival through the Cypriot Government Public Information Office, with whom I was developing a good rapport.

They were good reporters and asked pointed questions during their briefings, but at night they showed they really wanted to party. I didn't want to nor could I keep up. I told them on their second night out that we needed to be ready at 8:00 AM in the lobby to leave to go to the President's residence.

The next morning there was no sign of them in the hotel breakfast room. At about 7:15 I decided to go to the room that they shared. I knocked and no one answered albeit I could hear movement and knew someone was inside. The door was unlocked. I entered. What a sight. One of the reporters was sprawled on a chair on the balcony. No amount of shaking would wake him up. The other was staggering around the room looking like he was trying to find his bed. They apparently had not been in the room very long.

I grabbed the one who was moving, told him he was going in the shower. I called room service, ordered coffee and juice and told him to hurry. My staggering 'newsman' finished showering, dressed and downed most of the pot of coffee.

I looked at the other one who was now snoring loudly and concluded he was a waste of time. So I told his friend, "We are going to meet the President of Cyprus, Archbishop Makarios. You are not going to embarrass Canada. You are not going to embarrass the Canadian Contingent here. And most of all you are not going to embarrass me. Do you understand?" I got a nod, which didn't fill me with confidence. But it was a start.

At 8:00 AM I got him downstairs into the lobby where Cullen was waiting for us. As usual he had a big grin on his face. I was in no mood for his good humour. "What are you grinning at?" I barked.

Cullen said, "See you got this one on his feet. I found them downtown. Checked with one of the bars where I last saw them and they told me someone had taken them to a party," he said laughingly. "Heck of a job trying to get them back here. They didn't want to leave."

After a few short questions, Cullen admitted that he couldn't sleep and wanted to make sure that these guys were safe and back at the hotel. In fact as I was to learn, Pte Cullen considered it to be his job not go to bed until every newsperson or VIP was in bed. It didn't matter what I told him, he was going to do it anyway. How could I really discipline him for helping me in this way?

We drove to the President's residence and I kept talking to my charge, prompting him with questions and urging him to stay awake.

When we arrived he seemed to have sobered up somewhat. Maybe this wasn't an unusual situation for him, I thought. We were ushered into a large, beautifully decorated office where we met Archbishop Makarios.

The President was distinguished, gracious and spoke perfect English. If he detected that my reporter was suffering he made no indication. He offered us coffee and then asked for questions. Much to my surprise and relief, the questions asked were not only pertinent and pointed but ones which caused the Archbishop to reflect on occasion before answering. He was obviously pleased to have this opportunity to lay out his position on the Cyprus situation to this western journalist. Bringing media to visit the President was not on the usual week's agenda; but I felt after this I could probably get another audience if I wanted to.

In general the media visitors that we hosted in Cyprus during my tour were well behaved, but looking after a group for seven days and then replacing them with another was demanding for me.

Interestingly, I never felt concerned for the safety of my visitors or for myself even though the city of Nicosia was an armed camp. That did change for me when our intelligence staff discovered that there was a plot to kidnap a UN officer in the Nicosia area. Canadians were the largest group of UN officers so we considered we were at risk. In addition as the public information officer, I was a likely target since many combatants in the Middle East considered that the public information officer was most likely to be a spy. Consequently, all Canadian officers were issued with 9mm weapons and ammunition. Pte Cullen, as my driver was also provided with a weapon and I was assigned another corporal who with an automatic weapon rode beside Cullen in the front seat of the Mercedes wherever we went.

The first time we stopped for a drink and walked into a cafe in downtown, we each carried our weapons as ordered. Felt strange but no one else in the cafe really seemed to be worried or concerned about these three UN soldiers being armed when they were having their morning coffee. Maybe they considered that to be the price of not being at war.

I never told Shirlie about the threat. But I know she worried about my safety being in the 'Middle East.'

At the same time I was aware that there were problems in Canada, more specifically in Quebec. Before I left Canada there was a bombing of the Montreal Stock Exchange in Feb 1970, which resulted in extensive damage and injuries to 27 people. Other government establishments in Montreal were targeted and dynamite stolen from military and industrial sites.

In 1970, 23 members of the Front de Liberation du Quebec (FLQ) were in prison, four of whom were convicted of murder.

On Oct 5, 1970, two members of the FLQ kidnapped James Cross, the British Trade Commissioner from his home in Montreal. Five days later Pierre Laporte, Minister of Labour for Quebec was kidnapped from his Montreal home.

One week later, the Federal Government instructed the Canadian Forces to patrol around Ottawa.

On Oct 15, the government of Quebec requested the intervention of the Canadian Forces in 'aid of the civil power', which was supported by the three opposition parties in Quebec City.

Premier Bourassa requested the Federal Government on Oct 16 to grant the government of Quebec emergency powers, which in effect resulted in the implementation of the War Measures Act giving wide-reaching powers of arrest to police. PM Trudeau announced the imposition of the Act.

I was being kept up to date by Judy as she was receiving wire service reports in the Cyprus Mail newsroom. The news, which I passed on, was troubling to the troops albeit the large majority of their families were in Victoria, BC.

On Oct 17, the Canadian Ambassador to Israel, Charles McCaughey, who was also High Commissioner to Cyprus, was paying an official visit to the island. That evening the battalion held a cocktail party in the Officers' Mess in his honour with guests invited from several of the other embassies, high commissions and senior UN officials.

During the reception I was summoned to the bar to take a phone call. It was Judy. She wanted me to know that a report had just come across the wire service that the FLQ had announced that they had executed hostage James Cross. I knew from previous conversations with the Ambassador that James Cross and he were good friends. Both had been stationed in Kuala Lumpur, Malaysia, in the early 1960s when Mr. McCaughey had been the High Commissioner for Canada, and Mr. Cross had been Britain's Trade Commissioner.

I returned to the festive gathering and quietly made my way to the Ambassador and asked him if I could speak to him privately. I must have appeared very disturbed because he didn't question my request. Once out in the hallway, I broke the news to him. He was devastated. I felt horrible for telling him but felt it was my duty. He returned to the reception a much more sombre individual.

About 15 minute later, I was again summoned to the bar. It was an excited Judy on the phone. "There has been a correction," she told me, "The wire service has just advised that it wasn't James Cross but Pierre Laporte who has been executed."

I rushed back into the reception room and asked the Ambassador if he would come back into the hall. "What now?" he asked obviously upset. I told him the news. It was bitter sweet. His friend was still alive but a Canadian politician had been murdered.

Ambassador McCaughey probably understood that mistakes are made when stories are filed in such high profile cases. He had worked as a political correspondent for the Sudbury Star and North Bay Nugget in the early 1940s. In Oct 1941, he joined the Canadian Forces as a private and was discharged as a captain in 1947.

On December 4, 62 days after being kidnapped James Cross was released by the FLQ following negotiations with police which resulted in five known kidnappers being flown by the Canadian Forces to Cuba.

Shirlie told me in a letter that the soldiers were patrolling the streets nearby. We lived close to Rockcliffe, home for many of the foreign diplomats. Kids were not allowed to go out 'trick or treating' that year. She was worried about my safety in Cyprus, even though she didn't know about the kidnapping threat. I was worried about her safety and the kids.

Finally on December 28, three members of the FLQ were arrested and were later charged with the kidnapping and murder of Pierre Laporte. All troops were withdrawn in January 1971.

Ambassador McCaughey was a very gracious man and before he left he thanked me for keeping him up-to-date on the news. He also invited Shirlie and me to come and stay with him and his wife at his official residence in Tel Aviv when Shirlie came to visit me in November.

Each of us serving with the UN Forces in Cyprus was given two weeks leave during our tour. Shirlie arrived in mid-November on the Air Force Yukon aircraft. The flight was continuing to Israel so I joined her for the short flight to Tel Aviv. I had learned a few days before that the Ambassador had to accompany his wife back to Canada where she would have some surgery so he wouldn't be able to host us. However, he made arrangements for us to stay with our Canadian Military Attaché to Israel, Col Hugh Bartley and his wife Barbara.

When the aircraft stopped at the Ben-Gurion airport, the door opened and a young lady in an EL AL uniform came onboard and asked if Captain Dent would identify himself. I raised my hand and she asked Shirlie and me to accompany her. There were lots of other officers onboard, many higher ranking than I, so I wondered what was happening, as I am sure they were. Baggage was unloaded from the aircraft onto the tarmac and I identified our two pieces. We were then placed in a very official looking black sedan and whisked away... no customs, or immigration officials' check. Soon we arrived at a very impressive looking home in Herzliya, on the outskirts of Tel Aviv. This was the home of the Bartleys.

We were ushered into the house and shown our guest quarters. A note was left on the table saying that they were at a diplomatic function and would be home in about two hours. Meanwhile they had left a beef bourguignon simmering on the stove for us to enjoy and told us to have anything we wanted from their well-stocked wine cabinet.

We met our hosts next morning, and during breakfast they laid out the plans they had made for us for the week. Included were a trip to Haifa, Tiberias and the Ein Gev kibbutz on the Sea of Galilee. The Ambassador had also made arrangements for us to go to Jerusalem for three days. He had contacted one of his friends, a Jesuit priest who lived in the Church of All Nations. An amateur archeologist who had lived in Israel since 1948, he would be our guide in and around the Holy City.

After touring Tel Aviv and area the first day with Barbara, the Bartleys drove us to a Druze village close to the Lebanese border. The Druze are a relatively small group of religious people living primarily in Syria, Lebanon, Jordan and Israel. There are about six percent in Israel and most live in the village we visited.

The occasion had been organized by the Rockefeller Foundation to raise funds for a new school in the community. Accordingly, diplomats and attaches from several foreign countries had been invited hoping that they could influence their countries to donate money.

On the way to the village, Col Bartley told our wives that since we were invited guests, we might be invited to a special honour. "They might offer you the sheep's eyes," he said. "So don't make a fuss and insult them, just pop it in your mouth and swallow quickly," he chuckled, with a big grin. The ladies were aghast. Of course he was kidding.

The Druze were dressed in their finest clothes with many bright colours worn by the women and children. The young girls were very pretty and all wore make up. A feast had been prepared for us. Someone had even rented plates, knives and forks that we could use.

The centrepiece amongst the many salads and fruits on the large table inside a big tent was a large sheep that had been roasted. After helping ourselves, two of the Druze carried the roast around asking if we wanted more. A third man accompanied them to help. When Barbara said yes she would like a little more lamb, the man literally ripped a piece off with his hand, which didn't appear to have been washed for some time and put it on her plate. Not to insult anyone she had to eat it. Then came the entertainment with music and dancing.

The chief of the Druze took a liking to Shirlie, perhaps because of her very red hair, which was not common in the Middle East. He hugged her several times while smiling at me; I wasn't sure just what his intentions were.

It was a memorable event albeit I never found out how much money was donated or if the school was ever built.

One evening, the Bartley's took us to a cocktail party at the British Embassy in Tel Aviv. There were representatives from many countries including from Israel. While talking to one high ranking Israeli official and telling him about my role in Cyprus, I let it slip that my mother was Jewish. "Your mother is Jewish," he said, "You are an aviator and you are experienced in public relations. Oy vey, do we have a job for you already!" He was serious. I thanked him very much and respectfully declined. If I had accepted I thought, I might be buried in the Golan Heights today.

During the evening, we heard what sounded like rockets landing nearby. The seasoned guests seemed to take it in stride. One mentioned that the Jordanians were having a little fun tonight. Whether the rockets were coming from Jordan or not, I never did find out. But Shirlie and I did not find this very amusing. It is only 110 kilometres or 68 miles from Amman, Jordan to Tel Aviv, so I suspect we were well within range of any of their rockets.

We drove to Jerusalem the next day in the Ambassador's car. His chauffeur, an Arab, was very friendly and knowledgeable. He and his family were among the Palestinians who remained after the establishment of Israel in 1948. Reportedly, approximately 80% of the Arab inhabitants fled from the new nation to the West Bank and to Gaza, concerned about being massacred or being unwilling to live under Jewish control.

Some were accepted into neighbouring Arab states but some were denied. The latter were put into displacement camps. We drove by one such camp where our driver told us there were thousands of Palestinians and living conditions were precarious.

He also pointed out a field where there were many tanks that had been captured from the Arabs during the 1967 war. When I asked him if they were any good, he told me that they were excellent now that the Israelis had taken out the Russian engines and put in American ones.

On our journey we also saw many old rusted military vehicles left there since the fight for independence in 1948. These were the remnants of trucks, which were bringing supplies to Jerusalem when it was under siege and people were starving. Some of the vehicles had plaques with the dates when they were destroyed and the names of those who died in them.

Remembering that this had all happened a little more than 20 years ago was a very sobering thought, particularly because the situation was by no means resolved. In fact, events since 1948 demonstrated that realistically there would not be any solution to this problem between the Arabs and the state of Israel for a long time, if ever.

Our driver stopped at a beautiful old building, the American Colony Hotel, which had been a rich Arab's mansion at one time. This was to be our accommodation. He would come to fetch us back to Tel Aviv in three days.

The hotel calls itself an oasis of neutrality in the Palestinian-Israeli conflict. It is the preferred hotel for many diplomats, politicians and foreign correspondents.

Shortly after arriving, Father John, our guide appeared. His intent, in the next three days, was to show us as much as possible of Jerusalem and surrounding area. We soon found out that he was a walking encyclopedia. Of course his knowledge of the Bible was impeccable and almost embarrassing for us. He would show us a spot or a building, and quoting chapter and verse, he would proudly state that this is where it took place. In many cases, we vaguely remembered the story but had no idea of the chapter and verse.

Our first stop on this walking tour was the Church of All Nations where he resided. Located on the Mount of Olives next to the Garden of Gethsemane, it houses a rock where Jesus is said to have prayed before his arrest. Built between 1919 and 1924, the church was funded by many different countries, including Canada.

In the Garden, he showed us an olive tree, which was thought to have been there when Jesus walked through the area. It was memorable in that it appeared dead and had a large hollow in the trunk. And yet, at the very top there were green leaves and a few olives.

As inspired as we were by this church, it could not compare to how we felt when we entered the Church of the Holy Sepulchre. It is difficult to put into words the inner thoughts and feelings as one enters the site venerated as Golgotha, the Hill of Calvary, where Jesus was crucified. We entered the small room, or Sepulchre, where it is thought Jesus was buried. It left us speechless. We could only stand in awe. Words are not adequate to describe how we felt to be in this place.

Likewise a few moments later we began our walk up the Via Dolorosa. Thought to be the path that Jesus walked carrying his cross to his crucifixion, it winds up well-trodden and worn-stone stairs for about 600 metres or 2,000 feet. It has nine stations or stopping places of the cross each depicting a specific event in His walk to His crucifixion.

To be standing on a spot where Jesus stood carrying his cross so many years ago is beyond imagination. Again, it left us speechless and completely drained.

Father John took us back to our hotel and told us that in order to continue our tour the next day he needed to rent a car. Would we mind, he asked? It will cost about $16. That I can afford, I figured.

The next morning he met us in the lobby and told us he had a vehicle. Outside, a uniformed chauffeur greeted us, cap in hand and the back door open to the biggest white Mercedes stretch limousine we had ever seen. Yes, he confirmed, $16 for the day - the owner was a friend.

Our first stop was Bethlehem and the Church of the Nativity. Going to see where Jesus was born in this Holy City was spoiled to a degree by the fact that there is a field of TV antennas on roofs as we approached the church.

The original church was built in AD 339. It is thought to be located over the grotto that marks the birthplace of Jesus.

The Roman Catholic, Greek Orthodox and Armenian Apostolic churches administer the church. Apparently, this has caused some tension and even fights amongst monk trainees as they argued about the respect each other had for their prayers and the division of floor space for cleaning duties. We noted as we walked towards the stairs that would lead down to the grotto, that we had to navigate a circuitous route around chairs that had been set up in the church.

We stared in wonderment as we looked at the spot where Jesus was born. It is beneath an altar and marked by a 14-pointed star set into the marble floor and surrounded by silver lamps. There were just the three of us and we stood in silence and awe. We could almost feel the power of this sacred place to which, for centuries, millions of people from all over the world have come.

We quietly left but the feeling of wonderment at having been there remains with us today.

Our next stop was Nazareth and the Church of the Annunciation, which many believe was built on the site of the childhood home of Mary where she was told by the angel Gabriel at the age of 14 that she would become the mother of the son of God. It also became the hometown of

Jesus, Mary and Joseph after the Holy family returned from fleeing to Egypt to escape Herod the Great's soldiers.

Nazareth is about 80 miles from Bethlehem, which took us less than 1 1/2 hour by car. In Jesus' time it would have been about a four-day caravan trip, but Mary and Joseph probably took close to a week since she was so close to the birth of her child.

The lower level of the church is built around a sunken grotto that contains the traditional cave-home of the Virgin Mary. The first church on the site was built around 427 AD.

Nearby is a small church with steps that lead down to a small underground chamber which some believe was Joseph's carpentry workshop, although it is thought that he most likely worked with stone since that was the building material of the time.

We stayed for a couple of hours exploring the churches and the surrounding area of Nazareth and left feeling that we had seen another piece of this Christian story which we will never forget.

We journeyed back through Jerusalem. Our next stop was the Inn of the Good Samaritan. The monastery was built about 18 km from Jerusalem on the road to Jericho, on the site that was thought to have been a type of traveller's hostel, well before the time of Jesus. Though the Inn of the Good Samaritan existed only in the parable, a real life site was proposed and built in the early Christian centuries to strengthen the faith of pilgrims.

The remains of the building were surrounded by rocky desert terrain. Our driver pulled up and stopped as Father John told us the familiar story of a Samaritan, an enemy of the Jews, who stopped to help tend the wounds of a man who had been attacked by robbers, while just before, a priest and a Levite had passed by on the other side ignoring the poor man.

We left the limo and went inside the broken-down building. When we came out a few moments later, imagine our surprise to find ourselves surrounded by Israeli Defence Force soldiers all armed with Uzis and looking very fierce. Father John explained to them who we were. They told us rather curtly to be on our way. After all this was 1970 and we were close to the Jordanian border. The Israelis were very serious about guarding their territory.

An hour later we arrived at the Dead Sea, which borders Jordan to the east and Israel and Palestine to the west. Its shores are almost 1,400 feet below sea level making it the earth's lowest elevation on land. It is one of the world's saltiest bodies of water with a salinity of almost 34%.

Today, many people use salts and minerals from the Dead Sea to create cosmetics and herbal sachets.

Shirlie and I were offered the opportunity to go for a swim, because we were told that you couldn't sink. Shirlie was having a wonderful time with her feet and arms extended in the air floating on the water. Suddenly she did a back flip and her head went under water. She screamed and I yelled, "Don't open your eyes!"

I got an immediate lesson in the ingenuity and resourcefulness of the Israelis. There was no charge for swimming in the Dead Sea, but if you wanted a shower, and a towel, there was a charge of 10 Israeli pounds for each. Of course, virtually everyone who ventured into that body of salt needed both when they came out.

I led Shirlie to the shower and she quickly got the salt off her face. There was no damage; we got dried off, changed back into our clothes and headed for Jericho.

It is the place where, according to Joshua, Chapter 6 in the Old Testament, the Israelis defeated the city of Jericho after wandering in the wilderness for 40 years.

Today, there is a mammoth dig outside the town. A German team carried out the first major excavation in 1907. The piles of mud bricks that they found were later determined to be from the city wall when the city was destroyed.

We saw several layers of black material, which we were told, were towns that had been burnt and destroyed over the centuries.

Archeologists have determined that there were more than 20 successive settlements in Jericho, with the first dating back 11,000 years.

Jordan occupied the present city of Jericho from 1948 to 1967. When we visited, the city had been held under Israeli occupation since the war of 1967.

If only this dig could talk, I thought. Imagine the history that has taken place in this area. Beyond our imagination!

We were emotionally drained. Our day of visiting these historic sites in Israel was over. We were driven back to our hotel and said our goodbyes to our driver and more particularly to Father John. He had been a fount of knowledge for us and opened our eyes to an area like few other people could.

The next morning the Ambassador's driver picked us up at the hotel and drove us back to the Bartleys residence.

Barbara Bartley's plans for the day included taking us to Tiberias to see the Sea of Galilee and then to the Kibbutz at Ein Gev for lunch.

The kibbutz, located on the eastern shore of the Sea of Galilee, came into being in July 1937. The original settlers were from Czechoslovakia, Germany, Austria and the Baltic countries. It shared a border with Syria and was shelled during the 1948 Arab-Israeli War. It only became safer when the Israelis occupied the neighbouring Golan Heights in the 1967 Six-Day War. When we visited there were fewer than 500 residents in the kibbutz.

We ate in the lovely hotel where Barbara introduced us to St Peter's fish, which had been caught that morning in the Sea of Galilee beside the hotel. We were served the whole fish and while it was very tasty it was also very boney. Today I understand that this fish is also called tilapia, which we eat often and enjoy very much.

The next morning the Bartleys took us to the airport to catch our EL AL flight to Nicosia. It had been seven days which we still remember vividly to this day. To have seen where Jesus was born, lived and died, to have been in areas where he taught, were memories never to be forgotten. I would visit Israel several times in the future as part of my work but none would ever touch me as much as this visit with Shirlie.

Security at the Ben Gurion airport in Tel Aviv was very tight, as one would imagine. It was only three years after the latest Arab-Israeli War. But technology in 1970 was not as it is today. We walked through scanners but I didn't want my camera to go through because I thought the x-rays might ruin the film so I simply held it over my head above the scanners. Unbelievably, I was allowed to go through.

We had an approximate time for departure and waited in the departure lounge. We were called and taken to a bus with a handful of other passengers. Then, we drove a considerable distance until we turned behind a hangar; there was an old two engine prop aircraft, which looked like a DC3 aircraft, waiting for us. As we boarded I noticed what appeared to patches, presumably over bullet holes. I assume this aircraft had seen action in 1967.

The short flight to Cyprus was uneventful. Private Cullen was there to meet us when we arrived, smiling and happy as he always was. He had taken a week's leave while we were in Israel and had got a good tan on the beaches of Kyrenia.

He drove us to the Ledra Palace where I had booked a simple room with Andreas. We couldn't stay in my normal room, since it was being paid for by the UN. And I couldn't afford anything but the cheapest room in this hotel.

Andreas had a surprise for us when we arrived.

"Sorry," he said, "I had to give your room away this morning." "What?" I exclaimed, "But where are we going to sleep?" It seemed like our wonderful vacation together was going to take a sharp downturn.

"Not to worry," he said, "I have another room for you." He took us personally up to the third floor and opened the door. We walked into a beautiful suite consisting of a living room, dining area and a huge bedroom with a marble bathroom. My first thought was, I can't afford this!

I went back down with him to get the rest of our luggage. I asked Andreas what was the rate for this suite. He knew that the UN gave us $14 a day to supplement our two weeks of holidays. "Would $100 for the week be ok?" he said with a big grin. I couldn't believe it. "By the way, my wife and I would like you and your wife to join us for dinner in the dining room this evening."

"It sounds wonderful but could we take a rain check?" I asked him. "We're bushed after a week of travel in Israel and would like to get an early night."

"OK, but how about I send up some dinner to your room".

"OK," I replied.

"What do you like?" he asked.

"We like everything," I told him.

"Is 7 pm ok?"

"Great," I said.

Promptly at 7 pm there was a knock at the door. I opened it and there was a uniformed waiter with a trolley full of food. He wheeled it in to the dining room and started laying the table.

He told us that we had a large shrimp cocktail for a starter, chicken cordon bleu with small buttered potatoes and asparagus, a decadent looking chocolate dessert, and chilled in a silver chalice, a beautiful bottle of what I knew was a very expensive Cypriot white wine.

As he laid the table, he said with a huge smile, "My manager says to enjoy the dinner and the evening with his compliments." We were floored. We sat down and enjoyed this exquisite meal realizing it was the first time that we had really had any quality time together alone since Shirlie arrived in the Middle East.

We stuffed ourselves, crawled into bed, and were dead to the world in seconds.

The next morning Cullen called about 8 am and told us he was ready to take us anywhere we wanted to go. He had taken his second week of leave and wanted to just be with us. Since his fiancée lived in Victoria, BC, and she had no chance of visiting him, he told me this would be more fun than simply going out and drinking with the boys.

So for the next week, we treated Shirlie like she was a visiting journalist taking her to all the spots we would normally go, except for the meetings with the politicians and the official military briefings. During the day we toured Nicosia, Kyrenia, Limassol, Paphos and the beaches.

Shirlie had studied the books I had sent her. One was on the history of Cyprus, and the other, 'Bitter Lemons' written by Lawrence Durrell. We made a visit to the town of Bellapais, where he had written the book while sitting under the Tree of Idleness, a 200 year-old Robenia tree.

Durrell was a famed British author who moved to Cyprus in 1953 and lived in the village of Bellapais for three years. His book tells the story of the people he met and befriended on the island. It also charts the progress of the Cypriot 'enosis' or union with Greece and freedom from British rule, which plunged the island into chaos and violence.

Shirlie knew much about the history of the island and as we travelled to see various sites she would often tell me the history. So Cullen and I both learned from her studies.

All too soon the week was over and I was taking her to the Nicosia airport for her flight back to Canada. It had been two wonderful weeks together and I felt a huge pang of loneliness as I watched her go through the departure gate to catch the aircraft. But the loneliness didn't last long.

On the same flight had arrived a group of senior media men from British Columbia. Included in the group was Himie Koshevoy, a Vancouver raised journalist, who had written for various newspapers for five decades as well as writing several books. He was a columnist for the Vancouver Province, when he arrived in Cyprus, but there was no doubt that he was considered the dean of the group by the others.

Given their maturity, this group was a pleasure to be with and the week of their visit passed quickly without any problems for me. They were always in bed early, didn't want to drink all night and didn't want to go to 'girly' bars. They were a truly professional group. After they arrived home, Himie wrote me a letter inviting me to Vancouver. Following my return to Canada I had the opportunity to take up his offer. Himie and the others treated me royally to a dinner at his favourite club.

The next weeks flew by. Week-long visits by the Chief of Defence Staff, some officials from Foreign Affairs, a few newsmen, and a CBC entertainment tour, consumed any free time I might have had. I didn't have much time to think about being lonely.

The CBC group was great. There were about 30 people including the film crew who taped all the entertainment for a show that would run on CBC-TV network during the Christmas holidays.

There were a variety of entertainers including singers and dancers; the folk group The Travelers; Miss Canada; and, comedian and Nashville star Gordie Tapp. They did a show every night throughout the camp and in Nicosia at various locations. Members of other contingents as well as local dignitaries were invited to see them perform. To my knowledge, the entertainers were all volunteers and no one was paid for the week's work.

Just before they left to return to Canada, a cocktail party was held for them in the Officers' Mess. One young officer made a point of telling me that Gordie Tapp hadn't shown up. "I guess he thinks he is too good for us," he said contemptuously.

"Actually," I replied quickly, because I had almost expected this type of comment, "He is over at the hospital visiting with a couple of soldiers who are recovering from a serious illness and couldn't come to any of the shows. He asked me if I thought this would be OK since he thought this was a more important way to spend his time than drinking at a cocktail party. I told him I agreed wholeheartedly." The officer turned away and didn't say a word!

Suddenly, it was Christmas. It was a difficult time for most of the members of the Battalion, both officers and men. Many of us were married and had children and the thought of being so many miles away at this most treasured 'family time' was hard to deal with.

Capt Hassett, the Roman Catholic Chaplain, made a contribution which I will always remember. While visiting some of the soldiers on guard duty at an outpost shortly after he arrived in Cyprus, he had noticed a small Christian Chapel, which had been badly damaged during the fighting. Situated on the 'Green Line' between the Greek Cypriots and Turkish Cypriots, it had half the roof gone and at least a foot or more of rubble on the floor. There were no doors or windows left, plaster was cracked and some had fallen off. In some places grass was growing.

Capt Hassett decided this would be an ideal site for the Midnight Mass on Christmas Eve. Both the Greek Cypriot and Turkish Cypriot officials agreed that the UN troops could use the chapel for a service on Christmas Eve.

Members of the Battalion began cleaning up and by December 24 all was ready. Men began to arrive around 11 pm and by midnight the chapel was full. And the mass began.

I was there with Cullen and I am sure that many of those present were not Catholic but wanted to be part of this sacred event. I will never forget looking up at the sky as a gentle breeze drifted through the chapel with a comfortable temperature in the 20s (°C). Here we were looking at the crystal-like stars on a beautiful clear night, thanking God from a place only 300 kilometres from Bethlehem.

When the service was over, we all went to the Junior Ranks Mess where we enjoyed wine and some wonderful tourtières that the cooks had prepared. There was a glow in the mess and much hugging and shaking hands as everyone wished each other Merry Christmas. For a short time, being so far away from families was forgotten.

The next morning, at about 9 am, I got my gang together, Cullen, and the two photographers. I had told them that just because it was Christmas Day they shouldn't think they were getting a day off. They grumbled a bit and I heard a remark about a hard-assed boss, but they got their equipment together and we headed out.

We met the CO at the Officers' Mess and spent the rest of the day visiting soldiers standing guard at their outposts as well as going to all the messes. My photographers took photos that would be sent home to the individual soldiers' newspapers to show them being on guard during Christmas.

The soldiers were so appreciative of the CO coming to see them on Christmas Day. It didn't make it any easier, standing alone on guard, when they could see the families of the Turks and Greeks in their homes celebrating; that only reminded them of their own families at home.

At each mess the CO made his rounds wishing everyone a Merry Christmas and thanking them for all their support. Then we were all given a drink of Christmas cheer and toasts were made. At some messes we were asked to have some food and at others we joined in as everyone sang carols.

By 6 pm, when we had finished, my group was happy and full. We had a great day. I think they realized why I had made them work. Cullen told me later that, other than being with his family and fiancée, this was the best Christmas he had ever had. Unfortunately some soldiers chose to stay in their barracks by themselves and had spent the day drinking. Most of those who did, didn't make it past noon.

My Christmas present from Shirlie arrived on the next scheduled flight from Canada. I met the aircraft and the first to disembark were Hugh and Barbara Bartley returning after a Christmas holiday in Canada. She came running up to me and gave me a big kiss and a lingering, tight hug.

"That's from Shirlie," she told me, "and this is from the kids," handing me a parcel. It was a wonderful Christmas photo of the family including a grownup 'Bootsie' beside a Christmas tree. Nothing could have been better. But Shirlie knowing my sweet tooth had also included several Turtle chocolate bars. It is a present I have always remembered.

Early in the New Year I received another present. General Bourgeois sent me a message from Ottawa telling me that he was sending out my replacement and wanted to cut my tour short, because he wanted to send to me to the Middle East for two weeks to visit and write stories for Sentinel, the Canadian Forces national magazine, on Canadian soldiers serving with the UN in various locations. I had one week to get ready and then I was off.

It sounded like an exciting assignment but it was not to be. Less than a week later, another message from the General telling me that the assignment had been cancelled and Capt. Hilchie was going to arrive to replace me, and I would be on the next scheduled flight home. I don't know what happened and he never told me. Maybe he just felt sorry for me and wanted to get me home sooner. Perhaps Cdr Murray, who was one of his deputies and who lived on the same street as us, had told him that Shirlie needed me home. I was sad I wasn't going on the assignment but elated that I was going home to see Shirlie and the kids.

There was a round of goodbyes to both Greek and Turkish Cypriot friends that I had made during the last five plus months. Charlie had a party for me in his restaurant and wined and dined me all night long. Thankfully, Cullen was there to bring me back to the Ledra Palace along with a case of fine Cypriot wines that Charlie had given me. This I had to donate to the Officers' Mess, because I couldn't bring them home on the aircraft.

It was 81 °F at the Nicosia airport when I left on January 14, 1970. A clear blue sky and warm soft breezes caressed us as we headed to board the Yukon aircraft.

I arrived in Trenton the next day. It was 25 °C below zero. I took the short hop to Ottawa an hour later and a taxi home.

I walked in; Shirlie looked at me obviously completely stressed and said, "Thank goodness you're home, I have got to go to the drug store."

Welcome Home!!

Serving as a PIO in Nicosia, Cyprus.

Hosting a BC media group in Kyrenia, Cyprus.

188

CHAPTER 12 - PUBLIC RELATIONS AROUND THE WORLD

Not everyone was happy to see me home that day.

Shirlie had been coping with the largest snowfall for decades in the Ottawa area, more than 171 inches. She had struggled to keep everything going around home for almost six months including getting the kids to school each day, dealing with their occasional illnesses, paying all the bills, fixing a broken furnace and trying to act like their dad.

She was ecstatic to see me walk in the front door. She gave me a quick kiss and out the door she went. Apparently our two kids and the neighbour's two, whom she was looking after for a day, were all sick and she was off to get more medicine. Some 'home-coming,' I thought.

The six months I was away, Shirlie told me, seemed like an eternity for Susan and David. They wouldn't leave me alone for several days. Susan was eight and was curious about where I had been all this time and what I had been doing. She wanted me to keep telling her all the stories about Cyprus. David was five and he wanted me there to give him his piggyback rides which he had missed so much and which his mom couldn't do. For the first few days, it seemed like I walked around with a permanent attachment on my back.

Bootsie was now fully grown and weighed about 65 pounds. After I left, Shirlie had allowed her to sleep on the bed beside her for company. My first night home Bootsie and I had a falling out. She jumped on the bed and stretched herself out into her sleep position. She was as long as Shirlie. I asked her politely to get off. It didn't work despite coaxing her with her favourite treats. Finally I had to lift her struggling and kicking onto the floor. She growled at me during the process to indicate her displeasure.

She was not happy. It took a few weeks to make her realize that that spot beside Shirlie was MY spot.

General Bourgeois had told me before I left Cyprus that I could take a couple of weeks off, before reporting in for work, to reunite with family and get caught up with all my responsibilities at home. It really was the first time I had spent with them for a couple of years. During the past 12 months, I had moved from Halifax to Toronto, Toronto to Ottawa, Ottawa to Cyprus and Cyprus back to Ottawa. I was looking forward to some stability at my new job at National Defence Headquarters in Ottawa. Fortunately the family only had to move from Halifax to Ottawa.

The General had told me that he was appointing me as News Editor for the Directorate of Information Services at NDHQ. With the help of a small staff, I would be responsible for preparing all Armed Forces national news releases for external dissemination to the Canadian media, as well as preparing press releases to be sent to Canadian Forces base newspapers, and radio and television stations. I was happy and honoured. I had been accepted into the organization less than three years ago and now I had this responsibility. Besides which there was no travelling involved in this job. I could lead a normal life with the family, which in reality I had never done before.

During my time off, Shirlie told me that she had tried to maintain her sanity by looking at homes for sale. She had made it clear even before we got married that some day she wanted her own home. A new subdivision was being built in Orleans, in Ottawa's east end, and she had fallen in love with a split level bungalow, which she thought was in our price range. Since I had always wanted her to look after our finances, in case something happened to me, I trusted her judgment.

So before starting my new job, we all went out to see the model home. It was a three bedroom, 1 ½ bath, which would be ideal for us. It cost $21,000. The kids flew around the house and were laying claim to which bedroom would be theirs! The decision was made. I just had to be sure that we weren't going to be on the move any time soon.

Shortly after starting my new job on February 1st, I met with Gen Bourgeois privately in his office and used the opportunity to talk about my immediate future.

As politely as I could I told him that I had done a lot of travelling and moves since joining the organization a little more than four years ago. Now I was looking forward to some stability for a while. He looked me straight in the eye and said in a sincere voice, "Len, there isn't one chance in 10 million that you will move out of Ottawa in the next four years. You can bank on it."

"Great," I said, "Then Shirlie and I can buy the new house we are looking at." "Good for you," he said, shaking my hand.

I almost ran out of his office back to mine and called Shirlie immediately. "Let's buy our house," I said. There wasn't a happier girl in Ottawa at that moment.

We went directly to the sales office after work, asked for some changes to the model, signed the papers and made our deposit. The house would be ready for us in June, which fit nicely in ending our rental lease.

I enjoyed my new job and working with the staff in the directorate. I worked directly for Commander Stu Murray who was the Assistant Director of Information Services and who had coaxed me into the business. He had been a reporter for a number of years at a Saint John, New Brunswick daily, before joining the Navy. He would teach me a lot about being a news editor.

The kids were both in school, Shirlie was ecstatic and I enjoyed my work. Life was good.

There was a problem I had to solve which related to my tour in Cyprus. Pte Cullen had gotten engaged while he was there. One day I saw him busily working away in our office and I asked him what he was doing. He told me he was making a list of invitees for his wedding, which would take place in April. "I better be on the list," I told him. He looked at me incredulously and said, "But you will be in Ottawa, you wouldn't come out to Victoria, BC to my wedding."

"Don't be a smart-ass, Cullen," I said, trying to look serious. "You had better invite me." And so he had. Now I was stuck with an invitation and what amounted to a promise to be there.

I mentioned it to Cdr Murray and he told me to discuss it with the General. At the next opportunity, I told the General my dilemma. He looked at me for a moment and then smiled as if I had solved a problem for him. "Look, Len" he said, "The Queen's Own Rifles, my old regiment, is having a reunion in Victoria on the same weekend, and they want me to attend. Why don't you fly out and I will tell Capt Bill Mountain, the organizer, that I am sending you in my place. I just don't have the time to go and that will at least make them think I am interested. Then you can go to the wedding and attend the reunion. While you are out there drop in on a few of the newspaper editors you met in Cyprus and just renew acquaintances."

Wow, I thought what a great solution and what a great boss.

I sent a reply to Private Cullen accepting his invitation and made my bookings to fly service air from Ottawa to Victoria and Vancouver return. I made appointments in Vancouver to see Himie Koshevoy and several of the other newsmen I had met.

Meanwhile, there was a warrant officer on my staff who, coming to work, passed the site where our house was being built and every day he would give me an update on the progress. "Walls up today sir. Looks great." I could only thank him and grin.

The day before I was to fly out, I was working on a project for Defence Minister Donald Macdonald. Shirlie had called and said that we needed to go and sign some papers to approve the changes that were being made. Cdr Murray was not in that day, so I went and told the General that I would be gone for about an hour in order to sign some papers for my new house. "Captain Brown is working on the project and we will have it done by the end of the day," I told him.

"That's fine Len," he said. As I headed for the door, suddenly he said, "House, what house?"

"The house that Shirlie and I are buying," I said rather curiously.

"Len come in and have a seat," he said motioning towards the couch in his office. He sat down, looked at me, and said in a rather grave voice, "Len, I think I am going to have to move you this summer."

My heart sank. I looked at him and words tumbled out of my mouth, "Move Where? When? Why? I thought you told me a few weeks ago there wasn't one chance in 10 million of me being moved in the next four years."

"I know," he said rather sadly, "But things change."

"Where am I going?" I insisted on asking.

"I really can't tell you at this moment."

"What do you mean you can't tell me?"

"What do I tell my wife, what about our house?" I stammered.

"Well, I wouldn't buy the house if I were you. You just have to trust me and I will tell you more in time."

191

I got up, ran out of the office, because I knew Shirlie was waiting for me in the parking lot beside NDHQ. I reached the car and got in. She was bubbling. "Honey, I just came from Simpson Sears and found some wonderful furniture that will suit our house and they have curtains on sale that I want to order. This is all working out so well."

I looked at her and knew I was about to destroy her dream. "Shirlie, can you take a joke?" "Sure," she said, "What's the joke?" I took a deep breath and said, "I think we are going to be moved this summer." She was speechless. Her radiant smile left and her face seemed to turn to stone. She didn't say anything for about two minutes. I just watched her trying to digest what I had told her. Then a single tear began to creep down her cheek.

"Where and when?" she gasped. "I don't know the answer to either question. General Bourgeois just said to trust him."

She didn't say a word. In fact she didn't speak to me for the next 24 hours. We drove to the building site, told the salesman our problem and he was very understanding. We signed some pages; got our deposit back and our dream house was gone!!

She drove me back to NDHQ and dropped me off without a word. When I got home that evening, Susan asked me why mummy was so upset. I told her that mummy was very disappointed at something that had happened. "Just hug her and tell her you love her; we will tell you later what is wrong. It has nothing to do with anything you or David have done," I said.

The next morning I left for my week trip to the west coast. She still wasn't speaking. She told me later that she wasn't mad at me. She just had a lump in her throat and was afraid if she spoke the tears would come and she wouldn't be able to stop them.

I stopped at NDHQ before going to the airport to catch my military scheduled flight. Commander Murray and General Bourgeois weren't in their offices, so I went to see Colonel Morrison, the Director. I told him the situation and demanded as strongly as I felt I could under the circumstances that he had to tell me what was going on. He picked up the phone, contacted General Bourgeois and put down the phone. He looked at me for a moment and then said, "Len, I am going to tell you but if you mention a word of this to anyone except to your wife, I will personally see that you have a certain part of your anatomy removed. Understood?" I agreed and he proceeded. "This summer you are going to be promoted to Major and moved to Winnipeg to become the Senior Information Officer for the DND Office of Information responsible for NW Ontario, Manitoba and Saskatchewan. But no one can know until the promotion and posting list comes out. Agreed?" he said.

I was stunned. I was a four-year Captain being promoted to Major. Since the integrated information organization had been formed, promotions in Information Services had apparently been given by seniority. I was number six in seniority out of eight Captains. This would certainly be a departure from the norm. In fact, I knew that the most senior captain already had his two and one half stripes on a uniform hanging in his closet at his home. I had seen it there recently when we were invited to his place for a cocktail party.

I thanked the Colonel, left the office and immediately tried to call Shirlie. No answer. I tried from the airport, from Trenton when we landed there and from Winnipeg during our stopover. Finally I called from Edmonton and she answered the phone. I hardly recognized her voice. It sounded so low and despondent.

"I have good news honey," I shouted into the phone, thinking I could cheer her up with the news, "I am being promoted and we are being moved to Winnipeg." There was a pause and finally she said, "What's the good news?"

She told me she was happy for me and we would talk later. At least that's a step in the right direction I thought.

I arrived in Victoria, checked into my hotel just had time to make it to the Queen's Own Rifles party, which was being held at Captain Mountain's house. It was a small postwar home but kept immaculately. There were about 20 former members of the Regiment, most of whom were high-ranking including two generals.

Captain Mountain must have had a very understanding wife, because the living room had been repainted in the Queen's Own colours for the event, green and red.

The Battalion formed in 1860, had a distinguished history, but in 1970 the 1st Battalion of the Queen's Own Rifles of Canada was rebadged as the 3rd Battalion of the Princess Patricia's Canadian Light Infantry (PPCLI). The Queen's Own Rifles lives on as a militia regiment based in Toronto.

I was welcomed as a representative of, "good old Lou" and the welcome became more effusive as the drinks flowed. I finally was able to excuse myself telling them that I had a wedding to go to the next day for a private from 3PPCLI, which required another drink and toast before I could get out the door.

The next afternoon, I went to the wedding. The church was full and most of the pews were filled with PPCLI members of Ron Cullen's military 'family.' His new bride arrived in a beautiful, white stretch limo. She was petite and very attractive and looked about 18. Made sense because Ron was only 19. Wow, I thought, I was a Flying Officer when I got married nine years earlier and I couldn't afford such luxury.

The wedding went off without a hitch and then we headed for the reception. There was a free flowing bar and lots of food being taken around by servers. Suddenly someone grabbed my arm and I turned around; it was Private Cullen. He obviously hadn't seen me before. He was grinning from ear to ear. I got a huge bear hug. "You came," he said, "You came... I can't believe it."

I spent the next 30 minutes being taken around and being introduced to members of his and his wife's family and his close friends.

"This is my boss from Cyprus," he explained to everyone. "He came all the way from Ottawa to be at my wedding. Can you believe that?" I wasn't sure at that moment, whether he was more pleased about being married or the fact that I had come to his wedding. It was a great event and I am glad I went. Private Cullen and his wife stopped in Winnipeg about a year later when he was being transferred from Victoria to Petawawa and stayed with us overnight. I lost track of him after that, but I will always remember him.

I stopped in Vancouver for a couple of days and visited the media guys who had visited me in Cyprus. They wined and dined me royally and remained great contacts over the rest of my career.

When I arrived home, Shirlie was in a much better mood. I had promised her during our phone calls, while I was away, that I would buy her a house in Winnipeg when we moved. We sat the kids down and told them that we were moving and that it was a promotion for daddy and we would be buying a new house. They would each have their own room which they could decorate as they wished. It didn't seem to faze them that we were moving after only one year in Ottawa. Although Susan was only eight, moving to Winnipeg would mean that this would be the eighth house in which she had lived.

Going back to work was more of a challenge. Recalling what Colonel Morrison had told me, I didn't mention a word to anyone. But it wasn't easy. The Warrant Officer would give me updates on the building of 'my' house two or three times a week. I would have to thank him and sound enthusiastic about its progress.

As the time for the promotion and posting lists came closer, people began to congratulate Captain Russ McKee who was the top of the seniority list. Others obviously saw themselves moving up the promotion ladder. It was tough because there weren't many promotions available and they depended on either someone in Information Services retiring or quitting the Canadian Forces.

One captain, senior to me, had his next few years planned out. "I think I will get my promotion next year. Then I am going to go to Lahr, Germany and run that office."

"Gee, that would be great," I told him.

"Don't worry, Len," he said, "Your turn is coming. I think you have lots of potential. Just keep doing what you are doing."

When the lists came out, all hell broke out. It didn't take long for everyone in the organization to know what had happened. I don't remember any Captains congratulating me. Commander Murray was particularly pleased that his protégé was doing so well.

I found out later that three of the Captains senior to me had put in a 'redress of grievance' protesting my promotion. Imagine the promotion board selecting someone based on merit rather than on seniority. In

194

retrospect, I don't know how promoting the most senior officer in rank had worked each time, unless it was a strong recommendation from our senior officers on annual performance reports.

Commander Murray suggested I take a trip out to Winnipeg to meet with the person I would be replacing and to find accommodation. It seemed like a good idea to get myself away from Ottawa for a week.

During my visit I looked at several new sub-divisions being built. Armed with Shirlie's criteria for a new house, I was able to narrow it down to a couple of choices. The most promising was located just a few miles west of the base. It was a three bedroom split-level backing onto a man-made lake and a block from a new school that both kids could attend. Even better, it had a large double-car garage. The price was $21,500. I called Shirlie, described the house and she told me she had a picture in her mind. "Buy it," she said. And the next day I did.

When doing the paper work, I found out that I wasn't making enough money to get the mortgage. But my promotion to Major, which would only be effective in December, five years after my promotion to Captain, would effectively put me over the $10,000 a year mark, which would make me eligible. Colonel Morrison had to sign a statement to Central Mortgage and Housing Corporation verifying my forthcoming salary!

We moved to Winnipeg in July and moved into our new house, which wasn't quite finished on the outside. Shirlie was ecstatic; the kids loved their rooms, which were downstairs and close to what we made as the TV room. I was back in everyone's good graces.

The responsibilities of my new office were to provide public affairs advice, guidance and assistance to the Commander of Prairie Region as well as for Command, Base and Station commanders throughout Northwestern Ontario, Manitoba and Saskatchewan. We were also responsible for preparing and implementing public affairs plans and programs concerning DND and Canadian Force's operations across the region.

I had one young Navy Sub-Lieutenant, Barry Frewer; a senior, very experienced Warrant Officer photographer, Bill Cole; and, a Secretary/Office Manager named Marion Hess, as my staff.

Marion had been the Personal Secretary to a Brigadier General at Training Command Headquarters and was offered the job in our office after the Brigadier General retired and was not replaced. She wasn't pleased about her perceived 'demotion' reporting to a major. But after a month, she told me she loved the people she was working with and the atmosphere. She became the backbone of our office.

Ten years before, I had left Winnipeg as a brand new flying officer with new wings on my chest. I was back as a Senior Officer with considerable responsibilities.

I now had eight years experience as a public information officer at various levels, from a unit information office on a base to heading up the news editing section at NDHQ. What I had learned was that in order to be successful in my job, I had two audiences with which I had to develop credibility and who had to trust me. The first and perhaps most important were the leaders and people with whom I would be dealing within the military.

This was a challenge. Over the years, I had met many commanders at various levels as well as young officers who regarded me as a leaky sieve to the media. Once, when I was entering a briefing room, a young officer said loudly, "Watch what you say, the press is here." And of course there was the Company Commander in Cyprus who told me bluntly that he thought my salary would be better spent on getting new boots for his men.

Fortunately in Winnipeg, the Commander of Prairie Region and of Training Command, Major General Bill Milroy was very familiar with the importance of a well-informed public information officer and knew the benefit that person could provide to this Command and the Canadian Forces. Fifteen years previously he had held the position of Director of Public Relations for the Canadian Army. So all I had to prove to him is that I knew what I was doing. With his support, it would be much easier to get the support of the other commanders and officers.

The second group that I had to convince that I was a straight shooter and could be trusted were the members of the media. The difficulty was that the military often thought that a PIO was an open door for the media to get all the information that they, the military, didn't want made public, while the media thought that the PIO was the stooge who was protecting the military and only telling them what the military wanted to release.

My predecessor, Major Carl Fitzpatrick, a former veteran journalist, had obviously developed a great rapport with the members of the Winnipeg media. They had nothing but great things to say about him and it made my life much easier to build on that relationship.

My neighbour had been flying as a pilot with a commercial company out of Churchill and been transferred to Winnipeg where he married and bought the house next door. Shirlie and I were often invited to their parties, during which we met Peter Mansbridge, one of his friends whom he knew from Churchill.

Peter had been working at the Churchill airport doing a variety of jobs including announcing flight departures. Apparently, a Winnipeg CBC executive heard his announcements and offered him a job as a News Reader in Winnipeg. It was the beginning of an illustrious career. So Peter and I got to know each other socially and worked together sometimes professionally.

I spent the next year working on developing relationships with both the military and the media throughout the Prairie Region.

Indeed, throughout my three years in Winnipeg, I never had a problem with any member of the media. That wasn't to say that they weren't aggressive in going after a story which involved the military, but they were always fair and gave us a chance to explain our side of the story before going to press or air. That was the early 70's and in general the media, with whom I had dealt over the past 10 years, had always been sympathetic to the military and what its members were doing.

The situation was not the same in the US. Their military was still heavily engaged in Vietnam. The war in Vietnam was the first television war. In the US, by the fall of 1967, 50 million people watched the television news each evening and 90 percent of each broadcast was devoted to the war in Vietnam. Military reports that they were making encouraging progress were dutifully broadcast by the media and supported by the public.

On January 30, 1968, the North Vietnamese and Viet Cong forces attacked more than 100 major cities and towns in South Vietnam, in what became known as the Tet Offensive. It took two weeks for US and South Vietnamese troops to regain control of Saigon, and nearly a month to retake the city of Hue. While the US and South Vietnamese forces won, it did show Americans that the force they faced was much stronger than expected.

When the Tet Offensive occurred, the attitude of the media changed. They began to report that the war was unwinnable. Coverage became predominantly negative with more emphasis on the US defeats and on civilian casualties, as well as negative stories on what the troops were doing, including drug use and racial conflicts. Perhaps most damaging for the soldiers' reputation was the negative images coming from the massacre in the village of My Lai when it was revealed that 350 civilians had been killed.

Toward the end of the war, when the US withdrew in 1973, veterans coming home from Vietnam were treated horribly. Some were called 'baby killers,' spat upon and refused services such as cab rides. It took a tremendous toll; some never recovered. When I attended Staff College in 1979-1980, no wonder my course director, a US Marine who had three tours in Vietnam, hated the media so much.

This change in reporting did not go unnoticed by members of the Canadian Forces. After all, the US troops were really 'brothers in arms' and they had fought side by side in two World Wars and Korea.

In Canada, this anti-military sentiment caused members of the military to increase their distrust towards the media. It didn't help me as a public information officer. My belief had always been to get our side of the story out as quickly as possible to try and ensure we got the facts out, rather than having the media relying on 'sources' that perhaps had a distorted or limited view of the facts. 'Maximum disclosure with minimum delay' had been the creed I followed. But it was becoming increasingly difficult to get my colleagues to provide meaningful information, even if it wasn't classified.

Fortunately in the Prairie Region, there weren't many controversial issues involving the military during my three-year stay. The military had been deeply rooted within communities dating back to the beginning of the Second World War. Military establishments were a big source of jobs and revenue for many communities. In Winnipeg, the main newsmaker was usually the search and rescue squadron which, when called into service, was nearly always successful and the media and public were very supportive.

A few days after I arrived, the Snowbirds flew their first demonstration flight at the Saskatchewan Home Coming Show on July 11, 1971. Ever since, they have performed throughout Canada and the US, as well as in Mexico, and have become a premium showpiece for the Canadian Forces.

Perhaps one of the most challenging public relations issues during my stay in Winnipeg began in September 1973 when Headquarters in Ottawa announced that DND and the Canadian Forces had reached an agreement with West Germany for their troops to come and train at Canadian Forces Base Shilo, Manitoba, near Brandon. Some 5,600 German troops annually would train at Shilo for the next ten years. The West German Government had agreed to bear the full cost of this training, including the cost of any Canadian Forces administrative personnel.

Negotiations had been going on for two years before the agreement was reached. I was invited to attend some of these negotiating meetings at CFB Shilo. They were fascinating. On one side of the table were the German officers with Canadian officers on the other. In the midst of the group was a German civilian officer who acted as translator. I always thought he was the most powerful man in the room because only he knew what he was telling each group.

There were some unusual discussions, not related to the actual training. One involved the movies. In 1971, X-rated movies were shown in German theatres but were not allowed in Canadian movie houses. After some discussion, it was resolved that every Wednesday, the base theatre would be closed to Canadians and open to German troops who could watch any movies they liked.

When it came to the subject of food, a decision was made that German meat cutters and cooks would be included in their staff so that they would be able to cut and prepare the meat as the Germans wanted.

Helmut Schmidt, the German Defence Minister, announced that he would make a visit to Shilo in the summer of 1972 to inspect the training facilities that the troops might be using. Shirlie and I already had plans finalized for our holidays during that time so I assigned my assistant Lt Barry Frewer to accompany the Minister and look after the many media expected to show up.

Because of all our several summer moves and my training courses, we hadn't had a family holiday for four years. I doubt David ever remembered going on holiday with his family. This one would take us to Calgary for the Stampede, to Lake Louise and Banff, and to the Edmonton Klondike Days. Shirlie had bought a new little Mazda RX7, one of the first of its kind in Canada, and this would be its first long trip. The hotels were booked and paid for and everyone, particularly the kids, was so excited about going.

One day I had a call from Colonel Morrison in Ottawa to discuss the visit of Defence Minister Schmidt. "I want you to go with him to look after the media and any interviews he has," he said, "This is a very important visit."

"But I have my vacation booked at that time. Everything is booked and paid for." I told him. "I assigned Lt Frewer to go with him. He will do fine."

"What part about 'I want you to go with him' don't you understand?" he said emphatically. And the conversation was over.

One more time I had to go home and tell Shirlie that plans had to be cancelled and tried to explain to the kids that we would go another time. We never did! It also took six months and a lot of pleading to get all our money back from the hotels.

Germany had become a member of the North Atlantic Treaty Organization (NATO) in 1955, 10 years after the Nazis were defeated in May 1945. NATO was formed in 1947 as a mutual defence group aimed at containing the expansion of the USSR in Europe.

At the end of the war, the Americans, British and French held occupied zones in Western Germany and West Berlin. The Soviets occupied Eastern Germany and East Berlin. In 1949, the zones occupied by the British, French and US were combined to establish the Federal Republic of Germany. The Soviets responded by establishing the German Democratic Republic in East Germany.

The military occupation of West Germany by the Allies formally ended on May 5, 1955. Four days later, West Germany was made a member of NATO. Five days later, the Soviets established the Warsaw Pact, a military alliance between Russia, and its Eastern satellites, including East Germany.

Millions had died in the Second World War in Europe, many of whom were civilians. Thousands of Europeans, including Germans who had survived the Nazi death camps immigrated to Canada, and particularly western Canada after the war looking for a new and better life. Like my Mom and Dad and me, most had few possessions. But they brought their memories. The idea that a large group of German troops would be training on a Canadian base would not likely sit well with those who had suffered so terribly at the hands of the Nazis. The difficulty would be in convincing these people that the Germans were on our side!!

Fortunately, the media reported the story in a very balanced fashion. Following the announcement, there were negative letters to the editor, but basically the fact that they would be coming did not become a huge story. But I knew from feedback that there were large pockets of resentment amongst the many ethnic communities in Western Canada, particularly in Winnipeg.

One day I invited Peter Warren to lunch. Peter was a radio talk show host and moderated CJOB - Winnipeg's Action Line. He was a well-known and respected broadcaster who ran the daily three-hour, call-in show every weekday. He had thousands of listeners throughout the province and as far out as the radio station could be heard.

I discussed the concern we had about the German soldiers coming to train and the backlash that might ensue from the public. If someone had been living in Czechoslovakia or Poland in 1939, or in Leningrad or Moscow or Stalingrad during the war years, it would be difficult not to feel hatred and loathing towards the Germans. I told him that having been born in London and growing up during the war and losing my home three times, I understood why people would feel this way but there were several reasons why these troops should be looked upon differently.

Peter had been born in London in 1941 so he didn't have to be convinced.

First, most of these soldiers would not have been born in 1939, when the war began, or even in 1945, when the war ended in Europe.

Second, Germany was a member of NATO, our ally for the past 16 years, and indeed was on the front lines if the Soviets decided to attack.

Third, Canadian Army and Air Force units had been based in German since the early 1950s as part of NATO forces. Germans had had to put up with our troops on their soil for more than 20 years. On Army training exercises, it was not uncommon for tanks to go through German farmers' fields causing havoc. Years later when posted to Germany, I asked the mayor of a small town near the Czechoslovakian border, if he was upset with the tanks going through their fields. He told me that it didn't make him happy but he would rather have our tanks than those sitting 15 km to the east.

Getting the soldiers here, looking after them and the money they would spend, I pointed out, could mean a large infusion of money for businesses in Manitoba.

I also reminded Peter that German civilians had suffered horribly and died during the Second World War, some because of the Allies but many because of the incredibly cruel, vicious Nazi regime. It was claimed that approximately 1,100,000 civilians died due to military activity and crimes against humanity. Although hard to determine with any real accuracy, an estimated 400,000 to 2.4 million German civilian deaths occurred due to war-related famine and disease. No doubt family members of those who died now resided in Canada.

A couple of weeks later, with lots of pre-show promotion on the subject, Peter ran a three-hour program devoted to the subject of German troops coming to train at Shilo. He opened the show using my comments as the basis of setting a tone for the discussion. The lines were jammed. There were some hate calls damning the "Germans to hell" and stating they shouldn't be allowed in Canada. But many seemed to understand the points he had made. At the end of the three hours, which had given many an opportunity to vent, I felt that there would be greater acceptance of the troops coming. I used the same lines whenever I talked to members of the media about the subject. Given the editorials, it seemed to work.

The Commander of Prairie Region held a meeting a few days before the first troops arrived in March 1974 to discuss preparations for their arrival.

A concern discussed was the safety and security of the troops on arrival. One senior officer suggested that we put up temporary fencing so that the troops could walk from the airplane to the buses with no one able to get close to them. The negative images being shown on TV stations around the world flashed before my eyes.

I protested and fortunately the Commander agreed. The day the troops arrived, there were few people to greet them except for the official greeters and the hordes of media. All went smoothly.

The German troops would continue to come to CFB Shilo until 2000, with more than 140,000 being trained at the base during those 27 years. When they first arrived, RCMP Units in surrounding areas were apparently alerted to the fact that there might be trouble between the troops and the locals. A former president of the Brandon Chamber of Commerce was quoted as saying, "We didn't know what was going to happen when they arrived. But it turned out there was no trouble at all. They integrated into the community; some married local girls and stayed in the community. We are sorry to see them go," she told the media.

By 1971, I had worked with several ministers including Paul Hellyer, Leo Cadieux and Donald Macdonald, albeit not very closely. I had even been involved with helping to organize media coverage when Prime Minister Pierre Elliot Trudeau made a brief stopover in Cyprus in 1970 to pay his respects to President Archbishop Makarios. But I wasn't that aware of the personal side of politicians.

The start of my education in that area began in Winnipeg in 1972.

Edgar Benson replaced Defence Minister Donald Macdonald on January 28, 1972, and a few months later, paid his first visit to Winnipeg. At the end of his tour of the various facilities, a reception was held in his honour in the Officers' Mess. I will never forget his speech. He was so 'gung ho' and positive towards the military. He had served as a sergeant with the Royal Canadian Artillery during the Second War, and later graduated from Queen's University in Kingston.

He had represented the riding of Kingston, within which stood the Royal Military College, since 1962. He told us how proud he was to be Minister of National Defence and how he would do everything in his power to further the well-being of the Canadian Forces. He got a thunderous ovation. We needed that assurance because the Liberal government under Prime Minister Trudeau, in the late 1960s, had cut the Canadian Forces by 20% and frozen the Defence budget at $1.8 billion.

Officers at all levels left that reception optimistic that we had someone, a veteran, who would fight for us in Cabinet. Perhaps we (I) were naive or just desperately wanting someone who would stand up and fight for us. Equipment desperately needed replacing, our numbers had been significantly reduced, and our pay frozen.

On August 31, not long after that speech, Defence Minister Edgar Benson announced his retirement from the Canadian Government. Reportedly, he chose not to run in the forthcoming federal election, which would be held on October 30, 1972. He had been minister for seven months. One day after retirement, Edgar Benson was appointed as President of the Canadian Transport Commission, a position he held for 10 years following which he was named Canadian Ambassador to Ireland.

This no doubt added to the growing concern amongst military personnel about how important the military was to the government and was probably the beginning of my being very cautious about any promise made to me by a politician.

To make matters worse no replacement was named. Rather, Jean-Eudes Dubé, Minister of Public Works, was appointed acting Defence Minister for six days, from September 1st to September 6, when MP Charles Drury was appointed for the second time as acting Defence Minister. He had served for a week, from September 17 to September 23, 1970 between the appointments of Leo Cadieux and Donald Macdonald. Finally on November 27, 1972, after the Liberals had won a minority government in the election, James Richardson was named as Defence Minister.

In early June 1972, I received a phone call from Ev Cowan who worked in Ottawa in Parliamentary Affairs, which was part of the Director General Information Service Organization. He was organizing a 10-day tour of military installations across western Canada for the Standing Committee on External Affairs and National Defence. He wanted my photographer, Warrant Officer Bill Cole and me to assist in the escort of this group, which numbered more than 20 members of parliament. He had already cleared this with my boss.

Ev Cowan told me later that he had organized this tour as a result of a number of senior officers, including generals, complaining to him that politicians did not understand or appreciate what the military was doing, and the problems serving members had to face.

The Air Force Cosmopolitan aircraft devoted to the group landed in Winnipeg and picked up two local MPs, along with WO Cole and myself and we headed west. I would spend almost all my waking hours with this group. We visited all the major bases across the west, had great briefings and met many senior regular force and militia officers who were anxious to take advantage of this opportunity to brief this important parliamentary group. Our last stop was in Yellowknife, NWT, and next we were dropped off in Winnipeg.

Along with the members of the Committee, I had learned a great deal about the military and the day-to-day problems they faced under the present day budgetary constraints. But equally, I learned a lot about the parliamentarians themselves.

This group was all male. They represented a slice of Canadian society: farmers, doctors, lawyers, businessmen, ex-military and used-car salesmen. They were members of the Liberal government, the Conservative opposition party, as well as the New Democratic Party, and the Social Credit Party. I believe they were all serious about meeting their responsibilities as members of the committee, which basically was to examine issues of External Affairs and Defence policy with a view to making sure they were the best for Canada.

Being a Member of Parliament brought considerable pressure on each and every member. They had to respond to the demands of their party and its leader. They spent long hours in meetings during the week and, for most, had to travel long distances on Fridays to be in their constituencies for the weekend. Here they were expected to be available for their constituents, to solve problems, listen to complaints and take part in endless functions. More often than not, their families got last priority. I had one member of the group tell me later that if you could be elected to two terms of office and still keep your marriage together, you must have angel's wings on your back.

They held these responsible positions, but I discovered that they were also very human. They seemed to react to this pressure in different ways. On this trip, there were those who swore, told off-colour jokes; some who needed to have a 'Bloody Mary' in their hands as soon as the 'wheels were in the well' of the aircraft. Some drank a little too much. One carried a little black book and when we would arrive in a major centre would disappear as soon as the official agenda was over, not to be seen until the next official event. Perhaps, this trip was a welcome chance to let their hair down. I would find out more about the impact of the pressure on individuals being Members of Parliament as my career progressed over the years.

The 2nd Battalion, Princess Patricia's Canadian Light Infantry, based in Winnipeg was assigned to a six-month tour of peacekeeping duties in Cyprus in October 1972. Naturally the Winnipeg and Manitoba area media were very interested. In November, accompanied by WO Cole, I escorted a group of 12 senior media representatives to the island to see 'their troops' in action.

Canadian troops wearing the blue beret on peacekeeping duties had now been in Cyprus for more than eight years. LCol Jim Allen, the commander of 2nd PPCLI, had served previously in Cyprus in 1967. He had made a reconnaissance visit to Cyprus prior to deploying the Battalion, and 25 years later he stated in a book he wrote that, "Peacekeeping progress had almost been nil from July 1967 to October 1972. He suggested that, "Leaving UN officials in one mission for too long results in failure to come up with new approaches."

During my six-month tour on the Island, I had taken many media visitors to meet with the two peace negotiators: Glafcos Clerides for the Greek Cypriots, and Rauf Denktash for the Turks. The briefings were separate and always followed the same pattern. Denktash played the part of the spokesman for the 'threatened minority' representing about 20% of the population. He would express his immense gratitude for the presence of the Canadian troops who, he noted, were among the finest UN soldiers, and emphasize his confidence in the contingent's ability to keep the Turkish community safe from further atrocities that had already been inflicted on his people in the 1964 fighting. Although the negotiations had been going on for years, their talks were stymied for many reasons: by fears of giving away too much, by pressure from Athens and Ankara and by walls of mistrust between their communities.

Mr. Denktash told the Manitoba media group that the problems of the 1960's were, "as difficult to solve as they were in the beginning. A solution that would assure the Turks of their sovereignty must be found, as anything else would be enslavement for us."

At the end of the interview, he had the group taken to an abandoned crumbling building where, supposedly, the blood stains of victims remained on the walls of what had been their homes in 1964.

Clerides was much blander, stating only the facts. I am sure he knew what statements Denktash had been making to us. He told the group that he was, "considerably optimistic that a solution will be found within a reasonable amount of time." Asked what such a time period might be, he said between December 15, 1972 and June 1973. He based this time frame on the fact that although he and Mr. Denktash had been unable to arrive at a common proposal, a two-man team of experts, one Greek and one Turkish, had now been able to do so and would shortly be presenting a joint paper.

Talks between the two long-time acquaintances had been broken off, but because this new proposal was reported to have found common ground, negotiations were set to resume.

That was November 1972. In 2018, Cyprus remains a divided island!

Notwithstanding the attempts to find a peaceful solution, the presence of peacekeeping forces was a huge economic boost for Cyprus. Millions of dollars have been spent since 1964 to keep the peacekeepers on the island. Indeed, it was not uncommon that when the UN mandate for keeping peacekeepers in Cyprus was drawing close to an end, there often would be a series of skirmishes that were touted by both sides as those that could easily lead to another outbreak of fighting if UN troops were not left there. Cyprus is a complex issue.

The media group was given access to virtually all aspects of life for the Canadian soldiers serving as peacekeepers. They also travelled extensively around the island to see many of the historic sites and attractions. They met ordinary people who allowed them to get an insight as to how the average Cypriot lived and what they thought about the current situation. Although senior experienced journalists, they were over-awed with what they had seen and learnt in just one week. Their respect for the Canadian Forces, and more particularly their home battalion, was elevated considerably.

Shortly after arriving back in Winnipeg, I had the opportunity to meet our new Minister of Defence, James Richardson, at a function at the Officers' Mess. He had been appointed on November 27. In the past five years, we had had three full-time ministers and three acting ministers. I am not sure if that was just because of circumstances or an indication of the importance given to the Defence portfolio by the Federal Government. Mr. Richardson would stay for four years.

James Richardson was born in Winnipeg in March 1922. After attending Queen's University, he joined the Royal Canadian Air Force and flew Liberator bombers on anti-submarine patrols from Labrador and Iceland during WWII. After the War he joined the family company James Richardson and Sons and became Chief Executive Officer and Chairman in 1966. He ran for election in 1968 and served in several portfolios in the Trudeau cabinet until his appointment as Defence Minister.

Minister Richardson lived in St James-Assiniboia, a well-to-do section of Winnipeg and not that far from the base, but spent the majority of his time in Ottawa or on official visits to Canadian military bases.

It wasn't until May of 1973 that my association with the Minister became much closer. He was headed to Ankara, Turkey, for the annual Nuclear Planning Group meeting, which would begin in mid-May. A decision had been made in Ottawa that the Minister, accompanied by a group of national media, would stop in Cyprus while en route to visit our troops and make a courtesy call on President Archbishop Makarios. My boss, Col Morrison, called me from Ottawa and told me that he wanted me to fly over in advance to help set up the program and escort the media group and bring them back to Ottawa, since they wouldn't be allowed to cover the meetings in Ankara.

I only had a couple of days notice so I quickly made flight arrangements. When I arrived in Frankfurt, FRG, I was told that the Cyprus Airways aircraft was broken. There were only eight passengers on the direct flight to Cyprus so arrangements were made for us to stay in a hotel and fly out the following day. This made me a day late and I only had 24 hours to work on the plan for his visit. The Battalion had a draft plan which included a formal mess dinner on the night of his arrival.

Recognizing that he would have worked all day in the House of Commons and then flown in the slow Yukon aircraft from Ottawa to Lahr and then Lahr to Nicosia, I knew he would be exhausted. I strongly recommended that they change the dinner to the following evening and just give a supper in his hotel room and let him get some rest.

The group arrived and the Minister followed by the media toured the Canadian outposts and received in-depth briefings from the battalion officers and men on their responsibilities.

A hastily arranged meeting with President Archbishop Makarios went well. The President was very cordial and, in front of the Canadian media, expressed his gratitude to the Minister for the presence of, "the wonderful, experienced Canadian troops" in Cyprus.

205

Minister Richardson meets Archbishop Makarios at the Presidential palace.

The Minister and his small entourage left for Turkey, and the media and I waited one day to catch the scheduled flight back from Cyprus to Ottawa.

We got back to Ottawa and I jumped on a flight to Winnipeg. When I got back I was exhausted. Shirlie and the kids met me at the airport. I was cross and not very receptive to their enthusiastic greeting. The kids were upset.

Later, Shirlie told me bluntly, "Don't ever come home like that again. Next time stay in a hotel somewhere so you are more like a human being when you get home." From that day on, I followed her advice!

One Sunday morning, shortly after getting back, I received a call from Mr. Richardson at about 10 am. He wanted to know if I was busy. Not sure what to say, I said no, wondering why he was calling me at this strange hour. "I want to discuss something with you, but are you sure I am not interfering with you and your family, maybe going to church?"

"Certainly not sir," I replied. "When do you want to see me?"

"Could you come over to my house now?" he said.

Moments later I was in my car and headed across the river. I drove down a street backing onto the river. The street was filled with huge homes on very large lots.

I arrived at an estate and drove through gates, past a small guesthouse or perhaps it was the gardener's house at the entrance. The long driveway ended at a large stately home, which might have been where he and his wife Shirley had been living since they were married in 1947.

He greeted me, invited me in and we sat down in his spacious, antiquely furnished living room. He wanted reassurance that he wasn't preventing me from doing something I had planned. Mrs. Richardson, came in, introduced herself, and said, "Well Jim, aren't you going to offer Len a drink?" He did, and I politely declined. 10:30 in the morning was a little early for me to have a drink, even with the Minister of National Defence.

Then the Minister began to describe his problem. As it turned out, it had nothing to do with the military or defence. It was an issue involving some First Nations people who lived in his constituency. He wasn't quite sure how to handle it and was obviously concerned about any public reaction to what he might do or say. He wanted my opinion from a public relations perspective. After considering the matter, I suggested what I thought would be best for him to do and say. He thanked me and about an hour after arriving I was on my way home.

I was floored! This man was rich, influential, and a Cabinet Minister. He could have called upon a host of people to help him. But he chose to call me on a Sunday morning to discuss his problem and seek my advice. I had obviously gained his confidence.

A month later, I made a visit to NORAD Headquarters in Colorado Springs, Colorado. I spent a couple of days meeting with members of the information staff with whom I would be dealing when any event involved NORAD. Over a drink one evening, I told the Director, a full Colonel, about the meeting I had had with the minister at his home. He was incredulous. That would never happen in the US he told me. If the Secretary of Defense wanted to talk to anyone in the Defense Department it would have to start with one of his staff calling the Director of Information in the Pentagon and going from there. "I don't think it would ever get to the level where a major would be talking one on one to the Secretary," he stated.

It just pointed out the difference in our two systems. A few years later, when Alan McKinnon was Minister, I was told that he personally telephoned a staff captain who had written the first draft of a paper which had been sent to him and asked the captain to come to his office. Apparently he had an issue with what was being recommended. He wanted to make sure this is what the captain had recommended and to ask him personally why he had done so. Although, he was only Minister for nine months in the Joe Clark Cabinet, apparently he did this on a fairly regular basis.

207

Minister McKinnon had retired from the Canadian Forces as a major some years before and knew how the system worked. He knew how briefing notes that were authored at the desk office level were changed for a variety of reasons as they made their way up the chain before arriving on his desk.

It was now almost a year since we had moved to Winnipeg and I had had little time to spend with my family. Indeed with all our postings and my courses, we really hadn't been on a holiday as a family except to visit Shirlie's mother in PEI and my parents in Creemore. Not much fun for the kids!

So I sat down with Shirlie and suggested we take the kids to Disney World in Orlando. It had opened less than two years earlier, on October 1st, 1971, and was getting rave reviews. She was enthusiastic; we told the kids. Susan was 10 and Dave was 8. They were 'over the moon.'

The next evening I attended a meeting of the executive committee of St James Anglican Church. I was a member of the committee and also editor of the church newspaper. I mentioned our plan to one of my colleagues, who owned a travel office franchise in the city, to ask if he could help us arrange the holiday. He said not only would he help but had a suggestion which would make the vacation that much more enjoyable. He told me that a new cruise ship was making its maiden cruise with selected passengers and he had been offered a cabin for him and his family at an extraordinarily low fare.

"We just can't go," he said. "So why don't you take it. I will give it to you at the same price they offered it to me." Wow! I thought. Wait until I tell Shirlie and the kids about this. We had never dreamed about going on a cruise.

Plans were made and in late June just after school closed, off we went. We stayed in a motel in Tampa, which had bus transfers to Disney World every morning. Not only could we visit Disney World but also other sites close to Tampa like Busch Gardens.

We had great fun. The kids were ecstatic. It was a wonderful time for us to spend with the kids and not worry about work. We couldn't wait to get on the ship.

I had told David that he could have anything he wanted when it came to food and even order meals to our cabin. "Does that mean I can order milkshakes?" he said. "As many as you want, every day if you want." The look on his face was worth the cost of the trip.

The last day before we were to leave for Miami to board the cruise ship, we went to Weeki Wachee Springs, the city of Mermaids, just north of Tampa. A petting zoo and a jungle cruise added to the wonderful show put on by the mermaids.

But all the kids could talk about on the way back to the motel was that we would be leaving in the morning to head for Miami and the ship.

When we walked into the room, the red light was flashing on our phone indicating there was a message waiting for us. Somehow I knew this was not good news. It was Shirlie's brother Robin. "Call immediately," he said, but didn't say why.

I called and he told me. "Our mom has died. She is being buried tomorrow. Can you get Shirlie home to PEI for the funeral?" My heart sank. It was bad enough to tell Shirlie that her mother had died. But perhaps even worse to tell our young children that their grandmother had died and now we couldn't go on the cruise.

With the help of a sympathetic airline staff, I was able to get Shirlie home in time for the funeral. The kids and I flew back to Winnipeg to be joined a few days later by Shirlie. What had started out as a planned family vacation never to be forgotten, turned out to be just that, but for the wrong reason.

A couple of weeks later, I received a call from MGen Gus Cloutier, the Chief of Staff to the Minister. He told me that a trip was being planned to visit the Minister's counterparts in a number of Commonwealth countries around the world. The trip would start in two weeks and take 28 days. The Minister had asked that I accompany him to look after a group of seven media who would travel on the aircraft. He also asked that I bring along two photographers, one for still-photography and one for cine.

Gen Cloutier told me that Mrs. Richardson would be on the trip and I was welcome to bring my wife Shirlie along to provide female company for her.

Shirlie was excited when I told her. But reality soon set in. Susan and David couldn't be left alone or with a sitter for a month. We had no family close by. My Dad was still working and Mom wouldn't be able to leave him and come out on her own for a month.

Reluctantly, I called Gen Cloutier and explained why Shirlie couldn't come. She has never forgotten that missed opportunity. We realized it is one of the facts that one must face when following a military career. Family is not likely to be close by. Another is that every time I moved, which was often, Shirlie would have to quit her job and try to find another wherever we moved. When she was successful, it usually meant she had to start at the bottom, certainly in seniority. She had gone from being a nursing teacher at the VG Hospital in Halifax to a low-level floor nurse in Ottawa. But she did get a good job in Winnipeg at the Health Science Centre where she helped to set up one of the first kidney dialysis units in Canada.

The 707 aircraft landed in Winnipeg on August 5 to pick up Mrs. Richardson, WO Bill Cole and myself, and we were soon off on the first leg of our journey, which took us to Hawaii. We stayed overnight and the next day continued on to Fiji where we spent another night. On the third day we flew to New Zealand, which was our first official stop on the tour.

Onboard we had seven newsmen including a CBC film crew, and several reporters from various papers across Canada. Geoff Scott worked for a Hamilton daily paper. His wife Priscilla, who would provide company for Mrs. Richardson, accompanied him. As a teenager, Geoff had been a budding impressionist. He formed a partnership with another budding impressionist named Rich Little. They were performing professionally in Ottawa by the age of 17.

Rich was an usher at the Elgin Street Theatre in Ottawa and mastered many of his voices at the back of the theatre. He made his American television debut on CBS's 'The Judy Garland Show' in 1964. He never looked back and has had a brilliant career.

Five years after our trip, Geoff Scott would run and be elected in Hamilton Wentworth as a Federal Member of Parliament. Our paths would cross numerous times, both professionally and socially, during his journalistic and parliamentary careers.

Priscilla was a star in her own right. Granddaughter of former Conservative Prime Minister Arthur Meighen, she had a North American hit song, 'Man in the Raincoat,' at the age of 14. The hit gave her an opportunity to appear on the Ed Sullivan Show, Perry Como, Soupy Sales and CBC-TV. The record sold a million copies and led to a recording contract, which included appearing beside Elvis Presley, Pat Boone, and fellow Canadians The Four Lads in a music documentary.

Her career faltered when apparently her parents objected to her rising fame. She went to the University of Toronto and worked in Geophysics before moving to Ottawa as Geoff's wife. She did make a comeback in the 1980s, re-recording her 1960s hit as well as making several albums and performing with Big Bands and symphony orchestras.

Mrs. Richardson had apparently spent some time in New Zealand and was familiar with the Maoris. She and Priscilla started changing slightly some of the words for 'Now is the Hour' to reflect our thanks to the Maori. The song has often been described as a traditional Maori song. They assembled the group in the aircraft en route to New Zealand and helped us practice singing the Maori words:

"Now is the Hour,
When we must say goodbye.
Po atarau, E moea iho nei"

Led by the wonderfully powerful voice of Priscilla, we managed to sing a respectable version by the time we landed.

That evening we were guests at the Canadian High Commissioner's home in Wellington. The featured entertainment was a group of Maori who sang and did their ritual dances. When they finished, Minister Richardson asked the High Commissioner if his group could sing a song. The High Commissioner had a quizzical look on his face but of course said yes. We assembled in front of the Maori and sang our version. The reaction was immediate. The Maoris grinned, laughed and then began to cry. When we finished, they came rushing forward and hugged each of us. The High Commissioner was ecstatic. Nothing we could have done would have led to a better relationship between Canada and this group, and what we had done would be soon transmitted to the whole Maori community.

210

The next day, the Minister met his New Zealand counterpart for several hours of talks and we were then off to Rotorua, a wonderful small city first settled by the Maori. Rotorua is famous for its geothermal features, including spouting geysers, bubbling mud pools and colourful, sinister terraces. Here we were hosted at a reception by the Mayor and entertained by another group of Maori singers and dancers.

We flew from Rotorua to Sydney, Australia. At the airport, a large contingent of media had gathered and the Minister gave an impromptu press conference. He emphasized the importance of the Pacific Rim Nations working together in a common defence and told them of his forthcoming meeting with his Australian counterpart, Lance Barnard.

Outside the airport, the Australian government had assembled a number of staff cars. Much to my surprise I was escorted to a big black car with a driver who introduced himself and told me he would be at my disposal 24 hours a day during our stay over the weekend.

We arrived at our hotel in downtown Sydney. Once inside, a petite, trim, white-haired woman rushed up and gave me a tremendous hug. It was my Aunt Lily. I hadn't seen her in 15 years.

I had sent a letter telling her when we would be arriving. She had found out where we would be staying and decided to be there with her new husband Lou to greet me on arrival. We went up to my spacious accommodation where my bags had already been deposited.

They had brought a bottle of fine Australian wine with them. We opened it, poured glasses and toasted each other. Bill Cole was in the room beside me and came over to take a photo of the reunion.

Aunt Lily reminded her husband that the roast in the oven would be done within the hour so he should order a cab. I was expected to come home with them for dinner. At this point, as Lou picked up the room phone, I said, "No need for that Lou, I have my car and driver waiting. I'll just call down and have him come up to the door to pick us up." Lou hung up the phone and Lily looked at me in amazement.

The car was at the door with the driver holding the door open for us to get in. Once comfortably in, Aunt Lily said, "Driver, what is your name?" "Albert," he replied politely. "Well, I will call you Albert," she said, not looking for his permission.

"Albert, this is a government car right." "Yes mum," he replied. "Paid for by my taxes no doubt," she snorted. "Well, Albert, I don't care how important this guy is," she said looking at me sideways, "I used to change his diapers, so from now on you will take direction from me." Albert looked in the rear view mirror at me and I gave him a quick nod. "Yes mum," he replied, suitably humbly with a grin on his face. And so we were off to Lou and Lily's apartment.

When we arrived, she invited Albert in for a drink. He thanked her but said he was on duty and refused. "Be back to pick him up in about three hours," she said and off he went.

The following day, a Saturday, the official party, which included the Minister, Mrs. Richardson, MGen Cloutier, the Minister's aide and myself, were taken on a tour of Sydney. It began with a cruise around the beautiful Sydney harbour. It is often called the most beautiful natural harbour in the world. Its 240 kilometres of shorelines encompass 54 kilometres of sparkling waters. On this day, the waters were dotted with hundreds of sailing boats and ferries.

We stopped at the Taronga Park Zoo said to have the best views of any Zoo in the world. Situated on a hill, it overlooks the harbour, the Sydney Harbour Bridge and the Opera House. We had a two-hour tour encountering fascinating Australian animals including the cuddly Koala bears.

The new Opera House was our next stop. It was finished but not officially opened when we took our tour.

The project began in January 1957 and it was seven years before the model of the structure was complete. Almost seventeen years passed before the building was finished. The original cost was estimated to be $7 million; the final cost was $102 million.

Naturally, there was some controversy, but the Sydney Opera house is a masterpiece of modern architecture, recognized and admired around the world and proudly boasted of by the Australian people.

The concert hall has 2,679 seats. Standing on the vast stage, Minister Richardson was encouraged to sing a few bars to demonstrate the phenomenal acoustics in the hall. He did so. Mrs. Richardson was the only one who dared tell him, "not to give up his day job."

Two months after we toured the building, Queen Elizabeth II officially opened the Opera House to the public on October 20, 1973.

The last stop was for a late lunch at the Royal Prince Alfred Yacht Club which had its founding in 1867. After a great lunch we were taken back to our hotel.

That evening, my Aunt Francis and her husband invited me to their house for dinner. There I met some of my cousins whom I had not seen since we left London more than 25 years earlier. They had a beautiful home situated on a hill overlooking the north end of the harbour.

In response to my Uncle's question during dinner, I told him about our wonderful tour that day concluding with the lunch at the RPAYC. He looked at me and said, "I consider myself to be quite successful and have a wonderful business, but with all my money, you did something today that I could not do, "Incredulously, I replied, "What could that be?" "Have lunch at the RPAYC." And before I could ask the obvious question, he looked at me with a wry smile and said, "I'm Jewish."

I never checked and can only assume it was true. Hopefully that has changed since.

Sunday, Albert picked me up at the hotel and Lily and Lou at their apartment. We did a drive around the city partly narrated by Lily and partly by Albert. That afternoon we dropped them off at their home. Lily said good-bye and tears began to stream down her face. I could read her thoughts. I will never see you again Len. It was true. She died nine years later on May 1, 1982, at the age of 76.

On Monday, we flew to Canberra, where meetings were held with Lance Barnard. During the meetings, Minister Richardson mentioned Canada's latest White Paper on defence, "Defence in the 70s", which had been released two years earlier. Mr. Barnard admitted he hadn't seen it. The Minister turned to me and said, "Len, would you run out and get a couple of copies for the Minister, please?"

I knew the books were safely locked away in the aircraft parked at the Canberra airport. Getting them was a challenge. First, I had a driver take me to the motel where the crew was staying. I found a sleepy warrant officer who complained that he had only been in bed for a few hours. But he had the keys to the aircraft and could get into the baggage compartment where the box of books was kept. It took about 15 minutes of searching to find the box. Then we drove back to the Parliament buildings where the meeting was taking place. About an hour after the request, I slipped into my seat and passed the two books to the Minister. He said, "Thanks, Len" and passed them to Minister Barnard, probably not even realizing how long I had been gone.

It would be 14 years, in 1987, before the Federal Government released the next White Paper called, 'Challenge and Commitment: A Defence Policy for Canada.' Some have said it reflected the low priority given to the military by the Federal Government. During that period, debate and discussion of defence issues were minimal.

Before we left Canberra, we were taken on a tour of the Australian War Memorial, the national memorial to all its armed forces. It was opened in 1941 and is regarded as one of the most significant war memorials in the world. Years later, Canadian officials came to scout this structure when looking to build the beautiful new War Museum in Ottawa.

The Memorial consists of the Hall of Memory with the tomb of the Unknown Soldier, the Memorials Galleries (museum) and the Research Centre (records)

Although all of it was magnificent, what struck me most was the Hall of Memory, which is a narrow courtyard with a memorial pool surrounding an eternal flame. Above the courtyard is the Roll of Honour, a series of plaques that name the 102,000 Australian men and women killed in conflict from the various wars in which Australia has been engaged. The plaques show only the names and not rank or any awards since, as it says, "All are equal in death."

The Memorial was a place that I knew I had to spend more time and promised myself that I would return someday and bring Shirlie. It took more than 30 years to fulfill that promise.

Our next stop was Brisbane where we were taken to the Canungra Jungle Training Centre. It was originally established during World War II to train troops for combat in the South West Pacific area. During the 50's and 60's it fulfilled a similar role.

When Australia began sending troops to South Vietnam in the 1960s, the Centre increased its training program. As part of the pre-deployment training, 10,000 soldiers were sent for training each year before undertaking their tour of duty.

Australia's commitment to Vietnam began in 1962 with a group of 30 military advisors. Over the next ten years that increased to a peak of 7,672 Australian troops deployed in South Vietnam or in support of the Australian troops there. The Vietnam War was the longest and most controversial war Australia has ever fought. It had widespread support in the beginning but as the size of the involvement grew, a vocal anti-war movement developed.

Withdrawal of the troops began in November 1970 and by January 11, 1973 Australian involvement in hostilities in Vietnam had ceased except for an Embassy platoon which remained until July 1973. Approximately 60,000 Australians served in the war; 521 were killed and more than 3,000 wounded.

When we arrived, there was a platoon of soldiers from the Princess Patricia's Canadian Light Infantry taking the training course. We watched some of our soldiers dragging themselves on their bellies through water filled mud holes and under heavy obstacles. It was evident that this course was designed to be as demanding and realistic as possible. The training, combined with the unfriendly, sometimes deadly, insects and wild animals abundant in the area, made it a course I was glad I would never have to take. Recalling the Winter Bush and Arctic survival courses I had taken in Alberta and the Arctic in 1961, made me realize that all I had to do was survive harsh weather conditions and a lack of food.

We left Australia and headed for Hong Kong. This was a difficult and emotional stop for the Minister. He had joined the RCAF but could just as easily have joined his hometown's 1st Battalion Winnipeg Grenadiers, which had been based in Winnipeg since 1910.

One thousand, nine hundred and seventy five members of the Royal Rifles of Canada from Quebec and the Winnipeg Grenadiers arrived in Hong Kong on November 16, 1941 to reinforce the Hong Kong garrison. The force did not have all of its equipment, as a ship carrying its vehicles was diverted to Manila, Philippine Islands. Many of the Canadian soldiers did not have much field experience before arriving in Hong Kong. But the task facing them was supposed to be one of simple garrison duty.

There has been considerable discussion since the end of WWII as to whether Canadian troops should have been sent to Hong Kong. Some argue no, citing that the British Army Chief of Staff viewed Hong Kong as incapable of a prolonged defence or of being relieved, although this was apparently never made known to the Canadian Government. Historian JL Granatstein says that at the time, when asked by the British, we were still psychologically a British colony and that Canada had no choice but to send troops to Hong Kong. However, he states that in hindsight, of course, this was a grave mistake.

The Japanese attack began three weeks later, on December 8, less than eight hours, in real time, after the attack on Pearl Harbour. It was a violation of international law, as Japan had not declared war on the British Empire.

The Allies were outnumbered four to one and had no significant air or naval defence.

Fighting was fierce and brutal. Seventeen days later, on December 25, the British Governor of Hong Kong surrendered. It was the first time that a British Crown Colony had surrendered to an invading force.

During our short stay in Hong Kong, we visited the Sai Wan War Cemetery, which is the last resting place for 228 Canadians who died during the fighting. In total, 1,528 soldiers, primarily from the Commonwealth, are buried there.

Minister Richardson laid a wreath and then walked down the rows of crosses stopping in front of almost every one. He read the names and looked at the ages, particularly of those boys from Winnipeg. I couldn't help but notice tears beginning to roll down his cheeks. I am sure he was thinking that it could just as easily have been him lying there.

Like all of us travelling on this trip, he was aware of the stories of what had happened to those Allied prisoners who had been captured by the Japanese during the battle.

The 1,975 Canadians, who landed in Hong Kong, either died, were wounded or captured during the fighting. The wounded and captured were placed in prison camps in inhumane conditions. Those who did survive after four years of captivity describe hard to imagine horrors. One veteran told me years later that he entered the camp weighing close to 200 pounds and when freed he weighed 87 pounds.

Japan had signed the Geneva Convention in 1929 along with 46 other nations. It dictated that a Prisoner of War, "must at all times be humanely treated." A prisoner's food, clothing and shelter were to be equal to that of the captor's own troops. Nothing could have been further from the truth for those living in abject squalor in Hong Kong. Lack of toilets, proper food, medical care and harsh treatment by military guards led to the death of many.

The violation of the treaty reportedly came from the ideology and attitude that the Japanese had about their own military fighters.

Under the ancient Bushido rule of conduct, or 'way of the warrior,' surrendering was considered to be shameful and these men who were captured were cowards. Starvation diets, brutal hard work and inhuman physical abuse were the result.

The prisoners were kept in Hong Kong until early 1943 and then moved to Japan where they stayed in work camps until liberated in September 1945.

215

When the prisoners were finally released, 322 Canadians had died. Considering their treatment, it is surprising that there were no more deaths. Of the 1,975 Canadians who landed in Hong Kong in November 1941, 550 never returned home.

The Japanese Government issued an apology in December 2011 for the way Canadians were treated. Many of the few remaining survivors were not prepared to accept it.

Kuala Lumpur, Malaysia, was our next stop. At the airport, we were met by our High Commissioner and the Military Attaché. I was 'wowed' by the beautiful airport terminal and mentioned this to the Attaché. It was much nicer than the antiquated one we had in Ottawa. "Well," he said, "you should be proud of this because it was built with CIDA funds."

MND Richardson, wife Shirley and some of our group with them at Sai Wan Cemetery

The Imperial Japanese Army had captured Kuala Lumpur on January 11, 1942. The city was occupied until August 15, 1945 when the Japanese surrendered to the British authority following the bombings of Hiroshima and Nagasaki.

The Federation of Malaya gained its independence from British rule in 1957. Malaysia was formed in Sept 16, 1963 with Kuala Lumpur as its capital.

We were taken to our beautiful hotel and found our rooms on the top floor. As we came off the elevator, there was a military guard armed with an automatic weapon. We were told that armed guards occupied the first three rooms on the floor, and that our party was the only one on the floor.

When the Minister asked why so much security, he was informed that it was for his protection. After all, Mr. Richardson was a Minister of the Crown for Canada and a wealthy businessman. A good candidate for a kidnapping. He found it hard to believe that anyone would be that interested in him. But three months after our return to Canada, we learned that the security chief responsible for our security had been assassinated.

The Minister and High Commissioner met with the Malaysian Minister of Defence in meetings I did not attend. That evening we were invited to the Ambassador's residence for a reception.

There were lots of military attachés including a good-looking, large, blond haired, blue-eyed Russian. He made sure my glass never got very empty. He was very interested in our trip, what we were doing, where we were going, whom we had been meeting and what had been discussed. He wasn't subtle at all. He was on a fact-finding mission. I gave basic non-detailed answers to his questions and left him as soon as I could. It wasn't my first encounter with a Russian on such a mission and it wouldn't be my last.

The following day we flew to New Delhi, India.

Although the British had been gone officially for more than 25 years, it appeared to me that much of the city was still trying to recover and India to become an independent nation.

The British handed over control to the Indian Government on August 14, 1947. On that day, Prime Minster Nehru raised the Indian flag above the Lahore Gate at the Red Fort and made a speech to celebrate the country's Independence. That ceremony, I am told, is repeated each year on the anniversary date.

The Red Fort rises some 33 metres above Old Delhi. It was built in 1638 as a palace to house the Mughal emperor when the capital was moved from Agra. The Lahore Gate faces the city's largest, most crowded and most diverse market.

On the first day of our arrival, while the Minister was meeting with our High Commissioner, a driver took me in an older model British automobile, for a tour of the old city.

Just outside the Lahore gate was what appeared to me to be a huge pile of rubble made up of housing material and sheets of corrugated metal that might be used as roofing. It looked like a large junk pile. As we drove around the area, I saw children climbing out from what appeared to be entranceways. My driver confirmed that this area provided shelter for many of the homeless, poor people who lived in the city.

At the same time, I saw a new, modern tour bus full of tourists being driven through the marketplace. At a stoplight, a rickety old cart appeared beside the bus, pulled by a horse, which was so thin, its ribs were protruding and each one could be counted

The juxtaposition of the magnificent fort, the state of the art bus and the wretched horse and cart and the housing development provided a mental image for me, which summed up the state of the haves and have-nots in this city. I have never forgotten that sight.

We crawled along a main street teeming with people who gave no thought to a car driving down a roadway. Huge crowds crossed the street anywhere they wanted without any regard for traffic, lights or intersections.

At a stoplight, I got another shock. A boy wearing only ragged shorts approached our big, black shiny car holding in his arms a naked little girl who looked to be less than one-year old. He pressed her tiny, emaciated body up against the window of the vehicle. I refused his motion to wind down the window. He was looking at me in my splendid uniform with gold braid on my sleeve no doubt thinking I was rich. He gestured at the girl and then at me. I am not sure to this day whether he was asking me for money or wanting me to take the little girl!

In an area swarming with people, I suddenly had the need to use a toilet. I asked the driver if he could take me to one. A few yards ahead, he stopped and pointed down an alleyway and told me I could find a place there. I opened the door of the vehicle and was hit by a confluence of smells, which ranged from strange foods being cooked, to spices, to human body odor. I wanted to get back into the safety of the car. But I had to go. It was above 40 degrees centigrade. I walked only a few feet before I began to sweat profusely. I pushed my way through a crowd of people who looked at me strangely. Probably, they had never seen anyone dressed in a Canadian Forces officer's uniform.

The stench in the alleyway was even worse than on the street. There was evidence that the whole alleyway was being used as a toilet. The lack of any other place and the urgency that I had to go made me decide that, 'when in Rome do as the Romans do.' As I made my way back to the car, I was accosted by a beggar. It was an unforgettable, grotesque sight. He was a leper. Some of his face had been eaten away and skin on his hands was rotting; one finger was missing. He gestured at me to give him something. I could only think about getting back to the safety of my automobile.

That night a number of us were hosted to dinner at the High Commissioner's residence. As we sat in this magnificent dining room, being served a gourmet meal by Indian waiters and drinking fine wine from crystal glasses, I couldn't help but think about where I had been and what I had seen that afternoon. It made the meal less enjoyable!

The next day, the Minister met with Defence Minister Jagjivan Ram. He was a powerful man in the Indian Cabinet and was ranked as number two in the government. He became the youngest minister to serve in Prime Minister's Nehru provisional government in 1947 at the age of 39 and went on to serve as a cabinet minister for 30 years.

He was from the Chamar caste and had led protests against discrimination in his country from his early years in school. While attending a public school, at the age of 14, he drank water from a pot set out for Hindus. As a described 'Untouchable' he was not allowed to do this. The Principal had a water pot set out for him. He broke it twice and the Principal decided not to replace it a third time.

An 'Untouchable' was described as a person tainted by their birth into a caste system that deems them impure and less than human. They were not allowed to drink from the same wells, attend the same temples, wear shoes in the presence of upper caste or drink from the same cups in tea stalls. They were normally regulated to the lowest paying jobs and lived in constant fear of being publicly humiliated, beaten and raped with impunity by the upper caste Hindus.

Minister Ram showed great determination to overcome the adversity he faced as an 'Untouchable' by pursuing his education. He finally graduated with a Bachelor of Science degree from the University of Calcutta in 1931. He was instrumental in forming an organization dedicated to attaining equality for 'Untouchables.'

After Independence in 1947, the Indian Government introduced a system to enable 'Untouchables' to have political representation and to be able to obtain government jobs and education.

By the early 2000s, reportedly, there were still more than 160 million 'Untouchables' in India.

At the Ministry, I saw a number of poorly dressed Indian men simply sitting around in the hallways outside of officials' offices. Given the security at our Canadian National Defence Headquarters in Ottawa, I was surprised to see that they had this access. But perhaps they were workers who had been given the appropriate security clearance.

The Minister, his wife, the Chief of Staff and I were invited to Minister Ram's private residence for dinner. A Canadian from the High Commission hosted the other members of the official party.

We drove into a neat, tidy residential area and stopped in front of a small house which reminded me of the approximately 850 square foot homes that were built in Canada at the end of the World War II. Once inside it looked even more like one. We could see a small kitchen, a comfortable, plainly furnished combination living room and dining room. I was told it had two bedrooms and one bathroom.

The Ministers and their wives were seated at the small dining room table. There were two card tables set up in the living room. I was seated at one with three Indian gentlemen. One was a four star General, the Chief of the Defence Staff for the Indian military, resplendent in his uniform, and the two others were civilians, one of whom I soon learned was the Minister of Finance.

It would be an interesting evening of discussion with these individuals picking my brain about how the Canadian military operated. Foremost in the mind of the CDS was our military salaries. He wasn't bashful and asked me directly how much I was paid as a major. When I told him he looked shocked, whether real or put-on, and said to the Finance Minister, "He earns more than me. We need to look at the pay scales for our military." I am not sure if it was true but the CDS was obviously using me to make a point.

Dinner was a buffet set out on two tables in the kitchen. One table was set out with all vegetarian dishes and one with meat dishes. I believe the Indian Minister and his wife did not eat meat. I tried both and all the dishes were quite tasty.

Before leaving Delhi, we were taken to the beautiful memorial marking the spot where Mahatma Gandhi was cremated. He was assassinated on January 30, 1948 while standing on the steps of a building where a prayer meeting was to take place.

Gandhi was the pre-eminent leader of Indian nationalism in British-ruled India. Using non-violent, civil disobedience, he led India to independence and inspired movements for civil rights and freedoms across the world.

He had spent more than 20 years in South Africa as a young lawyer fighting discrimination and assisting Indian communities struggling for their human rights in that country.

He is commonly referred to as the Father of the Nation. October 2, his birth date, is commemorated as a national holiday in India and worldwide as the International Day of Nonviolence.

Dar es Salaam, Tanzania, was our next stop.

Tanganyika became independent from British rule in 1961. Neighbouring Zanzibar became independent in 1963. The two countries merged in April 1964 and on October 29, 1964 became the United Republic of Tanzania.

We checked into our hotel and were immediately warned not to leave anything of value in our rooms. I brought several items to the front desk and was told they would be locked in a large safe, which I could see was installed behind a heavy, steel mesh door. Regardless, I was told, "We cannot guarantee their safety; there are some bad people here."

That first evening we were driven to a fine restaurant about a mile away and dismissed our government transport for the evening. After dinner we exited the building and the Minister suggested we walk back to the hotel. A doorman interrupted and asked us where we were staying. He told us we couldn't walk back to our hotel because we probably wouldn't make it without being attacked. It was the first time I had felt any sense of concern about our safety on the trip. We took a cab.

The next day there were meetings with the Tanzanian Defence Minister and his staff. Canada had had some close military ties with Tanzania since the mid-sixties. In 1965, Canada began a five-year program assisting the training of a professional Amy and Air Force and helping to build the Tanzania Peoples Defence Force from the ground up.

On September 3, 1965, Canada announced the donation of up to four Caribou and eight Otter aircraft and assistance to the training of 400 Tanzanian aircrew, ground crew and support personnel. Half of them would be trained in Canada and the other half in Tanzania.

The first two Caribous arrived in Dar es Salaam on May 19, 1966 flown by Canadian trained Tanzanian pilots and were handed over to the Government, marking the creation of the Tanzanian Air Force.

In the evening we were invited to a cocktail party at the Officers' Mess. After we arrived, the Tanzanian Defence Minister welcomed Minister Richardson and his party and then used the opportunity to launch into a passionate tirade about their need to be vigilant and ready for any attack. It sounded to me like a pre-war speech and left our Minister and the rest of us looking at each in wonderment.

I learned later that he had probably been talking about the situation between Tanzania and Malawi, situated on Tanzanian's southwestern border. Since Malawi had become independent on July 6, 1964, diplomatic relations with Tanzania had apparently been strained. The differences stemmed from the attitudes and policies of the two countries towards the white minorities' regimes, the concern regarding the Tanzanian government's perceived attitude towards the Malawi president and his government, as well as several border disputes.

The next day, we climbed into a Caribou, along with the Tanzanian Defence Minister and his party, and were flown by a Canadian trained aircrew to Serengeti National Park in northern Tanzania.

The Serengeti, established in 1951, lies 965 km north of Dar es Salaam, close to Lake Victoria. It is home to many different species of animals including the lion. There are approximately 3,000 lions in the park, the largest population in Africa, due to the abundance of prey species.

The Park covers 14,750 square kilometres and receives more than 350,000 visitors a year.

We landed in the southern portion, which consists of endless almost treeless grassland. Our transportation consisted of a number of four-passenger safari-type Jeeps that allowed an excellent platform for photography. Not long after we began our tour, we came upon a lion with three small cubs. Daddy was cleaning himself while the cubs were tumbling and wrestling each other in the grass. Our guide told us that 'mom,' the hunter, was out finding meat for dinner. Indeed a short time later we saw her nearby pulling pieces of meat off of a wildebeest, which she apparently had just killed.

We were so excited and shot many photos. But about 10 minutes into our shooting session, the lion looked at us, gave a great roar as if to say, 'that's enough.' Our guide ordered the drivers to move on.

It was fascinating to see elephants, giraffes, zebras, wildebeest and buffalo living in their natural habitat. Since that time I have had a difficult time going to a zoo where these beautiful animals are caged or at best, in recent years, situated in small plots of land surrounded by high fences.

We stopped in the middle of nowhere for a delicious box lunch. We ate standing up using the jeeps motor hoods as tables. After lunch, one of the ladies asked a guide where they could go to the bathroom. He looked around at the vast open grasslands and said, "Anywhere you want." The

221

lady thought for a moment and then said with authority, "OK, gentlemen, line up. Now face away until we tell you to turn around." It worked!

We flew back to Dar es Salaam after a fascinating tour of the Park. That evening the Minister and his wife were invited to the Canadian High Commissioner's residence for dinner. The remainder of the party was entertained at a cocktail party hosted by the Canadian Third Secretary at his home. It was a large house, no doubt occupied by a British diplomat before the independence of Tanzania.

The Secretary looked to be in his mid-twenties and his wife looked like she might have just left her teens. Regardless, they had several Tanzanian staff to serve drinks and hors d'oeuvres and to help with a buffet dinner. The young Secretary confided in me during the evening that his bathroom in this house was larger than his whole apartment he had rented in the east end of Ottawa.

Perhaps that's why many of the people that I met, who worked for our Foreign Affairs Department, preferred to serve abroad. It meant missing your family and friends and sometimes being in dangerous situations. But there were some real benefits including better lodging and allowances.

We left Tanzania and flew west across the continent of Africa but not in a straight line. The aircraft commander told us that it was not possible to get clearance to fly over some of the countries so we had to make detours.

Shortly after crossing over the west coast of Africa, we flew over the Atlantic Ocean for a brief time until we turned north and headed for our next stop, Dakar, Senegal. While over the ocean the skipper informed us that at that precise moment we were at, "no place on earth- zero degrees latitude and zero degrees longitude." It was a strange feeling. Something perhaps only a few people get to do in a lifetime. Although the point has no real significance, I will always remember that moment.

We arrived in Dakar to be met by a large contingent of Canadians from our Embassy. Apparently, we were the first Canadian official visitors to visit Senegal in more than six months. They were obviously starved for information about life at home. We were checked into our hotel and then taken to the Ambassador's residence for a party with the embassy staff. The hosts were enthusiastic, full of questions about Canada and wanted to continue the party by taking us out to dinner at a favourite downtown restaurant. It was 10 pm local time, 1 am the next morning for us. We had just flown nine hours and crossed three time zones. I excused myself from the Embassy Information Officer who was my host and told her I really needed to, "hit the sack."

Senegal became independent in August 1960 after many years of rule under the French. Canada established diplomatic relations with Senegal in 1962 when the Canadian Embassy was opened. A long-standing development partner of Senegal, Canada has invested more than $1.2 billion since 1962, as part of the Official Development Assistance Program. The two countries have maintained strong relations in the areas of regional and international peace and security, and have participated in many peacekeeping initiatives.

We had been met on arrival by a Movie-Tone news team who followed us throughout our visit, including our meeting with the Senegalese Minister of Defence and later a tour of the newly constructed beautiful Technological School, which had been built by Canada with CIDA funds. I received a letter from the information officer two months after we returned to Canada. She told me that the newsreel featuring our visit had played in local movie theatres for six weeks after our departure. The 1970's were obviously a different era than today when we are used to 24-hour-a-day instant news coverage of events around the world.

While driving through Dakar along the beautiful coastline, we stopped at a red light. I noticed a young Senegalese woman sitting on a park bench nursing her baby. She had the top of her dress pulled down to her waist and was sitting serenely looking over the water while her child suckled at her breast. What a beautiful, natural sight I thought.

A few months later, back in Winnipeg, I read a Reuter's story, datelined Dakar, that the local government had outlawed the nursing of babies in public because it was upsetting some of the tourists. How absurd, I thought. People have been living this way for hundreds of years. A few tourists come and bring their standards and morals and expect the local population to adhere to them. Something wrong in this!

Our next stop, and the last on our tour, took us directly across the Atlantic to Venezuela. Canada opened a Consulate General office in 1948 and elevated the office to an Embassy in 1953. Venezuela is Canada's second largest export market in South America.

The stop gave the Minister an opportunity to lay the groundwork with his Venezuelan counterpart for an agreement between the two countries whereby Canadian Forces aircraft would be used by the Venezuelan Air Force to train pilots and use some Canadian pilots as instructors. That agreement came to fruition a few years later.

I learned that Hank Morris, who had been one of my navigator colleagues during flight training, was one of the pilots selected to train the Venezuelans. He had retrained as a pilot and, because of his South American background and fluent Spanish-speaking ability, was an excellent choice for the task.

Our introduction to Venezuela was thrilling to say the least. We had an escort consisting of about a dozen motorcycle policemen who surrounded our convoy of cars. They sped along the highway at an incredible speed, which I estimated was close to 100 miles an hour. The large highway was full of traffic. Sirens wailed, cars in front of us scattered in all directions. No doubt all of us were scared.

We arrived at our hotel and tumbled out of the cars anxious to touch the safety of ground. We were all laughing, giggling, and talking at once, probably because we were in a mild state of shock. Is this the way the Venezuelan government treats a VIP, I thought?

Suddenly, the Minister said, "I am not happy." He did not have to explain the reason for his displeasure to the Venezuelan officials who were with us. On our way back to the airport less than 36 hours later, our motorcade had the same police escort but we moved along more like a funeral procession.

We flew back to Ottawa and our 25-day trip was over. We had flown 74 hours and more than 35,000 miles, crossed the Equator several times and our visits had included five Commonwealth countries. The trip had provided the Minister an opportunity to meet face to face with some colleagues. In addition to laying the groundwork for several bilateral agreements, he had established relationships, which would serve him well during his next three years in the Defence portfolio.

I flew back to Winnipeg the next day. Shirlie and the kids met me at the airport. I was just gushing about all my experiences. Sat on the beautiful, sandy beaches on a tropical South Pacific Island, toured the Sydney Opera House, flew over a volcano in New Zealand, toured the Taj Mahal, and went on a safari in Africa. They all listened, but I could tell from the expression on Shirlie's face they weren't impressed.

"So what did you guys get up to," I asked.

"Well," said Shirlie rather grimly, "aside from the normal stuff, we went to the lake for a weekend."

"That's great," I replied trying to sound enthusiastic.

"Yes," she said, "quite an experience. Remember that tent we thought was so cozy for the two of us when we went camping before the kids were born?"

I nodded yes.

"Well we took that and the three of us, plus Boots, our 60-pound standard poodle, all slept in that tent. It took us an hour to get it up properly. Then someone came along and told us to be careful swimming in the lake because it was deep in places just off shore and that a woman had just drowned there that afternoon. Then it started to rain and it rained all weekend."

My enthusiasm for all my recent experiences disappeared to be replaced by guilt.

"I am so sorry," I said to them, giving them a hug. "I will make it up to you, I promise."

The first opportunity I had to keep that promise with Shirlie came a few weeks later. A message from Headquarters informed me that an information officers conference would be held in Ottawa on Thursday and Friday of the following week and I was expected to attend. In addition, there would be a party on the Friday evening to say goodbye to BGen Bourgeois who was retiring. Colonel Morrison was being promoted to replace him as the boss. We were welcome to bring wives to the party.

"How would you like to go to Ottawa with me for a few days," I asked Shirlie when I arrived home that evening. I had already booked my Priority 2 duty passenger seat on the Air Force 707 scheduled flight as well as a Priority 5 standby seat for her. Apparently there were lots of seats and it wouldn't be a problem getting her on the Wednesday flight to Ottawa, but it might be more difficult on the Sunday flight back.

"We can get our usual lady to sleep over to look after the kids for a few days. I booked us into the new Park Lane Hotel and you can go shopping and relax while I'm at my meetings."

"OK," she said, although I didn't think she sounded that enthusiastic. I think she was still thinking about the round-the-world flight she had missed. I knew in her mind, four days in Ottawa wouldn't measure up.

We arrived in Ottawa; I attended the meetings and Shirlie relaxed. As we were getting ready to go to the party on Friday evening she told me that she had been scanning the new homes section of the Ottawa Citizen. "I would really like to go out and look at the homes being built in Ottawa," she said. "And there are only a few being built at the moment," she added.

I was puzzled. Why was she interested in looking at houses in Ottawa? We had only been in Winnipeg for a little more than two years. There was no indication that we would be moved any time soon and I couldn't imagine coming back to Ottawa as my next posting.

Guilt!

"OK," I said. "Honey, if that's what you want to do, let's go out Saturday and look at new homes being built."

At the party, I mentioned this to my colleague Carl Fitzpatrick whom I had replaced in Winnipeg and who was now back in Ottawa. He told me that he had a car he never used and that he lived two blocks from the hotel. "You're welcome to borrow it," he said.

The next morning, bright and early, we headed for Carl's apartment. Armed with the key we went to the basement garage. Shirlie was bouncing and looking forward to the day. I was less enthusiastic. We found the car, got in, put the key in the ignition and turned it. Nothing! The battery was completely dead. My first thought was, well I tried. Now we could go back to the hotel and relax. I saw the look of disappointment on Shirlie's face.

Guilt!

"Well," I said, "There is a Hertz rent-a-car place nearby. We could go and rent one for the day." Was I really saying this? I couldn't remember renting a car for anything in the past except when I was on duty somewhere and the Government was paying for it! And renting one to drive around looking at houses seemed absurd. Shirlie's faced brightened up. We made our way to Hertz!

Five hours later, I was exhausted and tired of traipsing through half-built homes, being told by eager young salespeople how happy we would be in one of their homes.

It was 4 pm and we were driving back from the east end of Ottawa. I told Shirlie that I thought it was time to go back to the hotel for a rest before going out for dinner. Before she could answer, we saw a huge sign telling us that just a mile away was a new development being built by, "Prestigious Cadillac Homes."

225

"OK," she said, "But couldn't we just take a quick look and see what they are building?"

Guilt!

We drove into a parking lot and stopped in front of a single trailer surrounded by about a dozen cars. Inside people were milling around and pushing each other trying to get to see the schematic diagrams pinned up on the trailer wall. There were designs for five doubles and five singles homes. A sign told us that 54 homes were being built - 18 singles and 18 doubles.

Shirlie quietly made her way along the line, carefully reading all the information. Finally she called me and said, "You can buy me that house on that lot. Let's go look at the lot."

I looked. It was the biggest and most expensive house on the biggest lot, pie shaped with a large backyard. Sales price $59,995. Was she nuts, I thought? That's almost four times my annual salary. I was about to tell her so and then saw the look on her face. She seemed so happy, like she was looking at something she had dreamed about all her life.

Guilt!

"OK," I said. I spoke to Alan Silverman, the salesman and told him that we were interested in that particular model and lot and were going to look at it. "These houses are selling like hotcakes," he told me motioning to people who seemed serious about buying. "Can't guarantee it won't be sold when you get back." He saw the look of disappointment on my face and said, "Ok, I will put a hold sign on it for one hour but you have to get back to me by then." I thought it was a sales pitch but listening to the eager voices around me, I realized he was telling the truth. In retrospect, I think it was because these homes were bigger and selling at a lower cost than anything else we had seen in Ottawa that day.

We climbed over piles of clay and walked along what we thought would be the road with a few poured basements on each side until we reached what we thought was the lot. It backed onto a hydro easement. So we would have no other houses in our backyard.

By the time we got back to the trailer, it was almost 6 pm and everyone else was gone. I told Mr. Silverman that we were interested, that we would like to think about it and that we had to fly back to Winnipeg at 1 pm the next day.

"Here's my phone number," he said, "Call me tomorrow, if you wish."

We drove back to the hotel. Shirlie was ecstatic. "It's the beautiful home I have always wanted," she said. "The open concept is wonderful. It has four bedrooms, which means we will have a guest room, 2 1/2 bathrooms, we can build a recreation room downstairs for the kids, and even put a big swimming pool in the backyard." All I could see were dollar signs.

We went to dinner and spent the next two hours talking about the house. The talk continued when we got back to the hotel. Shirlie argued about all the positive aspects. I argued that we didn't know if we were coming back to Ottawa and besides which we couldn't afford it. "But all we have to do is put $500 down and it won't be built until, next summer," she said. "We can figure out how to afford it."

Finally about 3 am, exhausted and tired of telling her the same excuses why we shouldn't buy, I gave up and told her we would put the $500 down.

The next morning I called Mr. Silverman and he agreed to meet us at the building site. When we arrived I told him our decision. He told me that, since we had a plane to catch, there wasn't time to fill out a sales contract. He asked me to sign a blank contract and he would fill in the details later. We signed at the bottom of the contract, gave him our $500 deposit and headed for the airport.

I knew I had a seat on the aircraft because I was on duty. But I wasn't sure about Shirlie who was travelling on a space available basis. I had dropped in to the office of the Minister's Chief of Staff on Friday just to say hi. We had developed a friendship over the past two trips I had made with the Minister and his staff. He asked me when was I going back to Winnipeg and I told him on Sunday but I wasn't sure about Shirlie. He told me he could find out. I heard him identify himself on the phone and ask the question. He hung up and told me that her chances looked good.

We got to the military side of Uplands airport and I joined the check-in line at the Air Movements Unit. When it was my turn, I provided my identification, told the Corporal I was travelling on duty and asked him if he thought my wife could get on the flight. I wasn't sure what I would do if she couldn't. He looked at the passenger manifest and told me, "She is on, no problem, she is Priority One." He added, "But I am not so sure about you getting on." He grinned and said, "Sir, I was just kidding, you're both on."

It was then that I realized that when a Major General in the Minister's office calls and expresses an interest in a passenger getting on a flight, it was going to happen. I thought, in future I had better be careful. There might come a day when I really needed help with a big problem.

My first day back, I made an appointment to see my lawyer. When I showed him the blank contract I had signed with Cadillac, he looked at me incredulously and said, "Are you crazy. They can put any figures they want here. $500,000 and you will be liable for that amount."

"I can't believe a company as big as Cadillac with their reputation would do that," I said hopefully and rather meekly.

A week later, we received a letter in the mail from Cadillac. The contract had been completed with the agreed price and interest rate and signed. My only problem now was that I owned a home in Winnipeg and a home in Ottawa.

My next call was to my boss in Ottawa. I told him the situation and suggested it would be great if I could be moved next summer back to Ottawa. He didn't sound particularly pleased but said he would look at the draft posting plot and see what could be done.

Career managers handled the postings for most individuals in the Canadian Forces. Information officers were a small group in the 1970s, less than 40 in total. It was most important for the harmony of the office to have officers who could get along working together. Individual idiosyncrasies in this tight-knit group were known by senior information officers. So a Career Manager normally left it up to the organization to provide a proposed list of moves which usually was rubber-stamped. It was some years later that I learned that I had been slated to go to Lahr, West Germany from Winnipeg to head the Information office there.

In early December, I received a call from my boss telling me that we would be moved next summer and that the plan was to move me back to Ottawa. He agreed, when asked, that I could sell my house in Winnipeg.

So, my round-the-world trip and my guilt for not being able to take Shirlie with me had resulted in a significant change in my career path, albeit I didn't know it at the time.

We had never sold a house before. I called four different real estate agents. They all promised me the best possible price. One even said that if his company couldn't sell it in three months, they would buy it themselves. I guess it was a seller's market. The average listing price suggested by the agents was around $45,000. The company who would buy the house after three months said they would give us a guaranteed $42,000.

Arrangements had been made at National Defence Headquarters (NDHQ) for an entertainment group to go to our northern bases to put on shows for the various Canadian Forces bases spread out from coast to coast. The group would be gathering in Winnipeg and then be taken north on a military C130. I knew many of the group from previous shows with which I had been involved. My boss asked me if I could set up a reception for them before they headed north. Because no entertainment by the group was slated at CFB Winnipeg, the base commander was less than enthusiastic.

Following a long discussion with Shirlie, I approached Rear Admiral St George Stephens, the Commander of Training Command and Prairie Region Commander, and told him the situation. I suggested that we could host the party at our home, but needed some financial help. He agreed to provide funds from his entertainment allowance for food and drinks. He also said he would convince the Base Commander to provide a steward who would serve food and pour drinks.

We were having a recreation room built in the lower level of our house but the day before the party, it wasn't complete. When I called the company and told them my plans they responded well and managed to have it finished by 6 pm the next day. Shirlie and I were just finishing cleaning and vacuuming when the doorbell rang at 7:30. About 30 members of the CBC entertainment party had arrived. They included a host of great entertainers and the reigning 1973 Miss Canada.

Miss Canada cut the ribbon to officially open our bar and the party began. Lots of photos. Our daughter Susan had her picture taken with Miss Canada and I think, at that moment, might have thought to herself, "I could do that." It might be why, six years later, with our encouragement, she took a modeling course. While she never opted to enter the Miss Canada pageant, she did modeling ads in Ottawa for various stores.

Susan was offered a contract in Toronto with a modeling agency. She was 17. I wasn't anxious for her to go but what can a father say. Thankfully, once she got there, she saw it through different eyes. Two weeks later she came back to Ottawa to continue her formal education, which would keep her in school until the age of 34. When I asked her why she came back, she told me that she felt like, "a piece of meat" at the modeling agency.

The morning after the party, the house was a shambles. Dirty dishes upstairs and downstairs, empty liquor and wine bottles, ashtrays full of cigarette butts, and a burn in the centre of our new recreation room rug, I soon found out.

Shirlie and I both had to go to work and the kids to school. We could clean up later I told them. That afternoon, one of the real estate salespersons to whom I had given a house key called and told me she had someone interested in looking at the house. I hadn't hired her yet but she had impressed me and talked me into giving her a key, "just in case a buyer came along," while I was making up my mind whom to hire.

"It's a mess," I told her and explained what had happened the evening before. "Can't you wait until we get it cleaned up?"

"Don't worry about it. I'll call you later." And with that she was gone.

About two hours later she called and said she had an offer to purchase. I was floored. "How much?" I quickly asked.

"I'll come over tonight at seven," she said, "and tell you then. I think you will be surprised."

She arrived promptly at 7 pm We were anxious to know the details. She explained that this woman was only in town for the day. She was visiting from Thompson, Manitoba. Her husband was an executive with a company there; they wanted to buy an investment property in Winnipeg.

"OK," she said. "She has signed an agreement to purchase with a 48-hour limit."

She paused for effect and grinned. She knew we were dying to know the price. "She has offered you $52,000." We were speechless. We had expected somewhere between $42,000 and $45,000. We had only paid $22,500, two and one half years ago. This was three times my annual salary. Suddenly Shirlie's determination to buy a much bigger, more palatial home in Ottawa didn't seem as much of a burden.

I looked at Shirlie and told our real estate lady, who now had the job, "I think our answer is 'Hell, yes!' but let me talk to Shirlie and I will call you in the morning."

Needless to say we accepted the offer.

Six months later we said our farewells to all our media friends in Winnipeg. They held several parties for us to say goodbye and it was emotional as we left. Perhaps a different type of relationship between the media and a military information officer was to be seen in those days from what we have now in the 21st century!

In early July, Shirlie and Susan climbed into a loaded Mazda and David, Boots and I into our Pontiac Parisienne. We headed east to begin our new adventures in Ottawa!

Editor of Winnipeg weekly newspaper "Metro One" presents Shirlie and I with a going away gift.

CHAPTER 13 - A FIGHTING EXPERIENCE

"Sorry sir, but we don't have any room."

"What do you mean, you don't have any room?" I gasped.

We had travelled for four days and put Boots in a kennel. Now we were checking into the Park Lane Hotel. I had been in Ottawa several times during the past six months slowly taking on the responsibilities of my job as Head of Media Relations and Operations at National Defence Headquarters. About four months previously, I had booked a two-bedroom suite complete with kitchen in the hotel that was within the budget allowed for our move to Ottawa. We were to stay three weeks because our new house would not be ready until August 1st. On each visit to Ottawa, I had gone to the Park Lane Hotel and confirmed that the suite was being held in our name.

The gentleman at the reception desk whom I knew, was sympathetic. He told me that a NATO representative had called the hotel management a few weeks ago and asked to book the whole hotel for a conference that was to be held over the next week.

"I guess the management couldn't turn down NATO," he said with an embarrassed look.

"I don't know why you weren't informed earlier and I do sincerely apologize."

"So where are we supposed to stay?" I growled.

"This is July in Ottawa and hotels are pretty much full, but let me check and see what I can find," he said, obviously trying to be helpful.

He went away, came back a few minutes later from the office behind the desk and told me that they did have a large room that would accommodate four people at a hotel on Rideau Street. I knew of this hotel. It had a reputation for renting rooms by the hour!

Disgusted and dejected, we climbed back in our cars and headed east along Montreal Road. Not sure what to do, I thought I might as well check out the available room. I wouldn't let Shirlie and the kids get out of the cars. I went in and asked to see the room. It was about what I had expected and certainly not a room nor atmosphere that I was going to subject my family to for the next three weeks.

We continued to drive east, not bothering to stop at some of the motels we saw. Finally at the corner of Montreal Road and St Laurent Blvd we saw a large motel, which didn't have many cars parked in front. I wasn't sure if that was a positive or not. I stopped at the reception desk. They did have a room for four people. I checked it out. Four single beds lined up in a row in a long narrow room. It looked like an army barracks.

I showed Shirlie the room; she wasn't impressed. Three weeks with two kids in one room. "It will be like camping out," she said, obviously disappointed.

I didn't know what to say or do. To make matters worse the price per-night was the same as what it would have cost us to stay in the suite at the Park Lane. Summer time - supply and demand!

Reluctantly we agreed to take the room.

We took the kids to see our new house. They saw their respective bedrooms and already had ideas of what colour they wanted the walls painted and the colour of the carpets. White and purple for Susan, and beige and green for David. Given that we had done so well on the selling price for the old house, we told the kids we would put in an 18 x 36 foot in-ground swimming pool. They had agreed this would be in lieu of buying a cottage or a travel trailer.

A meeting with the builders proved that all of this was possible.

So the angst about staying in our rustic accommodation faded in the background as we all looked to the day we would move into our new house.

In the second week of July, I started my new job as Head of Media Relations and Operations at National Defence Headquarters. Headquarters had just been relocated from the 'temporary buildings' at Laurier Ave and Elgin St to 101 Colonel By Drive overlooking the Canal.

I thought it a strange place for a Defence Headquarters, particularly from a security point of view. Vehicles drove underneath the building and it was easily open to attack by, as an example, hand-held missile launchers from buildings across the street. The Minister's office was on the 13th or Executive floor as it was more commonly called.

I was told later that the building had been meant for the Department of Transport. But Don Jamieson, the Minister of Transport and a close friend of Prime Minister Trudeau, didn't like the building so it was 'offered' to Defence, which had been clamouring for a new headquarters for some years to consolidate employees spread throughout the National Capital Region. So now we were in 22 buildings instead of 45.

It was early summer and many people were on holidays, but it didn't take long to get very busy, particularly responding to the media. In my section, I had two media relations officers, one of whom was fluently bilingual, a regional operations officer who was the liaison officer with all the regional information offices and a general inquiries officer. We were a small but busy group. But I wouldn't be there for long.

On July 15, 1974, the Cypriot National Guard, in an Athens-backed coup, removed President Makarios from office. He was saved from probable death by an RAF helicopter that whisked him away to the British Base Akrotiri on the south side of the island. From there he went to London and on to New York to address the UN Security Council concerning the Cypriot problem.

On July 17, after the coup, the Greek military junta chose Nicholas Sampson as president. The coup and Sampson's assumption of power set the stage for a Turkish invasion three days later in which Turkish forces occupied the northern third of the island, a State which continues, despite the efforts of the UN Peacekeepers.

Nicholas Sampson was a well-known member of Eoka who had been working for years for Enosis - union of Cyprus with Greece. Eoka was a Greek Cypriot nationalist paramilitary group that fought for the end of British rule in Cyprus and for union with Greece.

For years, Sampson worked as a correspondent for The Cyprus Times in Nicosia. The British Army and police knew him as a ruthless and feared gunman.

In 1970, he became a right-wing member of the Cyprus Parliament. On one occasion, while stationed there in 1970 and living in the Ledra Palace Hotel, I was having a drink at the bar when he came up and sat on a stool beside me. I recognized him immediately. We exchanged pleasantries and I left, my drink unfinished.

Someone told me that once he had shot someone on the infamous Murder Mile where, in the late 1950s, British soldiers and their wives were often killed while walking along Ledra Street, a main shopping street. Reportedly, he then walked away only to come back a short time later as a reporter who had discovered a body.

It was obvious to Turkey that Athens was behind the coup. For the Turkish Government, Sampson and his government posed an imminent threat to the security of the Turkish minority on Cyprus. Turkey called for Sampson's removal and for the Greek Army forces in Cyprus to leave, and the island to remain independent. Reportedly at that time, neither the British nor the Americans were prepared or willing to take action.

At 4:35 am on Saturday, July 20, air raids by the Turkish Air Force began when a jet attacked two Greek Cypriot gunboats west of the coastal town of Kyrenia. Following a series of air strikes against military targets in Nicosia and Kyrenia, paratroopers were dropped onto the plain north of the capital. Shortly after, the Turkish army came ashore near Kyrenia unloading tanks, artillery units and troops.

Well supported by air forces, the Turkish landing operations had no major problems. The air force had destroyed the planes at Nicosia airport, including the six commercial Cyprus Airways aircraft sitting on the field. The runways were bombed and made unusable. The main opposition for the Turkish land forces was the Cyprus National Guard.

The Turkish invasion came as a complete surprise to the Greek Government, as well as to the members of their armed forces, many of whom were on summer leave. The Greek junta could not decide whether or not to become involved on Cyprus.

The indecision on the part of the Greek military junta led to its collapse on July 23. At the same time Sampson resigned in Nicosia and was replaced by Glafcos Clerides.

Sitting in the middle of these two opposing forces on July 20 were the members of the Canadian Airborne Regiment who had been stationed there since April. Canadians first arrived in Cyprus in 1964 and had always

233

been in the most difficult areas to monitor and patrol. At first, they were stationed in the Kyrenia district where much of the fighting had taken place in 1964, and now in the midst of Nicosia District, which included the downtown and surrounding areas.

When the fighting broke out it was an untenable position for the Canadian-UN forces. Their observation posts were sometimes caught in the crossfire. Turkish troops and Greek National Guard troops both began to wear UN blue berets. Some Turkish troops wore Canadian combat uniforms, no doubt stolen from the laundry, which was in a sector they controlled. As a result, on occasion, both sides fired at the Canadians.

The rules of engagement for the UN was that they could only return fire if their lives were considered to be in danger; even then they had to be cautious. Under these conditions, Canadian liaison officers were trying to negotiate with both sides to orchestrate a ceasefire. Some ceasefires were agreed to but never lasted for long.

The Ledra Palace Hotel was in a strategic location overlooking the Green Line dividing the two sides, as well as the Turkish quarter. There were Greek Cypriot National Guard troops in the hotel along with 380 civilians, including a large contingent of international media. The hotel was subjected to small arms and 50 calibre machine-gun fire.

On the second day, the Canadians evacuated all the civilians from the Ledra Palace. The Greek Cypriot troops were finally convinced to leave the hotel and, as agreed, the Canadians occupied the hotel. It became a UN post; a UN flag was hoisted over the building and the Turkish Forces so informed.

The UN initiated a ceasefire to take effect at 4 pm on July 22, the third day of fighting. After a few delays, the fighting stopped at nightfall.

However there were sporadic firefights during the following days. On July 23, Private Plouffe and Capt Normand Blacquiere were both wounded. Capt Blacquiere was hit in both legs and Pte Plouffe came to his aid. While he was giving the Captain aid, a bullet ricocheted off his helmet and into his jaw. He spat out the bullet and several teeth and went back to putting on tourniquets.

Blacquiere and his men were trying to escort some Turkish Cypriot Force officers and men to safety after they had tried to take refuge in a UN camp. Each time they tried to make their way to safety, the group was fired upon from a National Guard position.

The local Greek commander was advised of the mission and told to order his men to stop firing on the UN troops. But each time the group moved they got shot at. Finally, after three warnings, the Canadian commander advised that the next time the position opened fire on his troops, the Canadians would return fire. Perhaps the Greek Cypriot troops didn't believe that the Canadians would actually fire at them. The group tried to move and they got shot at again. The Canadians opened fire. Reportedly, two Greek soldiers were killed. They didn't open fire again. The Turkish troops were led to safety.

234

Capt Blacquiere was later awarded a Medal of Bravery for his actions and Pte Plouffe, the Star of Courage.

On July 24, the ceasefire was holding and the situation seemed to have stabilized.

Reports had been coming back to Canada from Col Clay Beattie, the senior Canadian, who was the Deputy Chief of Staff for the United Nations Forces in Cyprus. (UNFICYP). Canadian media from the international media located in Nicosia were also carrying stories. Obviously there were many queries about the safety and well being of our Canadian troops and what they were doing to stop the fighting.

In the midst of all this, Shirlie advised me that our house had been deemed 'ready' to move into. We made a date for our furniture to be moved in. At the same time, we had to deal with another problem involving my mother and father.

A couple of months before leaving Winnipeg, I had been responsible for ending my father's working days. One day, my mother had called and told me that dad had had a heart attack while at work. He had spent two days in hospital and was now home resting but was expected to be back at work the following week. When pressed she reluctantly told me that this was the second time that this had happened in the last year.

I was able to speak to him and asked him if he would consider retiring on a disability pension. After all, he was 62 and had been working with DND for 22 years. He told me that he would speak to his Civilian Personnel Manager when he went back to work.

The next week I called Dad. He told me that his Manager had told him that unfortunately he couldn't grant his request for retirement and that he would have to keep working. Dad took it as a 'fait accompli'. But I was upset.

Coincidentally, down the hall from my office in Winnipeg was the office of the Training Command Personnel Director who was responsible for all the personnel managers in the Command including those at Base Borden. I walked down to his office and said casually, "Bob, do you think it would be good for our image if a dedicated employee who has worked for 22 years and has had two heart attacks in the past year was to unfortunately have a third and die while working?"

"Not really," he said, looking slightly puzzled, "Why doesn't he apply for a disability pension?" he added.

I confessed and told him the situation. He called his Secretary and asked her to get the Base Borden Personnel Manager on the phone.

"Jim," he said in a calm voice, "I understand that you have a Bill Dent working for you who has had two heart attacks on the job in the past year. Don't you think he would be a good candidate for a disability pension?" He nodded and said, "Yes Jim, I am glad that you agree. I am sure that you can arrange that in the next couple of weeks."

I called my Dad that evening to tell him that effectively, I had had him fired. He wasn't unhappy!

Shirlie and I discussed the future and agreed it would be great if they could move to Ottawa and get a small apartment near to us. It would be good for the kids to have grandparents close by. It would be the first time, Shirlie said.

So I called Mom and Dad and made the suggestion. I told them we would help find them an apartment condo in Ottawa close to our new house. They were ecstatic.

On a weekend in mid-July, we hired a moving van and headed for the village of Creemore. They had sold their house. But when we arrived nothing had been packed. Between Shirlie, the kids, and I, we packed the belongings they wanted to move into the van and drove back to Ottawa on a Sunday afternoon. They would stay with us until their condo was ready in about a month.

It had been a busy summer so far.

One day, early in the last week of July, we met for our daily 4 pm debrief. General Morrison brought us up to date on the situation in Cyprus. He also told us that a decision had been made to send the remainder of the Canadian Airborne Regiment to Cyprus immediately.

"As you know," he said, "the national media are anxious to go. There isn't enough room for everyone so we are going to have a media 'pool'," he added. "They are going to be added to the first flight out of Edmonton tomorrow evening."

"We need a volunteer escort," he continued with a slight smile, "Someone who has been to Cyprus recently, who knows the senior officials on both sides and who can look after the media in this delicate situation. Someone like you Len," he said, as he turned at looked at me directly.

I was stunned.

"I would like you to make arrangements for a photographer of your choice to go with you," he added, "and we have Major Bob Lockhart, a Reserve Public Information officer, who has volunteered to go with you to help. I think you know him."

Indeed. Bob was a well- known, well-respected, newsman and the current Mayor of Saint John, New Brunswick. A smart, fearless, go-getter with whom I had worked when stationed in the Atlantic region. But I didn't think he had been to Cyprus and since he didn't know the situation, I wasn't sure if, under the circumstances, he would be a journalist, politician or information officer or combination of all three. Would he be able to help me or be someone else to look out for?

I wanted to explain to General Morrison that we had really just moved into our house and my parents were living with us and it was a very unsettling time for Shirlie.

He was already leaving the room. As he went through the doorway he looked back and said, "Good luck, let us know when you get there." The decision was made and I was wasting precious time needed to get ready to go.

I immediately called Warrant Officer Bill Cole in Winnipeg and asked him if he would go with me. He jumped at the offer. "Get yourself to Edmonton tomorrow," I told him.

I made sure that Bob Lockhart was in the loop; booked my flight the next day to Edmonton; and, headed home to tell Shirlie the news.

To say she was underwhelmed would be an understatement. This was the second time in three years that we would be arriving in Ottawa and then me leaving her to get settled. This time it appeared my time in Cyprus might be more dangerous.

I saw her shoulders slump and a few small tears roll down her cheeks. Then she stood straight and said, "OK, we'll manage." She came close, gave me a long-held hug and whispered in my ear, "Be careful."

When I got to Canadian Forces Base Edmonton, I was glad to see Bill Cole and Bob Lockhart already there. I soon met the group of newsmen who had been selected to be part of the pool.

We gathered that evening on the tarmac with the Regiment lined up ready to board the airplane. Col Guy Lessard, the commander of the Canadian Airborne Regiment gave an enthusiastic speech emphasizing that they were off to support their brothers as well as underlining the importance of the mission. He ended by telling them that the aircraft was heavily loaded and that they should leave anything that they regarded as non-essential and it would follow shortly on a Hercules supply aircraft.

Twenty-four hours later, after a gruelling flight, we landed at RAF Base Akrotiri, one of two Sovereign Base Areas in Cyprus. They were created in 1960 when Cyprus achieved independence from the British Empire.

During a refuelling stop at our Canadian Forces Base in Lahr, West Germany, I was greeted by my colleague Major Pierre Dupuis, who was the senior information officer for the Canadian Forces in Europe. Unfortunately, I had to be the bearer of bad news. A storage building in Ottawa, which contained many households of furniture for Canadian Forces members serving overseas had been burnt down, reportedly by an act of vandalism. Later, two youths were caught and convicted.

Pierre's wife was originally from France and much of their furniture was antique, had been in her family for generations and was very valuable. It was all gone. Obviously there was insurance but none of this furniture could be replaced.

We boarded buses and headed towards the capital, Nicosia. Occasionally, there would be bright flashes and streaks in the dark sky. It could be lightning I thought, but a soldier sitting beside me told me it was artillery fire. Welcome to Cyprus!

We dropped the media group at the Hilton and continued on to the Ledra Palace, which was now completely occupied by Canadian peacekeepers. The duty NCO showed me to a room in the recently renovated part of the hotel. The first thing I noticed as I walked in was the smell and the heat. I quickly learned that the room was not finished.

Plumbing was not hooked up and the air conditioner wasn't completely installed. "Sorry," I was told, "but all the other rooms are full. You can use the public washroom down the hall." I was too tired to argue.

The next morning I was invited to an initial briefing which would bring the new officers up-to-date on the situation. It was evident from the outset that LCol Manuel was not happy about the arrival of Col Lessard and the rest of the regiment.

LCol Manuel and his troops had been in Cyprus since April. They were handling the situation well and the Commander was regarded as a hero by many locals for his actions during the fighting, particularly in saving the civilians who were trapped in the Ledra Palace.

But the decision taken at National Defence Headquarters was based on intelligence and concerns that fighting might erupt again and more troops would be needed. When the fighting stopped on July 23, the threat of war between two NATO allies was over. But the Turkish Army was now on Cyprus and the Turks had most of northern Cyprus in their hands.

The first meeting of Foreign Ministers from Cyprus, Greece and Turkey, and Great Britain, as a guarantor, was held in Geneva on July 25, with no firm results. The second conference began on August 10 and this time included now Cypriot President Glafcos Clerides and Turkish leader Rauf Denktash. The latter's demand to form a federation were rejected. On August 15, the Turks launched a new offensive.

I had spent my time during the past 10 days meeting with Canadian senior officers, visiting where our troops were positioned and setting up interviews and tours for the media.

An interview with Rauf Denktash provided a very different side of the Turkish Cypriot leader. In all the previous interviews I had listened to over the past four years, he had always been relatively meek and almost pleading for help and recognition for Turkish Cypriot rights. On this occasion, now that he was backed by the Turkish army troops on the island, and given the fact that they occupied more than a third of the island, he was much more forceful and demanding for the establishment of a Turkish Federated State.

On February 19, 1975, he unilaterally declared the formation of the Turkish Federated State of Cyprus and became its President. It failed to gain international recognition from any foreign power other than Turkey as did its successor, the Turkish Republic of Cyprus, when Denktash declared independence in 1983.

My periodic stays in Cyprus had been generally peaceful with only the occasional bullets being fired in anger. This was different. It was interesting to see the reaction of the media.

One day, shortly after we arrived, I went to find a two-man TV crew who had chosen to stay in a smaller, cheaper hotel. They were sitting at a small table in front of the hotel, enjoying the brilliant sunshine while sipping their coffee. I asked them if I could set up any interviews for them.

They told me not yet as they were waiting for their TV equipment to arrive. "Where is it coming from?" I asked, taken aback.

"Oh, we left it in Edmonton, when the Colonel asked us to take only essential material with us." I didn't say anything. To me TV equipment would have been the last thing I would have left behind in this situation.

Unbeknownst to me at that moment, a Global TV crew was inside Turkish territory looking for stories. How they got across the 'Green Line' I still don't know.

But Don North and his cameraman were going around filming until they got caught by some Turkish Army soldiers.

That evening I was standing at the Ledra Palace bar having a beer before dinner. Suddenly the two of them stumbled into the bar, ashen faced and unable to talk except to ask the bartender for two double whiskeys. These they immediately downed and ordered another. Finally Don was able to talk. He told us about his adventure. When they were caught they were threatened with all sorts of reprisals including being shot. Fortunately, a young Turkish officer came along and ordered them to be taken to the Turkish Cypriot Public Information Office.

When they arrived they were shoved into a small, windowless room and left there for what seemed like hours. They had no idea what was going to happen to them. Finally the senior Turkish information officer came into the room. He questioned them as to who they were and where had they came from. Don told them that they were part of a pool of Canadian newsmen who had recently arrived in Cyprus.

"Who brought you here?" asked the PIO

"Major Dent," Don replied. Don said he thought he saw an ever so slight smile cross the officer's face. Then he looked at them and said sternly, "You are very lucky. I am going to have you escorted to the Green Line. But don't ever come back or I will not be able to guarantee your safety."

I told Don that this was probably the best officer he could have met under the circumstances, because I had known him for more than four years and we had always had a good relationship.

What amazed me was that, although they had been so threatened, the Turkish authorities did not take the film from the camera.

A few days later, I received a message from NDHQ that Don's boss at Global wanted them to return to Toronto immediately. Global TV was a new network built primarily to provide regional news. Don told me that his boss probably wasn't happy because he hadn't been able to send any stories home since arriving.

This was a particularly difficult problem for some news people, since there were few ways to get a story off the island. Some of the big American networks had apparently hired aircraft to fly to Israel from where stories would be filed. I can recall when fighting broke out again, driving through a rather dangerous route from the Hilton to our communications section at the airport carrying a story written by Doug Small, the Canadian

239

Press correspondent in our media pool. It was sent through our CF communication system back to NDHQ and then forwarded to Canadian Press.

I was able to make arrangements for Don and his photographer to get onboard a military aircraft that would take them to Ismailia, our base in Egypt, where they could board a military flight two days later back to Canada.

Don related to me later that this was a layover that they would never forget. On August 9, 1974, while in Ismailia, he met the captain of a Canadian Buffalo aircraft assigned to the United Nations Emergency Force. The officer told him that, after breakfast, he and his crew were headed out on a routine supply trip from Ismailia to Beirut to Damascus and back to Ismailia. He suggested the Global team come along.

The Captain assured him he would have them back in time so they could catch the flight to Canada. Don pondered the offer and thought it would be a great story. But then he weighed the odds; if they were delayed for any reason, he would miss the Canada-bound aircraft. Given the mind-set of his boss at the moment, they would probably lose their jobs. He regretfully declined the offer.

Later that morning, Don was in the Officers' Mess having a coffee when they got the news. The Buffalo aircraft had been shot down by surface-to-air missiles reportedly launched from a Syrian base. All nine crewmembers onboard were killed. The loss was the largest single incident loss of life in the history of Canadian peacekeeping operations.

A board of inquiry launched by DND was unable to determine if the missile attack was accidental or done intentionally to put pressure on the United Nations to curtail Israeli flights over Syrian airspace.

Needless to say Don and his photographer were shocked and traumatized. In less than a week they had been in two situations, which could have cost them their lives. He told me that when he got back to Toronto, he didn't have a chance to speak before his boss was giving him 'hell' for not producing and getting stories back. He said he threw all his tapes on his boss's desk and said, "Look at these," and added "I quit." I understand he headed for Los Angeles to continue his media career.

There were more than a hundred international correspondents from all over the world covering the situation in Cyprus, while negotiations were going on in Geneva and there was a lull in the fighting. Most were staying at the Hilton.

I met the appointed United Nations Forces in Cyprus (UNFICYP) public information officer, a 48-year old Reserve Army Lieutenant from a European nation. It didn't take long to realize that he was 'out of his depth' in coping with this calibre of media in this situation.

Each afternoon at 4 pm a media briefing and question session was held which included a senior UNFICYP officer, usually civilian, and the PIO. The media quickly labeled the meeting as the 'four o'clock follies' because nothing much was divulged. The briefers seemed loath to answer even the simplest question.

One day, it became obvious that the tension was getting higher between the two sides as the talks in Geneva didn't seem to be going anywhere. We were told to go to a different level of alert, which meant that the military peacekeepers were ordered to wear combat gear including flak jackets. When I arrived at the hotel wearing mine, it certainly caught the media's attention. "What's up?" asked Doug Small. I told him we had been ordered to the next alert stage.

So when the question period began, Doug asked the briefers if it was true that the UN had gone to another state of alert, why, and what did it mean. The answer: "No comment!"

I was floored. Any decent journalist would be able to find out, in short order, why we were dressed as we were, so why not tell them the truth at this briefing, I thought. I leaned over to Doug and told him that there were four stages of alert and we had been just ordered to the next state or second highest level. Doug posed another question to the briefers, "Am I correct in believing that there are four states of alert and that the UN is now at level two?" The response: "No comment."

Next day, a number of journalists had left Cyprus, including two Canadians. I asked someone who knew them, and was told the reason they left was to go to Greece to do a story on what the Greeks thought about the situation. Strange, I thought, particularly when it seemed like there could be an escalation into full-scale fighting again on the island very soon.

That happened the following day, as predicted by Col Lessard. Following the collapse of the Geneva talks, at 5 am on August 14, the Turks launched their second offensive.

Given the commander's warning, I found it hard to sleep and was up much earlier. Standing on my balcony, as the sun began to rise, I could see movement of large vehicles coming across the plains to the east. It was very quiet, until the bullet struck the railing of the balcony in front of me. I couldn't see where it had come from. I wasn't going to wait to see if I could determine whether it was a Greek or Turk who fired. I just bailed out and ran down stairs. I could hear more shots thudding into the wall of my room as I ran through the door and headed downstairs.

I was scared. This had not been part of any training I had been exposed to as an Air Force officer. But when I got into the dining room, several officers and Senior NCOs were calmly talking and drinking their coffee. They seemed unruffled at the sound of the occasional burst of gunfire hitting the outside of the hotel wall. They had been trained to expect gunfire and this situation didn't seem to faze any of them. One even commented about the exhilarating sound of what they suspected was a 50-calibre machine gun. The commander asked the two padres and me to get out of the hotel and head back to Camp Blue Beret. Blue Beret was located close to the airport, and was the home for most of our support units and administration personnel. I wasn't going to argue with the commander. I decided I would get my belongings later.

Major Zuliani, the Chief of Staff to Col Lessard offered me the use of his jeep and driver to take me back to Camp Blue Beret. I thanked him and jumped in. He gave me a casual salute and said, "Good luck." I think he actually meant it but he was also smiling. Maybe he was just trying to throw a scare into an already frightened Air Force officer. If so, he did it!

We arrived at the Camp without incident and the driver dropped me off at the Public Information Officer's (PIO) shack. WO Bill Cole was there and had signed out a jeep, which came with a young corporal driver. He knew I was coming so had arranged a room for me in the same building as Bob Lockhart.

Bill told me that a Greek National Guard unit was camped very close to Blue Beret perhaps thinking that it would be safer from any Turkish attacks. We headed in that direction. We got to a ridge where we could see the Greek soldiers. Suddenly out of the sun came two Turkish fighter jets. The next thing I knew, bombs were released. They seemed to be coming straight at us but their trajectory carried them over our head and they exploded in a huge ball of fire close to but not in the Greek Cypriot group. There was no mistake it was napalm. Fortunately, we learned later, there were no casualties.

Bill Cole was filming the attack. A few weeks later when I got back to Ottawa, I had this film with me. It was distributed to the media and carried worldwide.

Until this point, the Turks had denied ever using napalm.

We headed downtown to the Hilton. We met one of our media guys who was just as scared as I was. He said to me, "Len if I don't make it, call my wife when you get back to Ottawa and tell her I loved her." I felt like telling him, do the same for me, but didn't. Wasn't a good thing, I thought, to let him know how I felt.

The reaction of the media under the circumstances was interesting. As mentioned, some had actually left the island when they realized that fighting might break out again soon. Those that remained either where 'gung-ho' and wanted to get into the thick of things or were happy to stay in the hotel and report what they were being told.

Driving through the streets of Nicosia that day, I met a British reporter who pointed at a street where there was much activity. Apparently fires were burning on the Greek Cypriot side of the Green Line and Greek fire trucks going down to put out the fires were being shot at by Turkish soldiers.

Canadian soldiers in armoured personnel carriers were going in to protect the fire trucks. The reporter wanted me to take him down into the area so he could get better photos. I told him I wasn't going in there; the last thing the peacekeepers needed was a reporter getting in the way of what they were trying to do. He reluctantly agreed to shoot his photos from where we were relatively safe.

I was told later that day that a reporter from California who was working for Hearst Publications had been severely wounded. Apparently he had strutted down to a Greek National anti-aircraft position while the Greek Cypriots were engaging Turkish fighter aircraft, to do an interview about the situation. A bomb exploded and he was hit by shrapnel. I never did hear what finally happened to him except that he was in a local hospital for some time. He seemed to think that as a journalist he was immune from any possible injury.

In the 21st century, journalists covering conflicts are very much at risk. In 2016, at least 115 journalists were killed while on the job around the world. I did take more interest in a wounded journalist from Germany. My colleague in Lahr, Pierre Dupuis had received a message from the West German Government asking for our help in locating Dr Robert Held. Dr Held was a well-known and highly regarded journalist working for the Frankfurter Allgemeine Zeitung, a major national German newspaper. The editors had not heard from Dr Held in a couple of days and they had asked the federal government authorities in Bonn to help find him.

I did find him and he had been wounded. Fortunately none of the wounds were life threatening. I made arrangements for him to be flown out on one of our Hercules transport flights back to Germany as soon as the hospital would release him.

On the second day of fighting, I was at the Hilton Hotel late in the afternoon when the UN PIO told me that the Greek Cypriot authorities were arranging for the release of a group of Turkish Cypriot high-ranking officials who were being held by them as prisoners. They wanted the release to be seen as a sign of good will on their part and wanted the international media to cover the release and depict it as such. The PIO said that he had an important press release to write so was heading back to his room at Blue Beret. He said, "You can look after this, Major Dent." Before I could answer he was gone.

Almost immediately I was swarmed in the lobby of the hotel by a host of international journalists who wanted to know what was going on. I told them all I knew. I sought out a Greek officer whom I had seen earlier. He said that he wanted the media to come to the camp where the prisoners were being held to see how they had been treated; then to follow them, after they had been put into a bus to the release point at a checkpoint on the 'Green Line' beside the Ledra Palace Hotel.

I went back to the lobby and told the reporters. A senior Reuters reporter seemed to speak for all of them when he said, "We are not going to be traipsing around the city at night at their bidding. If they are serious, take the prisoners to the release point and we will cover the story there." It was dangerous to be 'traipsing' around the city. There was a curfew that started at dusk and ran until dawn. No unauthorized traffic was allowed on the roads. The city was full of checkpoints manned by armed military personnel. I went back and told the Greek officer how the reporters felt. He disappeared without a word, only to come back about five minutes later. He

243

told me that the prisoners would be taken to the release point. I told that to the gathered journalists who were getting a little grumpy. "Wait here," I said, "I'll get back to you as soon as everything is arranged."

I phoned and was lucky to reach my Turkish Cypriot PIO friend. I told him that I would be leading a caravan of vehicles carrying international press from the Hilton to the 'Green Line'. "For heaven's sake," I said, "make sure all your people know that we are coming and that when the prisoners are released there will be lots of camera flashes and video lighting." He told me not to worry and that he would pass the word down the line. But I was worried. I wasn't sure how long it would take to get word to the checkpoint where we would arrive.

About an hour later, the Greek officer came and told me all was ready. The bus was leaving the camp and would be at the checkpoint in about 30 minutes. I went to tell the media. Meanwhile, my driver was tying a flashlight to the pole that held the UN flag flying above our jeep. The light would remain focused on the flag as we made our way through the various Greek Cypriot checkpoints. The journalists loaded up and about 35-40 vehicles lined up behind our jeep. Next step was to get them safely to the release point.

Our little convoy started off and each time we approached a Greek checkpoint we were challenged by, primarily, a very nervous young teenager in uniform armed with an automatic weapon. It seemed that they had been alerted to the fact we were coming. They were hesitant, but after a short delay to inspect vehicles we were allowed to proceed.

We arrived at the checkpoint and the media gathered at the line. About five minutes later, the bus pulled up and a dozen very worried looking men dismounted and began to walk towards the line. Night was turned into day as camera flashes and video lighting lit up the whole area. No one would dare stop to answer any of the questions being thrown at by the reporters. In a few moments they had all crossed into Turkish held territory. They were greeted with hugs and kisses by a large group of officials, family members, and well wishers.

My next task was to get all the reporters back to the Hilton. It was the same routine with stops and checks at each checkpoint. By about 10 pm everyone was safely back at the hotel. I received thanks from many of the reporters, but I never heard a word from anybody in the Canadian contingent. I think they knew, but were just too occupied carrying out their duties to be interested in what the PIO had done.

Within two days, the Turks had control of more than 35% of the island. They drew a line from Morphou Bay in the northwest, to Famagusta in the east, which they called the 'Attila Line', and then declared a ceasefire. The Turkish forces built a barrier of barbed wire fences, concrete wall segments, watchtowers, anti-tank ditches and minefields.

The UN expanded its role to patrolling the United Nations buffer zone in Cyprus - a demilitarized zone - and even today the UN continues to seek an amicable diplomatic solution to the Cyprus dispute.

For the next month, our public information team assisted the media to cover the story. As relative peace settled in, media interest diminished and many reporters started to leave the island. The Canadian contingent's role was to deny any troop movement across the buffer zone, in order to prevent an escalation of fighting. They also assisted with the delivery of relief supplies to refugees and helped to organize the exchange of prisoners of war.

One afternoon, Bill Cole came into the PIO hut, breathless and white as a sheet. He told me that he had just come back from a mission with Maj Lockhart. Bob had taken them through the buffer zone and into a Turk community to get an interview with several of the Turkish civilians who had been caught in the crossfire during the fighting near the 'Green Line'. He thought it would make a great story for the Sentinel, the Canadian Forces national magazine.

Bob was fearless and when suddenly surrounded by fierce looking Turkish soldiers told them very aggressively that he was UN and to back off. Fortunately they did. Bill Cole said he saw these young soldiers with their fingers on the triggers of their automatic weapons and figured this was it. But they made it back safely to camp Blue Beret. I am not sure if that was the journalist, politician, or information officer in Bob Lockhart. But I saw him later than day. Without trying to curb his enthusiasm I told him to please be careful. "The paper work involved if a reserve public information, who was also mayor of Saint John, got shot would be horrendous," I said, trying to look serious.

He grinned and said, "Don't worry about me." I did.

In late September, I received a message from my boss in Ottawa telling me that the fun was over. It was time for me to come back home and get to work! My replacement was arriving on the next scheduled flight.

I couldn't say I was sorry. It had been a difficult and very scary experience for me. But it was more difficult for the Airborne Regiment. During the fighting, three Canadian peacekeepers were killed and 17 wounded.

A week later I was back in Ottawa with a much-relieved wife. I had a week of vacation given to me as a bonus for being in a 'war ' zone. Interestingly no one in my organization had bothered to tell the administrators that Bill Cole, Bob Lockhart and I had been in Cyprus, so we weren't considered eligible for any 'danger' pay. I learned that we were not officially there. I have often wondered what would have happened if one of us had been killed. Probably no benefits for our survivors!

The time had provided some harrowing experiences. Seven weeks of being shot at and living through some dangerous situations. I needed a quiet week away. So Shirlie and I headed for the Bahamas. It would give me a week to get reacquainted with my wife and get prepared for the next chapter in my life in Ottawa, which hopefully would be more relaxing.

CHAPTER 14 - AN INTRODUCTION TO POLITICS

"Join the National Press Club," my boss told me. "It will give you lots of chances to develop a good relationship with the media guys and it will be fun," he added.

I was back at my old job as Head of Media Relations and Operations for the Canadian Forces and DND. Our small group consisted of six officers and support staff. We were responsible for answering questions from the national and international media; providing information and direction to our seven regional offices across Canada and in Europe, and maintaining a good working relationship with similar organizations in other departments, particularly Foreign Affairs.

In addition, we wrote the public relations plans for all the major national events and activities in which the Canadian Forces and DND were involved. We also handled all the general inquiries coming from the public. One warrant officer had become extremely proficient at answering written questions sent to us by a variety of Canadians, ranging from school children to business leaders. On average, he received and answered more than 6,000 requests for information on an annual basis. He prided himself in the fact that letters received were answered in less than 24 hours.

It took tact and diplomacy to do our job and keep all our contacts happy, particularly the senior officers and minister's staff within the Department. Once again, we were in the middle where the officials within the department thought we were providing too much information to the media, while the media thought we were just providing them the propaganda that the department wanted us to put out.

So joining the National Press Club and establishing a rapport with the appropriate media representatives seemed like a good idea. I had started going to the Press Club occasionally in 1966 when I first came to Ottawa to be considered for a position within the Information Organization.

In the 1960s the Club was located in an intimate room over the Connaught Restaurant on Elgin Street. If I recall correctly there were only about 75 members. What I do recall was going there one Friday evening when Gordon Lightfoot was singing a song he had written about Gerda Munsinger.

Ms Munsinger was at the heart of a political sex scandal, which became public in 1966. An alleged East German prostitute and Soviet spy, she was accused of sleeping with several ministers in Prime Minister John Diefenbaker's government in the late 1950s. She had left Canada in 1961, but the case was brought up in the House of Commons in March 1966 after Diefenbaker criticized the Liberal government for their handling of a security breach involving two Soviet diplomats.

The rebuttal by the Liberals, which raised Munsinger's name, caused a sensation and became a major distraction. It disrupted normal proceedings in the House for some weeks. "Making Canada look like something other than dull and unexciting will possibly attract more attention to the forthcoming Expo 67," offered Charles Lynch, then chief of Southam News. Although Lightfoot became famous, his Munsinger song was thought to be a 'one off' and was never heard again. A royal commission criticized the manner in which Diefenbaker had handled the matter but found no security breach.

So, I became a member of the National Press Club. In 1967, it had moved from its Elgin Street address to much larger surroundings at 10 Wellington Street. The Club was full of journalists, lobbyists, politicians and public information officers.

It was an active place particularly during the lunch hour and in the evening. Poker games and drinking went on often into the wee hours of the morning. Importantly, at that time, any comment made in the Club was understood to be off the record.

I made many worthwhile contacts, including with senior well-respected personalities such as Charlie Lynch, Don Newman, Craig Oliver, David Halton, and renewed relationships with people like Peter Mansbridge and Mike Duffy, with whom I had worked years before.

The Club was a great place to socialize and to establish a working rapport with the media. It also helped to cement my credibility with members of the media. I could also have conversations 'off the record' which often helped them to understand what the Canadian Forces were doing, or problems they were facing. This helped me to develop a sense of trust with the media. Never was I burned or betrayed by telling a contact something I had told them off the record.

In my whole career as a public information officer, I do not remember lying to a member of the media. My belief was that your credibility is like your virginity, once lost it is gone forever. There were times when I couldn't answer media questions 'on the record' for a variety of reasons, often involving security. I believe that because of the credibility I had established, they accepted, but were not always happy with my non-answer. I know that, not satisfied, they went searching for an answer from someone else, but I was never criticized in media reports for my lack of an answer.

Each year the Club would hold the Annual Follies using the great talent which was available from its members. The biting humour and satire would be aimed at members and guests, including some of the most senior politicians, as well as on occasion the Governor General when he or she was in the audience. These remarks went unreported. Basically, what happened in the Club stayed in the Club! Unfortunately, as the years went by, this began to change. No longer was it a place where the media, politicians or lobbyists let down their hair and just enjoyed themselves without fear of it being front page or in a gossip column. I experienced a damning example of that which cost a cabinet minister his job when I was stationed in Germany in the mid-80s. But more about that later.

I settled into my new job. It was a different experience from my last eight years in regional offices in Winnipeg, Halifax and in Cyprus where there were no real hours and various functions and activities that kept me busy at all hours. Here, I came to work at 7:45 each morning and usually got to go home at 5 pm unless there was an emergency situation in which case necessary members of our operations group stayed as long as we had to. However, there were sometimes long days involving activities of our Canadian Forces around the world, which sparked interest from national and international media and which required us to work long hours. Two significant incidents that put our public information organization at the forefront come to mind.

On January 24, 1978 the Soviet satellite Cosmo 954, a reconnaissance satellite, fell from outer space and entered Canadian airspace. The radioactive debris scattered over northwest Canada in an area the size of Austria. Concern of the hazards to the environment raised fears worldwide. Immediately an operation to recover the radioactive material was launched.

Dubbed 'Operation Morning Light', it was a joint-Canadian-American effort using primarily military forces from both countries. The area containing the debris was 'swept' by foot and air during the period Jan 24 - April 20, 1978. A second phase ran from April 21 - Oct 15. During the operation, 12 large pieces of the satellite were recovered, and all but two were radioactive. Subsequently the Canadian government billed the Soviet Union for expenses totalling over $6 million; reportedly, the USSR eventually paid $3 million.

News of the Cosmo 954 crash and the discovery of radioactive pieces became front-page news around the world. Our media liaison centre became the hub for media questions, pouring in at all hours of the day and night from all corners of the world, as well as from many environmental organizations.

Just as Phase 1 was ending another incident occurred that focused worldwide attention on our Information Services, although this one lasted less than 10 hours.

About mid-afternoon on April 20, 1978, our media liaison office was advised by the NDHQ operations centre that a Korean Air Lines flight was overdue while flying over the Arctic region of Canada en route from Amsterdam, Netherlands, to Anchorage, Alaska, and then to Seoul, South Korea. The aircraft was a Boeing 707 with 109 passengers and crew onboard.

As a former member of a Search and Rescue Squadron, it was a call that I had always dreaded. A passenger plane lost or down in the Arctic with a large number of passengers in sub-zero temperatures. What could we do even if we did find the location of a downed aircraft with survivors? In most cases, it would be difficult, if not impossible, to get helicopters to their location in a reasonable amount of time to rescue them. We could drop emergency supplies including blankets, clothes and food from fixed wing aircraft if we could find them in such a vast search area. But even with

249

supplies and food, how would a group of untrained civilians ever survive such conditions for any length of time while awaiting rescue?

Search and Rescue squadrons across the country had been alerted. By 5 pm more than 20 SAR aircraft were in the air headed to the immense search area, which covered most of northern Canada. Canadian aircraft from across the country including one that was in Thule, Greenland, and US aircraft from Anchorage were assigned search areas to cover.

The fact that the aircraft was missing soon became known to the media, and the calls began to come in, first from Canadian journalists, then the US, then from Korea, and gradually from media all over the world. Our two-man media liaison cell became the focal point for all queries regarding this search and rescue mission. Col Boulet, our Director, told us that he thought we could handle the matter, so at 5 pm left to go home. Our response team now consisted of the two media liaison officers, Major Geoff Haswell, Lt (N) Doug Caie, and me.

Throughout the evening, I visited Operations frequently to keep abreast of developments that could be passed to the media. At about 10 pm, I walked into the Operations Centre and was met by a small group of senior officers including the Chief of Defence Staff and the head of the Air Force. Their faces showed a mixture of relief and concern. The CDS called me over and told me that the search was over. They had been made aware that the aircraft was forced down in Russia, close to Murmansk, near the Finnish border allegedly for violating Soviet air space. Asked how we knew, the CDS told me that the Pentagon had just advised him. At this point the Air Force Commander told me that all Search and Rescue aircraft were about to be recalled.

My PR instincts immediately kicked in. I knew if this order was given, somewhere across the country a reporter would find out that the aircraft were returning to their bases and the pressing question would be... Why? I didn't believe that we, the Canadian Forces, could announce to the world that the Pentagon had told us that they knew what had happened and where the aircraft was. After all, given the circumstances, an announcement would have to be couched in a sensitive manner and made by the appropriate authority in Washington. I made my concerns known to both the CDS and the Air Force Commander.

"So what are you saying?" the CDS asked me. "Keep flying the aircraft on their mission, until the US makes an announcement That's all we can do," I stated, watching as the red colour rose up in the face of the Air Force General. "I will call the Pentagon, explain our problem and see what they intend to do," I said. Much to the chagrin of the Air Force Commander, the CDS agreed but told me, "Sort this out as quickly as possible."

I raced back to our media centre, called the Pentagon and asked to speak to the duty officer expecting to get a junior officer on the phone since that is what our Duty Officer at National Defence Headquarters would be. Much to my surprise an officer quickly answered the phone and identified himself as a Major General. "I am so sorry sir," I said, "I was looking for the duty officer." "I am the Duty Officer," he replied rather curtly. I quickly told him our dilemma. He told me he understood and would, "get on it." I conveyed this to the CDS and waited.

The clock was ticking towards 11 pm when all the major news networks in Canada would be carrying the story of the ongoing search. About 10:45 pm, I received a call from the 'Duty Officer' in the Pentagon. He told me that a White House spokesperson was issuing a statement to the media, as we spoke, confirming that the Korean Airliner 902 was known to have been forced down in Russian territory.

"You can release this info to the media," he told me. We immediately called all the major news networks. At 11 pm, it was the lead news item on all broadcasts.

We later found out that the aircraft had indeed been fired upon by a Soviet interceptor, who reportedly initially identified the aircraft as a USAF reconnaissance 707, the same aircraft type as the Korean airliner. But then the Russian pilot corrected himself telling his superiors that he could see a red stork with wings spread on the aircraft's tail which was not a symbol carried by NATO aircraft.

There are conflicting reports about events that followed, with the Soviets stating that the intruding aircraft flew over Soviet territory and ignored commands to follow the interceptor, while a Finnish Air Traffic control centre indicated that the Korean pilot tried to communicate with the pilot of the intercepting aircraft.

According to reports, despite attempts by the fighter pilot to convince his superiors that the plane was not a military threat, he was ordered to shoot it down. He fired two missiles, one which knocked off about four meters of the wing and punctured the fuselage causing rapid decompression in the aircraft. The airliner quickly descended and flew about 40 minutes looking for a place to land. The pilot finally brought the plane down on a frozen lake 140 kilometres from the Finnish border.

Two passengers were killed on the landing. Soviet helicopters rescued the 107 survivors. Two days later the passengers were released. The crew was held for questioning and finally released after offering a formal apology. Apparently a navigation error, which is not uncommon near the Magnetic North Pole, caused the plane to make the turn which took it over Russian territory. In the end the Soviets were said to have sent South Korea a bill for $100,000 for the cost of looking after the passengers and crew. I do not know if the South Koreans ever paid the bill!

Worldwide media attention had been focused on our media liaison officers during these two incidents. They performed their function extremely well considering that they sat at separate, individual desks taking phone calls with no technological equipment to keep them abreast of ongoing developments, particularly those being reported by the media. The decision was made by Commodore Laurie Farrington, our new Director General Information to address this problem.

Given the amount of attention the Canadian Forces had received in the media around the world, it didn't take much to convince the senior 'grownups' in NDHQ that we needed money to build a better facility. Thus, shortly thereafter, a DIS Centre of Operations or DISCO was built in the centre of our public information organization. Televisions, radios and tape recorders provided the opportunity to monitor television and radio stations. Canadian Newswire gave immediate access to news items. Interestingly, it was not long before other organizations, including the Intelligence Branch, were coming in daily looking for copies of news and news summaries.

This revamping of our media liaison section was only one part of what Commodore Farrington wanted to do as part of his plan to revitalize our Information Services division. Commodore Farrington, a trained educator, had been appointed as DG Information in 1976. His vision resulted in some major changes over the next five years that would impact how Information Services operated and importantly, how senior management viewed us.

Early in 1977, a Task Force was formed to conduct a review of how our organization functioned and what changes could be made to better provide the level and quality of services that the Canadian Forces and Department of Defence required. Captain Al Ditter, an experienced army officer and public affairs officer and I, were tasked to carry out the review. After three weeks, we wrote our report, which concluded that a more comprehensive study was needed and should be conducted by a private public relations agency. Part of our reasoning was that senior management would be more likely to put stock in what an outside civilian firm told them since they would regard these individuals as being completely unbiased.

Tisdall, Clark and Partners Limited, a Toronto based PR firm, was selected to carry out the study. Joseph A.P. Clark, a WWII veteran who finished the war as a lieutenant commander, started the company. He came from a family with a prominent journalism and PR background. His father Joseph W.G. Clark was a decorated flyer in the First World War having been awarded the Distinguished Flying Cross and had served as a military director of public relations during WWII. His uncle Gregory Clark had served in the trenches for three years during WWI, returning to Canada in 1918 with the Military Cross for conspicuous gallantry at Vimy Ridge. He returned to a job at the Toronto Star, where his father Joseph T. Clark had worked as an editor.

Gregory was too old for active service in WWII so returned to the battlefields as a reporter. He was considered by his peers to be the dean of Canadian War Correspondents. He received the Order of the British Empire (OBE) for his service as a war correspondent and later became one of the first recipients of the Order of Canada. Joseph A.P. Clark's son, Tom Clark, is a well-known and respected Canadian television journalist.

Al Ditter and I were assigned to be on call to help the firm as needed in their study. In late 1978, the company submitted a report to the Canadian Forces entitled 'The Armed Forces and The Public'. It would be the catalyst

252

for a number of significant changes in the division, including the formation of a Policy Evaluation and Plans' (PEP) cell which was responsible for developing suitable public affairs plans and programs in support of department operational programs as well as writing the public affairs input into Cabinet submissions.

Meanwhile, my relationship with the Minister and his office continued. In early 1975, I received a call from Clive Batten, an official in the Minister's office. He related that the Minister, Jim Richardson, was going to visit our troops who were taking part in a NATO winter exercise in Norway. He told me that plans were being made with CBC and CTV to carry the story on their national news broadcast. No media were coming so there was a need to get a story and film, which could be provided to the media. The story would be filed from Norway and the film carried back to Toronto as quickly as possible.

My job, he told me, was to pick a photographer and come on the trip aboard the Minister's aircraft, which would leave early on Saturday morning. We would stay in London until Monday morning and then make our way to Bardufoss in northern Norway.

"We will fly back to Oslo late Monday afternoon and you can write your story and file it back to Canada to NDHQ from the Canadian Embassy," he said. "Tuesday morning you can fly back commercial from Oslo to Toronto. We will have you pre-cleared through customs and have a car waiting for you to drive you to the photo lab," he continued, "but you have to have the film to the TV stations before 6 pm"

I immediately went down the hall to tell General Morrison, our then Director General Information, about the order I had been given. He was not particularly happy that I had been called directly. I sympathized with him, suggesting that Mr. Batten was new to the Department and perhaps didn't know the protocol. Gen Morrison was not impressed and when I told him I was supposed to fly back commercial, he got red in the face and shouted at me, "I have never flown commercial across the Atlantic and you are not going to."

I went back to my desk, called the Minister's office and told Mr. Batten what the General had said. He said, "Leave it to me." About 10 minutes late, the General's secretary called and told me the General wanted to see me immediately. He was furious when I arrived in his office. He had just got off the phone with the Minister's office and had been told that I would fly commercial back to Canada and furthermore the cost would come out of the General's travel budget. He yelled at me for having called the Minister's office and then told me to, "get the hell out" of his office.

Needless to say I stayed away from him for the few days before I was to leave. The photographer and I joined the Minister's party early Saturday morning and flew out on a Canadian Forces Boeing 707 for London. When we arrived in London late Saturday evening, the Minister's small party was picked up in a staff car and taken from Gatwick to the Dorchester Hotel on Park Lane, in downtown London. No arrangements had been made for the photographer and me. We were told we could take the train into the city.

As I watched the lights of the staff car fade into the distance, I was not impressed. We were left on the tarmac with our luggage and photography equipment. Lugging it to the train station and then getting from the train station to our hotel, The Cumberland, would not be easy and it was already approaching midnight. I had not dared book us into the Dorchester hotel, where the Minister's party was staying, because the rates far exceeded that which our Canadian Forces travel rates allowed.

I asked one of the ground crew if they could help us take our stuff to the closest taxi stand. "A taxi will cost you," he said." Probably about 50 pounds." "I don't care," I replied, albeit not knowing what kind of reception I would get when I submitted my claim. But since I was already in trouble for flying commercial, I didn't think it much mattered if I spent another 50 pounds on a taxi ride.

About an hour later we arrived at The Cumberland. I had stayed there before during my flying days. It was a good hotel centrally located at Marble Arch in downtown and close to the Dorchester.

We walked up to the reception desk, tired and cranky. I asked to check in. There was no record of a reservation. To make matters worse the desk clerk could speak only limited English. He didn't seem to understand that I had made a reservation several days ago. Here I am in my hometown of London, England, I thought, and I am having problems getting someone to understand me. Finally, with my insistence, the clerk called a colleague. I explained the situation again. He checked and a few minutes later told me that there was no reservation on file. But they did have a small room with two single beds they could provide for two nights. Perfect end to the day!

We walked to the Dorchester on Sunday morning, found the Minister's party and made arrangements to be picked up early on Monday morning to go with them to the airport.

A three and a half hour flight from London to Bardufoss and we arrived to be greeted by LCol Kent Foster, the battalion Commander, and Lt Tim Dunne one of our information officers assigned to the exercise. We were immediately whisked off by helicopters to the 'front.'

Norway shares an approximately 200-kilometre land border with Russia. During the Cold War, it was one of the two land borders between NATO and the Soviet Union; the other being the Soviet Union-Turkey border. Patrolling the border was the responsibility of the Norwegian Army.

The Minister was taken to visit a number of troops. Our troops, all dressed in white winter snowsuits, were camouflaged into the white snow trenches they had built. The Minister appeared to genuinely enjoy getting down in the trenches. These were also excellent opportunities for our photographer to get great photos and video footage. It took about two hours for him to make his rounds. The troops seemed happy that he had come, but were anxious to get back to their routine.

The Minister's party was taken to a temporary mess in a tent where hot toddies were served to all. Then we were back on the 707 and headed for Oslo. I had the rolls of film that my photographer had taken, along with one that Lt Dunne had given me that he had personally shot during the visit.

In Oslo, I was taken by a Canadian Forces Warrant Officer to the Military Attaché's office where I wrote a news story outlining the Minister's visit to the troops on the Russian border. As far as I knew, it was a first. I was then driven to the home of the Norwegian Minister of Defence, where Mr. Richardson was being wined and dined. It was close to midnight by then, but the Minister interrupted his evening to come and carefully read and make changes to the release. The warrant officer and I then raced back to the Canadian Embassy where we asked the communicator on duty to send the story back, marked priority, to NDHQ Operations Centre with instructions to have the message delivered to Mr. Batten as soon as possible.

The Warrant Officer dropped me off at the hotel. I was exhausted. I emphasized to the clerk on the desk that I needed a wakeup call at 6 am since my flight left at 8 am. I fell into bed looking forward to five hours of sleep.

I awoke with a start. I hadn't heard the phone ring but sensed something was wrong. I look at the clock beside the bed. Five minutes to seven.

I jumped out of bed, muttering unkind words about the efficiency of the hotel. I threw my clothes on and tossed all my belongings into my suitcase. Five minutes later I was in the lobby. The clerk apologized profusely and told me a cab was outside. I raced out, jumped into the cab and told him my dilemma. Fortunately we were only about 20 minutes from the airport. We made it in less.

The SAS counter for the London flight was empty. Everybody else had apparently already checked in. I raced up and the efficient clerk had me ticketed and headed for the boarding gate in two minutes. I raced to security and then to the gate. I arrived with 5 minutes to spare before the aircraft door was closed.

The flight to London was long enough for the stewardess to serve a great hot breakfast, which helped my hunger and frame of mind. I felt in my pocket just to make sure I had the rolls of film that were so precious. Without the film, the whole trip would be a bust, I thought and I would really be in cak cak!

In London, I had two hours between flights. I was able to clean up, brush my teeth and find a barbershop. Now I felt great.

Eight hours later, our Air Canada flight arrived in Toronto. I had the documentation that allowed me to be passed quickly through customs and immigration. Outside the terminal I found a staff car and driver waiting for me. I instructed him to take me to our information office located on Yonge Street, downtown. We arrived about 4:30 pm I immediately gave the film to our office photographer for processing. Feeling great, I called Mr. Batten to tell him I was back and all was well. Little did I know!

He answered the phone on the second ring. I identified myself and he started yelling. He swore and cursed at me and told me I was through as an information officer. Between his curses, I tried to ask him why was he so upset.

"CBC and CTV have just closed the space they had saved on tonight's national news for the story...because they had no story," he screamed at me. "Why in the hell didn't you send me the story?" I tried to calm him. I told him that I had sent the story at roughly midnight Oslo time from the Embassy and made it priority. "Well I never received it," he said and slammed the phone down.

To make matters worse, if that could be, the photographer came out of the dark room and told me that for some reason all of the photos on the rolls of film I had given him were overexposed. "Nothing worth printing," he said. I was shocked. The Warrant Officer was probably my best photographer. What could have happened? Then I remembered the roll in my other pocket that Lt Dunne had given me just as we were leaving Bardufoss.

"Try this," I said, not really expecting much. A short time later, he came out of the dark room. He had a smile on his face. He told me that there was one great photo of the Minister in the trenches with a few of the troops.

"Make me six copies, ASAP," I told him. I typed a quick caption and made copies. Photos in hand, I had the driver take me first to the Canadian Press office and then to the offices of the Toronto Telegram and Toronto Star.

The photos made front page in the next morning papers in Toronto and in many daily papers across Canada.

I told Lt Dunne later that, "I think you might have saved my 'bacon.'"

I flew back to Ottawa. The next morning, I called the Minister's office. I didn't dare face Mr. Batten. I found out what had happened to my news story. The message with the story had arrived back in NDHQ and had been passed to the NDOC in the early morning hours. Apparently, the corporal on duty saw that it was a news release, didn't think it was that important, even though it was marked priority. It was thrown into a basket for delivery in the morning and got buried with other messages. For some reason it was never delivered!

The newspaper coverage in the major papers and others across the country was a little salve on the wound. So my meeting with Clive Batten later that day wasn't that painful. He didn't apologize but he didn't bring up the subject of my being fired. I was told later that the operations officer on duty that evening was invited to Batten's office for a 'talk'. I am glad I wasn't there. I never heard if anything happened to the corporal.

All the time, effort and money spent on this plan by many people, up to and including the Minister, over a period of 96 hours, had gone for naught because one individual had not done his part. It reinforced my belief that a chain is only as strong as its weakest link!

The incident didn't seem to impact on my relationship with General Morrison; he was even quite pleasant to me. I am not sure if it was because of my relationship with the Minister's office or because this mission had gone awry.

In July 1976, Commodore Farrington replaced General Morrison as Director General Information Services. Late one afternoon, shortly after he arrived, he and Colonel Boulet, our director, met with me and told me that in order for my career to progress I would have to become bilingual.

In 1969, a bilingual policy for federal departments had been set by the government and reiterated by the Chief of Defence Staff in a directive in February 1970. A bilingual policy advisor to the Chief of Personnel was created to oversee implementation of the legislation. By 1975, additional goals, which included the designation of bilingual positions, had been defined. No doubt senior positions in the Information Services Division would be included.

There was a one-year course in Ottawa starting shortly. I was being booked on the course starting in September, I was told. I wasn't crazy about the idea but knew they were correct. Without being bilingual, there would be no promotion for me.

It actually was a welcome change. Classes from 8 to 4, a little homework, and the school was nearby to our home. I would have much more time to spend with Shirlie and the kids; I would be under a lot less pressure and much more relaxed.

That all changed in early January 1977. Barney Danson had replaced James Richardson as Minister of National Defence, officially, in November 1976. Cdr Don Lory, my direct boss, had been called up to the Minister's office to work as his Press Secretary. Mr. Danson decided he wanted to keep him and he did for almost three years.

My bosses called me in to NDHQ in late December. They told me that I would have to cease the course. I would be coming back in the New Year and taking over Cdr Lory's role as Deputy Director Information Services.

In this role I would be responsible for the management of the financial, personnel and administrative aspects of the division, as well as looking after its operations. It was a very demanding job for a Lieutenant Colonel.

I had been rated as the most capable Public Affairs Major in the Public Affairs classification on my last annual personal assessment. I obviously thought that a promotion would go along with the responsibilities. But that was not to be.

There were four Lieutenant-Colonel positions in the Branch. None of those were currently filled by a Francophone. When the promotion list came out, I did not get the promotion. It went to a Francophone officer. And I was left in the same Lieutenant-Colonel position. It seemed ironic to me. I had been taken off a course which would make me bilingual, and placed in higher-ranking position, but I wasn't promoted because I wasn't bilingual. It wouldn't be the last time I would face such a challenge. And it was a challenge because several of the officers now reporting to me were Majors. But thankfully, in most respects, they recognized the position I was in and worked hard to support the organization rather than getting tied up in a battle over rank.

I carried out these duties for the next three years. Interestingly, whenever I would ask the Director if I could be sent on a French course to reach bilingual status, I was denied because he told me he couldn't afford to let me go from my position.

In the spring of 1979, my bosses called me and told me I had been selected to attend the Canadian Forces Staff College in Toronto. I was the first Public Affairs officer to be selected to attend this demanding year course.

I had been in Ottawa for five years, had worked hard and had learned a lot about politics and the media at the national and international level. This would give me a break, or so I thought. Little did I know that what I was getting into wouldn't be any easier than what I was doing.

CHAPTER 15 - AN 'EYE-OPENING' EXPERIENCE

"There are 24 hours in every day. The first 18 belong to us. The rest, you do with as you wish."

This was highlighted in one of the armload of instructions we were issued on our first day at Staff College. We found out all too soon that the directing staff was serious!

There were 130 Majors on the course, including 27 exchange students from NATO and Commonwealth countries. The selection criterion was to pick Majors who were seen as likely to become very senior officers in the Forces. In our case it proved to be true. Two of our Majors became successive Chiefs of Defence Staff in the 1990s. A number of others became high-ranking Generals in very senior positions.

The course ran from August 1979 to June 1980. Shirlie and I decided that it would not be appropriate to have her and the kids move to Toronto for a year. Susan was now in Grade 12 and considering where to apply for university. David was in Grade 9 and just getting used to high school. They had lived in Ottawa in the same house for five years. The longest they had ever lived anywhere in their lives!

I found an apartment close to the College on Avenue Road. Shirlie and I devised a system whereby each weekend one of us would be on the road. Susan and David would come to Toronto on their own, by bus, and I would pick them up at the bus station. Then, when I was free from my assignments, usually by Saturday afternoon, we would go to hockey games or movies that they wanted to see. On Sunday afternoon I would put them on the bus home to Ottawa. On the third weekend, Shirlie would do the same. On the fourth weekend, I would usually catch a ride with one of my colleagues back to Ottawa. It made a difficult year easier to handle.

I learned from some of my colleagues that it was tough for a number of them. They had moved into apartments in the huge city of Toronto with their families. There was no support organization as most had experienced when living on military bases or close by. Wives and children now found themselves having to cope in new surroundings for a year, with dad either too occupied to be able to help or gone on a trip somewhere. Unlike being on a military facility, there was no one nearby who appreciated their situation or cared.

The course was tough. There was lots of pressure. In the first week we were given several writing assignments, most with due dates of four to six weeks. Given that much time, a few students didn't bother to start the assignments immediately. The next week more assignments were given with four to six week deadlines. Suddenly, for some, there was the realization that there was only a week left and four major assignments had to be turned in. Handling the stress and managing time was part of the course. One student couldn't take it. Just before Christmas he tried, thankfully unsuccessfully, to commit suicide.

259

Many of the assignments revolved around planning and writing staff papers on strategic operations, something that I had never done. Virtually everybody else on the course was an 'operational' type person. So I probably had to work harder than most. I set up a daily schedule. Classes ran from 7:45 am to about 4 pm I had dinner and watched the news from 6 to 7; then worked for four hours each night. At 11 pm I would watch the news, then go to bed. Awake at six, the day would start again.

We were divided into 16 syndicates. There were many syndicate discussions on military tactics and strategies, which were often over my head. I found that my syndicate colleagues were most helpful to me when they realized that I didn't always understand what was being discussed. They were also of great help when we got into Course exercises, which would involve several syndicates working together to tackle an operational exercise, usually involving our Cold War adversaries, the USSR.

In one exercise, we played the 'good guys' and were provided real time intelligence information by US Armed Forces officers who had come from the US to help run the training. The college staff played the 'bad guys'. In another similar five-day exercise, the students played the role of Soviet military advisors in the Kremlin pondering a potential attack on North America, once again with actual intelligence provided by the US. What fascinating experiences; ones which helped me understand the potential risks facing the West at the time and, more importantly, ones which provided excellent training for those operational officers who would become senior officers in more responsible positions in years to come.

Our syndicate director, LCol Jack Kelly was a US Marine Corps officer. He had served several tours in Vietnam. He hated the media and openly blamed them for the manner in which Americans had turned against what the military was doing in Vietnam. He was an extroverted, 6'3", handsome soldier, in the fighting shape that one would expect of a US Marine officer. We developed a good relationship even though I was a public information officer who dealt with the media. But he didn't always support my choices in assignment topics.

Early on in the course we were asked to write a major paper discussing the impact of a modern weapon on the military and on war. Each chosen subject had to be agreed to by the syndicate Director. I chose to write about television. He laughed at me and told me that television was not a weapon of war.

"Just let me write it," I urged. He said, "Alright Len, but I can tell you now that you won't get a good mark."

For me, it was a no brainer. Less than five years before, on April 30, 1975, television screens across North America and around the world were filled with scenes of the last US military and civilian personnel escaping from Saigon. It was the end of the Vietnam War... the first televised war in history.

From 1965 to the Tet Offensive in 1968, 86% of the national CBS and NBC nightly news covered the war in Vietnam. Reports were generally positive until Tet. Journalists then realized that the war was not being won as they were being told by the US military. Stories began to become more negative.

There was no military censorship. Journalists could follow the military and report their observations as they wished. Editorials rose from less than six percent before Tet to 20% after Tet. Most were negative. Stories became more frequent regarding US troops. They focused on the increasing drug use, racial conflict and troop disobedience.

Families sat in their living rooms nightly watching death and destruction. The bombing of the village of My Lai, which news reports suggesting that up to 350 civilians (some said more) had been killed by Lt Calley and his task force, became one of the war's leading stories.

Although not able to determine exactly how many Americans changed their opinions because of what they saw on their TV screens, it is known that public opposition to the war effort became more vocal in 1968.

Thousands of modern weapons were dropped on North Vietnam, Laos and Cambodia. Perhaps the television coverage was not as lethal as the thousands of tons of Agent Orange that were dropped on these countries. But it certainly was a deciding factor in bringing the war to an end.

Indeed, on April 1, 1968, the day after he announced that he would not seek re-election, President Lyndon Johnson met with the National Association of Broadcasters and told them in effect that television coverage of the war made it impossible for America to win the war in Vietnam.

I had lots of material for my project. I finished it and handed it to LCol Kelly. A few days later, I got it back. From what he told me, I believe that he agreed with my premise; but could not agree that television was a 'weapon of war.' My mark, 'Meets requirements.'

In late September we were tasked by our syndicate director to select a subject on which we would write a major paper due the following May. My topic was, "Gaining Public Understanding and Support for the Canadian Forces in the 1980s."

Once again, LCol Kelly told me that this was not a suitable topic. Despite his urging to pick something more 'military', I insisted. He finally agreed but made it clear that I shouldn't expect to get a good mark.

For the next couple of months I conducted my research. Much of it was done by gathering information from appropriate individuals rather than reading previous written material. I interviewed three former Ministers of Defence with whom I had worked, Paul Hellyer, Barney Danson, and James Richardson. I also had interviews with senior military reporters, including Ron Lowman of the Toronto Star, John Best of Canada World News, and Jo Anne Gosselin from Southam News Service.

I met Paul Hellyer for dinner one evening in Toronto and conducted my interview during a relaxing meal. Aside from my questions, the former Minister revealed something that I or perhaps no one else had ever known. Paul Hellyer was serving as Defence Minister when the Liberal

Government introduced the concept of Integration and Unification of the Armed Forces in 1964. Unifying the Royal Canadian Army, Royal Canadian Navy, and Royal Canadian Air Force into the Canadian Forces and putting all members into one uniform was widely opposed, particularly by serving military members. But on February 1, 1968 three proud military services ceased to exist.

Mr. Hellyer told me that one day he had a meeting with three officers representing each of the services all of whom were wearing a 'green' uniform. His first reaction when he saw the uniform was that, "the Navy will never accept this." He told me that the three officers, on a committee to come up with a common design, had apparently patterned the uniforms on a US military uniform and were very positive and enthusiastic about what they were proposing.

"My choices were to say no, go back to the drawing board and see me in six months or to agree to what they were proposing," he told me. He went on to say that morning he had already said 'no' to several proposals to implement the policy of Unification. "I sat there for a moment and then I approved the new 'green' uniform," he sighed. He took a long sip of his drink, sat back in his chair, looked at me and then said, "Len, it was the worst decision I ever made as Defence Minister."

I had my first draft written well before Christmas. I put it in a drawer in my desk in the apartment, but then made the mistake of taking it out about once a week, reading it and making changes trying to improve upon the content. By the time I handed it in late April, I truly believe the first draft was the best.

Nevertheless I got the paper pack from Col Kelly a couple of weeks later. My mark 'Meets minimum requirements.'

I was shaken but not surprised. He had warned me. The next day I was called into the Commandant's office. Brigadier General Gordon Kitchen said, "Len I have read your paper. I think it is great. I know the mark Jack Kelly gave you but don't worry about it. That's just him being Jack. I have directed that your paper be one of those essays printed in the College Review."

It was bad news-good news. A bad mark but it would be one of the 10 best selected from 130 submissions to be printed in the 1980 College Annual Revue.

I suspect that Col Kelly was looking for me to write something similar to some of the subjects chosen by other students such as, "The Neutron Bomb and European Defence" or "The Utility of High Performance Warships."

Another phase of our course, which provided outstanding learning experience for the students, came from guest lecturers. During the course, we had 240 senior military, industrial and business leaders primarily from North America speak to us. Admittedly, all were amongst the best in their respective areas, but not all were the most stimulating speakers. By the middle of the course a rating system had been devised by the students, giving speakers a rating based on 5 being the best. About mid-way in the theatre, cards would be held up reading 4; 4.2; 4.3, etc. The scoring sometimes caused a ripple of laughter. No doubt the presenter, who could not see that far back in the darkened theatre or might be facing the screen, would wonder what he had said that caused this reaction!

For me, the presentation that I will never forget came from retired Vice Admiral James Stockdale, United States Navy. There was no laughter or card scoring when he spoke. The whole student body and staff listened in awe for two hours.

Adm. Stockdale had recently retired from the USN. On retirement, he became president of The Citadel. The Citadel is the Military College of South Carolina and one of the six senior military colleges in the US.

He graduated from the naval academy as a pilot in 1946. On September 9, 1965 at the age of 40 he was the Carrier Air Group Commander aboard the USS Oriskany. He was launched that day on what would be his final mission over North Vietnam. He flew on more than 175 missions during his service in South East Asia.

On his return from the mission he was hit by anti-aircraft fire. He ejected and broke a bone in his back. His hard landing dislocated his knee. It went untreated and left him with a distinctive gait. He spent the next seven years in Hoa Lo prison, which became known as the Hanoi Hilton. He was the highest-ranking Naval officer and led the resistance against attempts by the Vietnamese to use prisoners for propaganda purposes.

Despite being in solitary confinement for four years, two of them in leg irons, he was able to develop a communication system between prisoners. "The system made us use our brain and kept us from going insane," he told us. His determination and acts of self-mutilation made him unattractive to parade in front of foreign journalists. The Vietnamese became convinced of his willingness to die rather than cooperate with the communists, which reportedly caused them to cease the torture of American prisoners and led to the gradual improvement of the treatment of prisoners of war. His heroism became widely known after his release from prison in 1973 along with 591 of his comrades. He was later awarded the Medal of Honor by President Gerald Ford.

"We were beaten every day," he said. "The beatings we could take," he told us. "You would always submit to your torturers but still know you could take more beatings. If you ever got to the point where you couldn't take more, then they had broken you. But worse than the beatings," he continued, "was an incident that occurred one day when we were all paraded out into the stockade and stood to attention. Then a female voice burst forth from the loud speakers. This obviously American woman berated and condemned us for what we had done to these poor North Vietnamese people. She told them how ashamed she was to call herself an American when men like us could do such acts. She called us war criminals."

263

All the beatings, the solitary confinement, the lack of medical treatment and the poor food could not equate to hearing Jane Fonda speaking on that day, he told us.

But he survived that day and came home to many honors. According to his Alma Mater, the United States Naval Academy, he was one of the most highly decorated officers in the history of the Navy.

He wore 26 personal combat decorations, including two Distinguished Flying Crosses, three Distinguished Service Medals, two Purple Hearts, and four Silver Star medals in addition to the Medal of Honor. He was the only admiral in the history of the Navy to wear aviator wings and the Medal of Honor.

He told us that, once a year, the remaining prisoners who survived were taken by the Federal Government to Washington to meet in a downtown hotel for a weekend. No wives, no families, just fellow prisoners. "No one else could really understand what we went through." "At these annual events," he said, "Comrades told stories, drank, cried, and laughed."

Vice Admiral Stockdale went on to serve in several prestigious positions while writing many articles about his Vietnam experience. In 1992, he was selected by his old friend H Ross Perot to stand as Vice Presidential candidate for the Federal election.

This honorable man who obviously had meant so much to his fellow prisoners had certainly left a mark on us as serving officers. He died in 2005 at the age of 81.

Another phase of our course involved visiting military installations and business facilities in Canada, the United States and Europe. They were extremely educational trips, but sometimes exhausting. In addition to the long flights, we often had to continue to work on assignments that were due when we returned to the College.

One visit took us to the Space Centre in Houston, in the fall of 1979. We were given a tour of the facility and briefed on various planned missions. A bonus for us was the opportunity to meet the members of a flight crew training for a future mission. We were standing in a large hangar type area when a group of clean-cut, men and women, all wearing jeans and t-shirts, approached us. They were the current crew in training. They looked like teenagers. But all had exceptional educational backgrounds, which qualified them for their training.

Their enthusiasm was infectious. But I think all of us were probably too old and maybe not qualified enough to be part of this team. They couldn't wait to launch on a mission.

One of the crew was 30-year-old Judith Resnik. Ms Resnik had been selected as a NASA astronaut in Jan 1978, the first group to contain women. She was well qualified to train as a shuttle mission specialist. She had worked in several professional positions with major companies including RCA Corporation and the Laboratory of Neurophysiology in

Bethesda, Maryland. She completed her Ph. D. in Electrical Engineering at the University of Maryland in 1977.

I didn't think much about them until more than five years later. On Jan 28, 1986 the Challenger Shuttle was launched from the Kennedy Space Centre in Florida about 11:40 am EDT. Seventy-three seconds into the flight the Shuttle exploded, the result of a leak in one of two Solid Rocket Boosters that ignited the main liquid fuel tank.

The seven astronauts, representing a cross section of the American population including race, gender, geography, background and religion, were all killed. Included in the crew was Judith Resnik.

Christa McAuliffe, was a gifted teacher and the first educator to fly in space. She was selected to communicate with students from space. I learned of the accident while in Damascus, Syria. I was horrified.

But my thoughts soon became what untimely deaths for such talented people who could have contributed so much to the good of the world. Tragic!

A month later we were headed for Europe to visit our Canadian Forces stationed in Germany.

The weekend before leaving, it was my turn to be back in Ottawa. On the Saturday, I was doing some shopping at the nearby Shoppers East Mall when I met my Dad, who was sitting at a table having a coffee.

"Sit down and have a coffee with me," he said. "I can't Dad," I said. "I have just so much to do before I go back to Toronto and we leave on Monday for Europe."

"Just have a quick one," he pleaded. And I did. Little did I know at the time that this would be the last time we would ever be able to do this.

On Monday, we flew to Europe and arrived at Lahr, West Germany, the headquarters of Canadian Forces Europe and home of 4 CMBG, the Canadian Army Group stationed in Europe. The next morning we drove to Baden where the 1st Canadian Air Group was based. We were taken to the Officers' Mess for lunch. As we entered the bar, an officer who identified himself as the Duty Officer approached me.

"Are you Major Dent?" he asked. I told him I was. He went on to tell me that he had a message for me from Ottawa. "Your Dad is doing fine," he said. "The operation went smoothly and he is recovering nicely. No need to worry."

"What operation?" I shouted. "I just left him a couple of days ago. He didn't say anything about an operation."

It was until I got home and talked to Shirlie that I found out that Dad had suffered a fractured hip, albeit there didn't seem to be any cause. But we soon did find out the problem. On Dec 23, his 68th birthday, Shirlie and I prepared his favourite dinner, roast beef and Yorkshire pudding with all the trimmings. He hardly touched his food. Shirlie's experience as a nurse kicked in. She knew something was wrong. A doctor's visit and a couple of tests confirmed her suspicion. Dad had cancer! Unfortunately it had spread throughout his body.

265

I was back in Toronto in early January when I learned that he had been admitted to hospital. I came back the following weekend to see him. He had told the doctors that he didn't want any more tests or treatment. Three days later, on Jan 20, 1980, he died. I was devastated!

Dad had worked for more than 22 years at the Joint Nuclear Biological Chemical Warfare School at Base Borden as a cleaner. My first thought was that he had been exposed to something at the school over the years and that had caused the cancer. I wanted to sue. But then I thought, what difference? Even if I won, any settlement would not bring my Dad back. Shirlie also thought the world of my Dad. But she pointed out to me that Dad had been a heavy smoker for years and that most likely could have been the root cause of his cancer. It was hard for both of us and Susan and David, who loved their grandfather. His death was so unexpected. He was never sick and never complained about not feeling well. It was hard to get back to my studies at the course.

The heavy schedule helped. We were so busy in those final few months. Visits to the headquarters of North American Defence Command (NORAD) in Colorado Springs, and Strategic Air Command in Omaha, Nebraska; the USAF Staff College in Montgomery, Alabama; Camp Lejeune, US Marine Training base in North Carolina; missile launch sites in North Dakota; the United Nations in New York, amongst others, as well as domestic sites like the Pickering Nuclear Power plant outside of Toronto, were packed into our already busy schedule.

By the end of the course I had learned so much. It was the best training I had ever had. Perhaps the most significant lesson came during our writing exercises when we were tasked to prepare briefing notes and staff papers which, in real life, would be sent to senior echelons.

In the early 1800s, Prussian General Carl von Clausewitz laid out his version of the principles of war. We were taught the 10 principles as slightly modified by the United Kingdom and which were taught to the Royal Navy, British Army and Royal Air Force.

The master principle of war, we were told, was the Selection and Maintenance of the Aim. A single unambiguous Aim is the keystone to successful military operations!

This was my guide during everything I wrote or did during the College year. I then carried it into my every day work life and also used it as a template when planning anything in our private lives at home.

Determining a definitive aim is not easy, as I would find out. Many people do not concentrate on determining an aim because it is difficult.

When I was finishing my career with the Public Service in the late 1990s, I was asked to attend a weekend planning meeting at Veterans Affairs Headquarters in Charlottetown. Senior members of the Department were gathered to establish a Directorate of Commemoration. Almost immediately the coordinator began asking individuals questions about how many staff members they would need for Operations, Administration, Communications and the like. How large a budget would each section need? The idea was to design an overall proposal to be sent to the senior policy makers for approval.

Early on I raised my hand and asked, "Could you please tell me what the aim of the proposed Commemoration Directorate would be?" The Coordinator looked at me rather amused and said, "Well, Len that should be fairly obvious." " Please treat me as stupid," I said. "Can you tell me the aim?"

We spent most of the rest of the weekend trying to get the group to agree on what the aim should be!

The course finished in June. We had grown close and there were many heartfelt hugs and goodbyes. Then we headed to our respective postings.

Graduating from CF Staff College.

I came back to Ottawa, as I was told I would before leaving the Information Division, but to my surprise I was posted to head up the recently created Policy, Evaluation and Plans (PEP) Cell which reported directly to the Director General. Our job was to assess departmental policies, plans and programs, in order to develop suitable public affairs policies to support them. It also included preparing public affairs considerations for input into departmental papers, such as submissions to Cabinet. It was an interesting job. It made good use of what I had learned at Staff College.

267

But Col Boulet, our Director, was not happy at me being taken away from his team. At one point our relationship had been very close. In fact, several years previously while acting as his Deputy, he told me that we could get rid of everyone and he and I could handle the job! Not true, but an indication of his respect for me at the time.

That began to change when Commodore Farrington took over and began his sweeping changes. Suddenly, I was being asked directly by the DG for input and opinions rather than the issues and questions being directed through my boss. Commodore Farrington even took me to a meeting of NATO defence ministers in Brussels as well as to an annual meeting of national heads of public affairs at NATO headquarters.

It was during this latter meeting that I learned an important and interesting lesson. With 16 Nations represented at the table, the amount of input that each country was allowed was directly proportional to its contribution to the Alliance. In other words, since Canada was not making the sought after percentage of GDP, we were not expected to intervene in the discussions as much as other Nations who were contributing more. It was an unwritten rule but one that was generally followed. At this meeting, an issue arose in which Canada did have considerable experience and expertise. The British General told the assembled group that he would defer his time to his Canadian colleague, Commodore Farrington, who, "Would be able to make a more meaningful contribution."

I am not sure why Commodore Farrington was treating me this way, albeit it might have been an issue between him and the Director. I never found out, but it did put me in a difficult position; one which would have an impact for me in the future.

Nevertheless, I continued doing my job as best I could. I also continued my involvement with community organizations. From 1976 until 1982, I spent six years as chairman of the Pineview Community Advisory Committee. The community where we lived consisted of more than 1,200 homes. There was a constant challenge working with the city to develop suitable recreational facilities and to ensure that the community was not over-burdened with too much development.

From 1976 until 1983, I served as the Chairman of the National Public Relations Committee for Boy Scouts of Canada. During that time I was also asked to chair the Canadian Committee for the 75th anniversary of Scouting. From 1981to1983, I served as the Camp Chief of Public Relations for the World Boy Scout Jamboree, which was held in 1983 in Kananaskis, Alberta.

All of these volunteer jobs added to an already heavy workload. More importantly, it meant a lot less free time to spend with Shirlie, Susan and David. But they never complained, Shirlie just had to spend more time solving problems at home while also working full-time as a Victorian Order of Nursing Nurse, visiting patients and providing care in their homes. It seemed the right thing to do at the time. And she always supported me.

Indeed, we often had my committee meetings in our house where she would provide the coffee and home baked cookies!

In 1981, Brigadier General Lionel Bourgeois replaced Commodore Farrington. He had no direct experience as a public relations officer but had commanded several bases in Canada and Europe. It seemed that this operational and command experience was what the senior officials wanted to direct the Information Branch, rather than an officer who had spent much of his or her career in Public Information.

In the summer of 1981, I was promoted to Lieutenant Colonel. Shortly after, I was moved from the PEP cell, back to my previous position as Deputy Director Information Services responsible for media relations, operations and general enquires. I now had the correct rank for the position. But the relationship between the Director and myself remained a frosty one. There was a period of six weeks when he chose not to talk to me even thought we had adjoining offices and attended the same daily meetings with the staff. He would send me notes and I would answer. Not good for the organization!

It didn't help when General Bourgeois started taking me on trips with him including to a Defence Minister's annual meeting at NATO Headquarters in Brussels. He hadn't been to one before, so my thought was he considered that I could contribute my knowledge from having attended one with Commodore Farrington. Colonel Boulet had never attended such a meeting.

The meeting was held in early May 1982. The war between Great Britain and Argentina over the Falkland Islands had been raging since April 2 when the Argentinean military invaded the remote UK colony in the South Atlantic. Argentina had some difficult domestic economic issues at the time. Apparently, the military junta in charge hoped to restore public support by taking back the islands, which they said had inherited from Spain in the 1800s. The Falklands were also close to South America.

Margaret Thatcher, the tough, no-nonsense British Prime Minister, said the 1,800 residents of the Falklands were of British stock and dispatched a task force 8,000 miles to reclaim the Falklands.

The fighting was short but bitter. It lasted 74 days. The Argentineans surrendered on June 14, 1982. Six hundred and fifty five Argentineans, 255 British servicemen and three Falkland Islanders lost their lives.

At NATO Headquarters, Ministers were preoccupied with issues involving the Cold War. But this war in the South Atlantic involving Great Britain, a major NATO partner, was also of concern. There was some concern that Argentina might turn to the Soviet Union for help, which would make this issue much more complex.

On May 9, I was asked to set up a session for the media, covering the meetings, to meet with our Minister Gilles Lamontagne. Canadian Ministers did not normally attract much media attention during such meetings. Despite efforts to attract as many media as possible, historically, three or four would be considered to be a reasonable turnout, unless there

269

was a major announcement being made by Canada. I was involved in this several years later when Canada announced the introduction of the CF-18 fighter jets to be stationed at CFB Baden in Germany.

Much to my surprise more than 40 media personnel representing major international outlets showed up. To this day, I am not sure why! There is not normally a slow news day in these surroundings and certainly not with the War going on in the Falklands. Why so much attention to a Canadian Defence Minister??

Strangely enough, the questions weren't focused on the Falkland conflict. Rather one reporter, who had obviously done his homework, set the tone by asking the Minister about his experience as a prisoner during the Second World War.

Minister Lamontagne had flown as a bomber pilot with the RCAF. He was shot down over the Netherlands in 1943 and spent the rest of the war in a German prisoner of war camp. His experiences in the POW camp seemed to be intriguing to the journalists, perhaps because not many Ministers of Defence had had this experience.

The Minister was elated at the turn out and the questions that were asked. Many Ministers dread these media sessions because of their concern about where the reporters want to take them with their questions. Mr. Lamontagne's Chief of Staff congratulated me for doing such a good job. I felt great. Until the next morning!

On May 9/10, HMS Sheffield sank. The first Royal Navy vessel sunk in action since World War II.

On May 4, the ship was hit by an Argentine missile fired from a fighter-bomber. British Minister of Defence Secretary Ian McDonald announced it to a shocked nation. Two missiles had been fired at the ship; one missed but the other scored a direct hit and ignited raging fires in the ship. The ship was abandoned. Twenty men died and 24 were injured. The ship was taken undertow, but high seas caused flooding through the ship, and on May 10 she went to the bottom.

On May 10/11, the sinking was front-page news and led TV and radio news reports around the world. There was not one word of Mr. Lamontagne's hardships in a POW camp to be found anywhere.

The Chief of Staff sought me out and spent several minutes berating me in public about, "Where is the coverage?" I tried to explain that the Sheffield dominated all news reports. He wasn't interested.

"Here we are with the Director General of Information and a senior experienced Public Affairs officer and we can't even get a story in the media about the Minister," he shouted. "I want a written report on my desk when we get back to Canada as to why you failed to get coverage."

I contacted the NATO Headquarters Public Affairs division, but they had not seen any coverage.

Back in Ottawa a few days later, I contacted my counterpart at the information division of External Affairs. I explained my dilemma and rather embarrassingly asked him if they could contact all our embassies around the world to see if there had been any story carried about the Minister's interview. I already knew there had been nothing in Canada.

He didn't laugh at me and was rather sympathetic to my plight, although I suspect he had a big grin on his face. Twenty-four hours later he called and said rather gravely, "I am sorry Len, but it appears there was no coverage."

I finished the memo, which included the negative results of my search, and sent it to DG Info for signature and forwarding to the Chief of Staff. We never heard another word. I wonder if the whole approach by the Chief of Staff had been a CYA, to make sure he didn't get any blame for what had happened?

Indeed, I had dealt with several chiefs of staff, most relatively young civilians appointed by the Minister, who were political loyalists working their way up in the party. As a result, they really wanted to make sure that the Minister was kept happy, regardless of the cost.

In one such case, the Minister was scheduled to visit CFB Shilo, an Army base close to Winnipeg. He would fly into Winnipeg by jet and then go by helicopter. His Chief of Staff called NDHQ Operations and told them that he needed a Boeing Vertol helicopter to transport the Minister to Shilo. We only have the Bell Jet helicopters at Winnipeg, which are much smaller, but it will be just fine, was the reply. The nearest Boeings are in Petawawa.

"What don't you understand about the Minister wanting a Boeing Vertol helicopter?" said the young aide.

So, two helicopters had to be flown from Petawawa to Winnipeg, one as a backup. The cost and time involved to move the two aircraft and crews back and forth in order for the Minister to take the short ride to the nearby Base was substantial. But the Chief of Staff was able to show the Minister that his preferred helicopter was there waiting for him. I knew the Minister well. I am certain that if he had known, he would have never agreed to this happening!

General Bourgeois knew that my relationship with Colonel Boulet was difficult. I am sure that he also knew that his coming to me for advice, rather than going through the Director and taking me with him on visits wasn't helping.

In late 1982, he came to me and told me that he was going to have me posted to Germany "For my own good, " he said. "Get you out of Ottawa for a while." I knew he meant away from Colonel Boulet.

I was shocked. It was a position that I had always wanted, but the Senior Information Officer was a Major's position. Moving from Deputy Director of Information at Defence Headquarters to head a Regional Information Office seemed like a demotion.

I went home rather dazed and told Shirlie. She had mixed feelings. She liked the idea of living in Europe for three years, but it meant giving up her job as a VON Nurse, which she had enjoyed for the last 10 years. We also knew that we would have to leave Susan behind since she was now in university. It would be the start of the breakup of our family.

271

Susan was not happy to hear that we would be leaving her behind. In addition, my mother who was now living alone, although close by, would not have us for any support.

After a long discussion, Shirlie and I agreed that the move would probably be good for me. Having said that, I don't know what would have happened if I had told Gen Bourgeois I didn't want to go!

We started making plans for our move. We loved our home, so decided to rent it. We needed to find a place for Susan to live, and to find someone to keep a check on my mother. We were only allowed 20 boxes of belongings to be shipped to Europe, so some major decisions had to be made about what to take and what to put in storage.

The time needed to plan was not helped by the fact that the decision was made to send me on an 18-week French course in CFB St Jean, Quebec starting early in January 1983. I found this interesting, studying French but moving to Germany. The rationale provided to me was that I needed to become bilingual if I hoped to be promoted.

I also had my responsibilities as Assistant Camp Chief responsible for Public Relations for the World Scout Jamboree, which would be held for 10 days in July in Kananaskis, Alberta, near Calgary. What little free time I had, had to be devoted to working on that 'volunteer' job. It culminated in my going out to the Camp for three weeks and taking David with me.

It was an incredible experience. The Jamboree had originally been scheduled to be held in Iran in 1979. It was cancelled because of the political instability in that country. So in 1981, Reg Groome, the International Commissioner on our National Committee, attended a World Boy Scout meeting in Geneva during which he volunteered that Canada would host the Jamboree and would be ready in 1983 - two years away.

A week later, at a National Council meeting in Montreal he triumphantly announced to us that we, Canada, would host the Jamboree at the Alberta site. Some complained that four years was the norm for organizing such an event and two years wasn't enough time. His quick retort, "We are wasting time. Let's get on with it."

He was not a man that backed away from a challenge. At the time, Reg Groome was the Chairman and President of Hilton Canada and Vice President of Hilton International.

Reg was a self-made man. He had been helped greatly by a Scout leader when he was a struggling young boy. He never forgot. He became completely devoted to scouters and the Boy Scout organization. We often had our meetings in and stayed at the Queen Elizabeth hotel in Montreal, where he and his family lived in a large suite.

Completing the arrangements for the Jamboree was a challenge. But on July 5, 1983, we welcomed the first of 15,600 boy scouts and girl scouts from 102 countries into the Kananaskis campsite for 10 days of fun, excitement and learning in the Canadian Rockies. It was the first time that girls were allowed to attend as official participants.

272

The Theme that my staff colleague Bob Milks and I had drafted and proposed to the National Committee was "The Spirit Lives On." It was meant to show the international brotherhood of scouting living on despite the tension that caused the cancellation of the Jamboree in Iran.

I had a staff of about 60 public relations professionals, most of whom were volunteers, including a large group of more than 20 from across the US. Amongst our many activities was the production of a daily newspaper. The paper carried stories and photos of the daily events around the camp, along with what would be happening the following day. It was finalized each evening and taken to Calgary, an hour's drive away, where it was printed in approximately 16,000 copies. Each morning before 8 am, every scout and leader was provided with a copy of his or her own eight-page daily paper.

One of my "team", as he called himself, was Lord Robert Baden-Powell, grandson of the founder of Scouting. He was given the title of Deputy Camp Chief, but spent much of his time in the PR tent helping us with our initiatives to obtain appropriate media coverage for the Jamboree. In all, more than 260 media from around the world attended. He was an excellent communicator, easy to deal with and had no pretensions about his title or who he was.

"What can I do, Len?" was his normal greeting each morning. I was too busy to be deferential; I treated him as another member of the team.

Lord Baden Powell and I at a press conference at the Boy Scout World Jamboree.

273

He wrote me a wonderful letter after the event, telling me how much he had enjoyed the Jamboree and the fact that I had treated him as an ordinary individual during the event.

During that time Shirlie was on her own and had to make some horrible decisions. Our pet poodle 'Boots', who we had had for 13 years was ill and the Vet told Shirlie she would not survive the move to Europe,. "Putting her down would be the most humane thing to do," he told Shirlie. To make matter worse, Mom's cat who she loved and was her only companion since my father died, also had a disease and again the recommendation was to put it down. So, while Dave and I were away, Shirlie had to take responsibility for putting down the two beloved pets!

By the time we came back from Alberta, she had everything organized including winding up her responsibilities at her work. We were set to go. Unfortunately, no medals for wives!

I had decided upon hearing about the move that I wasn't prepared to simply be the Senior Information Officer in the office in Lahr, West Germany. The responsibilities were pretty much confined to providing information support to the Headquarters of Canadian Forces Europe as well as to the 1st Canadian Army Brigade Group in Lahr and the 1st Canadian Air Group in Baden.

I was told by my photographer during a preliminary visit, "This is a great place. Once the fall exercises are over, there isn't much to do for the rest of the year. Great place to ski."

I knew from my visits to NATO Headquarters in Brussels that not many people knew what the Canadian Forces were doing in Europe. Indeed, in some cases I was made aware that some residents didn't know we had military forces based in Germany. When asked about the Base Lahr, where our CFE Headquarters was located, many military allied personnel said they knew that there was a great Canadian Exchange where one could shop with excellent prices.

I had asked Major Ray Windsor, who would be my second in command, to set up a visit so we could meet with senior Canadian military and civilian officials in Heidelberg, Bonn, Brussels and Supreme Headquarters Allied Powers Europe (SHAPE) in Mons, Belgium. He wasn't sure why but did as I asked.

I knew there were Chiefs of Public Information appointed for all the other countries in NATO, except for Canada. My aim was to set up a similar position in Europe for Canada.

I flew to Europe in late May for a week visit and followed the itinerary that Major Windsor had set up. In all the meetings, I explained that I wanted to expand the profile of Canada in Europe and would be seeking their help to do so. The reception was great.

....

On July 15, Shirlie and I, Susan and David boarded a CF Boeing 707 in Ottawa bound for Europe. Since Susan was in her university summer break it seemed a great opportunity to bring her over. Perhaps she wouldn't feel as rejected by us leaving her. In fact, during our three years we had her fly over six times for summer and Christmas breaks. That way we didn't miss her as much.

I had found a wonderful furnished house in the small village of Ottenheim, population 2,000, about 15 kilometres from the base. Our landlord, who was a carpenter, had built this house, and he and his family lived in it for seven years while he built a dream home across the street. When we moved in they had left all their old furnishings and bought new ones for the new home. We were fortunate because most military people renting houses from the locals had to supply their own furnishings, including electrical fixtures and sometimes bathroom equipment.

It didn't take long to realize that living in Germany was going to be much different than living in Ottawa.

Our rented house would not be ready for the first week, so the four of us were offered an attic apartment in one of the government-operated married quarters' buildings. In reality it was no more than a long room under a peaked roof with four cots side by side and no air conditioning. In the middle of July, the temperature in that room must have been more than 40 degrees Celsius.

On our first night we all tossed and turned trying to get to sleep. I lay sweating on my cot thinking why didn't I book us into a local hotel, and pay the cost. After all I had to be in the office at 0745. I wanted to be bright, cheery and upbeat. It would not be good for the new boss to show up late on his first day. Finally, mercifully I slept.

Someone was pounding on our door. I sat straight up wondering what the heck was going on. Shirlie was closest; she jumped out of bed and opened the door a crack. Before she could even ask what was the problem, a burly military policeman shoved open the door and screamed, "SNOWBALL!" He turned and ran down the stairs.

I had no idea what he was talking about. So we all tried to go back to sleep.

I managed to arrive at my office at 7:45. Not quite as cheery as I would have liked to be. I was met by Major Windsor. He looked at me at the door with a slight smile. "You missed an Alert this morning," he said. Mea Culpa, I thought. Nobody had told me that 'Snowball' was the code word for a general alert for all of Canadian Forces Europe. Every serviceman and servicewoman was expected to respond because there was no way to know if this was a practice or the threat of a real attack on our facilities from the forces of the Soviet Union. And with the flying time from Czechoslovakia to Lahr well under one hour, no one wanted to take any chances.

Each person had an assigned place to go. Mine was to be with the Commander of CFE in a bunker where he would be able to direct operations. I would be his communications advisor.

I knew Ray Windsor was not pleased with me being in that position. After all, the Senior Information Officer had always been a Major. He had been led to believe this would be his office to run. Now suddenly this Lieutenant Colonel had been sent from Ottawa to run the office; he would be second in command. Nevertheless, Ray was a consummate professional. I could not have asked for better support than he gave to me and to our office.

It was the first of many 'Snowballs' during my three years in Lahr. They were 'no-notice' and came up sporadically in order to ensure that we were always ready to go.

A few weeks after we moved into our new home in Ottenheim, the telephone rang at about 4 am It was a 'Snowball.' I dressed and immediately drove to the Base. I felt proud. Here I was as part of a group dedicated to protecting freedom and democracy, keeping the world safe. Our German neighbours could sleep soundly.

As I was leaving the village, I saw an elderly lady all dressed in black, driving her old rickety bike towards the next village of Allmannsweier about five kilometres away. I later learned she did this every morning. She worked in a bakery and had to be there in time to make sure all the fresh bread, rolls and sweets were ready for the first customers who came at 6 am. It made me realize that lots of people had important jobs to do!

Nevertheless, we were in Europe close to the front lines. Military training exercises were conducted on a regular basis usually culminating in the fall with a major exercise involving troops from all sixteen NATO nations.

Canadian media were often invited to fly over on Air Force aircraft and spend time covering the Canadian involvement. It was a busy and sometimes difficult time for our Public Affairs Office. Those conducting the exercises, particularly the senior officers, were focused on their training. They took it very seriously and didn't appreciate any interference from what some saw as unnecessary visitors. The media representatives wanted to go everywhere and interview everyone. They sometimes wanted to dictate where they went and when.

On one occasion, the producer of a series that Gwynne Dyer was making, arrived in Lahr with her cameraman in advance of her boss. Gwynne was a well-known syndicated columnist and military historian whose articles were published worldwide. He had also produced several award winning documentaries.

I was taking the two of them around and describing what the itinerary would be, where they could go to shoot footage photos, and, where they couldn't. "Oh no," she said, "Gwynne wants to rent his own vehicle and we will just go and shoot where he wants."

"Not bloody likely," I replied. I heard the producer in the backseat of the car whisper to the cameraman, "Don't worry, Gwynne will fix this when he gets here."

Gwynne arrived the next day on a military aircraft. I met him at the airport and greeted him politely. Before he could say anything I said, "Mr.

Dyer, we have a brand new Brigade Commander here working on his first major NATO exercise. The last thing in the world he needs is a film crew running around in the exercise area where they could interfere with the exercise and risk getting shot or blown up. The paper work would be horrendous. So you have two choices. Either follow the itinerary that we have prepared for you or take your crew and leave when this aircraft departs." Without hesitation he said, "OK, Col Dent, we will do whatever you wish."

He completed his series and when aired by CBC nationally it received high ratings. Called the 'Defence of Canada' it came out as an argument, according to Gwynne Dyer that, "The Alliances and commitments that Canada had made in the course of the twentieth century were unnecessary for our security and often directly contrary to our interest, even if the politics of the time had made them inevitable." He extended that criticism to, "Include Canada's then current Alliances and overseas military Alliances." This of course did not sit well with the Canadian military history establishment. By this time I was back in Ottawa as the Director of Information Services.

The senior officers in DND were not impressed. It actually helped those of us in the Information Branch who wanted to be more proactive, to convince our bosses that we needed to get our story out far and wide. They hadn't always been convinced we needed to be proactive, but this series and the publicity it got across Canada was a wake-up call.

As a counter to this negative perception of Canada's military policy, we established a National Speakers Bureau and used several other tools, including active and retired members of the military speaking with the media and at various conferences and educational facilities across the country. It ran for several years, and in my mind enhanced the image of the Canadian Forces and our role in keeping the world a safer place.

Gwynne and I got along just fine. After all, we live in a democracy. As someone famously said, "I do not agree with what you have said, but I will defend to my death your right to say it." We had several dealings in the years ahead. The last time I met him was at an education conference in Edmonton in the early 2000s where he was the guest speaker. He even invited Shirlie and me to come and visit him in London, England where he and his producer Tina Viljoen were now living.

Most of the media came to visit the Canadians in Germany to report objectively on what they saw and heard. But not all. Some came with preconceived notions of what they would see or, in some cases, already had their stories written and wanted to come to confirm what they believed was happening with Canadians troops and their families in Europe.

Shortly after I arrived in Lahr, I was asked if I would serve as the Vice President of the Canadian Club of Southern Germany. At the end of the first year, the President was posted and I became the President for the next two years.

The Club was designed to bring speakers from Canada who could keep those of us, who were interested, abreast of important issues of the day at home. We would invite a speaker each month who would arrive on the weekly schedule flight from Ottawa and return to Canada a week later.

During my tenure, we invited a number of outstanding media correspondents, many of whom had also had served with the military or had covered the military over the years. Journalists like Charles Lynch, Peter Mansbridge and Peter Newman.

They would give a speech in Lahr and an interview on the CF Radio Station and then we would take them to the air base at Baden for the same procedure. They were then free for the rest of the week. I didn't have time to look after them so I recruited Shirlie to be their guide. She would pick them up in staff car and take each person to various historic and scenic locations in Alsace Lorraine. It was a break for Shirlie.

Shirlie escorting CBCs Peter Mansbridge on a tour in the Alsace.

But one of our speakers, an enterprising editor of a national women's magazine, advised us in advance that she wanted to do a story about how wives were being treated by the military in Europe. We set up several interviews and took her to various clubs and facilities that were there to make life easier for the wives, particularly the young ones, many of whom were living outside of Canada for the first time. In fact, shortly after we arrived in Germany, Shirlie and the wife of the senior medical officer had prepared a comprehensive slide briefing for the new arrivals, which

278

provided them with a great amount of information on how to handle their lives in Germany.

Nevertheless after all the information that was provided, along with the personal testimonials, when the story appeared it centred on the issue that wives were not being treated well. Another case, I suggest, of the writer having her mind made up and didn't want to be confused with the facts. That seems to become more prevalent in the 21st century, as the reporters write more opinion pieces and editorials than factual stories.

In my first two months, I wrote a detailed plan, the aim of which was to enhance the image of Canada and the Canadian Forces stationed in Europe amongst Europeans and other NATO Allies. I gave it to Major General Wightman the Commander of Canadian Forces Europe. Although, in reality, I reported to Colonel Boulet in National Defence Headquarters, MGen Wightman was the Senior Commander and if I wanted to be able to do anything in Europe I would need his cooperation and support.

He was 100% behind my initiative and told me that he would help in any way he could.

I immediately set out on a trip around Germany and bordering Europe countries to meet with senior Canadian military commanders and diplomatic officials in our embassies and at NATO, some of whose I had met during my earlier visit in May. In Bonn, I met my longtime friend Everett Cowan who was now Defence Counselor in the Canadian Embassy. He arranged a meeting for me with the Ambassador Don McPhail. I briefed the Ambassador on what I was trying to do. He said, "I wish I had someone doing that for me." I looked at him, pointed at the Canada insignia on my shoulder and said, "Sir, I am doing this for you. This is for Canada." He beamed, reached into a draw and pulled out a card and said, "This is my personal number. Call me direct anytime you think you need to and you think I can be of assistance."

The reception from the Canadian senior military and civilian officials was much the same wherever I went. I sent a copy to my boss in Ottawa, told him what I was doing and that now I was changing my title to Chief of Public Information for Europe and the Middle East. I told him about all the support and backing I had from senior Canadians in Europe for what I was doing.

My next visit was to the Headquarters of the British Army of the Rhine, located near Dusseldorf. Here, I met with Colonel Bittles, who was the British Chief of Public Information and perhaps the most senior military Public Information Officer in Europe. I discussed my plan to increase the profile of the Canadians stationed in Europe. He assured me I could count on his assistance.

At the end of our meeting, we had agreed that we should try and form a group of CPIs from the sixteen NATO nations. The idea would be to meet every three months to discuss public affairs plans for the next quarter to see how we might work together to promote NATO and our activities.

Colonel Bittles agreed to take the lead and contacted each Chief of Public Information.

We first met in Stuttgart, Germany, hosted by the US CPI. Over the next three years, these meetings proved to be most worthwhile in helping achieve a more coordinated approach to telling the NATO story. It also advanced my aim of making the efforts of Canada and Canadian troops much more noticeable.

During the next three years our office hosted many media from Canada as well as other nations who came to cover the events and exercises in which the Canadian Forces were involved.

The Canadian media ranged from the very senior reporters and national columnists to military beat writers and those who wanted to do TV and radio documentaries on what we were doing in Europe.

One of my first groups consisted of ten senior weekly newspaper editors from western Canada, most of whom owned the paper they represented. I always appreciated working with weekly newspapers. My experience had been that they wrote more articles and genuinely wanted to learn, and seldom had any preconceived notions about what they would see. In addition, weekly newspapers often got read cover to cover, whereas with daily newspapers readers were usually more selective about what they read, so even great stories about the military might be missed.

One of their first requests for their unscheduled time was to be taken to Tiffany's Bar, a girly bar on the outskirts of Lahr. It was the one bar that most newsmen had heard about back in Canada and it wasn't uncommon for them to want to see what went on there. I don't think it had anything to do with covering the military because I don't think many military personnel went there. I had never stepped inside the bar but knew its location because I passed it on the way to and from work.

"I am not going to take you to Tiffany's," I told them. "If you want to see a girly bar go see one in Canada; I want to take you on a 'volksmarch'." "What's that?" I was asked. "Well on Saturday morning we will drive out to a village, each pay five marks and walk for ten kilometres up and down the hills through beautiful countryside in the Black Forest. At the end, each of us will get a medal and there will be bratwurst and beer, and an 'oompah-pah' band to entertain us," I told them. "Sounds hard," said one editor who was probably the youngest but also about 50 pounds overweight. Indeed I did have some concerns about whether he could make it.

There was some grumbling but finally they agreed. Shirlie and I picked them up in a bus on Saturday and off we went. I wanted Shirlie along because with her nursing experience, she would be most valuable if we needed some CPR or such.

With some huffing and puffing by some, we finished the walk. Our youngest member was completely red in the face and had struggled but didn't want to give up and embarrass himself in front of his fellow editors. Each received a medal and each wanted their picture taken with the medal.

Later I received copies of the stories they had written. Featured on the front page of each newspaper was a story about their wonderful volksmarch in Germany prominently displaying their picture with the medal.

I never heard another word about Tiffany's from them. But Tiffany's would be part of a major incident that occurred a couple of years later.

During my tour I worked with three Ministers of Defence. In May 1984, Jean Jacques Blais, who had been Canadian Defence Minister since August 1983, came to Brussels to attend the two-day Defence Planning Committee meeting. It was the 35th anniversary of NATO. I went to NATO headquarters to provide public affairs assistance.

After the meetings, we came back to Lahr. I had arranged an interview for the Minister on the Lahr Canadian Forces Radio Station. I briefed him on what questions I thought would be thrown at him and he felt quite comfortable in answering them.

The interview, which ran just before the 5 pm newscast, was going smoothly. I was watching through the glass into the booth where the Minister and the interviewer were sitting. Suddenly, someone opened the door and handed the interviewer a piece of paper. He paused looked the Minister in the eye and then asked, "What do you think of the announcement that Foreign Affairs has just made?" He went on to read a bulletin that had just come over the wire service. The Minister looked like a deer in the headlights. He looked around saw me through the glass and glared. He then went on to say he didn't know about the announcement and was visibly upset.

Minister Blais had a very short fuse, I found out. Not wanting to embarrass the Minister further, the interviewer ended the session. After all, the station was part of a DND-funded service to the troops and this was the Defence Minister.

I immediately called my contact in the Canadian delegation in NATO Headquarters and asked, "What the hell is going on? Why didn't you tell us? Minister Blais has just been sideswiped." I almost heard a sense of glee in the gentleman's voice when he told me, "Why would we tell him?" I was shocked. But it wasn't the first and it wouldn't be the last time that I saw the rivalry between the Foreign Affairs and Defence Departments."

But the shock waves were going to come for me from the Minister. The interview was over. He opened the door, saw me and began to yell. I tried to assure him I didn't know anything about the announcement. His answer, "You should have known; you're the Information Officer!"

Minster Blais yelled at me the whole way driving in the car from the radio station back to CFE Headquarters, getting redder in the face every minute as he fumed about his interview, which could be heard in many parts of Europe. By the time we got back to Headquarters, MGen Wightman was waiting for us. Then, the Minister started yelling at him telling him he wanted this totally incompetent, SOB, Information Officer fired immediately. Gen Wightman took him by the arm politely and said,

"Yes, Minister we will deal with this later" and walked into his office and shut the door. I did not see Minister Blais before he left the next morning to return to Canada. The interview was live and was not played again. Nothing was made of the Minister not knowing about the announcement.

As soon as I could, I briefed Gen Wightman on what had happened. He told me to, "forget it." But I was shaken and had no idea if this would impact my career. I could understand why the Minister was so upset. It wasn't my fault, but would he tell my boss back in Ottawa?

Almost ten years later, I was working at Privy Council Office and Jean Jacques Blais was working as a lobbyist. We met on the street one day, just outside our office building. He came up grabbed my hand, shook it and said, "Good to see you. Let me take you to lunch at the Rideau Club some day." Apparently he had forgotten the incident in Lahr. But no doubt he knew where I now worked. I hadn't forgotten our last meeting in Lahr. We never had lunch!

While still in Germany, I discovered that a sense that Foreign Affairs was the major player and Defence a minor also existed in Germany. A very senior member in the Ambassador's office in Bonn had apparently convinced the Ambassador that there should be more control over what was being done by Canadian Defence Forces stationed in Europe. The suggestion was that messages from Canadian Forces Europe going back to Defence Headquarters should go through the Embassy in Bonn. Major General Wightman was asked to come to Bonn to discuss the matter. He assembled a small team, which included his Deputy, the Senior Legal Advisor and myself, to accompany him. There had already been 'fireworks' in several phone conversations so everyone knew this might not be a pleasant meeting, so much so that the Ambassador decided to host the meeting over a long dinner at his personal residence.

It was a difficult discussion and I thought at one point that the senior member and our senior legal advisor would come to blows. The evening ended with no change in how Canadian Forces Europe communicated with National Defence Headquarters, but it took a change of personnel to begin healing the rift between the two groups.

In September 1984, Robert Coates was named to replace Jean Jacques Blais. In late November, Robert Coates, along with his Chief of Staff Rick Logan and Press Secretary Jeff Matthews, came to Lahr en route to Brussels to attend the Defence Planning Committee meeting. It would be some time before I learned about their exploits in Lahr during their short visit.

I went to Brussels in advance since we were planning a major press conference for the minister who would address the arrival of the new CF-18 fighter aircraft that would soon be based in Germany.

I met Rick Logan on his arrival at the Hyatt Regency hotel in Brussels. I had heard that he could be a bit of a bully so his opening line didn't surprise me.

"Who the hell are you?" he exclaimed.

"I am Colonel Len Dent, Chief of Public Information for the Canadian Forces in Europe and the Middle East. And who the hell are you?"

"I am Rick Logan, Chief of Staff to the Minister."

"I am completely underwhelmed," I said, forcefully.

He looked at me for a moment then smiled and said, "Do you want to go for a drink?"

I got along with him fine from that point on. But I did see that when he could bully someone who did not fight back; he could be mean. His manner when talking to the military senior officers was considered to be boorish and inappropriate and did not win him any friends amongst that group.

More than 40 international press members attended the press conference, which was an unusually high number to attend when a Canadian Defence Minister held a press conference. I am not sure if it was a slow day or there was just interest in the arrival of the CF-18.

Just before the start, Rick Logan came up to the Minister and said, "Bobby, Jeff and I are going to SHAPE (Supreme Headquarters Allied Powers in Europe - located in Mons, Belgium.) We are going shopping at the US PX. We will be back soon." What struck me was that he called the Minister 'Bobby'. I knew their relationship went back a long way but this seemed a little too familiar, particularly in this setting. The Minister looked startled and said, "What about me?" Logan replied, "It's Ok, Lennie will look after you and the press conference." I was not sure if this was a tribute to me or they just didn't want to be there when the Minister had his press conference!

The first question regarding the new aircraft came from a Southams wire service stringer based in Paris and was very technical in nature. I saw the look in the Minister's eyes and knew we were in trouble. In fairness he had been Defence Minister for only a short time and couldn't be expected to know some of these technical details. He stumbled through answering the first question. A supplementary one from the same reporter wasn't any easier.

I saw the look on the faces of some of the other professional reporters and knew they sensed the Minister might be a little out of his depth.

I took a gamble. I went up to the table where he was sitting and whispered in his ear. Then I turned to the media gathering and said, "I am so sorry ladies and gentlemen but the Minister has been called to a meeting with the Secretary General. We will have to stop the press conference. However, I do have a detailed backgrounder on the CF-18 and its pending stationing in Germany which hopefully will answer all your questions."

The Minister stood up. I quickly escorted him to the door. There was no grumbling from the media. Perhaps this wasn't such a big deal... and a Canadian Defence Minister wasn't that important to them. I doubt a US Secretary of Defense would have been allowed to get away as easily!

I handed out the excellent backgrounder, which had been prepared by the ADM (Policy) group back in Ottawa. The next day there were several short stories carried by national newspapers in Europe. None mentioned anything about the Minister having to leave after the first two questions.

I learned that evening from Rick Logan that Minister Coates was very happy with the way I had handled his 'press conference.' Over a drink, at the hotel bar, Logan said to me, "I want to have you moved back to Ottawa and work with Jeff and me. You will be the Minister's military press Secretary."

I was taken back. I had only been in Europe for a little over a year. The last thing I wanted to do was to move back to Ottawa and to work in the Minister's office. I expressed my gratitude for his confidence in me but told him, I really wanted to stay in Europe and briefed him on how I hoped to raise Canada's Defence profile. I told him I thought I would be of greater value where I was. By the time he finished his last drink, he had agreed. What a relief!

It wasn't until about three months later that I realized how wise it was to turn down this invitation to work in the Minister's office.

In February, Shirlie and I had taken the weekend and gone skiing in a wonderful resort in Switzerland near the Italian border. We had rented a chalet at the bottom of the hill and enjoyed two days of unbelievable skiing conditions and weather.

When we arrived home at about 8 pm on Sunday evening and opened the door, our phone was ringing. I answered and heard the rather upset voice of MGen Wightman. Apparently he had been trying to reach me for hours.

"There is a reporter named MacDonald in town who is bugging the life out of me," he said. "Apparently he has the lowdown on something the Minister did while he was in Lahr last November. He wants to interview me about the visit. I told him I wouldn't talk to him until I had talked to you. Next time he calls I am going to give him your number and have him call you." He sounded relieved that he had finally got me. He hung up. I knew a Neil MacDonald. If it was who I thought, he was a young aggressive reporter working for the Ottawa Citizen. What could have brought him all the way to Lahr??

It didn't take long for me to find the answer. About ten minutes later the phone rang.

"This is Neil MacDonald from the Ottawa Citizen," the voice growled. "I am trying to get an interview with MGen Wightman and he tells me that I have to talk to you first." He sounded frustrated.

"So what is this all about?" I replied.

"I don't have time for all this bureaucratic BS," he snapped.

"Either tell me what this is about or you won't get an interview with the General," I snapped back.

"OK," he said, "Can I come to your house?"

"No," I replied, "But there's a Gasthaus just outside the main gate of the Base. I will meet you there in about 30 minutes." I hung up before he could answer.

Twenty-nine minutes later I entered the Gasthaus. MacDonald was at a table nursing a beer.

I ordered a beer. I told him to brief me on why he was here.

It only took a few minutes for him to lay out the story. He had learned back in Ottawa that Minister Coates and two of his advisors had visited the famous Tiffany's Bar here in Lahr. He didn't tell me how he had first heard about the visit. He told me he had visited the bar, had spoken to some girls who had met the Minister. Now he wanted to interview MGen Wightman about what he knew about the story. Why did he let the Minister go to the bar?

I was told later that Logan and Matthews had been in the National Press Club bar at lunchtime one day and had talked about their visit to Tiffany's while in Lahr .

Of course, many of the media who had come to Lahr over the years to visit the Canadian troops had, mostly by curiosity I suspect, visited the same bar. It was a girly bar where the girls tried to get you to buy them overpriced drinks. These types of clubs were not uncommon in Europe. Strange as it may seem, our landlord and landlady, who lived across the street from us in the small village of Ottenheim, sent their 16-year old son to a similar local bar as a birthday present. A coming-of-age present perhaps. So, no big deal to most people in Europe, I understood.

MacDonald was in the NPC bar and overheard the story. When he got back to his desk at the Ottawa Citizen, I was told, he called Matthews to confirm the story. Matthews was terribly upset that he had taken what he had heard in the NPC and intended to use it and reportedly hung up. Apparently MacDonald told his News Editor about the story and convinced him to let him go to Lahr and research this story.

So regardless of how he had heard about the incident, he was here and had a story which could be very damaging to the Minister and potentially to the Canadian Forces.

I told Mr. MacDonald that I would speak with MGen Wightman and get back to him in the morning.

About 11 pm, I knocked on the door of MGen Wightman's residence. Much to my surprise he answered the door in his pajamas. There might have been security somewhere, but I didn't see any. I did know that during the raid of a Red Army Brigade apartment near Frankfurt by German officials, some newspaper articles were found which featured our Canadian Commander, which suggested to me that he was a high-ranking officer of interest. Indeed, on an ongoing basis, we had unscheduled exercise alerts at the Base simulating an attack by these terrorists.

MGen Wightman invited me into his living room. I related to him what Neil MacDonald had told me.

He told me that during the short visit of the Minister to Lahr, the previous November, he had planned a formal Mess Dinner for the Minister in the Black Forest Officers' Mess. The dinner ended about midnight and the Minister and his two aides retired to their VIP quarters in the Mess.

Only those three would know who brought up the subject, but obviously someone suggested that they go for a visit and a nightcap at Tiffany's Bar. It is only conjecture but perhaps this suggestion came after a long day and a long evening featuring lots of good food and refreshment. Personally, I doubt it was the 56-year-old Minister who would have made this suggestion.

So reportedly, Mr. Logan commandeered General Wightman's staff car and driver and drove to the bar. Later Gen Wightman told me that the driver came back and told him what had happened. The General was able to get a big burly military policeman in civvies into the bar to look after the Minister's personal safety. As Mr. MacDonald learned from his visit to the bar and stated in his article, Mr. Coates had a drink and talked to some of the girls.

The next morning the Minister and his Aides climbed aboard their aircraft and flew to Brussels for their NATO meetings.

I suggested to MGen Wightman that he should give an interview to Mr. MacDonald in order to make it clear what the involvement of the Canadian Forces had been. If not, it could be taken that we were trying to cover up a very simple, straightforward event. He agreed, but asked me to find out what DGInfo (Director General Information) back in Ottawa thought of the idea.

The next morning about 8 am Ottawa time I called for BGen Yvon Durocher, our DGInfo. I was told he was at the morning meeting. I wasn't able to speak with Col Boulet as he was unavailable.

I called MGen Wightman and told him what had happened and advised him we should go ahead with the interview. He agreed. I called Neil MacDonald and told him to come to the General's office at 4 pm

We met at the General's office at the agreed time. I came with my tape recorder. Mr. MacDonald said, "What's that for?" I told him I was going to tape the interview. He said rather abruptly, "I don't allow my interviews to be taped." I said, "Fine, then there will be no interview." So he agreed to the taping. Interestingly a couple of hours after the interview, he called and asked me if he could borrow the tape. He wanted to check his quotes!

The interview was straightforward. Obviously he knew the story but focused on what the Minister and his Aides had done before the trip to the bar and why the General had let them go. The General told him about the Mess Dinner and offered that once they went back to their VIP quarters, it was not his responsibility to monitor their movements. When pushed several times under MacDonald's questioning he did allow that he had learned where they had gone but also had been advised that at no time was there any question regarding the safety of the Minister.

Following the interview, I went back to my office and called home. Shirlie told me that Rick Logan had called several times and wanted to speak with me urgently. My first thought was that, "I am toast." Rick had learned about the interview and probably wants me fired!

I drove home and paced up and down for a few minutes in front of my house trying to figure out what I could tell Logan. Finally, I decided to just tell him the truth as the story had unfolded for me.

I called and he answered after the first ring. "Len," he said. "How are you, how are things going over there?" He sounded very cordial and my immediate thought was that this was not the man who was going to have me fired.

"Well," I exclaimed, "We have a problem. By the way do you know that this phone call is being recorded?" I had called through the NDHQ Operations Centre where all calls are recorded.

"What is your private number?" he said. I told him and he hung up. About five minutes later, my phone rang. Logan was on the line, as where Jeff Matthews, the Press Secretary and Paul Dunn, a Political Advisor to the Minister.

I then went on to tell him what Neil MacDonald had found out, giving him all the details I knew. I also told him why we had had the interview with General Wightman and what he had said.

He was furious. Not at me but at MacDonald. "This is all b... s..," he yelled into the phone. "Maybe, but if you say this isn't what happened you better get on to the editor of the Citizen and talk to him," I said as calmly as I could.

"We'll sue if they print this story," he yelled. "Don't talk to me," I said, "Call the Citizen's editor."

Shortly after I hung up, I received a call from Paul Koring, who was the CP correspondent based in London. He told me he had heard that a Citizen reporter was in Lahr working on a story about the Minister. I had worked with Paul a number of times and respected him as a reporter. He was hardnosed but a very fair journalist. Since Mr. MacDonald already had his story, I didn't think it unfair to tell Paul that Neil was in Lahr and what he was after.

Paul said he wanted to put me on hold. A few minutes later he came back and told me that he had talked to CP Headquarters. CP wouldn't touch the story, he said, because of the possibility of a lawsuit. But, he continued, if the Citizen runs the story then we will be running with what they have printed and, "I will be back to you with questions." "Fair enough," I told him.

The next day, Feb 12, 1985, the story ran in the Ottawa Citizen and was carried by news agencies around the world.

The New York Times ran the story stating that The Ottawa Citizen had quoted an unidentified Canadian intelligence officer as speculating that the nightclub visit by Mr. Coates might have jeopardized his top security status.

Years later, in 2012, Neil MacDonald wrote a story on the death of Archie Barr who, at the time of the Coates affair, was the Deputy Director of the Canadian Security Intelligence Service. According to his story MacDonald stated that at the time he had interviewed Barr, "I'd been told that Robert Coates, Brian Mulroney's new Defence Minister, had compromised himself and a briefcase containing national secrets somewhere in Europe. Apparently hookers were involved." Barr assured him that CSIS was not investigating any such story. Though, he said, some other agency might be and, if it were, it might not have seen fit to tell CSIS. "So I got digging," said MacDonald.

MacDonald continued that, "We found out that Coates and two assistants had been in a bar featuring strippers and hookers outside the Canadian military base in Lahr." He added," There was no briefcase of secrets involved."

At the time, I had heard the story of a briefcase with secret material but had no idea where it had come from. But, it certainly did make the story more sensational.

Later that day, Robert Coates stood in the House of Commons and announced, "I have resigned as Minister of National Defence effective today." The Minister called the story inaccurate and libelous but did not elaborate.

Mr. Coates told a hushed session of the House of Commons, "I recognize the fundamental importance of my portfolio, one which is as sensitive as any in Government. I'm a man of honour who respects Parliament and I especially respect my Prime Minister."

Prime Minister Mulroney told the House that an investigation had determined that at no time was the national security of Canada compromised in any way. Opposition leaders commended Mr. Coates for his decision to step down.

Meanwhile, in Lahr, it was evening and I had really no information about what was happening in Ottawa. I had learned from a news report that the Minister had resigned but knew nothing of what the Prime Minister had said in the House or what his Press Secretary Bill Fox had responded to questions from the media.

As soon as I reached the office the next morning the avalanche of calls from media outlets all over the world began. One of the first was from Paul Koring. I am not sure why, but thankfully he briefly brought me up to date on what the Prime Minister and Bill Fox had said the previous day. Then he asked me a question concerning what the Prime Minister had said. My response was easy. "If that is what the Prime Minister said, then who am I to dispute that? To this day, I believe if he had not told me what the PM had said I might have answered in such a way that could have embarrassed Mr. Mulroney and probably would have been the end of my career.

My greatest problem with answering questions from the media, particularly the European media, was trying to explain to them what Mr.

Coates had done wrong. I explained countless times that he had gone to a girly bar at 1 am in the morning.

"We know that was the answer but what did he do wrong that made it necessary for him to resign?"

And that really was an impossible question to answer. From what I was told his only mistake was going to the bar. His conduct in the bar was something he could have told his wife about and probably did. Apparently given the activities of many European politicians, according to European journalists, his actions were not unusual.

Obviously the Canadian moral standards were different and more was expected of a Minister of the Crown. I can't blame Neil MacDonald. He was a young, keen journalist following a 'hot' lead. But in retrospect, this story ended a 28-year career in politics and cost a man his career as a Minister. A visit to a bar that perhaps should not have happened!

Mr. Coates did sue the Ottawa Citizen. Since I was in Germany for another year I never did learn of the result of that lawsuit. He remained as a backbencher but did not run for re-election in 1988.

The next day, Erik Nielsen was named Minister of Defence. It was a heavy load for him to carry. He was already serving as Deputy Prime Minister, but having served for 30 years in Parliament, he was well experienced and an excellent choice to take on this difficult portfolio.

I first met Minister Nielsen in May 1985, when he came to the spring session of the Defence Ministers' meeting at NATO Headquarters in Brussels. He and his wife and group had arrived early in the morning having flown overnight from Ottawa. Unfortunately, External Affairs officials in Brussels had not booked his suite for 'check-in' in the Hyatt Regency until that afternoon. When asked, the occupant, a Texas oilman, refused to leave his suite, until the actual departure time. The hotel was fully booked, but the manager finally found a small standard room that the Nielsen's could occupy until the suite was ready.

The Minister had had virtually no sleep on the way over. As I realized later, he had stayed up all night on the flight reading the briefing book prepared for him by Defence officials. His hope of getting a few hours of sleep, before his briefings that afternoon didn't materialize. So he was a little grumpy when he arrived at the Canadian Delegation offices in NATO Headquarters. He was also rubbing his eye continuously, which we determined must have been as a result of his lack of sleep. We found out later that he had an eye infection.

The two-hour briefing dragged along with the Minister not commenting and just rubbing his eye. What appeared to be a lack of questioning by a Minister being briefed was not unusual. There was just so much detail that, in my experience at these meetings going back 10 years, most Ministers didn't question what they were being told.

Suddenly Minister Nielsen stopped rubbing his eyes and said, "Wait, you just told me something that is completely different in the briefing book. Which is correct?"

The Ambassador, his senior staff along with all of us in attendance were shocked. Not only had the Minister read the briefing book but he remembered the details. We were impressed!

"I want to know the proper information before our Defence Ministers' meeting starts tomorrow morning at 10 am," he said.

That night he joined the other 15 NATO Ministers at the home of the Secretary General for dinner. Reportedly, it was about midnight when he got back to the Hyatt Regency. By this time he and his wife had been moved into a suite. But he must have been exhausted.

About 1:30 am one of the senior Canadian reporters who had come to Brussels to cover the meeting decided that he needed to speak to the Minister immediately. I am not sure why, but it couldn't wait until morning. No doubt, having gained some false courage for the liquid refreshments he might have consumed at a bar in downtown Brussels, he called the hotel. The hotel operator obviously did not know who Erik Nielsen was so she connected him to the Minister's suite. His wife answered the phone. Perhaps, not used to the protocol and not knowing if the call was important, she woke up her husband and told him he had a call. One can only imagine Erik Nielsen's reaction when a not-so-sober reporter greeted him asking a question.

When I arrived at NATO Headquarters the next morning I was confronted by the Minister's Chief of Staff. He was furious. He told me what had happened and then chastised me for not having more control of the 'press.'

About an hour later a rather 'hung-over' reporter showed up at NATO headquarters and found me. He asked rather sheepishly if I thought he could still have an interview with the Minister. I told him that for both our sakes, he should avoid even letting the Minister see him.

At the meeting, just before the Minister went into the formal session, he got the information he had asked for the day before. Then he looked at me and said, "Other than that idiot that called me in the middle of the night, are there any other media guys that want to talk to me?"

I told him that Paul Koring from Canadian Press was anxious to discuss the forth-coming NATO exercises in Northern Norway, and more specifically how Canada would be able to meet its commitments to NATO. He looked at me and said, "Tell him I don't want to talk to him." Turning to the Ambassador, he said, "What about you Mr. Ambassador?" to which he replied, "Me neither, I don't want to speak to Koring."

Obviously, Koring's reputation as a hardnosed reporter was well known to the Minister who was sometimes referred to as "Velcro lips." He had this nickname dubbed by the media because of his tight-lipped reluctance to speak out while in office. He had the habit of stonewalling questions in the House and with the media.

In this case, I was told to tell Koring that the Minister did not want to talk to him. I met Paul in the lobby and rather diplomatically told him that the Minister was very busy with briefings and meetings, and that he would be leaving early that afternoon to fly back to Ottawa for a late vote in the House that evening, which in fact he did. I am not sure if Paul believed what I told him, but accepted the explanation from me graciously.

The next time I met Minister Nielsen was later that year when he came back to take part in the ceremonies introducing the CF-18 to squadron service in Europe. The ceremonies were held in Lahr and attended by Canadian and German dignitaries as well as NATO officials. There were many international media in attendance for this auspicious occasion.

Leading the German delegation was Defence Minister Manfred Wörner. He gave a moving speech highlighting the importance of the addition of the new aircraft, lauding the contribution it would make to NATO while underscoring the great relationship between Germany and Canada. He presented it flawlessly in his second language and got a warm round of applause from the assembled crowd. Nielsen took the microphone and, reading from a speech prepared for him in National Defence Headquarters, gave an unmoving and uninspiring 10 minutes of primarily boring facts and figures. His speech was greeted with polite applause.

Later that evening, officers and their wives gathered at the Officers' Mess for a formal mess dinner for the Minister and his wife. After dinner he stood up to say a few words armed with his Ottawa-prepared speech. The Minister was a veteran of such occasions and no doubt realized that his speech that afternoon had not been a barnburner. He rather unceremoniously dropped the notes on the table besides the dais and began to speak off the cuff.

Within minutes he had the whole gathering roaring with laughter, and the laughter continued for the next twenty minutes. Then I realized that this was Leslie Nielsen's elder brother. In his career, Canadian actor and comedian Leslie Nielsen appeared in 100 films and 1,500 TV programs, portraying more than 220 characters. Erik no doubt could have had a career in acting but then some would say that his working in the House of Commons for thirty years was a 'career in acting.'

I only wish Minister Nielsen had thrown away his speech this afternoon, but then he was new to the Defence portfolio and probably felt more comfortable with the prepared text. Regardless, although I had only been with him on two occasions, he was one of the smartest Ministers with whom I had worked.

The Canadian Forces base at Lahr was home for the Headquarters of Canadian Forces Europe, and attracted many high-ranking visitors particularly from Canada. They were royally wined and dined during each visit, and I am sure this became known throughout the Cabinet in Ottawa. We did seem to get a lot of visitors each week. It was wonderful for those coming for a short stay, but for the small group of senior officers who had to host them at small lunches and dinners, it became, frankly, tiresome. It also took valuable time away from our normal workload, which often meant staying beyond normal working hours to catch up. More troubling was the impact on our bodies from consuming so much rich, heavy German food and wine, which was normally served.

One such visitor who came several times during my tour in Germany was Governor General Jeanne Sauvé. She had served as a Member of Parliament for fourteen years, and in 1984, was appointed Governor General by Queen Elizabeth II, on the recommendation of Prime Minister Pierre Trudeau.

On her first visit to Lahr she was hosted to a luncheon by MGen Wightman, and ten senior officers. I sat across from her. There was polite conversation throughout the meal, but I couldn't help but feel, as we chatted, that she would have rather been somewhere else. I wondered just how well she was. She had been hospitalized just before being sworn in, which delayed her installation ceremony. The rumor was that she had some form of cancer, but she was quite secretive about her actual illness stating that it was a private matter. Nevertheless she took on all the demanding responsibilities of the office on May 14, 1984.

After lunch she was scheduled to be interviewed on our local Canadian Forces Network radio station. We were riding in the backseat of the staff car and she asked me what the interviewer might want to ask her. Since this was her first visit, I told her that they were interested to know how she felt about being the first female Governor General of Canada and her responsibilities as Commander in Chief of the Canadian Forces.

"Good Lord," she exclaimed with just a hint of a twinkle in her eye. "What are my responsibilities as the Commander in Chief?"

I wasn't quite sure if she was kidding me or not. She was an astute woman who had been a journalist and broadcaster with Radio Canada and CBC before becoming a Member of Parliament in 1972.

I had done my homework about her role with the military in advance of her arrival. So I played along. We discussed some of the things that I thought were most important including her being the most senior officer of the Canadian Armed Forces; her requirement to approve and sign all declarations of war; her duty to appoint the Chief of the Defence Staff; approve new military badges and insignia; visit Canadian Forces personnel serving at home and abroad; and, her duty to sign all commissioning scrolls.

She smiled and thanked me. I still don't know if she was just testing me or not. Perhaps that was the old reporter in her, seeing if this Public Information officer had prepared himself for her visit.

The interview went smoothly. She was very elegant and impressed the Station staff and those who heard her interview.

I took her to visit and mingle with some of the troops as they worked on the base. She was very regal and seemed genuinely interested in talking with them. At her request we went to the CANEX, the military 'general store,' where she could do some shopping. The next day she left Lahr and continued on her tour of Europe.

292

She came back twice while I was serving in Lahr. Each time was much the same: a short stay, which included an official lunch, sometimes a dinner, talking to the troops and then off.

During the three visits I spent a lot of time with her. She could be very charming but on some occasions would seem to be aloof and not that interested in what she was doing. I continued to wonder if this apparent lack of interest was a result of her trying to cope with an illness.

There were many important individuals who made their way to Lahr during my tour in Europe. One such was the Secretary General of NATO. I had just arrived in my office one morning when MGen Wightman called and told me that Lord Carrington would be arriving in about an hour. He was flying in from Brussels for a short visit to the base. The General told me that the 'Sec Gen' just wanted to have a tour of the facilities and to meet some of the soldiers and airmen at work. Most of all he didn't want any media to be aware of his visit. So, "Just take some photos of him and the troops," the General said. "He is Ok with that."

An hour later I picked him up at the base airfield terminal building. We began our tour with a stop at the tank compound, since I knew that Lord Carrington had served in tanks during World War II. He landed on the beach at Normandy on D-Day and was later awarded the Military Cross for holding a strategically vital bridge at Nijmegen in the Netherlands. After the war he entered politics and served from 1946 to 1982. He was Britain's Defence Secretary from 1970-1974 and Foreign Secretary in 1982, when the Falkland Islands were invaded by Argentina.

But by his actions and demeanour, one would never know he was anything but an average man on the street. He saw a corporal working on the track of an old tank and asked him what he was doing. "Trying to put this piece of this ******* thing back together," the young soldier said without really looking at whom he was speaking. " This ******* tank belongs in a museum, we spend more time trying to fix it than driving it," he blurted.

"Know how you feel, old chap," said Lord Carrington, "Had much the same thoughts when I was in tanks." The Sec Gen walked away.

I said to the corporal, "Do you know who you were talking to?"

"No, but he seems like a nice guy," he said continuing to tug at the tank track.

"That is the Secretary General of NATO, Lord Carrington."

He turned, looked at me and gulped, "And I talked to him like that."

"Never mind," I said," I am sure he has heard worse."

This easy going and unpretentious manner was typical of the way in which he talked to all those we met. Then, after a three-hour tour, we headed for the Black Forest Officers' Mess for lunch, hosted by MGen. Wightman and six other officers. During the meal, we discussed NATO, some of its problems and even his thoughts on getting a better image for the organization. Throughout, he was down to earth and genuinely interested in hearing our opinions on his thoughts on NATO.

Following lunch it was back to the airfield and he was gone. An interesting experience for me with a very impressive man. An experience I have never forgotten.

Because our office had taken on many more responsibilities, there was never a lack of things to do. In fact, we had to prioritize. We had made an obligation to get more exposure for our troops stationed in the Middle East. But with only three officers and one photographer in our office and distances being so far, it was difficult to give our peacekeepers the attention they deserved. There was one of our public information officers always stationed with the Canadian contingent with the United Nations Forces in Cyprus. But troops in other parts of the Middle East got less attention.

I sent our photographer Sergeant Margaret Reid with the Minister when he visited the troops. But when the aircraft arrived in one capital, Sgt Reid was denied permission to leave the airport because she was a woman and dressed as a soldier. She was furious. I know what she told the authorities and I thought afterwards she was lucky she wasn't taken to jail, and it didn't change their decision not to let her leave the building. Fortunately she did not experience that treatment anywhere else on the tour.

In January 1986, I had the opportunity to 'hitch' a ride with LGen Charlie Belzile, the Commander of Mobile Command. In effect, the Commander of the Canadian Army. He was on a trip to the Middle East to say 'good bye' as he was soon retiring from the Canadian Forces.

We left Lahr on the Commander's CFE Dash 7 and headed for Damascus. Our Canadian Military Attaché met us at the airport.

While waiting for our bags, he took me aside and told me that they had changed my title for my visit within Syria. "For this visit you are the Executive Assistant to General Belzile," he said. "But why can't I just be the Chief of Public Information?" I said rather innocently. "Believe me, it is much better for your health and well being " he said. "Your title is interpreted as you being an intelligence officer or spy." It worked for me. I didn't want or need any problems during our stay.

In that vein, I asked if it was safe to walk the streets of Damascus. I was told that if you dropped your wallet on the sidewalk, no one would even pick it up to give it back to you. That struck me as rather odd until it was explained that every Friday there was a gathering at the main square in Damascus and that thieves were brought in and in a very public demonstration their right hands were cut off. What an incentive to cut down on petty crime!

That evening we were invited to the Attaché's house for dinner. During a pre-dinner drink, he told me that news reporting in Syria was just a lot of propaganda. He switched on the Syrian government TV channel for the 6:30 news broadcast. As the announcer was reading the news, he suddenly read a bulletin stating that the Space shuttle Challenger had just blown up. He then went on to other news.

"See what I mean," our host said, "that's the kind of garbage we have to listen to."

After dinner, he turned on the Christian TV station from Beirut, Lebanon, where he told me that they got fairly accurate news. It was then that we learned the truth. Indeed the Challenger had disintegrated at 48,000 feet over the Atlantic Ocean off Cape Canaveral, 73 seconds after takeoff from Florida at 1139 EST. It was Jan 28, 1986.

Seven crewmembers including five astronauts and two payload specialists died. Christa McAuliffe, one of the payload specialists would have been the first teacher in space.

An intensive investigation revealed that the disintegration apparently began after an O-ring failed at lift-off. It was a tragic accident that resulted in a 32-month hiatus in the US space program.

It was a sobering end to our evening!

The following day we were driven out into the Golan to the border area separating Syria and Israel.

During the six-day war in 1967, Israel captured the western Golan Heights from Syria, and Syrian control was reduced to about one-third of its size. After a failed attempt to recapture the territory by the Syrians in the Yom Kippur war of 1973, a UN supervised Demilitarized Zone was established between the Syrian controlled territory and the Israeli occupied Golan Heights in 1974.

UN troops came from Austria, Peru, Canada and Poland. The Canadians were based at Camp Ziouani located on the Israeli controlled side of the Golan Heights. They were at the Headquarters of Logistics and the Canadian troops were responsible for performing general transport tasks, rotating troops, controlling and managing goods and maintaining heavy equipment.

There was no official border crossing. However, UN troops had one gate near the town of Quneitra where they could cross between the two territories. So we drove to the border and were close enough to see our Canadian soldiers in Camp Ziouani, but because we were not UN soldiers we were not able to visit the camp.

That would take more than 24 hours. We drove back to Damascus and flew to Tel Aviv via Cyprus because we could not fly direct across Syrian territory to Israel.

We were driven from Tel Aviv to Tiberias to spend the night. Aware of the visit of LGen Belzile, the Israeli Defence Force (IDF) General in command of Northern Israel had made plans to host us for dinner that evening in a private hotel dining room.

Our small group assembled in the hotel bar at 6:00 pm for a pre-dinner drink. A young Israeli officer came in, went to Gen Belzile, saluted smartly and said, "The General sends his regrets but he will not be able to join you for dinner this evening; he has a bad cold. He hopes you enjoy the dinner that has been prepared for you."

He saluted again did an about face and marched out of the room. We looked at each other. A hardened Israeli general couldn't make it to a dinner for the commander of the Canadian Army because he has a cold. Sounded a little incredulous!

The meal was superb and the excellent wine made in Israel flowed freely.

The next morning we came down to breakfast and were told by the hotel staff that overnight the IDF had successfully raided a Palestinian Liberation Organization (PLO) camp just across the Lebanese border. While we were eating breakfast the same young officer came in to the dining room. He was carrying a gift-wrapped parcel, which he handed to Gen Belzile.

"The Commander regrets his not being able to join you last evening," he said, "But he wants you to have this little gift and hopes that you will understand the circumstances." Once again he saluted and was gone. Of course we understood why he had not been able to join us. But the gift was not unwrapped by the General so I have no idea what the IDF commander had offered as a token of his apology.

We left the hotel and headed for the Golan Heights. Once up on the Heights we could easily understand the problems the Israelis had faced with the Syrians occupying the western edge of that territory.

The northern half of the border between the two countries was very steep, with the escarpment climbing to about 2,000 feet. Syrian forces occupied the plateau behind it, the Golan Heights.

Prior to the 1967 Six-Day War, Syria had continually shelled Israeli communities from the Golan. In the spring of 1967, a large number of troops were massed along the 40-mile border. There were more than 265 artillery pieces aimed down at Israel. By the outbreak of the Six-Day War, Syrian forces in the Golan totaled over 40,000 troops with 260 tanks and self-propelled guns.

During the fighting, heavy artillery barrages were launched against Israeli communities from the Golan. Two infantry companies crossed the border to attack a Kibbutz. The defenders held off the attackers for 20 minutes until the Israeli Air Force arrived and drove the Syrians back.

On the fifth day of the fighting, Israel launched an offensive aimed at driving the Syrians from the Golan Heights. After almost 36 hours of fierce fighting, the Syrian resistance collapsed. With the end of the fighting on the Golan Heights, the Six-Day war was over. Casualties had been high on both sides, but much more so for the Syrians. Israeli forces had 115 killed and 306 wounded. Syrian losses included an estimated 2,500 deaths, 5,000 wounded and 591 taken as prisoners of war.

We arrived at Camp Ziouani just about 24 hours after being a few hundred yards away on the Syrian side of the border. We spent the remainder of the day being royally hosted by the officers and men serving at this remote base. Gen Belzile was well respected and well liked by the army troops and they were most pleased that he had made the effort to travel all this way to see them as part of his farewell tour. It was the highlight of the six-month tour for many, we were told.

The next morning we said our goodbyes and headed for Jerusalem. Once again I got to stay in the beautiful American Colony Hotel.

That evening Israeli military officials hosted us at a dinner. The following morning, after meetings with a few Canadians stationed in Israel, we were driven back to Tel Aviv, climbed into our Dash 7 and headed for Nicosia, Cyprus.

General Belzile had commanded the Royal Canadian Regiment in Cyprus in 1969 and was very knowledgeable about the island and the situation that the troops faced.

I think the General must have met every officer and man stationed in Nicosia during our 24-hour stay. Once again it was clear he was a soldier's soldier! The manner in which this high-ranking officer was greeted by all, down to the youngest private, demonstrated their loyalty to and affection for him.

The next morning we flew back to Lahr, ending an informative trip that would help me to better direct interested Canadian and foreign journalists who wished to visit our troops stationed in the Middle East.

The military base at Lahr was opened in 1967 when RCAF #1 Fighter Wing was moved from Marville, France. France had opted out of NATO and required all NATO bases to be closed. Later, a squadron from Zwiebrucken, Germany was moved to the base. In the early 1970s, the RCAF squadrons were moved to Baden-Solingen, about 45 minutes north of Lahr.

In 1970, the Canadian Army, located in several bases in northern Germany, was brought to Lahr except for the PPCLI, which was moved to Baden-Solingen.

By the time we arrived in 1983, there were about 10,000 military and civilian personnel and their families living in Lahr and the surrounding areas. We Canadians made up about one-quarter of the population of the city. Canadians frequented the Gasthauses and restaurants and pumped considerable dollars into the local economy. In general, we were well liked and appreciated by the local community.

Most of us took advantage of our location to travel to the nearby countries when we had time off. Lahr is located in the southwest corner of Germany, on the edge of the beautiful Black Forest, and close to the French and Swiss borders. One goal we had when we first arrived was to have breakfast in Germany, lunch in Switzerland and dinner in France. One day, we did just that, driving through some scenic countryside and were back home by 9 pm. During our three-year stay, Shirlie, David and I, took some skiing trips at fantastic resorts in Germany, France, Switzerland, Italy and Austria, all of which were only a few hours' drive away.

Life was good. There were a few scary moments. We knew that there were cells of the terrorist group Red Brigade operating not that far from the Base.

Occasionally there would be full alerts when a suspicious package was found on the base or an intelligence report indicated the possibility of some terrorist act. Sirens would sound the base evacuation order. The all clear would sound and later we would find out that someone had left their lunch sitting on a bench, or had forgotten a package. But it kept us alert. Of course, there were always the 'Snowball' exercises when we had to react as if it was an actual attack. After all, it was only about 600 km from Prague, Czechoslovakia to Lahr, or less than an hour by fighter jet.

But perhaps the scariest moment for military personnel and their families came not from the threat of a bombing or an attack, but rather from something that happened in the Ukraine many kilometres away.

On April 26, 1986, a reactor at a nuclear power plant in Chernobyl, Ukraine, blew up. This led to a series of steam explosions and a fire, which sent a plume of highly radioactive fallout into the atmosphere.

The plume drifted over large parts of the western Soviet Union and Europe. From 1986 to 2000, 350,000 people were evacuated and resettled from the most severely contaminated areas of Belarus, Russia and Ukraine.

Two plant workers died on the night of the accident. Twenty-eight died within a few weeks as a result of acute radiation poisoning.

Today, resettlement is still ongoing. In 2011, Chernobyl was officially declared a tourist attraction.

Apparently, the 1986 accident is the only accident in a power plant using nuclear power to cause fatalities from radiation. According to a paper published by the US Nuclear Energy Institute, "It was a product of a severely flawed Soviet-era reactor design combined with human error."

According to a United Nations study published in 2011, most emergency workers and people living in contaminated areas received relatively low whole-body radiation doses.

However, there is some evidence of a detectable increase in leukemia and cataract risk among workers who received higher doses when engaged in recovery at the site. Monitoring of these individuals is ongoing.

News of the accident went worldwide. Lahr is located about 1650 kilometres west of Chernobyl. But it didn't take long for a great deal of concern to be raised amongst local residents including many of the military wives living in Lahr and the surrounding area.

Military officials at the base were aware of the concerns and first thoughts were for the safety of all members of the population in the area, both Canadian and German. A call was made to Canada and two scientists from the National Research Council with appropriate testing equipment were immediately dispatched to the base. Their orders were to make a wide variety of tests to determine the level, if any, of radiation that might be in the local area. Over a period of several days they found nothing to indicate that the area had been impacted by radiation as a result of the Chernobyl explosion.

My office used all media outlets to keep the general population apprised of the results of these tests.

The Base had its own radio station, Canadian Forces Network or CFN Lahr, which carried Canadian news provided by CBC, Radio Canada and other news outlets, as well as local news and programming from a small staff employed at the station.

This station, along with articles in the weekly base newspaper, Der Kanadier, would reach most of our military and civilian families as well as the local German listeners and should have brought some degree or reassurance, or so I thought!

There was one young female reporter working at CFN Lahr who chose not to believe what we were telling everyone. She managed to find a local German 'scientist' who became the voice of doom. She interviewed him on her afternoon program. It was not helpful.

He painted a horrible picture of impending disaster and predicted many cases of severe illness leading to possible death for local residents. He strongly advised mothers to not let their children play outside or touch the grass, and under no circumstances to allow them to drink milk from local cows. It started a small panic.

I immediately went to talk to the young interviewer. I tried to reassure her that the entire scientific tests pointed to no level of danger. Incredibly, she told me she thought I was lying. "Cover up," she said, "So people, will not be afraid."

Why would I do this I asked her? I have a wife and a son living here in the area. If I thought there was a danger for them I would have them on the next plane home. Nothing I could say would convince her. Because CFN was part of my responsibility I went to the station manager and suggested to him that since this reporter could not be balanced in her coverage, she should not be allowed to cover this story in any manner in the future. It sounded like censorship. But it was our military base and what was being told to our listeners was a wild prediction not based on any facts and that was causing unnecessary upset. So, in my mind it was justified.

In the next couple of weeks nothing happened, no one became ill and gradually the residents began to feel more comfortable. To the best of my knowledge no one in the area ever became ill or had any effects from this disaster.

There is ongoing debate about the impact of the Chernobyl disaster. In 1986, some experts predicted as many as 40,000 extra cancer deaths from radiation poisoning. But it has been difficult to say how many people have died as a result of being exposed to radiation from the explosion. The exception might be amongst children, with nearly 7,000 cases of thyroid cancer having been diagnosed by 2005 in Belarus, Russia and Ukraine. A very rare disease in youth, reportedly scientists are sure that the radiation caused the high numbers of cases, 12 of which were fatal.

By mid-May, life had returned to normal in the Lahr area. About that time I received a message from Ottawa that Brigadier General Terry Liston, Director General Information wanted to visit, and asked me to arrange and accompany him on a series of meetings with officials in Supreme Headquarters Allied Powers of Europe (SHAPE) in Mons, Belgium, and at NATO headquarter in Brussels.

BGen Liston had taken over as the new head of Information Services in the summer of 1985. He was an experienced, articulate and no-nonsense army officer.

A week later we were checking into the Officer's quarters at SHAPE. The General suggested we meet at 6 pm in the Officers' Club for a pre-dinner drink. The waiter delivered us our martinis; the General took an approving sip, sat back in his comfortable lounge chair and said, with a smile, "Well Len, I have good news for you and bad news."

I hadn't expected this evening to be about me. So I looked him straight in the eye and said, "OK, so what is the bad news?"

"You are not going to be promoted." He still had a smile on his face, which I thought was odd under the circumstances. Was he happy giving me this news?

"So who is going to be promoted?" I asked having absolutely no ideas what he was going to tell me.

"Geoff Haswell," he said. I wasn't surprised. Col Boulet had given me only average annual assessments while in Lahr. MGen Wightman had sent several letters back to Ottawa giving me a high rating for my contribution in Europe and recommending me to be promoted and made Director. But these letters had not made a difference.

I didn't have anything against Geoff. He was about seven years younger than me, a Royal Military College graduate, and had worked for me on several occasions. I considered him a friend.

"So what is the good news?" I said, almost afraid now to ask.

"You are coming back to Ottawa as the new Director of Information Services to replace Col Boulet."

I was stunned!

"But what about Geoff? Why isn't he taking over as the boss?" I stuttered.

"He has been chosen for a NATO job in Brussels. He will be the Information Officer working with the Canadian Ambassador to NATO and his staff," the General replied.

"Why not send me? I know the Ambassador, all the information officers, the media that work around NATO headquarters. Then Geoff could be DIS."

"Len," he replied. "You are coming back to Ottawa as DIS. Now pay for the drinks and let's go to dinner."

Two days later, I was putting Gen Liston on the plane back to Ottawa. I drove home. Shirlie met me at the door and was anxious to know how the trip with the General had gone.

She was elated to hear that we were going back to Ottawa. She would be close to our daughter Susan, and wanted to get back into the work force. And she was happy for me that I was going to be the Director of Information Services. But she was dismayed that I had not gotten the promotion. We had talked about this in the months before I found out and I had told her that I thought, based on my annual assessments and the issues raised by General Wightman over the report, that I wouldn't be promoted. But I never expected to get the top job.

Two months later after a round of good-by parties given to us by our military friends and the locals with whom we had become close, we were on the military Boeing 707 bound for Ottawa.

It would be the start of a whole new chapter in my life.

Our DNDOI Team in Lahr (at a Gasthaus).

CHAPTER 16 - LIFE AT THE TOP

"If you had to do it all over again, would you do anything differently?"

I was standing in my new office on the 12th floor of National Defence Headquarters in Ottawa.

Col Jean Boulet was cleaning out the last few remnants of his desk in an office he had occupied for 12 years. When he spoke, he seemed to be serious.

"Not for one damned moment, Colonel," I said, although I was not quite sure what he was inferring. Maybe it had something to do with me not getting promoted!

In retrospect, I didn't dislike Col Boulet. In fact for several years he and I had been rather close. As mentioned earlier, he had told me on one occasion that he and I could run the whole Information Division; we didn't need anyone else. Not true, but an indication of his trust in me.

My problem began when Commodore Farrington, a new Director General of Information, began asking me, the Deputy Director, for my opinion directly.

I can only guess that he wasn't convinced that he was getting the guidance or advice that he wanted from his Director or wanted a second opinion. Commodore Farrington was an educator and believed strongly in his subordinates getting as much education and training as possible, even if they were information officers.

My being selected, in 1979, as the first Information Officer to go to Staff College was set in motion by Commodore Farrington.

When I returned a year later, Commodore Farrington made me the head of his newly created Policy, Evaluation and Plans cell. As such, I reported directly to him. I think that Col Boulet felt that sometimes my advice was being relied upon more than his. I understood how he felt. In his position, I would have felt exactly the same. But when asked by the Commodore for my opinion, I felt I had to tell him what I thought.

The Colonel picked up his box of belongings then put it down again on the desk. He held out his hand and said, "Good luck, Len."

I gave him a firm handshake and wished him a happy retirement. He took his mementos and left the office. I couldn't help but notice a small tear on his face. After all this had been his fiefdom for more than a decade. Now his days of ruling his little empire were over. He continued to use his expertise for more than 25 years, principally as an editor and French translator with the Royal Canadian Legion, until he died in 2012.

I stood for a moment and looked around at my new surroundings. Almost 20 years ago to the day I had been in the Director's office telling him why I would like to become a Public Information Officer. Today I was the Director. I couldn't believe it!

I wasn't wearing the rank. But I knew I could do the job!

I believe that most of the Information team felt the same. It wasn't long before the two other Lieutenant Colonels came in to my office shook my hand and welcomed me. For me, this was the pledge of support I needed, since I was their boss at the same rank level. They would have to show the rest of the team that we all needed to work together.

And we would need to work together to meet the challenge that General Liston was throwing at us.

It didn't take me long to realize why he wanted me as the Director. He was very much a gung-ho army officer who wanted to take a more proactive stance towards spreading the word about the Canadian Armed Forces to the Canadian public and the world. His initiative was no doubt driven in part by the current federal Government whose communication policy was to be more open with the public.

I had always been a pro-active type of Information Officer. In all the regional offices, Halifax, Winnipeg and Lahr, I had always wanted to be out developing positive relationships with the media, and developing trust and respect for our organization.

When I took over in Winnipeg as Senior Information Officer for the Prairie region, my predecessor had apparently never left the city, even though the area of responsibility stretched from Thunder Bay to the Alberta border. I made it a point in my first few weeks to visit all the bases and stations in the region as well as to visit as many media outlets as I could across the area. Interestingly the editor of the Portage La Prairie newspaper told me that he didn't know we had an Information Office in Winnipeg.

My establishing these relationships resulted in some very positive media coverage for our Canadian Forces in the Western Provinces during the next three years. However, I hasten to add that if the military was found to be doing something wrong, it was reported. Perhaps the difference was that the media called us first to get our side before printing or airing the story, and the stories were usually balanced and fair. Of course, this was in the early 1970s.

This pro-active approach in 1986 meant much more work for us at NDHQ in Ottawa, and for the small staffs in the regional offices. One of the first things we did was set up a Speaker's Bureau. It wasn't hard to convince the seniors in Ottawa and across the country, particularly since Gwynne Dyer's documentary on CBC was running nationally and gaining much attention. The Radio-Television section was given more staff, and much effort was devoted to preparing promotional material to be distributed nationwide.

A cell was established to provide media awareness and media interview training. This training was offered to newly appointed generals as well as base commanders and project managers. Lectures were also given by senior information officers to those attending the Canadian Forces Staff College, Canadian Forces Staff School, and to militia commanders across Canada. LCdr Doug Caie, whom I had recruited in the early 1970s in Winnipeg, headed the cell. He did exemplary work and deserved much of the credit for the increased positive relationship between the Canadian Forces and the media.

Added to our workload was the fact that the Defence White Paper was being prepared to be submitted to the government for approval. Many long hours were spent going through the drafts and preparing an analysis on how the document would be accepted by the government and the general public. The document entitled 'Challenge and Commitment: A Defence Policy for Canada' was released by the Federal Government in 1987.

This would be the first Defence White Paper since 1971, when the Defence Review entitled 'Defence in the 70s' was released by the Government. There were suggestions at the time that the sixteen-year gap between the two White Papers was indicative of the low priority that the Federal Government and Canadian Parliament gave to the military.

Prior to the release of the White Paper there had been minimal discussion of defence issues. Following its release, there was an immediate response, particularly from the media. Articles and commentaries were, in the main, supportive of the direction of the new Defence Policy, although some were skeptical about specific proposals such as the commitment to equip the Navy with nuclear powered submarines.

I still remember a meeting that I attended with the Chief of Staff to Minister Perrin Beatty and the Deputy Minister Bob Fowler. It appeared to me that for the DM, the purchase of the nuclear powered submarine was the cornerstone of the White Paper.

The subject of the possibility of Canada entering into the nuclear submarine field had been discussed often in many areas before the White Paper was released. Just before the meeting, I had had lunch at the National Press Club, where I went to talk to national reporters to get a sense of how they were leaning on particular issues.

At one point during the post lunch meeting when the DM was waxing eloquently about the submarines, I added a comment, "I was told by some of the senior national reporters that if DND really wants to get those submarines, they should stop talking about them."

Bob Fowler was furious. His face went red. He told me in no uncertain terms that we had to keep telling the public how important these submarines were and how much they were needed. I told him I was only telling him what I was told.

One huge problem was the cost. And the more the public heard about the price, the more the opposition to their purchase would grow.

When released, on June 5, 1987, the White Paper announced that Canada would spend $8 billion to build 10-12 nuclear-powered attack submarines to defend the Arctic against the Soviet submarine threat and to patrol the Northwest Passage and territorial waters over which Canada claimed sovereignty.

The nuclear powered submarines would never be built. There were a number of factors involved, including the cost. When announced, 50% of Canadians were in favour of building the subs, with 37% opposed. A little more than a year later the opposition had increased to 60% and by 1989 that number had grown to 71%.

This decrease in public support was no doubt aided by the media coverage given to the program regarding the cost. Many reports argued as to the affordability and wisdom of spending this much of the Defence budget in this manner.

On one occasion, a national TV network had asked for an interview with a senior military program official as well as the Minister. In the morning, I attended the interview with a General who, in response to questions, outlined the positive aspects of this acquisition and why it would be so important to the Canadian Forces. Given the interviewer's questions and given the state of the world at that point, I could sense where he was going regarding the submarines' overall cost and raison d'être.

The interview with Minister Beatty was set up in the late afternoon after question period in the House. I knew he would be coming back about 3:30 pm, so I waited for him in the lobby of National Defence Headquarters. When he entered, I said, "Mr. Minister could we sit down and have a few words before you go up to your interview?"

"So, you want to brief me on what to say Len," he said with a big smile on his face.

I had been working with Perrin Beatty for more than a year. We had developed a good rapport and I believed he trusted my judgment.

"We'll sir, I just wanted to tell you what the interviewer is likely to ask and where I think they want to take this interview given how they interviewed the General this morning, what questions I think you might want to avoid, and what answers you might want to give."

So I briefed him and we went to his office and the interview.

Perrin Beatty was very bright. He graduated from the University of Western Ontario and Upper Canada College in Toronto. He once told me that at 22 he wasn't quite sure what he wanted to do as a career. Some colleagues suggested that he run in the upcoming federal election. He did and was elected. Seven years later, in 1979, he was appointed as the Minister of State for the Treasury Board, the youngest person at the time to serve in a federal cabinet position. He held several other important portfolios and was appointed Minster of National Defence in 1986.

After about the third question, he glanced my way and his slight grin told me that the interview was unfolding as I had told him it would.

The interviewer was trying to get him to compare this purchase of submarines with the purchase of the CF18. In 1977, the government had set up a competition to replace the CF-104 Star fighters, with a budget of $2.4 billion to be paid to the winner, for 130-150 aircraft. From 1982 to 1988, the Air Force received 138 CF18s from McDonnell Douglas for a capital cost of approximately $4 billion in 1982 dollars.

I knew that Finance Minister Wilson had been reported to have some concern about the cost of the submarine program. With the chance of delays and cost over-runs in such a complex nuclear submarine program, it seemed to me that the interviewer was trying to box the Minister into a position where he would be seen to be opposed to what Mr. Wilson was saying. I had advised Minister Beatty in advance that this could happen and suggested he not get into comparing the purchase of the CF-18 to this new program, which he did not. But there was no doubt that the TV program being put together and aired later was not designed to gain any more public support for the program.

Subsequently, the proposed numbers of subs to be built was decreased by the Government to about one half of the original announcement, but even then the cost was deemed to be prohibitive. With a budget squeeze, lack of public support and the decline and eventual collapse of the Soviet Union, it became more difficult to justify the expense of continuing with such a project. In May 1989, the Government cancelled the nuclear submarine project.

But senior officials didn't always like my comments or advice. When General Liston was not around, as his Deputy, I would attend 'morning prayers', a daily meeting of senior military and civilian officials in the department.

Sitting around the table were mostly two and three star generals, the Deputy Minister and civilians at the Assistant Deputy Minister level. The meeting was chaired by the Chief of Defence Staff, a four-star General. Except for a few aides, I was usually the lowest rank in the room. Certainly, at my level, you were not expected to speak unless you were asked a question. But regardless of rank, at those meetings I was representing the Director General Information, and on one occasion I felt I just had to speak.

The CDS was berating my old media friend CP correspondent Paul Koring for a story that had appeared in all the major papers that morning regarding a very large expenditure announced by the Department for the purchase of radios for the Army. The story outlined the basic facts of numbers and cost of radios to be purchased. It went on to say that the average price of these radios would be more than $70,000 each, whereas a radio could be bought at Canadian Tire for $19.95.

The difficulty had arisen because our press release had been very short and lacked many details on the type of radios that would be purchased. Unbeknownst to me, before he wrote the story, Paul Koring had spoken to one of our junior media liaison officers asking for more details, including the types of radios and why they were so expensive, which was not in the release.

Unfortunately, my liaison officer told Mr. Koring that they were radio radios and that all the details were in the press release. Incensed, Mr. Koring decided to write the story even though I am sure he knew that the radios were sophisticated pieces of equipment needed by the army for very specific missions.

Heads nodded in unison as the CDS condemned Koring and the media for such negative reporting. Without any thought to the consequences for me, I said, "Sir, we can't really blame Koring. First of all after the press release had been massaged and edited throughout the Department, it carried very little details about the radios."

The CDS shot back, "Well he could have called and asked for details".

I replied, "Sir, he did and unfortunately, my liaison officer was unhelpful. That is my problem and it won't happen again. But we really have to try and put out more comprehensive press releases."

Heads swiveled as they looked at this exchange between such a low-level officer and the CDS. But the CDS simply said, "OK, let's move on."

I never heard another word about the incident. I think what saved me is that I had a reputation of always telling the senior 'grownups' what they needed to know and not always what they wanted to hear.

In fact, it wasn't long after that incident that I received a summons to the CDS's office to meet with the CDS alone. I thought to myself, I must be in trouble because this is the first time this has happened to me. I wondered what I had done to deserve such an invitation.

As I entered the CDS's chambers a Chief Warrant Officer met me. He took me into the next office to be greeted by a Major who then escorted me to the office of a Colonel. He ushered me into the CDS's office. The Chief was sitting at his desk working at a personal computer. "Have a seat, Len," he said. I sat.

After a couple of minutes he turned away from the computer and offered me a sheet of paper. "Read this," he said, not unkindly. So I did. It was a letter to the editor of the Globe and Mail, which addressed an article that had appeared in the newspaper that day.

After I had read it I looked at him and he said, "Well what do you think?"

"I don't understand the first paragraph," I replied.

"Well, both the Deputy Minister and Assistant Deputy Minister Policy have read it and liked it," he stated rather emphatically.

"I am sorry, sir," I said, "But the first paragraph still doesn't make any sense to me."

"So what would you say?" he asked. I told him.

He listened, turned to his computer, and said, "OK repeat that" and began typing as I spoke.

I am not sure that I was on every one of the senior official's Christmas card list but I believe I did have their respect.

My job didn't get any easier when BGen Bertrand replaced BGen Liston as Director General of Information, in the summer of 1987. He was an Air Force officer who had recently commanded CFB Bagotville. He was a tough commander and I am not sure how happy he was to be posted into a position as an Information Officer. For many 'operators' this was not a prize position. I soon learned that he didn't appreciate me suggesting to him how to tackle public information issues even though he didn't have much experience in the field. At one point he told me that he was getting tired of me telling him how to do his job. After all, he was a General and didn't need my advice.

However, this wasn't something I had to deal with for long. In February 1988, BGen Bertrand had a heart attack. I am not sure if was the stress of the job or some other factors that caused this. Regardless, I was now elevated into the position of acting DG Info - as a Lieutenant Colonel! I was fortunate to have some very competent officers to support me, including LCol Ralph Coleman who became my Deputy during this period. I first met Ralph in 1969 when he was the Information Officer at CFB Gagetown. He had gone on to work in the PM's office and had become an Information Officer working with PM Pierre Trudeau.

Nevertheless, it added more stress, but perhaps not as much as having to cope with Generals who had never been in an Information Officer's position before. In fact, when I knew that the search was on for a new DG Info to replace BGen Bertrand, I contacted the Chief of Staff to the CDS and asked him if the CDS was happy in the manner that I was handling the job as DG Info.

"Very happy," was the reply.

"Then please, don't appoint another DG Info for a while. Just let me do the job. I don't even need to be promoted."

But I believe it was too late to stop the process. In late April, I answered the phone and a voice said, "Hi Len, it's Al Geddry, how are you?"

"Who is this?" I replied.

"Al Geddry, the Base Commander at CFB Gagetown. I'm the new DG Info. I will be there in about a week. Len, you and I are going to 'kick-ass' and make this organization work."

I was stunned. This was how I learned who my new boss was going to be!

Interestingly I did get some recognition from Bob Fowler, the Assistant Deputy Minister for Policy, a source I didn't believe it would come from. He was a very smart, accomplished bureaucrat who had served at Foreign Affairs for many years, and before coming to National Defence, was the Assistant Secretary to the Cabinet (Foreign Affairs and Defence) in the Privy Council Office. He would be appointed Deputy Minister of National Defence in May 1989.

He tended to try and ride roughshod over some of the senior officials in DND. But I had found that when you stood up to him he was prepared to listen.

On one occasion his Deputy (a General), and I, had been discussing how to handle a particularly sensitive PR problem, which involved a number of UN countries and most particularly the Soviet Union. After about an hour, we had reached what we both agreed was the best approach. At that moment Mr. Fowler walked in and asked what we were up to. The General told him the problem. Instantly he said, "That's easy, let's do this," and provided his solution. It was diametrically opposed to what we had just agreed on.

The General said, "OK."

I couldn't help it. I immediately said forcefully, "What do you mean OK? We just agreed to do it this way," telling what we had agreed upon. Bob Fowler looked at us and said, "OK, do it that way, mine was only a suggestion."

In late May, General Geddry forwarded to me a note that he had received from Bob Fowler.

It read in part:

"As you know, from the time that BGen Bertrand was taken to the hospital on Feb 27, 1988 until your arrival on May 2, Len Dent was Acting DG Info. He was, of course, somewhat handicapped as a Lieutenant Colonel having to work with and, indeed, sometimes talk sense to the senior management of DND and the Minister's staff. He frequently received contradictory and seemingly irreconcilable instructions and advice from a number of these people - including myself. Nevertheless, he persevered and performed remarkably well. I found him to be cooperative, quick to grasp the essence of issues and efficient in the handling of public affairs during this period. I know that the members of the Minister's staff, who worked closely with him during this period, share this view.

In short, Len Dent did a highly commendable job as Acting DG Info. Please pass along my appreciation and congratulations."

It was a tough job, trying to deal with the increased interest from the media and the public because of the White Paper and all it envisioned for the Canadian Forces and Canadians. Certainly, there was increased pressure on our information organization to do more with perhaps the minimum number of trained Public Information officers.

Adding to our workload was the requirement to bring in the new training program for information officers, as well as new commanders and general officers. We also had to deal with a more interested group of senior officers and members of the Minister's staff, all of whom had their own particular view on when, how and what information should be released to the media and to the public. Fortunately, all the members of the Information Division were 'full-shoulder to the wheel,' and I never felt any animosity or lack of co-operation because, on occasion, I was the boss at a lower rank, or when the General was away, two ranks below what was called for.

There were also some rewards.

On January 29, 1988, I was truly honoured to accept, on behalf of the Public Affairs Branch, the new Public Affairs badge from General Paul Manson, who was Chief of Defence Staff. The transition to a separate officer classification for Public Affairs officers began in 1977, when it was split from the Administration Branch. This marked the final step in the process. It was a process that I had been engaged in for some years.

General Manson and I unveil the Public Affairs Branch Badge

On a more personal note, on June 20, 1988, I was informed by letter from the Secretary to the Governor General that Jeanne Sauvé, Governor General of Canada, on behalf of Her Majesty Queen Elizabeth the Second, had appointed me as an Officer of the Order of Military Merit (OMM).

The Order of Military Merit was established on July 1st, 1972 to recognize outstanding merit, achievement and service in the Armed Forces. It consists of three levels of membership: Commander, Officer and Member. The Advisory Committee, made up of senior members of the Armed Forces, and the Secretary General of the Order, review nominations and submit names of the most meritorious candidates through the Chief of Defence Staff, to the Minister of National Defence, who recommends appointments to the Governor General.

I was provided with a copy of the recommendation which stated in part, "Lieutenant Colonel Leonard David Dent, CD, Director of Information Services and Deputy to the Director General Information, fully deserves an appointment to the Order of Military Merit for his professionalism, for the high regard in which he is held by his fellow officers, for his exceptional devotion to duty and for his outstanding service to his military and civilian community."

An investiture was held late in the fall of 1988 at the Governor General's residence at the Citadel, in Quebec City, since Rideau Hall in Ottawa was undergoing repairs.

Receiving the OMM for Governor General Jean Sauvé

Shirlie and I flew to Quebec City and I joined with 13 other recipients and their significant others for the presentation of the medals by Governor General Sauvé.

It was a meaningful day for all of us, which included a wonderful lunch hosted by the Governor General. Although the Order had been in existence for 16 years, our medals were numbered only in the mid-400s. We all felt very proud.

It was my last contact with Madame Sauvé. A little more than a year later, in 1990, she was succeeded as Governor General by Ray Hnatyshyn. She died on Jan 26, 1993, reportedly after a long battle with Hodgkin's lymphoma.

I actually had received another medal from the Governor General five years earlier. In 1983, I had been advised that I had been awarded the Silver Acorn, which is presented to recognize 'Especially Distinguished Service to Scouting.'

A Boy Scout Executive presents me with the Silver Acorn award

I never saw the recommendation but assume it was based on my work as Boy Scouts of Canada National Public Relations Director for eight years and as Assistance Camp Chief for Public Relations for the World Jamboree held in the Spring of 1983 in Kananaskis, Alberta, where we hosted more than 16,500 scouts from 102 countries, and my work as head of the Canadian 75th anniversary of Scouting Committee, in 1982. At the

313

time of the announcement, we were living in Germany. So a presentation ceremony was held in Lahr and the medal presented by MGen David Wightman, Commander Canadian Forces Europe, who was also the Honorary Commissioner of Maple Leaf Region for Boy Scouts of Canada. It was later presented to me again at a ceremony back in Canada.

1988 was a good year for the family and me. Gen Geddry, although a full speed ahead kind of officer, was willing and appreciative of my public affairs advice, so we had a good relationship. We were very busy. Shirlie was enjoying her new job as a cardiac crisis nurse at the National Defence Medical Centre. Susan was starting her final year at McMaster School of Medicine, and in August, she and her long time boyfriend Steve were married. David had graduated from basic infantry training in the Canada forces at Cornwallis, Nova Scotia, and was now stationed as a member of the Princess Patricia's Canadian Light Infantry in Calgary.

On January 29, 1989, after two and one half years in the portfolio, Defence Minister Perrin Beatty was replaced by Bill McKnight. Mr. Beatty, although having no military experience had been very interested in, and a fighter for the military, shepherded the White Paper through the Cabinet.

Likewise Mr. McKnight had no military expertise. It was joked in the Department, that Mr. McKnight was appointed because he was born in Wartime, Saskatchewan. Nevertheless, he would face some difficult issues during his two years in the portfolio. These included the standoff with Native warriors at Oka, Quebec, in 1990 and the deployment of the Canadian Forces to the Gulf War in 1991. It was also the time of cut-backs in the Government and he had the additional task during his two years in office of overseeing the closure of military bases and the cancelling of planned defence spending, as well as cancelled equipment contracts.

Blair Dickerson, a tall, vivacious young woman and Carleton university graduate with a degree in Political Science arrived with Minister McKnight and would serve as his Press Secretary. On our first meeting she appeared suspicious of me. I was to learn soon that she felt my loyalty would be to the Canadian Forces and any advice given to her and the Minister would be to first benefit the military. Once I realized this, I assured her that my loyalty was also to Mr. McKnight. "As the Minister goes," I told her, "so go the Canadian Forces."

We developed a great working relationship and she came to trust what I was telling and advising her. She was close to the Minister and so my stock also went up with him.

Not everyone in the Department of Defence was happy with the fact that the Director General and Director of Public Affairs could pass advice directly to the Minister and his staff. This reporting network had been in place since the mid-sixties following the integration of the three services when the newly formed Directorate of Information Services stated that the Director reported to the Chief of Defence Staff, the Deputy Minister and the Minister Leo Cadieux, the Minister at the time. The Minister had come to rely heavily on advice from Col Lou Bourgeois, then the Director. Col

Bourgeois became a very powerful force within the department. At that time, for example, every General Service message from NDHQ providing information to the troops that was sent out Forces-wide had to be cleared through Information Services.

I was aware that several very senior officers were trying to change this relationship. They wanted the Public Affairs advice to be filtered through the top military and civilian officials before it went to the Minister's office.

Later in 1989, the Department appeared to make its move. A position of Assistant Deputy Minister Public Affairs was created and the incumbent would report to the Deputy Minister. A civilian would be the head. Calls went out for applicants. Finally, Bill Young, an acquaintance of mine with whom I had worked, was appointed to the position.

Bill had been head of Public Information at NATO Headquarters in Brussels, a prestigious job that involved working with 16 nations and the world's press. I was not so sure however, that even with this experience, he would be prepared to deal with the inner workings and intrigue that he would face at National Defence Headquarters. It provided a great deal of pressure. Cdr Doug Caie, who was very familiar with the seniors in the Department and had worked with most of them, was appointed as his Chief of Staff and tried to help him stick handle through the waters.

Bill would have a heart attack a few months later. When it was known that he could not return, the position of Assistant Deputy Minister of Public Affairs was done away with, and the Branch moved to and under the Assistant Deputy Minister of Policy, who reported directly to the Deputy Minister. Thus information advice now would filter through the ADM Policy to the DM and then on to the Minister's office. Both of these positions were held by civilians. Frankly, that meant that those in the Public Affairs Branch did not always know if their considered advice was the advice that reached the Minister's office.

But fortunately for me, all this happened after I departed the Branch.

As we entered 1989, I knew things would have to change for me. I had been told that in the summer of 1990, Col Haswell would be returning from Brussels to take over as the Director. Of course, it raised the question of what would happen to me. Hard to move from being the boss to a lower position, and at age 49, I still had a potential five and a half years that I could serve.

Early in the New Year I received a phone call from a General with whom I had worked previously and was now the Deputy Commander of NORAD in Colorado Springs. He told me that the current Director of Public Affairs would be moving that summer and wondered if I would be interested in taking over the position, not as the Deputy, he added, but as the Director. This floored me.

Historically, top positions in NORAD were filled by US officers, with the Canadian being the Deputy. Apparently the General had spoken to the Commander of NORAD and explained my situation. The NORAD

Commander had agreed for this one time that I could take over the position. It was never discussed if I would be promoted.

Why the US General would have agreed I have no idea. However, I was known within the communications organization in the US military, including in the Pentagon.

I took the offer home and discussed it with Shirlie. She was, to say the least, underwhelmed! She had moved back into her own home after three years in Europe, got it fixed up again to her liking, could see our daughter again on a regular basis, had taken updating courses for her nursing profession, and gotten a job she really liked. She just wasn't prepared to move again outside of Canada so soon.

So, I called the General in Colorado and reluctantly declined.

But, in my mind, God does work in mysterious ways.

A few months later, I had a call from Greg Gertz who was my contact at the Privy Council Office. He told me that Mary Gusella, his boss, the Assistant Secretary for Communications wanted to have lunch with me, but didn't tell me why. Naturally, I agreed but was very curious as to why this very important lady would want to take time out of her busy schedule to buy me lunch.

A few days later we met at a downtown restaurant and spent a pleasant hour talking about current events and the communications challenges facing DND at the moment. Towards the end of our lunch as we were sipping coffee, she looked at me and said, "Len, how would you like to come and work for me?"

I was puzzled. "To do what?" I asked.

"You have been recommended to me to take up the position as a Senior Policy Analyst on my staff," she said. "You would be responsible for providing communications advice and assistance to the Prime Minister's Office and the Cabinet for matters pertaining to Foreign Affairs, Defence, CIDA, Veterans Affairs, Public Works and Government Services."

I was speechless!

Finally, I told her that I was incredibly honoured to be offered such an opportunity, but I would like to discuss it with my wife. She said, "Of course. Get back to me in a few days."

That evening, Shirlie and I sat over dinner and took a long time to consider this opportunity. Neither of us really knew what the job entailed, what the workload would be, nor how much time it would take me away from our time together. But Shirlie was working, the children were both gone so that didn't seem to be a problem. What it presented was an incredible opportunity to get away from DND, where I faced the possibility of a posting out of Ottawa and demotion of responsibility within the next year.

The next day, I told BGen Geddry about the offer. I also called Ms Gusella back and thanked her and told her I was very interested in her offer.

A few days later General Geddry called me into his office. He told me that he had spoken to a senior officer in the 'personnel world' and it just seemed like it would be hard to make this happen.

"Don't worry Len," he said. "We will find you another good position."

I was devastated. I must have related this all to Blair Dickerson and she must have told the Minister. The next day I met Mr. McKnight in the hallway and he told me: "Len, I have heard about your offer to go to PCO. I think this will be really good for you and DND. I don't normally get involved in these types of things but in this case I will, if I have to."

When I got back to my office, I called a very senior officer who I knew in the Posting and Careers Branch and told him what I had been told.

I am not sure how this situation got resolved. Presumably there was correspondence between Ms Gusella and Deputy Minister Bob Fowler. In any event, I finally received word that my secondment to PCO had been approved and I would start there in February 1990.

I was to enter a whole new world!

CHAPTER 17 - LIFE AT THE CENTRE

"Len, come with me. I'm going to a meeting at 10:00 in the Langevin Block and I want you to be there."

Inviting me was Bill Pascal the Chief of Staff to Ms Gusella. He had greeted me when I arrived on the 6th floor of the Blackburn building on Sparks St two hours earlier. He took me to my new office, which was about the same size as the one I had left in NDHQ.

The office had several filing cabinets, which were all full, left, no doubt, by my predecessor. I had a big desk and a computer. The lady who would be my secretary was in a smaller office down the hallway.

As we made our way from the Communication Secretariat offices to the Langevin Block via an elevated walkway between the buildings, Bill briefed me on the meeting. We would be discussing the issue of a protestor who had been sitting on the lawn close to the Centre Block of the Parliament Hill for several days.

Equipped with a bullhorn, day after day, he had been shouting vociferously at the building condemning the Prime Minister and his government, alleging corruption and bribery and calling for all members to resign. I was familiar with the story having read it in the Ottawa Citizen.

We walked into a small conference room on the first floor of the Langevin Block close to the Prime Minister's office. Bill quickly introduced me to the gentlemen sitting around the oval table. Seated at the head of the table, and chairing the meeting, was Norm Spector, the Chief of Staff to the Prime Minister. I had heard of him. A smart, no-nonsense guy by reputation. I was told he had earned three degrees by the age of 23 and later received his doctorate in Political Science from New York's Columbia University. Two of the other gentlemen were from the Senior Legal Advisor's office, along with the Prime Minister's Press Secretary.

Mr. Spector quickly summed up the problem telling us that the protestor's constant ranting was causing upset within the building and making it hard for some to work. He wanted to know what solutions we could offer.

The Senior Legal Advisor made the case that amongst other things he could be charged with disturbing the peace and arrested.

The Chief of Staff looked at Bill Pascal and said, "So what do you think of that idea?"

Bill immediately turned to me and said, "Len, this is your file, what do you think?"

I was stunned, at least for a few seconds. Here I was two hours into my first day at PCO sitting in a meeting with very senior members of the Prime Minister's Office and being asked my opinion.

I wasn't sure why it was my file. But I learned later that because it was taking place on the lawn of the Parliament Hill, it was considered to be the responsibility of Public Works and Government Services, and by extension, 'my file.'

As I would realize quickly there was no learning curve, there was no one to hold your hand in this job. You hit the ground running. Fortunately, my communications experience, accumulated over nearly 30 years in many situations around the world, would help me to respond quickly. Perhaps that was why I was asked to come to the Communications Secretariat.

"Arresting him would make great press but wouldn't be great for the PM or the Government," I said.

Mr. Spector looked at me with steely eyes and said, "Ok, then what would you suggest."

"Have the RCMP move him back on the lawn close to Wellington St. and let him rant away. It's doubtful he will be heard within the building," I said.

Much to my surprise there was a nodding of heads around the table and shortly the meeting was over. According to one report I have read since, the individual continued to protest for quite some time on Parliament Hill but from farther away from the Centre Block.

On our way back to our offices, Bill looked at me and said, "You did good in there. Mary and I knew you could do it; that's why we wanted you to be part of our team."

I had passed my first big test. But I was sure that there would be many more and I doubted that bad advice would be tolerated.

Within our Secretariat, he told me, there were six senior policy analysts. Each analyst was responsible for a number of related government departments. In addition to the analysts, Mary Gusella, the boss, and Bill, there was a small cadre of secretarial and support staff.

We reached my office and he said, "Take the rest of the day to get settled and make your introductions. Tomorrow morning at 8 am we have our morning brief when we discuss the issues facing us for the day. See you there."

A few minutes later he dropped by and handed me a background note, which included a list of my responsibilities.

I read the first three:

"Provide communications advice and guidance to the Prime Minister's Office, Cabinet ministers, senior executives and officials on the communications dimensions of proposals to the Cabinet and to the Committee on Priorities and Planning, particularly those related to Foreign Affairs and Defence, International Development, Emergency Preparedness and follow-up with Departments, and monitor decisions and communications plans ratified by Cabinet;

Prepare briefings for Cabinet Committees and the Chairman of the Cabinet Committee on Communications for use in meetings of that Committee as well as in meetings of the Priorities and Planning Committee and the Cabinet; and,

Undertake as a representative of PCO, or on behalf of the Cabinet Committee on Communications, specific projects related to Communications."

WOW!! Is that all? My immediate reaction was what have I got myself into? I had been briefed in a general manner and told that it was a challenging job; that individuals were selected for these analyst positions because they were considered the appropriate person to be able to do the tasks and do them well. But this was scary.

I made my way around the office and introduced myself. Everyone was friendly but no one had time to talk. They were all too busy. In 24 hours I would be the same.

At 8 am the next morning, eight of us, the analysts, Mary and Bill, plus our Office Manager who took notes, sat around the table in the small briefing room. Analysts, in turn, provided an update of issues with which they were dealing and any communications challenges with which they were faced.

This meeting provided a snapshot of what was happening throughout the Federal Government departments. A real benefit was that any potential interpretation or differences regarding government policy and procedures that could arise within or between departments, or how and when to make an announcement, became evident.

In fact, PMO had decreed that all media releases of major announcements needed to be sent to PCO Communications before their release. Individual departments would not necessarily know what other departments and the PMO were doing, or about to announce. This process provided an opportunity to co-ordinate the release of information being made by Departments, often on the same day; which otherwise, could have them competing for coverage.

Thirty minutes later I was back in my office and reading my first submission to Cabinet sent from Emergency Preparedness Canada. It dealt with the development of a plan to outline National Emergency Arrangements for Public Information in the time of International Tension, Crisis and War. This was a responsibility of Senator Lowell Murray who was the Chairman of the Cabinet Committee on Communications. I had to read the document and then provide a summary on two pages or less that outlined the background, along with my comment and recommendation as to what was being proposed.

These briefs normally had to be two pages or less, regardless of the size and content of the submission. The PM, PMO and Cabinet ministers, inundated with information, could only devote so much time to reading a summary. So it was mandatory to write very tightly and explicitly on every subject.

Each note that left the Secretariat was signed by the Assistant Secretary Cabinet (Communications) or her appointee, usually Bill Pascal. However, each also had, typed at the bottom of the brief, the name of the person who had drafted it. Whether the recipients placed a certain amount of value on who wrote the note, is not something that I ever learned, although, in one case that I will describe later, it might have caused me to be seated at a meeting of the Cabinet Committee on Communications beside Senator Lowell Murray.

Sen. Murray, a graduate of St Francis Xavier University and Queen's University, went on to become a distinguished individual well respected by those with whom he worked and who made a significant contribution to public life over a period of 50 years. He was an executive assistant to Justice Minister Davie Fulton; Chief of Staff to Robert Stanfield; and, New Brunswick Richard Hatfield's Senior Advisor. He was appointed to the Senate in 1979 and remained there holding important portfolios until he retired at the mandatory retirement age of 75 in 2011.

Both Mary Gusella and Bill Pascal were very helpful when I would bring notes for their signature. They would give me hints on how to improve the note I had drafted, so in effect I was getting some on-job-training.

My next daunting task was to develop a relationship with the officers with whom I would be working within the departments for which I was responsible. I knew many of the communications officers with whom I would be dealing, particularly in Foreign Affairs and Defence. So that wasn't a problem. The problems began when having to deal with the operators and policy people.

I also had to establish a good working rapport with the appropriate individuals within PCO and the PMO.

In 1990, PCO or Privy Council Office was made up of a number of secretariats including Operations; Plans; Intergovernmental Affairs; Foreign and Defence Policy; Security and Intelligence; Social Affairs; Economic Affairs; Machinery of Government; and Communications. These secretariats were responsible for coordinating the day-to-day issues for government and providing policy advice to the PMO and Cabinet.

We used to say that, "PCO is policy orientated and politically sensitive, while the Prime Minister's Office is politically orientated and policy sensitive." The Clerk of the Privy Council organized the PCO secretariats to deliver on the PM's agenda.

During my time, the Prime Minister's office was staffed mostly by political appointees. At the lower advisory levels, some were quite young. These were often university graduates who had majored in political science and had worked for the party sometimes since their teenage years. They were keen, energetic and faithful to their leader and on occasion would provide some difficulty for me. Their advice, usually based on what they thought would be best for the party and the PM, sometimes would differ from mine. My advice based on 30 years of experience in public affairs was based on what I thought would be best for the government as well as the PM. It would prove to be an interesting issue later in my first year in the job.

There were a few senior appointees who were brought into the PMO from Federal departments. Some examples are Chris Davis who worked in the Press Office; Mark Entwistle who served as the Press Secretary and Director of Communications to the PM; and Paul Heinbecker who served as Chief Foreign Policy Advisor and speechwriter for Prime Minister Mulroney, and then as Assistant Secretary to the Cabinet for Defence and Foreign Affairs in PCO. All three came from Foreign Affairs. All three were very smart and very capable in their roles.

Chris went on to be the chief spokesman at the Canadian Embassy in Washington, and later became the chairman of the board of an international import and export firm. Mark would become Canada's Ambassador to Cuba and later managing partner of Acasta Cuba Capital, an advisory service for the Cuban market. After his time at the Centre, Paul served as Permanent Representative of Canada to the United Nations in New York. Later, as a Distinguished Fellow, he joined the Centre for International Governance Innovation, in 2003, contributing to the Global Security and Politics program.

All three were great to work with. They all understood the importance of communications and welcomed my input into what they were doing.

But developing good working relationship with some of the individuals within PCO and the departments was not always easy.

Those working within PCO were civil servants who usually were being honed towards taking over executive positions within their departments and government. Working at the Centre would give them a broader perspective of government from the Prime Ministerial level.

Virtually everybody I would have to deal with, working at the high levels of Departments or at the Centre, was an over-achiever or an A-type personality.

Perhaps that is why they were in their positions. Everyone was tremendously busy. And some didn't think they needed the input of a communications analyst to produce something for the PM and Cabinet that they felt they were quite capable of doing themselves.

For me, this was particularly a problem with the Foreign and Defence Secretariat. Most officers came from the Department of Foreign Affairs. I knew from my interaction with the Department, while I was in DND, that many in Foreign Affairs considered that if they were able to pass the difficult tests to become a Foreign Services officer they were certainly capable of considering the communications aspects of any issue with which they were dealing. However, there was a senior officer from DND working within the Secretariat, with whom I had worked while in Europe when he was serving at NATO Headquarters. He was sympathetic to my role and was very helpful. We did establish a good working relationship.

I believe it also became easier to work with the various Secretariats when our Communications Secretariat was 'upgraded'. In the summer of 1990, Mary Gusella was moved to become the Associate Undersecretary of

State, Department of the Secretary of State. A year later she became the Deputy Minister Multiculturalism and Citizenship Canada and two years later President of the Atlantic Canada Opportunities Agency. And her career continued. A very smart lady.

She was replaced by Dan Gagnier, an experienced senior top advisor, who had recently served as the Chief of Staff to Ontario Liberal Premier David Peterson. Dan was brought in as Deputy Secretary to the Cabinet for Communications and would sit at the Cabinet meetings beside the Prime Minister as his Communications Advisor.

This obviously raised the profile and gave more clout to our Secretariat. It also made it easier for us as senior policy analysts to get information from other Secretariats.

At about the same time Bob Parkins, a senior national and well-respected journalist, was brought into the Communications organization. He would work as a 'right hand' man and advisor to Dan. He was also a great help and someone to whom I could go for advice when dealing with a difficult issue.

Not long after Dan arrived, a communications issue arose concerning a cutback in Defence Production spending by the Federal Government, which would mean the loss of a considerable number of jobs in Quebec. There was bound to be some negative feedback from that Province, albeit the cutback would affect other provinces as well, but perhaps not to the same degree.

I wrote a briefing note directed to Senator Lowell Murray, which outlined the situation and provided some communications advice. When I took it to Dan he said, "Do I have to read this or should I just sign it?" It would become the norm. He was just so busy that he relied on his analysts and wanted them to tell him when he needed to know more about what was being sent to the PMO and Cabinet. The answer was either, no it is routine just sign, or yes this is sensitive and likely to come up in your discussions with the PMO.

In this case, I suggested he read it before signing.

A day later, Sen. Murray called together a meeting attended by six Cabinet Ministers from Quebec. As they were on the way to the meeting, Dan and Bob came by my office and Dan said, "Come with us Len, we want you to see how this works." It would be my first Cabinet Committee meeting.

We arrived in the Centre Block on Parliament Hill and went to a Cabinet room. I sat down on a chair next to the wall behind the large oval table around which the Ministers would sit. Dan and Bob sat in the same row but a few chairs away. I wasn't sure who else would attend but as it turned out, we were the only observers.

The Ministers arrived followed by Senator Murray and his Chief of Staff. The meeting began; much of it was in French. My French was cinquante-cinquante (50-50). So, with the fast-speaking Ministers I wasn't always getting all the nuances, but I knew they were not happy. Their concern was what and how were they going to tell their constituents, many of whom would lose jobs because of this announcement.

Each of them made their case. At one point, Senator Murray looked at me, and motioned to me and then at an empty chair beside him at the cabinet table. I looked back at him. I obviously didn't understand. He pointed at me again and then at the empty chair. I looked over at Dan. After all he was the Deputy Minister and my boss. Why was I being asked to sit beside the Senator? Dan looked back at me, and shrugged his shoulders as if to say, "I don't know."

So I moved up to the table. Immediately I put on the headphones, which provided instant translation so I could now understand 100% of what was being said.

Finally the last Minister had spoken.

Sen. Murray sat for a moment and didn't say anything. Then he turned looked at me and said, "OK Len, so what do you have to say."

I was stunned. My first such meeting! I was at the table with six powerful Cabinet Ministers and now I was being asked to give them my advice. I now knew why the analyst's names were on the bottom of briefing notes. Sen. Murray knew that I had written the note regarding this issue. He wanted me to speak about it.

Thank heavens, like a good boy scout I was prepared.

"Well," I began and then paused. I could see the Ministers looking at me rather curiously. "In general terms, the Province of Quebec has been doing very well with its share of defence production dollars compared to other provinces. I have a chart, with a copy for each of you, showing what each of the provinces has been given. I have also included the amount of money spent in each of your constituencies over the past few years for your use as you see fit. And these are quite good. But frankly, for those of you who will have spending cuts in particular towns, these figures are unlikely to satisfy the ones who will no longer have a job."

I stopped, got up and began to distribute the copies to each Minister.

Senator Murray said, "Thank you Len. Any questions?" There were none. Then the Senator said that there were a couple of other issues to discuss. "Dan, Bob and Len you can leave." We left. I never heard if they continued to discuss how to address the situation.

As we walked back to our offices in the Blackburn Building, Dan didn't say much about the meeting but I could tell he was happy. I believe I had passed another test.

This was confirmed that afternoon when I received a call from Senator Murray's Chief of Staff. "Senator Murray was very impressed with how you conducted yourself this morning," he told me.

Only a few weeks later, I attended another committee meeting, chaired by the Senator.

An issue had arisen that involved Canada and the US. It had legal overtones and as such the briefing note sent to PMO and PCO was primarily authored in the Legal Division of Foreign Affairs. Apparently, the communications advice had also been prepared by lawyers.

While I understood and agreed with the position being put forth, I didn't believe that the proposed explanation to the Canadian public would be convincing or supported. In my briefing note to the Senator Murray and the Cabinet, I advised that I believed there was a communications position that would likely be more acceptable to Canadians.

The issue was discussed at a Cabinet meeting which the PM chaired and which Dan attended. Dan told me that after some discussion, the PM had told Foreign Affairs Minister Barbara McDougall that there was agreement with the policy but that the communications approach needed some more work and suggested she confer with Senator Murray.

Dan told me to prepare a briefing note on the matter for the Senator, which could be used in a forthcoming Cabinet Communications meeting.

There were several Ministers involved. I called each of the Chiefs of Staff including Foreign Affairs and discussed what they thought the position would be of their Minister. To my surprise they were all quite cooperative.

Based on their input, I prepared a briefing note, which included a suggested introduction that Senator Murray could use to open the meeting. I then proposed that he offer each Minister an opportunity to speak and suggested the order. After each Minister's name I wrote what I thought that Minister would basically say. I ended the note with a wrap-up for the Senator and a conclusion that he could provide to the meeting.

On the morning of the meeting, the Senator's Chief of Staff called me and told me the Senator wanted me at the meeting and I was to sit at the table beside him.

That afternoon, the meeting began. I sat beside the Senator with five other Ministers around the table.

I should note that most, if not all, of the Members of Parliament and Senators, particularly those who have additional responsibilities such as chairs of committees have incredible workloads. They work long hours. In some instances they have only a few minutes to consider an issue before a meeting where decisions have to be made. It is one reason why briefing notes need to be concise and to the point.

The Senator began to speak paraphrasing from my briefing note. He then asked the first Minister to speak. As he went around the room and heard their inputs he looked at me rather incredulously as if to say, "How did you know what they were going to propose?"

The Senator summed up the meeting and it was over.

Of course Dan, who was close to Senator Murray, received his feedback directly from him. My work had apparently raised my stock with both Senator Murray and my boss.

Dan's s faith in me became more evident when, a few months later, he told me that there was a meeting that afternoon to discuss a Foreign Affairs-Defence issue which would be attended by the respective Deputy

Ministers, and chaired by Paul Heinbecker, now the Assistant Secretary to the Cabinet for Foreign Policy and Defence. Dan said he couldn't go but wanted me to go in his place. "My seat is at the table," he said, "and I want you to sit there. Whatever you say I will agree with. You know more about this Defence stuff than I do anyway," I seriously doubted that! But I was honoured that he would trust me to this extent. I would have to be on my toes.

I went to the meeting and took a seat next to Paul Heinbecker. Bob Fowler, now the Deputy Minister at Defence walked into the room, saw me sitting at the table and said, "Hi Len, I must have the wrong room." Paul grinned and said, "No Bob this is the right room."

I don't think Bob Fowler could believe that he was coming to a meeting at PCO and would be across the table from this junior person. I'm sure he expected Dan Gagnier to be there.

The meeting got underway and Bob began a long dissertation on the subject. At the end of his comments, Paul looked at me with a slight smile and said, "So Len what do you think of what Bob said?"

I knew I was there sitting in Dan's chair. He expected me to say what I thought. So I stated that while I agreed with much of what Mr. Fowler had said, there were a couple of points which I thought were quite important that I couldn't agree with and said why. I understood that Bob Fowler was making a case on behalf of the Defence Department, as he should. But I had to look at the issue through glasses that took the whole Government perspective into account. I could see Mr. Fowler's temperature rise as he started to redden in the face. It didn't help when the Deputy Minister from Foreign Affairs and Paul both agreed with me.

By the time the meeting was over, his temperature was back to normal and he said goodbye to me quite cordially. I suspect he knew I was at the table under Dan's instruction.

When I got back to the office I met Dan and briefed him what had happened. He grinned perhaps at the thought of Bob's displeasure with me being there, sitting in his chair. He told me, "Good for you. You did the right thing."

On August 2, 1990 Iraq launched an invasion into neighbouring Kuwait. Many in the West saw it as a move to take over the vast oil resources in that country. The invasion was condemned by the major powers around the world. On August 6, the UN Security Council placed a trade embargo on Iraq. Two days later Saddam Hussein, the President of Iraq, proclaimed the annexation of Kuwait. The following day the UN declared the annexation void. US troops arrived in Saudi Arabia, and on August 12 a naval blockade of Iraq began.

I was at home getting ready to go to bed at about 9:30 when the phone rang. It was Chris Davis, the Press Officer from the PMO. He told me that a meeting was just wrapping up and the PM and the committee had agreed on sending Canadian Forces to be part of the UN Task Force going to the Middle East. Paul Heinbecker was writing the speech for the announcement, which the PM would make the following morning at 10:00 in the National Press Theatre. He wanted me to come in immediately and provide Paul with any questions that I thought the media might address to the PM after the announcement.

On the taxi ride into the Langevin Block, I wrote 15 questions that I was sure the media would be asking about this mission. One would surely address the fact that the Navy vessels likely headed out to the Mediterranean were older than many of the sailors sailing in them.

It was a tense time. There were 35 nations involved in the US-led UN coalition. The aim was to demand an Iraqi withdrawal and prevent a further military thrust into Saudi Arabia. If fighting broke out between the UN force and Iraq, no one knew what other Nations could be drawn in or on which side.

UN resolutions authorized the embargo of Iraq as well as a naval blockade in the Persian Gulf to enforce the embargo. Also authorized was the use of, "all necessary means" to ensure Iraqi compliance if its forces were not withdrawn from Kuwait by January 15, 1991.

I met Paul and began going over the questions. Paul balked at one saying that he, and by extension, the PM, wouldn't want to discuss that. My point to him was that the Government might not want to discuss it but it was a most probable question from the media and it would be better if the PM addressed it head-on before it was asked.

Paul finished the speech about 3 am and we headed home.

Later that morning, PM Mulroney announced that a Canadian Navy Task Group would be sent to join the embargo forces in the Persian Gulf. The destroyer escorts HMCS Terra Nova, serving since 1959, and HMCS Athabaskan, serving since 1972, along with the supply ship HMCS Protecteur, serving since 1969, and five Sea King helicopters would make up the force. He acknowledged the concerns about the age of the ships but assured everyone that they were extremely well maintained and updated on an ongoing basis. They would be upgraded with new equipment "borrowed" from the new ships being built.

A new 'City Class' of destroyers was in the works. HMCS Halifax, the first of the program would be commissioned in 1992. But it had been a long process. The Canadian Patrol Frigate program that would eventually add 12 Canadian designed and built vessels to the fleet began in the mid-1970s.

There were fewer questions than usual from the media because he had addressed most of what they wanted to know.

Regardless of what he said, I wasn't sure that some in Halifax would be convinced of the safety aspects of the state of the ships.

The Task Group was scheduled to leave from Halifax on August 24. In my briefing note to PMO, I strongly advised that the Prime Minister needed to be in Halifax to say 'goodbye' to the ships and crew when they sailed away. Having worked in Halifax for four years, I knew that the media were very pro-Navy but not necessarily pro-Federal Government. Of course the wives would be concerned about their husbands sailing off to a possible warzone in these ships. Some saw the age of these ships as an indication of the priority given to the Navy by the Government.

There were some in the PMO who did not agree with my advice. One young staffer told me that the PM would be likely going into a," hostile crowd" if he went to Halifax and, "This is the last place he should be." "Better that the Governor General Ray Hnatyshyn go, after all he is the Commander-in-Chief."

I told the staffer that if the PM didn't go, the media would have a field day. "PM snubs Navy," would be the front-page headline on the Halifax Chronicle Herald, I predicted.

I'm not sure who made the final decision. I would bet the PM didn't see my recommendation. And possibly there were factors of which I was unaware that were considered in the decision-making process. But the Prime Minister did not go! To make matters worse, if I recall correctly, he and some Cabinet members went to a retreat in Quebec at the same time as the ships sailed, which became known publicly. Media coverage was much as I had suggested. The decision would not gain the Conservatives much support in the Atlantic Provinces in future Federal elections.

Once the ships sailed, I realized that if fighting did break out, it would be much easier to coordinate communications for the government if there were a Communications Command Centre. Where could such a centre be established? It wasn't likely that any of the ministries that would be involved would be happy about another ministry hosting such a centre, particularly Foreign Affairs and the Defence Departments, unless it was in their domain and under their control.

I discussed this with Dan and Bob and we agreed that Emergency Planning Canada (EPC) would be the ideal location. After all, they had just completed the building of such a facility in their headquarters in downtown Ottawa for use in case there was some type of national emergency that would require the national coordination of government communications.

I met with Lesley Lynn, an old friend who was EPC's Director of Information. She was delighted with the idea and told me that she would loan me Gerald Garneau, one of her Senior Information Officers, to help write a Communications Strategy in the event of fighting in the Persian Gulf.

I was busy with many other issues, but met every couple of days with the EPC 'pen' to discuss the development of this strategy. There were six Departments involved as well as PMO and PCO, so the strategy document was quite complex. When completed it would also include a large appendix of questions and answers that might be directed by the media to anyone of these organizations.

In early December we had a final draft. This was sent to those involved for their vetting, changes or corrections. Ministers were encouraged to take it home over the holidays to read so they would be familiar with what was being planned.

Meanwhile, on October 1st, the Canadian warships began their work as part of the Multinational Inspection Task Force in the central Persian Gulf. The task was to inspect all inbound and outbound shipping in the Persian Gulf to prevent exports from or shipment of weapons to Iraq and Kuwait, in accordance with the UN Security Council Resolution 661.

The Canadian vessels would carry out more than a quarter of the inspections by Coalition forces of cargo ships and other vessels suspected of trying to run the blockade.

In October, 24 CF-18 Hornet aircraft, most from CFB Baden Soellingen in West Germany, were sent as an Air Task Group to assist the Naval Task Group. According to DND, this was the first time since the unification of the Canadian Forces in 1968, that Naval and Air units were directly supporting each other in a 'war zone.'

On Nov 29, the UN passed resolution 678 which demanded that Iraq withdraw from Kuwait in compliance with 660, passed on August 6, which condemned the invasion of Kuwait. It stated that, "If not complied with by January 15, 1991, UN member states were authorized to use all necessary means to implement 660."

The situation was getting scary!

Shirlie and I were scheduled to go to our timeshare on Captiva Island, a barrier island off Ft Myers, Florida, for two weeks holidays over the second and third week of January. Because of what might happen in mid-January, I was loath to go. But Dan convinced me saying that I needed and deserved a rest and anyway, "They could work with DND."

I am not sure how much relaxation I had at Captiva. Every day I watched the US news reports. The US media and Americans in general seemed to be very concerned that we were headed towards war.

January 15 came. Saddam Hussein did not respond to the UN orders. Two days later, the US-led coalition launched Operation Desert Storm. A massive aerial bombardment of Iraq began.

For the first time, live news broadcasts were carried to those at home from the front lines of the battle, principally by the US network CNN.

Sitting, watching this unfold in this idyllic location made me feel that I should be back in Ottawa working with my colleagues. It didn't take long before I got my wish. On January 18, Dan called and told me I needed to come back as soon as possible. Apparently, getting information from DND was not as easy as they thought it might be. I was the one who would have to try and get their cooperation.

I wasn't sure how successful I would be. On one occasion when the ships were headed to the Persian Gulf, I had called DND for some information that needed to go into a briefing note for the PM. I was told that it was none of my business. I said that the information was for the PM and this particular individual, who I am sure thought the Chief of Defence Staff was the highest authority, told me, "It's none of his business either," and hung up. But I had many channels into the Department and on that occasion, did get the information that I needed.

When Dan and I finished talking, I immediately called American Airlines since I knew there were no Air Canada flights out of Ft Myers for a few days. I told them my situation and why I needed to get back to Ottawa as soon as possible. Their response was amazing. "Get here as soon as you can and we will get you on the next flight out headed for Ottawa. Don't worry about ticketing. Just give us your Air Canada tickets and we will sort that out."

Shirlie and I were at the airport within hours and headed home. The next day I was back in the office.

The Communication Command Centre was up and running at EPC. In fact, just a few days before January 15, the plan had been given a trial run. It had worked well.

At 6:30 am each morning representatives from all the ministries involved, along with those from PCO and PMO, would gather in the briefing room. This meant that usually there were Ministerial Chiefs of Staff and Press Secretaries along with those of us from PCO Communications Secretariat and, on occasion, the PM's Press Secretary.

In all there were 31 participants from various Departments involved in manning the 24 hour-a-day Communication Centre, including those who volunteered to work the night shift before going back to do their regular work in their home Department.

Dan chaired the meeting. It began with a briefing on what had happened internationally and domestically regarding the war during the past 24 hours. We were shown a five-minute video with highlights of TV news clips covering the war. Press clippings from that day's news coverage were provided. A communications plan for the next 24 hours had been prepared by those staffing the Centre. It was active 24 hours-a-day.

The plan provided what was thought to be the big issue facing the Government that day, along with a suggested approach including who should be the lead Department and spokesperson, along with a list of potential questions and answers.

Following a discussion of the plan, any changes were phoned into our Secretariat at PCO. Usually between 7:30 and 8 am the meeting was finished. Dan would then meet with Paul Tellier, the Clerk of the Privy Council, to brief him on the plan. If thought necessary, he would then go with Paul to brief the PM.

As soon as the OK was given by the Centre, the plan was sent to all Ministries and Departments involved, as well as to our Canadian Embassies and Consulates around the world. The system worked very smoothly and ensured great coordination of our efforts. Indeed, several senior Cabinet Ministers told Dan later that the daily plans provided by this group were as good as they had ever seen.

On February 24, Coalition ground troops and tanks went into Kuwait and then into Iraq. On February 28, 100 hours after the Operation

Desert Storm ground invasion began, US President George Bush declared that Kuwait had been liberated. An immediate ceasefire was ordered. This was formalized on March 3.

In all, approximately 4,500 Canadian Forces personnel had been involved in the war effort, with 2,700 in the region at one time. No Canadian ground forces had participated in the invasion of Iraq. However, 1 Canadian Field Hospital from CFB Petawawa was attached to a British army unit in Saudi Arabia. It marked the first time that Canadian fighter aircraft had been knowingly sent into a war zone since the Korean conflict in 1953. It was also the first time that women in the Canadian Forces were in a war zone in a combat role.

Reportedly, the Allies had lost about 300 troops in the conflict and the Canadians none. There were no official figures, but estimates of Iraqi military deaths ranged from 8,000 to 100,000.

Some of the CF-18s coming from the Persian Gulf were scheduled to arrive at the CFB Ottawa airport en route to their home bases. My briefing note suggested to PMO that the PM should not miss this opportunity to be there to greet them, even if he would seem to be playing second fiddle to the Commander-in-Chief. This time the advice was taken and the Prime Minister and Mrs. Mulroney sat quietly but prominently at the reception as the Governor General praised the aircrews for their role in the war.

The Gulf War marked a significant change for the Canadian Forces which for many years had been heralded for their peacekeeping efforts. This time they had actually been in a combat role.

Although they would continue their peacekeeping duties in various places around the world, it wouldn't be long before they would be thrust back into another very difficult situation, in response to the growing security threat caused by the civil war in the former Yugoslavia.

In February 1992, the UN Security Council authorized the creation of the United Nations Protection Force (UNPROFOR). Its mission was to create peace and security so that negotiations, which would lead to the overall settlement in the Yugoslavian crisis, could be carried out. Amongst other duties, UNPROFOR was responsible for ensuring the functioning and security of the Sarajevo airport as well as delivering humanitarian assistance in Sarajevo and throughout Bosnia-Herzegovina.

In the spring of 1992, 860 Canadian Forces personnel were sent to the Balkans as part of UNPROFOR. In September, a second deployment of 800 took place. For the next three years there would be approximately 1,600 Canadians in the Balkans.

In July 1992, the Royal 22nd Regiment and an infantry company from the Royal Canadian Regiment arrived in Sarajevo to secure the airport, which meant that international humanitarian aid could be delivered to that beleaguered city.

Canadian MGen Lewis Mackenzie, first commander of the UN Peacekeeping Forces in Sarajevo, later stated that, "For 30 days the

Canadian troops were operating in an extremely dangerous environment to facilitate the delivery of approximately 300 tons of food and medical supplies a day to a city that was short of both. Soldiers risked their lives rescuing Sarajevans who were wounded and exposed to sniper fire. Thanks to outstanding leadership and occasionally 'lady luck', the most serious injury sustained by the Battle Group over 30 days in the most dangerous city in the world was the loss of a foot to a land mine by a Corporal from Newfoundland."

In March of 1993, the 2nd Battalion Princess Patricia's Canadian Light Infantry (PPCLI) from Calgary was sent to Northwest Croatia where they would try to stop raiding operations by both Croat and Serb troops.

Our son David was a Master Corporal serving with the Battalion and would spend six months in a very dangerous place. The Battalion would come under mortar and artillery fire as they passed through Serbian lines. David wrote home to everyone he knew. Mom and Dad began to think that he felt he might not come home. We were both worried about his safety. It didn't help when one soldier, about David's age, hit an IED (improvised explosive device) while driving his jeep, which resulted in him losing both legs. He was sent back to the National Defence Medical Centre in Ottawa where Shirlie was nursing. He became one of her patients. Seeing this helpless 26 year-old lying there every day only made her think that it could be our son. During the period September 1993 to September 1995, 11 Canadians soldiers died during their service with this UN Force.

But others in Canada were worried about what our troops were facing, including Prime Minister Mulroney. On his direction, when the troops first left for Sarajevo, PCO was to provide him with a briefing note every morning at 24 Sussex, his residence, by 7:00 am The two-page note would provide him with a summary of the operational details involving our troops there over the past 24 hours. The last paragraph would give an overview of the media coverage both domestically and internationally, including which issue the media would likely be focusing on that day and advice on who should be the lead Minister responsible for providing responses to any queries about the situation.

The Foreign Affairs Secretariat would write most of the note. As the Communications Secretariat Analyst responsible for providing advice on Foreign Affairs and Defence, it fell to me to write the last paragraph. It meant some very succinct writing to get all the necessary information into basically four sentences and one paragraph. I was thankful for my year at Staff College, which had taught me how to write in this manner.

So each morning, seven days a week, I would be at the office by 6:00 am

I would listen to the late various newscasts at 11:00 pm each night and get up at about 5:00 am. Usually, Shirlie would drive me or else I would call a cab to work, writing the paragraph in my head as we drove. In the office, I would quickly review all the national and international news wire services, which were available on my computer and then update the paragraph if necessary. Pushing the 'send ' button on my computer at 6:30 am meant it would be in the Foreign Affairs Secretariat instantly. An analyst there would add it to the note and it would be sent to 24 Sussex to meet the 7:00 am deadline. This went on every day for more than five weeks.

The note was also sent to all the other Secretariats and Senator Murray. One day, not long after we started this process, he called and told me that Hugh Segal, the PM's Chief of Staff, had called him early that morning to discuss the note and the communications advice. Senator Murray had not seen what I had said. He asked if I could call him every morning at his home just before 7:00 am to tell him what I had sent to the PM.

All this added to my long day ongoing routine. But it was important work. And the note kept the PM satisfied. In the case of our troops positioned in Sarajevo, I believe Prime Minister Mulroney was genuinely concerned for their safety

Talking to Canadians over the years suggests that many believe politicians run for election only for what it can mean for them and that they are egotistic and full of self-importance. For my experience, having met and worked with many politicians at all levels, municipal, provincial and federal over the years, I would agree in part. Most have big egos, feel self-important and do get their egos fed by their positions of power. Yet, at the same time, I have realized that those with whom I have worked in the Federal Government over a period of more than 25 years have been for the most part very dedicated and caring. Yes, there are benefits including a salary higher than the average person makes, a great pension when they qualify after six years, often a chauffeured car. But many have difficult and often thankless tasks.

On one occasion, I was talking with Mary Collins at a PMO sponsored social event and she told me a little of her life. She was a Member of Parliament representing the constituency of Capilano-Howe Sound, between 1984 and 1993. She was currently the Associate Minister of National Defence, the first woman to hold the position.

Every Friday, she would take the last flight to Vancouver and arrive late. Early the next morning she would be in her constituency office. A multitude of her constituents wanted to see her to discuss issues they were concerned with or unhappy about. In the afternoon, she often had meetings to attend and usually there were some receptions or events that kept her occupied until late Saturday evening. Sunday morning she made time to spend with her family, which usually meant a late, long brunch. Then, back on a flight that afternoon to Ottawa. Early Monday morning she would be at an early Caucus breakfast meeting. Then it was morning, afternoon and evening in a succession of meetings, House of Commons sessions, Question Period and evening events. Friday evening came again quickly.

"Sounds terribly stressful on you and hard on the family. Maybe you should think about quitting," I said.

"Oh no," she replied quickly, "I still have so much I want to accomplish."

Cabinet ministers in particular face extremely difficult and onerous responsibilities. As an example, it is a huge responsibility to send a large group of our military into harm's way. Not one that is taken lightly!

I believe that this concern was reflected in how these decisions were made. I attended a meeting of the Standing Committee on External Affairs and National Defence (SCEAND), chaired by Barbara MacDougall who was the Minister of External Affairs. The issue at hand was whether to commit a battalion of soldiers into an African country under a UN mandate for a so-called 'peacekeeping' mission. But it was a very dangerous mission.

Because of the nature of the mission, Committee members around the table were expressing their doubts as to the wisdom of participating. At one point, Minister MacDougall asked one of the senior DND officials, if there could be Canadian casualties. The response was that, "Yes, there is a good chance that soldiers will be injured and some killed, but don't forget, that is what we are trained for."

After weighing all the factors, the final decision was that Canada would not take part in that particular mission.

The difficulty for the Government is that the media and the public are generally not aware of all the factors that go into making many of the decisions. The information being considered is often very sensitive, involving classified information, including that provided by other individuals and companies, and sometimes information of concern to or from other countries. Under these circumstances many of these details cannot normally be provided to Canadians. And if all the information were released, it would likely lead to others second-guessing the wisdom of the decision. This is often the case when the details are not known.

But, there is information that could be released, particularly info held by Ministries which, for a variety of other reasons, is not.

An attempt was made by the Federal Government to alleviate this problem with the Access to Information Act in 1985 that stated, "This Act is to extend the present laws of Canada to provide a right to access to information in records under the control of a Government institution, in accordance with the principles that Government information should be available to the public, that necessary exceptions to the right to access should be limited and specific, and that decisions on the disclosure of Government information should be reviewed independently of Government."

In 1998, many Canadians followed the Somalia Affair, an infamous time for the military, when two Canadian Airborne Regiment soldiers were tried for torturing and killing a Somali teenager. The trial and the subsequent Federal Government inquiry, led to a clause being appended to the Access Act making it a Federal offence to destroy, falsify or conceal public documents.

Of course, compliance involves a considerable amount of work for the Government ministries, which over the years have had to react to thousands of requests for information, many from the media. There is no doubt that there has been resistance to the release of information. A charge was levied for each request, ostensibly to pay for the work done. There have also been considerable delays in answering requests, which caused angst, particularly from the media. When I left Government service, it continued to be a source of upset for those trying to get information from the Government.

At another meeting of SCEAND that I attended, Finance Minister Don Mazankowski provided a briefing on a G8 meeting that he had just attended in Bonn. The information was crucial to the decision-making process being considered at that meeting. At the end of the meeting, Minister MacDougall stated the decision that she believed they had agreed upon. She went on to say, the media will crucify us when they hear this and as a result Canadians will think we are nuts, but given the circumstances it is the best decision for Canada.

Indeed the media are vigilant on reporting the actions of Government. But, in my opinion, the media seemed to be more critical of the actions of the Mulroney Conservatives than when the Liberals were in power. Some, including members of the Canadian public, said he deserved it. I was once told by an acquaintance that Brian Mulroney was, "The worst Prime Minister that Canada has ever had. But you know that," he added. I said, "Actually, I don't. Tell me why is he the worst Prime Minister." The person was at a loss to explain except to repeat that he was the worst PM. Pushed for an explanation, he finally said, "Well, I am always reading that in the media."

Indeed, PM Mulroney went from being quite popular when elected with the largest majority Government in Canadian history, in 1984, to very unpopular when he left in 1993.

The Government had its highs and lows in recognition from the media and the public. They were severely criticized when they introduced the Goods and Services Tax in 1991. Mr. Chretien campaigned against the GST stating that if they were elected it would be done away with. Mr. Chretien and the Liberals did win the election in 1993. But the GST was never done away probably because the Government realized the valuable source of revenue that it brought into the Government coffers. Interestingly years later when Conservative leader Stephen Harper began to reduce the GST, there was loud opposition from the Liberal opposition concerning the notion that it should be reduced. This dichotomy in thinking was seldom questioned by the media.

Brian Mulroney did get accolades from Canadians, including the media, for advocating economic sanctions against South Africa and their apartheid regime, which is said to have eventually led to Nelson Mandela's release from prison in 1991.

Mr. Mulroney was accused of cozying up to the Americans. He did have several visits with Ronald Reagan and then with George Bush Senior while I was working at PCO. Some members of the media, and by extension Canadians, were upset when Ronald Reagan and the PM joined together to sing, "When Irish eyes are smiling" in Quebec City at a St Patrick's Day event.

But PM Mulroney was widely respected by his colleagues outside of Canada. His trips to Washington were not, "to get his marching orders," as have been stated in the media, rather to provide the President of the US with some sound advice. And I am aware from my working at PCO that it was often listened to.

Reportedly, it was the friendship between Reagan and Mulroney that led to the US coming onboard with the North American Free Trade Agreement. The first Trade Agreement between Canada and the US was signed by President Reagan and PM Mulroney, and in late 1992 the North American Free Trade Agreement was signed by the PM, President George Bush and Mexico's President Salinas. Mr. Mulroney was quoted as saying about 10 years ago, "Anyone who fails to appreciate that there is an important connection between good personal relationships amongst leaders and success in foreign policy understands nothing about either."

But he could do little in the latter days in the PM's office to garner any positive reporting from the media. An Ottawa magazine ran a story concerning his 16-year old daughter suggesting a satirical advertisement for a contest inviting young Tories to, "Deflower Caroline Mulroney." Asked for his reaction during a TV interview, the PM replied, "I could strangle the guy who wrote that." He was criticized for not being prime ministerial. He said later, "I was talking as a father. What would you have said?"

Some years later when PM Chretien was walking through a crowd in Quebec, he reached out to a man who had been heckling him and grabbed him by the neck. The media loved it and he was cheered... a double standard perhaps?

I hasten to add that I worked during my career for Liberal and Conservative Defence Ministers and Government leaders. I always supported each one to the best of my ability. I just feel that during my working years, and perhaps since, the media in general have been more sympathetic to the Liberal members and governments than to Conservative.

I once asked Mark Entwistle, his Press Secretary, why the PM continued to stay in this job. After all it couldn't be for the money. He had been the President of the Iron Ore Company of Canada (1977-1983) and surely made more than the salary he was now receiving. Reportedly as PM his salary and allowances in 1990-1991 totaled approximately $150,000.

Mark looked me straight in the eye and said forcefully, "Because he thinks he can make a difference for Canada." Only time and the history books will tell what, if any, difference he made!

But the job as leader of the country is hard on anyone regardless of his or her political stripe. One only has to look at the facial features and hair colour when they begin and when they finish, to see the toll it takes. Look at photos of PM Mulroney in 1984 and 1993. At a Christmas party I attended for those of us working in the PMO and PCO offices, the PM appeared with his wife Mila. He looked tired and drawn. She stood beside him as he began to give his Christmas remarks to the group. She held his hand and stroked his arm. He said, "I woke up this morning and read several newspapers with my coffee in bed. After looking at the front page of the Toronto Star, Ottawa Citizen and Quebec Le Droit, I thought oh, what the heck, I didn't want to get out of bed this morning anyway."

He was a senior amongst the G8 leaders and was liked and respected amongst that group. I learned from working in PCO, that his advice and counsel on major international issues was valued by many leaders, including the White House and the US President.

I had some proof of that when I visited Washington for a round of meetings, which had been arranged by my friend Col David Burpee, Director of Defense Information at the Pentagon, in August 1992. He thought it would be worthwhile to share experiences gained through the Persian Gulf Crisis.

It was an interesting two-day visit to say the least. I was allowed to sit in on the daily morning public information briefings when the major issues of the day of interest, particularly to the media, were discussed, and decisions made as to who would handle questions at the noon media briefings and what should be said. One Major raised an objection to my being there. Col Burpee assured him he could speak freely in front of me. "He is our friend," he said.

He also expanded the nature of the visit to include other Departments and Agencies and the White House. So, in addition to meeting the senior information officers for the Army, Navy and Air Force, I met with some other very senior people. They included William MacDonald, Director of Freedom of Information at DOD; Walter Kansteiner, Special Assistant to the President and Deputy Press Secretary for Foreign Affairs at The White House; Kenneth Hill, Deputy Executive Secretary, National Security Council (NSC); Paul Clarke, Assistant Press Secretary for Foreign Affairs at the White House; Nancy Bearg Dyke, Director of International Programs and Public Diplomacy (NSC); Colonel Jeffery Jones, Director for Defense Policy and Arms Control, NSC; and, Robert Pines, Deputy Assistant Secretary for European and Canadian Affairs at the US Department of State.

The meetings were all cordial and each of these individuals took the opportunity to underscore their gratitude for the close relationship that existed between the US and Canada. It was fascinating for me to be treated in such a manner by people at such a high level.

In the meeting with Ms Bearg Dyke, she expressed great appreciation for Canada's efforts in opening up the Sarajevo airport and our military efforts in Bosnia-Herzegovina.

338

It was a wonderful insight into how the US Government functioned at the top level, the decision making process as well as how they handled day-to-day communications at the Pentagon.

Perhaps my most humorous meeting was with Mr. Pines at the State Department. I arrived at his office and was ushered in by his secretary. He sat behind a large rather imposing desk. He offered me a seat in front of the desk; then he looked at me and asked, rather sternly, "What the hell are you doing here?" I replied, "I really don't know. This meeting was set up by my host Col Burpee at DOD."

He stared at me for a moment and I thought he was going to kick me out of his office. Then he smiled slightly and said, "Do you like Chinese tea?" "Very much so," I replied. He pushed the intercom button and said "Sarah bring us in some Chinese tea and some of those biscuits I like."

We moved into a more casual setting on couches in his office and began to chat about a variety of issues that interested him about Canada, seeking my input as we talked while sipping our wonderful hot green tea and munching on delicious biscuits.

He was very open in his feelings towards Canada stating that he was very respectful of Canada's views. He said that sometimes Canada was a, "pain in the ass" but that more often than not we were right in the positions we took. This led him to tell me that he was very respectful of PM Mulroney and even more so of Joe Clark who had served from 1983 - 1991 as Minister of External Affairs and was now Constitutional Affairs Minister.

The visit to Washington also gave me an opportunity to meet with the US organizers of the Commemoration ceremonies marking the 50th anniversary of the end of the Second World War, which would run through 1994 and 1995. They were well advanced in their planning and quite willing to share any documentation, information and ideas that they were working on. They also assured me they were willing to work closely together with Canada to develop a similar program, if we needed any assistance.

In fact all of those with whom I met showed a great respect for Canada. I came back to Ottawa with a new group of very senior contacts with whom I could liaise if and when necessary.

Flying back to Ottawa, I thought, "What a great job I have." Sure, there was lots of stress and long hours, with some days starting at 6:00 am and ending at 8:00 or 9:00 pm and in worse cases much later. Some days, or more likely nights, I just wanted to throw my hands in the air and say, "I quit." But it was exciting and rewarding to be working at the 'Centre' of Government. I felt I was making a contribution.

Late one evening, the phone rang and woke me up. It was Senator Murray. He apologized for calling so late. Then he said, "Len, the Cabinet is going to make a decision in the morning to replace the CH-113 Labrador helicopters probably with the EH-101. Tell me again why we need this new helicopter."

I had written a briefing note to the Senator some weeks earlier on the subject. But, with a decision now pending, I was eager to reinforce my view.

"Well, Senator," I began, "I know you are aware that I crewed in those helicopters at 103 Rescue Squadron way back in 1964 almost 30 years ago. And I believe I told you I was in one that crashed in Newfoundland because we lost an engine and were too heavily loaded to fly on one. Besides which they were not great to fly in bad weather and icy conditions, which is not great for a SAR helicopter.

The EH-101 has three engines and all the modern technology, which will make a wonderful aircraft for the role. I think Boeing is being a little naughty when they say they can refit the CH-113 and make it as good as a new one. You can take a typewriter, clean it up, put in new keys and a ribbon and it looks great... but it is still a typewriter not a computer. We need a computer."

"Thanks, Len," he said. "Sorry again to disturb you," and hung up.

I have no idea if what I told him had any influence on the decision!

The next day the Cabinet met. The decision was taken to buy 15 EH-101 helicopters in addition to those that had been ordered to replace the Sea King Helicopters. The purchase would cost $5.8 billion for 50 helicopters. The joint purchase was smart because it simplified training, maintenance, and the overall unit cost per aircraft would be reduced. There were also a large number of jobs at stake, since many companies across Canada would have the opportunity to build parts for the aircraft.

The opposition, led by Mr. Chretien dubbed the aircraft a "Cadillac" that Canada didn't need and couldn't afford. He vowed that, if elected, he would cancel the program. In fact, it became part of the Liberal party's platform for the next general election.

I considered that DND and the Canadian Forces needed to go on a very proactive information program to tell Canadians from coast to coast to coast why the CF needed these new helicopters and the benefits to the country, particularly in their Search and Rescue role. For some reason, my former colleagues at DND didn't seem to agree. As far as they were concerned the decision had been made. They didn't need to go selling the program. I told them that contracts could be unsigned. It fell on deaf ears. I called the Minister's office to ask what they were doing. I was told that a PR firm had been hired to do the publicity; I didn't need to worry. They were not prepared to provide any details even though I asked several times.

One afternoon, Dan called me into his office and said in a kind voice, "Len, I just came back from a meeting with the PM's Chief of Staff. Your name came up three times in relation to the EH-101 helicopter. I know you are very supportive of this decision, but I am telling you for your own good, drop it. No more calling DND about the EH-101."

"But, I think if we don't convince the public why we need this aircraft, the Canadian Forces won't get it."

"That may be," he said rather sympathetically, "but I want to keep you around, so no more talk about the EH-101, OK?" This time he was a little more emphatic.

He didn't have to say it again. It was crystal clear. Keep pushing for a very active PR program for the helicopter and I probably would lose my job.

So I stopped talking about the EH-101.

To this day I am not sure why the decision was apparently made not to talk about the new helicopter program. Perhaps some considered that if the Government didn't talk about it, there would be less negative publicity. But that didn't work. The Opposition made it part of their platform for the next election.

When Kim Campbell became Prime Minister in June 1993 she reduced the order to 43 aircraft at a cost of $4.4 billion. But public opposition continued to grow.

"After all the Cold War was over and Canada couldn't afford these very expensive machines."

In October 1993, Jean Chretien and the Liberals were elected. The incoming Party ordered the immediate cancellation of the order. There was a cost attached. Some say $500 million to pay cancellation fees. Some say much less, some say closer to $1 Billion. I don't know who really knows what the final cost was.

But the biggest problem was that the Boeing Labrador helicopter and the Sea King, both 30 years old, still continued to fly. Reportedly by the mid-1990s the Sea King required 30 man-hours of maintenance for every hour in the air. No doubt that has increased. But Jim Cantlie, a retired Navy pilot, gives full credit to the work of the maintenance crew for being able to keep these old aircraft flying.

Successive Liberal and Conservative governments have struggled with the replacement program which has involved rebids, company strikes and renegotiated contracts, to name only a few of the problems.

In 2014, the Government signed a contract to buy 28 new CH148 Cyclone helicopters built by Sikorsky at a cost of $7.6 billion to replace the Sea Kings. But apparently the aircraft were not scheduled to be fully operational until 2018 at which time the Sea Kings will have been in service for 55 years.

Starting in 2002, the Labradors were replaced by the Augusta Westland CH149 Cormorant, a three-engine aircraft that was formerly marketed as the EH-101. Strange, to say the least, but that is politics!

My ongoing concern at PCO was that I didn't know how long I would be able to stay.

One year after my secondment to PCO, I received a letter, ironically from Colonel Geoff Haswell, who had replaced me as the Director, telling me that they could not extend my secondment beyond the current year. I

341

discussed this with Dan Gagnier who in turn spoke to Paul Tellier. Dan apparently told Mr. Tellier that he would like to keep me if I wished to stay.

I assume an interesting conversation took place between Mr. Tellier and Deputy Minister Fowler. I was called in to Tellier's office and asked if I wanted to stay with PCO. Mr.Tellier told me that Bob Fowler agreed that I could stay one more year. In the meantime, if I was interested, he told he would start the process that would allow me to become a staff member of PCO, filling one of the six permanent positions.

I couldn't believe my ears. The thought of going back to DND and the Canadian Forces held little appeal. After all, I had held the highest position in my profession. What could they offer me that would be better than becoming a full-time employee of PCO, one of the few!

In fact, I had already had received a call from my 'Career Manager' a few months earlier. He told me I was going to be posted to Halifax this coming summer.

"To do what?" I asked.

"To be the Public Affairs officer for Maritime Command," he replied gruffly.

"But I did that almost 20 years ago," I told him.

"I really don't care," he said, almost shouting into the phone. "I need someone there and you are it."

"Did you discuss this with your Deputy Minister?" I asked.

"He is your Deputy Minister too, Dent," he growled.

"Fine," I said in a loud voice." Then you tell my Deputy Minister what you have planned for me and see what he says."

I slammed the phone down. I never heard another word.

It wasn't easy. The position at PCO that I would fill had to be advertised. Anyone in Canada could apply. If they did not get accepted they would have to be told why.

Then, if I was approved, there was a six-month period when the process could be challenged by anyone who had applied for the job.

To add to my uncertainty, Paul Tellier left PCO shortly after our conversation to take up the position as President and Chief Executive Officer of the Canadian National Railway. Dan Gagnier also left to become President of the Brewers Association of Canada and two years later, Vice President of Communications and Marketing for ALCAN.

I felt abandoned.

But the process had been set in place. On April 30, 1992, I was offered a temporary position, which would run until February 1993. I hoped that by then the job could be made permanent. For me it was worth taking the chance. I wasn't going back to DND under any circumstances.

So, on May 5, 1992, I submitted my resignation to the Canadian Armed Forces. Because of retirement leave, my actual retirement date was February 1993.

I did get the permanent position. It became effective on Mar 1, 1993 just as my final days as a member of the CAF ended.

After 33 1/2 years, my service to Queen and Country had ended. But my deep feelings for, and allegiance to, the Canadian Armed Forces, had not.

We were fast approaching June 1994, which would mark the 50th anniversary of the D-Day landings on the beaches of Normandy, France.

One of my prime concerns centred on what Canada would do to recognize D-Day and all the various anniversaries, leading up to the end of WWII.

Having just been briefed by the Americans and having spoken to some British colleagues, I knew that both these countries were planning a big program to encompass the whole period of recognition. I also assumed that France would be doing much the same, particularly in June 1994.

These celebrations would draw much attention since most considered it would be the last time that many of the veterans would be able to attend such ceremonies, particularly those taking place overseas.

In early April 1993, I invited Information Officers from Veterans Affairs, DND and External Affairs to a meeting at PCO to discuss their intentions. I was underwhelmed by their plans and their enthusiasm. Both DND and External Affairs considered that they had more important issues facing them and were not prepared to devote a lot of planning time, since they considered it was a Veterans Affairs responsibility. Veterans Affairs told me that they would be doing much the same as in other years of celebrations albeit they intended to take more groups of veterans to all the various battle site celebrations in Europe.

I had a vision of a huge program, which would celebrate Canada's large involvement in a war that changed not only Canada but also the world. In my opinion, it was a grand opportunity to celebrate how this country had changed from an agrarian society into an industrialized nation. A wonderful chance to recognize not only those who fought overseas, but also the tremendous contribution of those who remained on the home front. I knew the Americans were going to highlight the efforts of 'Rosie the Riveter' and the millions of women who toiled so hard on the home front.

When I discussed my thoughts with the Veterans Affairs representative, his response was that the mandate for the Department was to recognize and commemorate the efforts of veterans and veterans only.

After the meeting I wrote a briefing note to Glen Shortliffe, who had replaced Paul Tellier in 1992 as Clerk of the Privy Council. I told him the results of the meeting including my view of what the program should cover. But regardless of Veterans Affairs intention to stick to their mandate, I proposed that Veterans Affairs be the lead on Canada's commemoration events. I added that this would give the Department some positive profile and I would work with them to try and convince them to broaden their program to recognize the efforts on the home front.

From previous conversations, I knew that he and some senior officials in the PMO along with some MPs, were very keen on these celebrations, and the idea of setting up a special Commemoration Committee to run the program had been discussed.

He came back to my boss and said, "OK, but tell Len to keep a close eye on the program."

I am sure there was some dialogue at high levels going on behind the scenes about this program. I had evidence of this in early June. I had a call from a gentleman who identified himself as Bruce Brittain. He told me he was a former Deputy Minister of Veteran Affairs and wanted to meet with me to talk about what I envisaged for the commemorations.

I apologized and told him I was very busy. He said he considered it to be important that we talk. So I suggested that he come to our home on Saturday at lunch time. I told him my wife would prepare lunch and we would have lots of time to chat. He agreed.

At 12:00 on the dot the door bell rang. It was Bruce Brittain dressed smartly in grey flannels, blue blazer and an Air Force tie. I had done some research on him and discovered that he had become a Squadron Leader with the RCAF during the war, flown the Halifax bomber, and had won the Distinguished Flying Cross. He was, I believe, the last veteran of WWII to hold the position of Deputy Minister Veterans Affairs from 1975 -1985. Obviously an excellent choice if he was to be involved in any commemoration program.

He told me over the lunch that he had bailed out of his crippled aircraft and landed on what he thought must have been, "The only paved road in that part of Norway." He was captured by the Germans and placed in a POW camp. He had severely injured his leg on landing and was taken to the camp hospital. There he was tended to by a Norwegian 'doctor.' He found out later that the doctor had attended medical school for one year in Oslo. The Germans took him out of the school and told him he could administer to the prisoners.

With the help of an X-Ray machine, the doctor determined where he thought the break was and treated it accordingly. But his leg did not heal properly and he was left with a painful limp.

Bruce was released from the Camp in 1945 and shipped back to Montreal. A Canadian doctor discovered that his break had not been treated and his leg had healed in poor alignment. The doctor speculated that what the Norwegian doctor saw was probably a hairline crack in the X-Ray plate. They had to re-break his leg and fix it. He was in hospital for almost a year.

We ate lunch and chatted for about four hours. I learned that Nancy Hughes Anthony, the current Deputy Minister of Veterans Affairs, had contacted him and asked if he would be interested in becoming the Executive Director of a special committee that VAC wanted to set up for the commemoration of the 50th anniversary of the end of WWII. Given that I thought that VAC would only concentrate on commemorating the veterans, I was very pleased at this initiative.

344

We discussed the ideas that I had for the celebrations and he was very much in favour of what I was suggesting. He thanked Shirlie for lunch and told me that he would be in touch.

About a week later, my boss called me into his office. He told me he had a call from Ms Anthony. She had briefed him on a new special Commemoration Committee being formed and said that, if I were interested, she would very much like me to be part of the team. It would mean a two-year secondment to Veterans Affairs Canada and she was prepared to cover my salary and expenses.

I wasn't sure why she had picked me, but later Bruce told me that after our meeting he had told Ms Anthony that, "He would accept the job as Executive Director of the new committee only if she could convince Len Dent to join the team." I still don't know if he was serious or just joking!

I was very much inclined to take this offer. I had been with PCO now for about three and one half years. I was enjoying it very much but it was stressful. This was also an opportunity to help shape a program that I was very passionate about.

My boss told me he would not stand in my way if I wished to go. I was on permanent staff at PCO now, so it would mean I could come back in two years.

That evening, I discussed with Shirlie the pros and cons of taking the position. She said it seemed like a wonderful opportunity and, as always, she told me if this is what I wanted then she would support me and I should take the offer.

The next day, I informed my boss that I thought I could make a significant contribution to this commemoration program and wanted to go.

Two weeks later, I cleaned out my desk, briefed my replacement and headed for Veterans Affairs Canada on 66 Slater Street.

It would be the start of another amazing chapter in my life.

CHAPTER 18 - CANADA REMEMBERS - A TIME TO REMEMBER

"Len, I'm going out to buy a coffee pot and you can buy the coffee."

Bruce and I were standing alone in a small block of empty offices in Veterans Affairs that had been provided to us by the Deputy Minister. At this point it is all we had. No staff, no budget. This was July 1993. The 50th anniversary of the end of WWII would be over in less than 24 months. We had to put together a program and have it up and running quickly. We needed a plan and people.

Bruce told me he would look for more members for the team and asked me to draft a document that would outline what we would hope to accomplish.

His first pick was a great addition to the team. Col John Gardam, O.C., O.M.M., M.SM. CD. John was born in England and immigrated to Canada at the age of 15. At 20, he joined the Canadian Army and served for 33 years. On retirement he was appointed to the Commonwealth War Graves Commission, Canadian Agency, as the Assistant Secretary General where he was responsible for all the War Graves in North America. Next, he was appointed as Project Director for the Canadian Peacekeeping monument where he remained until 1992. It was the following year that Bruce was able to secure his services and John became the Program Director for the Department of National Defence's component of our program.

Shortly after his arrival, Bruce, John and I, along with Don Ivy, a representative from VAC communications, sat down to discuss what we should call the program and what kind of logo we should adopt.

After about two hours of 'friendly' discussion we arrived at our conclusions. The program would be named 'Canada Remembers.' It would be defined as a National Program commemorating the 50th anniversary of the end of the Second World War.

The US had already adopted the name 'A Grateful Nation Remembers' and this seemed to dovetail. Canadians and the US had fought together, so it made sense to have a program similar in remembrance. Second, we came up with a design for the logo. It consisted of a gold maple leaf with a red poppy in front and a second red poppy half hidden behind the maple leaf. It was balanced and quite attractive, but I thought it needed some meaning to bring it to life. So I went back to my office and wrote:

"The maple leaf in gold symbolizes the 50th anniversary of the end of the Second World War. The foreground poppy is in remembrance of those Canadians who served and died overseas, and the background poppy commemorates those who lost their lives in Canada and reminds us of the wives, husbands, children and all those who played a vital supporting role at home. The intertwining of the three stems symbolizes the unity and strength of Canadians and their loyalty, dedication and sacrifice-enduring values that will sustain Canada in the future."

347

The Minister accepted the logo and the meaning. It would become a symbol that would be used in countless ways during the program.

At the outset, we ordered 10,000 lapel pins using the logo and another 5,000 with a slightly different version to be given to VIPs. At that time, I wondered how we could dispose of 15,000 pins over the 22 months of the program. I shouldn't have worried. By the end, with the help of the Royal Canadian Legion who sold them and used the proceeds for their Poppy Fund, we had given out or sold more than 500,000, both in Canada and abroad. After more than 25 years, these pins are still being given out by VAC as part of their ongoing Commemoration program.

In the weeks that followed we hammered out detailed objectives, developed action plans, started networking with other government departments and organizations, consulted with the media and related production companies, assessed what was possible, and developed contingency plans.

Bruce then approached me and asked me to write a communication strategy for the program. He had received one written by VAC Communications Division. It focused primarily on veterans and commemorative services overseas and did not include what he and I had envisaged for the program.

I was reluctant to write anything since I believed this was the responsibility of the Communications Division and did not want to upset them, as I was sure it would. But he insisted. After saying no to him twice, he told me it was no longer a request but an 'order.' It got me into trouble with the DG Communications who gave me a severe tongue lashing and told me I should have refused to do it. I stated that I had been ordered to do it, but the DG was not impressed.

Bruce felt that what we were doing was a separate program and wanted to do it his way. He considered that to a great extent the mandate of the Commemoration Committee was communications. As such, the communication strategy did lay the foundation for the subsequent development of the program.

When forwarding the plan to the Deputy Minister he wrote, "I had some difficulty in having this plan written – it required almost the use of a 2 x 4 on the head of the author before he acceded to my 'request' to produce it; this because he would be treading on the turf of someone else's position. However, the urgency to have a useable plan available so that we could do business with other departments and the private sector required unusual measures."

Shortly thereafter, Bruce decided to resign from the program. I do not believe that it was his lack of enthusiasm for what we were doing in the program. Indeed, on occasion, he would come to my office early in the morning and hand me a document looking for my comments. The final computer draft was often timed between 2:00 and 3:00 am. I consider he was passionate about this commemorative process. But, although he never told me, I sense he was running into opposition from some senior members of VAC regarding how he wanted the program to unfold. I thought his leaving was a great loss to the program.

However, in December 1993, Serge Rainville, an experienced senior executive and currently ADM Veterans Services, who was in a position to marshal the resources of the department, replaced him.

More members of Veterans Affairs were added to the team. I was named Director of Marketing and Corporate Relations. This was fine with me because it was what I thought I had been coming to the program to do.

Thus VAC could carry on with their day-to-day communications business regarding the program while I could work on the many projects that had been identified in the communications strategy. This included, as an example, the commemorative pin featuring the logo, flags, banners and decals; a number of introductory information and music videos; a youth video contest; posters; television vignettes for use as public service announcements; and a range of other paraphernalia and commercial products such as clothing and watches.

I quickly realized that I needed a financial commitment from the Canada Remembers program and some help to do all the work involved. I drafted a budget to cover the anticipated costs of all the various projects that I foresaw happening over the course of the program and submitted it to the Executive Director. Rather surprisingly to me, it was approved quickly.

I then sought out an assistant. Word spread quickly throughout the various Government departments and I began to receive many CVs from individuals, some whom I knew well, who wanted to work on the program. Most were quite capable of doing the job and some were senior to me in the hierarchy of the Public Service. One applicant who was working at the Privy Council Office had received his PhD in political science from UCLA.

My dilemma was that I wanted someone who was very capable, willing to work long hours and take a lot of responsibility. At the same time, I couldn't afford to have someone who would want to debate with me how a project should be done and slow down the process. There was a great deal to do in a very short period of time. I needed someone who would provide good input, but be quite ready to accept my decision and 'get on with it.'

One day, I received an application from a George Harris who was working in a clerk position in a Government department. He was 33, married with three children. He had a Master's degree in Political Science. I learned later that he had been trying to enter the Foreign Service but to date had been unsuccessful. I arranged to have him come in for an interview the following day at 1:00 pm. He apparently arrived on time, but I had been caught up in a meeting where we were discussing a problem and didn't get back to my office until 2:30. I apologized and explained the nature of the problem. I then asked him how he would handle this issue. We discussed it for a while and I was impressed by his insight and thoughtfulness. At the end of this discussion he handed me a lengthy paper he had written and finished in the pre-dawn hours that morning regarding his opinion of the Normandy landings.

I scanned it briefly. Then I sat back looked at him and said, "You're hired."

"But what about my interview?" he gasped. "You just had it," I said.

It was one of my best decisions. George would work tirelessly night and day throughout the program and became completely dedicated to what we were doing.

What was truly amazing to me was the amount of support for Canada Remembers from industry, organizations, veterans' groups and individuals from coast to coast to coast.

In August 1993, we received a call from the St Clair Group, a Toronto based international publishing group, who wanted to create a commemorative magazine for the program. The company would prepare all the editorial copy and find the necessary companies to finance the production of the magazine. They would pay for the costs of production and publishing and deliver it to wherever we asked. We also would have the right to approve all contents of the magazine. The first run would be 50,000 copies. It was too good an opportunity to pass up.

George and I worked closely with the editorial and advertising staffs. We each went through every word of every article and every advertisement to make sure that it was in keeping with the intent of the program. Sometimes, we had to take a "blue pencil" and edit out material that could be seen as offensive to veterans or could be construed as negative towards Canada's war efforts. After all, this entire program was designed to recognize the tremendous efforts that Canadians, both in uniform and civilian clothes, had made towards winning the war.

For whatever reason some Canadians authors had a propensity to finding the negative side of Canada's efforts and wanted to highlight our deficiencies. There was no place for this in the program as far as I was concerned.

The magazine was produced in May 1994, just in time to begin distribution both in Canada and overseas at the D-Day landing celebrations. It was taken by the PM's staff to be handed out to our allies during the ceremonies. It was a great summary of Canada's efforts during the Second World War, something that apparently was not known by some of our allies.

Shortly after the start of the program I approached the National Film Board asking them if they would be interested in producing a documentary for the 50th anniversary. A luncheon meeting was arranged to discuss my proposal. The NFB team of four arrived, headed by executive producer Don Haig. Little did I know how fortunate we were to have him heading the group. Don had been in the business for 30 years. He was called the 'Godfather of Canadian film' for nurturing young talent and producing many award films.' He had helped to create more than 500 films in Canada.

He had won many awards including Academy, Gemini and Genies. In 1993, while directing this project, he received the Governor General's Performing Arts Award.

I spent about three hours passionately telling the group what should be the focus of this documentary. The true stories of ordinary men and women who went overseas and fought; the difficult times faced by those on the home front including the more than one million women who went into the industrialized workforce for the first time; and, the difficulties faced by those returning from overseas after the war ended, as well as those families into which they were returning.

A writer took notes. Don told me that a one-hour TV production would probably cost about $700,000. I told him we could commit to one-half of that. I had already done some homework with NFB and put that amount into my budget.

Two weeks later Don called and told me he had a draft storyboard that he was sending to me. George and I both read it. We were amazed that the storyline was about 80% of what we wanted. We made our suggested changes and sent it back. Don agreed and production began. In fact, Don agreed to all of the production changes that we asked for, although some of his staff was not always as willing to go along with our suggestions. But Don prevailed.

He no doubt recalled the angst that the production of a documentary about Billy Bishop by the NFB some 10 years previously had caused. The producer of this documentary had gone to some lengths to discredit some of Bishop's heroics during the First World War. It had caused an uproar, particularly from veterans across the country.

Don invited me to NFB headquarters in Montreal to view some of the film footage that they had found. He told me that in their archives there were approximately 50,000 feet of footage that had never been aired. Some was tragic, showing the horrors of what these young men faced, both Allies and Germans. Some was funny. Like a soldier in dress uniform chasing a turkey around a French farmyard who might have been told, "Catch it and it's yours." Of course this was all silent film, which was a challenge trying to put sound over. On one occasion, technicians spent several hours trying to sync the sound of chimes over the video of Big Ben in London as its hands struck midnight leading into 1944.

The Film Board searched out 75 veterans and civilians who had been in the war effort and traveled across Canada to conduct interviews describing what they had faced. Their stories would form the heart of the production.

Not long after the start of putting the documentary together, Don called and told me that he was gathering so much material that it could not justifiably fit into a one-hour TV program. "It needs three hours," he said. I told him that was great but our budget was still only $350,000. He replied not to worry; he would find the rest of the budget either through NFB or sponsors. The actual cost, I was told, to complete the production was approximately $2 million.

The idea of NFB producing another documentary on the military was a concern to some. I had been asked to address a meeting of the Naval Officers' Association of Canada (NOAC) in Ottawa to brief them on the Canada Remembers program. When I outlined the production by NFB, a retired Vice Admiral stood up and strongly advised me that I should have the script and film viewed by the Parliament and the Senate before it was finalized. His comment was applauded by most in the audience. I told him that I was watching every word and every foot of film during the production, and as a former Director of Public Information for DND, as he knew I had been, I would not allow anything to be produced that would be detrimental to the military, and certainly not to veterans. Besides, I told him as politely as I could, the Canada Remembers program would be over in about 20 months and if we sent it to Parliament Hill, the program would be over before the review was completed!

Indeed, I did go to NFB Headquarters in Montreal at least once a month during the 18 months it took to produce the three-part series. It first aired on CBC nationally in early 1995. It received great reviews. It was subsequently aired several times by CBC as well as the History channel and several TV stations in the US.

Perhaps indicative of how it was received, the Royal Canadian Legion requested the right to use it in their education programs across the nation. Likewise, it would form the core of an education package that we would put together. The three-part series was repackaged into six 23-minute segments by the NFB and we added teaching material.

The National Film Board offered the education series for sale, and we were told that by the end of 1997, more than 20,000 units had been sold to schools across Canada.

Education was one of the principal objectives of the Canada Remembers program. Our Communication strategy included having students accompany pilgrimages to Italy, France, Belgium, Holland and Hong Kong. We also introduced a video contest whereby teams of two students across Canada were invited to prepare a 10-minute video featuring veterans of WWII or those who supported them at home. Somewhat to our surprise there were hundreds of entries.

In each of five regions across Canada, local judges, from VAC staff and members the Legion, selected three winning teams. Third prize was $500 to the team, second prize was $750, and first prize was $1,000, plus a DVD player donated by Philips Canada, which would be presented to the school. DVD players were just being introduced in 1995 and were quite expensive.

The best team selected in each Region would accompany the pilgrimage to Holland in May 1995 for the ceremonies commemorating the end of the war.

George and I joined the 10 winning students on what would be an unforgettable 10-day trip. We travelled with Lawrence MacAulay, the Secretary of State for Veterans Affairs, and a large contingent of veterans aboard a KLM aircraft. For some of the students it was their first flight. We also took along a film crew to record all the ceremonies and the students.

The reception for the Canadians in Holland was amazing. The Dutch have never forgotten the role that Canadian soldiers played in their liberation from the Germans. Thousands lined the streets for parades wherever we went. Particularly on May 5 – The Netherland's Liberation day.

Veterans marched or rode on wartime vehicles. Men, women, and children threw flowers and kisses; some ladies raced out and kissed the marching Vets. Tears flowed down the faces of those watching and those marching. It was an emotional time.

In the city of Apeldoorn, more than 1,000 Canadian veterans, along with some Allies, walked or rode before thousands of adoring Dutch men, women and children. The city had been freed by Canadians on April 16, 1945. In the fighting in the area between April 11 -17, 1945, 506 Canadians soldiers died.

As a result of the German occupation, from May 1940 until April 1945, 234,000 Dutch citizens lost their lives. By April 1945, the official daily ration for each person was 320 calories. Twenty thousand Dutch men, women, and children died during the 'hunger winter' of 1944-1945 and 982,000, or more than 10% of the population, was considered to be malnourished. While farmers and those in small villages could grow their own food, to a point, it was more difficult in the crowded cities. Beginning on April 29, 1945 and continuing for 10 days Allied Air Forces including the RAF, RCAF and US Army Air Force flew more than 5,000 missions and dropped over 11,000 tons of food to the beleaguered Dutch.

The Dutch have never forgotten. It was overwhelming to see the manner in which Canadians were revered.

Watching Dutch students their own age placing poppies on the graves of Canadian soldiers, at several cemeteries that we visited, brought tears to many of our students eyes as well as those of the visiting veterans. We were told that students attend to graves all year long.

Our visit to Westerbork was even more moving. Located in northeastern Netherlands, this camp was set up by the Dutch in late 1938 to house Jews fleeing from Nazi Germany. Ironically it was partially financed by Dutch Jewry. The camp was taken over by the Nazis on July 1, 1942 and turned into a deportation camp. It was designed by the Nazis to make inmates comfortable to avoid problems when they were sent on the trains. Many thought their living conditions would be the same in the camps in Poland.

The first train left on July 16 with more than 1,000 Jews sent to Auschwitz. In total, more than 100,000 Dutch Jews, and about 5,000

353

German Jews, were sent by train from this camp to their deaths in occupied Poland.

It was here that Anne Frank and her family stayed for two months in mid-1944. They boarded the first of the final three trains on September 3, 1944 and arrived in Auschwitz three days later. Anne and her sister were moved to the Bergen-Belsen concentration camp where Anne died in March 1945, reportedly from typhus. She was 15. Her sister Margot, 18, had died a few days earlier also from typhus. Their mother Edith died in Auschwitz in February of starvation, 10 days before her 45th birthday.

Anne's father Otto survived Auschwitz and made his way back to Amsterdam where he found that a 'helper' had saved Anne's diary, which she had written over two years while hiding with her family. The diary was first published in 1947 in Dutch, and in English in 1952. It has been translated into more than 60 languages.

The Canadian 2nd Infantry Battalion liberated the several hundred remaining inmates of Camp Westerbork on April 12, 1945.

The single train track, which stopped outside the camp, was redesigned as a memorial and opened by Queen Juliana in 1970. The end of the track was bent to point to the sky and signifies it will never be used again for such a purpose.

One of our students, a Chinese-Canadian, stood on the track and with tears pouring down her face said, "I never thought I would be standing on the rail where the train took Anne to her death." It was a moving, unforgettable moment for all of us.

Years later, I met a woman singing in a concert in Hollywood, FL. A beautiful lady in her 60s, she was dressed in a gorgeous flowing, long sleeved gown which covered both arms. She sang passionately, soulfully, some of the WWII songs that meant so much to those who suffered during the war years. I went to congratulate her and realized that she had only one arm. She willing showed me her other arm which bore a tattooed number. She told me that she had been shot by a Nazi guard when she was in a camp and had to have her arm amputated. She was 16 at the time. I told her I had helped produce a documentary involving students visiting Holland and told her that we had visited Westerbork and knew what had happened to Anne Frank. A few tears began to trickle down her face. She told me she had slept in a big bunk with Anne, her sister and her mother at Auschwitz. No doubt those memories came flooding back to her now. Anne and Margot had died; she had survived.

The tributes to Canadians continued wherever we travelled throughout our visit.

In one town, after the parade, we took our student group into a small Café for drinks and cake. I went to pay the bill and was told by a large bar owner, who said rather sternly but with a big smile, "No bill today for Canadians."

It was a visit that neither the students nor any of us Canadians attending would ever forget.

Once home, we worked with the film crew to produce a 20-minute documentary narrated by two of the students. That documentary was going to be part of the education package we were building to place in schools across the country.

Part of our education package also included producing four posters that were reproducible, for inclusion in Teach magazine during the school year. Developing four pieces of art work depicting the various stages of the war from beginning to end and then writing in-depth teaching material which was placed on the back of each poster, was a huge task in a relatively short period of time.

A Teach magazine hired artist produced the initial artwork. We hired a teacher to draft the teaching material. The vetting was up to us. It was only with the help of several teachers that we were able to do this. One of our main supporters was Allan Bacon, a high school Principal, who at that time was President and CEO of the Canadian Teachers' Federation. He would prove to be an invaluable resource during the Canada Remembers program and beyond, as we continued developing education material.

It was a great opportunity to reach teachers at all levels. The magazine was distributed to 18,000 elementary school teachers and 7,000 high school teachers. The first poster, featuring a family at the start of the war as dad was heading overseas, fit well with the theme of the International Year of the Family. This edition was sent to an additional 25,000 teachers, courtesy of the organization's Canadian committee. French copies were also sent to 2,100 elementary schools in Quebec, 2,200 French language schools across the country and 1,200 French secondary schools.

To reach even more schools, teachers and students, we worked with Canada Post to develop a poster with teacher's activities on the reverse, which would be included in their May 1995 issue of Heritage Post magazine. This slick magazine produced by Canada Post was sent to 56,000 teachers across Canada.

The NFB series, the videos, posters and magazines were just some of the products that were produced for schools across the country. I hasten to add that the production and distribution of all the products would not have been possible without the tremendous support that came from so many different civilian and veterans' organizations across Canada including teachers and teachers' groups.

We were able to involve teachers and authorities from provincial school boards, teaching associations and university faculties of education across the country. Prof Jon Bradley from the Faculty of Education at McGill would prove to be an enormous help. He became enamoured with the program from the first time I briefed him on what we were trying to accomplish. He was able to harness a number of other professors at the University to help along with each of his approximately 180 students.

355

George Harris and I with our display at a Teacher's Conference.

During the next two years they would provide invaluable assistance into what they considered would be appropriate and a fit into provincial and territory curriculums. Since curricula are a provincial responsibility, producing teaching material that would be acceptable to all was a definite challenge.

Even with all the support, I felt that we really needed to get a major national teaching organization behind us. So I targeted the Canadian Teachers Federation. Allan Bacon, the president and CEO, was a very busy man. I flew to Halifax where the CTF Annual Conference was being held. It took almost a day before I could corner him and get ten minutes of his time. I told him about our program and asked him for his advice and help. He was 'onboard' from the beginning. He became an enthusiastic and active participant, helping us to develop and write material, and providing his counsel and experience in all of our products, well beyond the official end of Canada Remembers.

To increase the awareness of and support for Canada Remembers, it was also important to get business, industries, veteran groups and the media involved.

I was invited to address the annual meeting of the Conference of Defence Associations being held in Ottawa. The association represented 24 defence influential groups and 50,000 individuals, plus the Royal Canadian Legion. Later, I was invited to speak to 600 representatives of the Canadian Aerospace Industry Association representing 250 top aerospace industries and the annual meeting of the Corps of Commissionaires, attended by 300

356

governors, representing 25 districts and 18,000 commissionaires in Canada. Importantly, I went to Charlottetown to address the 75th Annual Convention of the Canadian Community Newspapers Association whose members represented 750 newspapers.

Another influential audience that I was invited to address was the Canadian Society of Association Executives. Nearly 800 executives who represented 250,000 businesses and two million Canadians attended these meetings. The interest in our program at all these meetings was very positive and supportive.

In fact, the interest in our program from so many different areas was something that astounded us. As a result, I believe that in reality, although we started the program, we really were only the catalyst and played a small part in what Canadians across the country did to recognize the sacrifice and efforts of so many Canadians both overseas and at home during the turbulent war years.

Many veterans who previously would not talk about their personal memories of the war, began to talk. They went to schools, sat down with the kids and told them about their experiences. It was so important to so many of the veterans that today's children learn about what happened. Many wrote books and, in some cases with their own funds, had them published and placed in schools.

It seemed as if in every town, village and hamlet across Canada, events were held to recognize the end of the War. Dances, suppers, plays and parades were only some of the events featured. Canada Remembers truly captured the imagination of Canadians across the nation and the profile of veterans was raised considerably.

Even sports teams wanted to be involved. The Toronto Blue Jays offered 2,500 seats to veterans for a Blue Jays vs. Kansas City Royals night game. They also provided a large VIP box and invited one couple each from the Army, Navy and Air Force, Merchant Marine and Women's Corp. David Collenette, the Minister of National Defence and a Toronto M.P. was invited to assist a disabled veteran in a wheelchair to throw out the first pitch. We provided patches featuring the Canada Remembers logo, which each player wore on his shoulder for that game. The evening was a huge success with all the veterans' seats filled, more than 40,000 in attendance, and Toronto winning in a 16th extra-inning game.

The Montreal Expos, Toronto Argonauts, Hamilton Tigercats and Ottawa Rough Riders all held similar events to honour the veterans.

But perhaps the most remarkable effort was that coordinated by the Canadian Football League. The marketing head from the CFL called me and told me that they wanted to honour the veterans by gathering together former members of the 1944 Grey Cup Champions and taking them to the 1994 championship game in Vancouver. He told me that 50 years ago the St Hyacinthe-Donnacona Navy team defeated the Hamilton Flying Wildcats 7 – 6 at the Civic Stadium in Hamilton to win the coveted Grey Cup. The Navy team was mainly made up of a group of sailors who liked to play football, but at least eight members of the Toronto Argonauts professional team were players. It was the last time that two Eastern Canadian teams would play in the championship.

The CFL had located 14 members of the original team and 10 of their spouses. The plan was to fly everyone into Calgary and from there, take the Rocky Mountain Rail train to Vancouver. Former noted CFL players like Peter Dalla Riva, who played 14 years with the Montreal Alouettes, and Terry Evanshen, who also played for the Alouettes during a 13-year career, along with a few current team members, would be part of the group. John Tory, commissioner of the CFL, would also be on board, as well as a crew from ESPN to record the adventure.

The CFL coordinated the arrangements with the Palliser Hotel in Calgary, Rocky Mountain Rail tours, Canadian Pacific Airlines and CP Hotels. Fortunately, there was little that we at Canada Remembers had to do, but I was invited to join the group.

The two-day train trip itself was outstanding. Most of the veterans were in their 70s, but still generally lean and fit. There was only one complaint. The organizers had decided that there should be no alcohol on board. They wanted the 'Vets' to arrive in good shape for the big welcoming ceremony in Vancouver. Peter provided some relief from the 'prohibition.' At each stop he would rush off the train and somehow find a liquor store. Back on board he would invite the Vets one by one to come into the small bathroom for a quick 'nip' from the Mickey's he had purchased. Fortunately there wasn't enough to do any serious damage to anyone.

We stopped in Kamloops and stayed in a local hotel overnight. The veterans were feted in the town arena by military and civilian bands and a huge local crowd who came out to applaud their visitors.

The next morning I had taken my breakfast from the buffet and sat down when Terry Evanshen came and asked if he could sit with me. Of course I said yes. Once seated, he looked at me and asked me if I knew his story. I wasn't sure what he meant but told him no. He then told me 'his story,' which has stuck with me ever since. For me it is another, 'Do you believe in God?' story.

Terry had completed his football career and was working with a firm in Toronto in July 1988. Having just finalized a big deal, he called his wife and told her he would be home soon to break out the champagne. He was happily driving his Jeep from Toronto to the small hobby farm near Peterborough where he, his wife and three daughters lived.

About halfway home on a rural highway, that Friday afternoon, a van ran a red light and broadsided his vehicle, throwing him through the back window. Miraculously, a driver in a car behind him saw the accident and had a hand-held mobile phone. A 911 call revealed that an 'off duty' ambulance crew heading back to their station, was less than five minutes away. They arrived and administered aid to the severely injured Terry. He was in a coma, had suffered brain injuries and was hovering near death. The ambulance rushed him to a nearby hospital east of Toronto.

It was about 6:00 pm. By tremendous luck, a highly skilled brain surgeon was still in her office doing some final paper work before leaving on vacation. An operation was immediately performed. Terry remained in a coma for two weeks. When he awoke he was unable to walk, or perform basic life skills. His emotional state was that of a young child. He was suffering from retrograde amnesia and had no idea who he was or where he was and had no recollection of anything in his past. Everything that he had known for the past 44 years was gone.

But without the mobile phone, the ambulance nearby and the skilled physician available, no doubt he would not have survived.

Terry told me that it had been an incredibly difficult past six years. Particularly for his wife and daughters. He didn't know who they were and treated them, "horribly." "I don't know why they stayed with me," he said.

Terry told me that he was trying to learn how to live and laugh and love. His brain damage was such that he could not remember anything from the previous day, so he had to keep repeating his actions to determine what was right and what was wrong. Each step was encouraged, with much patience by his wife and daughters.

I was left limp. My breakfast sat cold on the plate in front of me. This fit 50 year- old, was calmly describing what he had been through and continued to battle. I don't know if I would have such courage.

Terry has gone on to be an inspirational speaker telling audiences across Canada how he is rebuilding his life and his confidence one step at a time; inspiring them to recognize the power of the human mind to overcome obstacles.

We arrived in Vancouver days in advance of the game and were greeted by a Navy band, a host of dignitaries, and a mass of TV cameras. For the next four days the veterans were invited to parties and receptions throughout the city.

On game day, the CFL provided each one of them with a shirt which was a replica of those they had worn 50 years ago including their own numbers and names. Before the game started they were each introduced and ran the length of the football field to the roar of the more than 80,000 fans gathered in the stadium.

The game itself was outstanding. For the first and only time an American team would battle a Canadian team for the Grey Cup. Fans across the country would cheer for the BC Lions representing Canada,

The larger, stronger Baltimore CFLers led throughout much of the game but it was tied 20-20 at the end of the third quarter. With 1.02 minutes left on the game clock, veteran field goal kicker Lui Passaglia had what seemed like a sure tiebreaker from the 38-yard line. He missed and it was run out of the end zone. No point. In the last minute Baltimore gave up the ball and with no time left on the clock Passaglia had another attempt from the 37. This time he didn't miss. Final score 23 – 20 BC Lions. The stadium went nuts. Fans poured onto the field. The stage set up for the

359

ceremonies couldn't be reached. The Grey Cup had to be presented in the BC Lions locker room.

For everyone lucky enough to be at the game, and particularly the veterans, it was a moment never to be forgotten. Indeed, this 82nd Grey Cup game has been billed as one of the ten best Grey Cup games of all time.

A 1944 Grey Cup Champion and I holding the Grey Cup in Vancouver.

It was now only six months until the huge ceremonies marking the end of the Second World War in Europe. Time flew by. It seemed like George and I were working seven days a week trying to complete the projects we had initiated. The bulk of the Canada Remembers team was totally occupied addressing all the challenging issues they were facing while organizing pilgrimages of veterans to ceremonies in Europe and the Far East, as well as ceremonies across Canada. In addition to those included in the pilgrimages, in 1994 and 1995, thousands of Canadian veterans returned to the countries they helped to liberate 50 years earlier. They were greeted as heroes. As a result it appears that many Canadians began to realize what these men and women had done so long ago. There was a renewed interest in veterans, which continues to this day.

May 8, 1995 was a moving day in Canadian villages, cities and on Parliament Hill. At each ceremony, the aging faces of those who had fought were prominent, some with missing limbs and disfigurement still evident.

Tears of remembrance poured down their faces. They had come home but many of their buddies had not. A difficult question for many of them was, "Why did I survive and not Joe?"

The documentaries, books and events held leading up to the day had made most Canadian aware of the sacrifice. From a population of less than 12 million, one million men and women served in uniform, more than 47,000 died and more than 55,000 were wounded; 11,000 taken prisoner.

But in those six years, between 1939 and 1945, much had changed. Canada had moved from an agrarian society to an industrialized nation. Canada had developed into a land of opportunity. It would be start of a whole new era for this country.

For George and me, there was much left to be done. While we had managed to get some materials into some schools, there was still much left in our plans to be produced and distributed.

My two-year secondment from Privy Council Office was up, but the new Deputy Minister David Nicholson was aware of the progress of the education program and was much in favour of it being continued. In May 1995, he called me in to his office and asked me if I would be willing to accept another two years at Veterans Affairs to work on the program. I had anticipated the offer and Shirlie and I had already agreed that I would accept. There had been too much time and effort spent to allow this program to end. So I told him I would be very pleased to accept, on the condition that he would also extend George's contract. We were a two-man team and I really needed him if we were going to be successful.

One of the major challenges facing us was the fact that education in Canada is a provincial responsibility. As such, each province has its own curriculum and determines what and how subjects would be taught. Trying to develop material that would fit into all of the 10 provinces and two territories would be a real challenge!

But we had an excellent resource working with us... Allan Bacon, who was still head of the Canadian Teachers Federation.

I discussed the problem with Allan who immediately suggested that we needed to have all of the Provincial Ministries of Education on side. He offered to write to each of the Ministries. Two weeks later, in June 1995, he had sent personal letters as President of the CTF to each of the Ministers, underscoring the support of the CTF, outlining what we were attempting to do, and asking that an official be named who could be our contact into the Ministry.

Much to our surprise, within several weeks we had replies from each of the Ministers and all were most supportive. I believe it was due to the high regard in which Allan Bacon and the CTF were held by those organizations.

Eight days after the letter was sent to the Honourable Willard Phelps, Minister of Education for the Yukon, a signed reply addressed directly to me stated in part: "I commend you for the time and dedication required to undertake such a massive project. I agree that the contributions of Canada should be recognized. The toll of the Second World War and the merit and sacrifices of Canadians are important aspects of our history and social order." He went on to name one of his officials who would be responsible for reviewing our material and providing suggestions for its content.

Having the Ministries on board was a huge step towards making this program successful. Armed with this backing we were able to approach the Canadian School Board Association, provincial School Boards and Teacher Associations across Canada. There was support from all. I think this support can be attributed to the subject that we were addressing as well as the fact that we wanted their input in the development of the product, rather than giving them a final product that did not have any of their input.

We packaged our first series of products into a cardboard suitcase about the size of a large briefcase. It contained the NFB series, videos of the students in Holland, the posters as well as the Teach Canada Remembers magazine and some vignettes that we had prepared. The core item was a 155-page Teachers' guide written in large part by Allan Bacon. We titled the kit, 'Canada's Coming of Age 1939-1945.'

Distribution was our next challenge.

I approached a leading publisher of education material for schools, in Toronto, to ask them if they would be interested in marketing the product across Canada.

The person who I met showed interest, but then said, I thought rather condescendingly, "Of course we would have to read and check everything before we could agree to becoming involved." I said, "Do whatever you have to," feeling confident that with all the input we had had from teachers, they wouldn't find much wrong in content or in grammar to disagree with.

Two weeks later, the representative called and asked if I could come to Toronto for a meeting. She told me that all the material had been checked and that there was nothing that needed to be corrected or changed.

So, now we needed to talk about a contract for the company to market and sell the product to schools and anyone else who was interested. I had spoken to a number of teachers across Canada regarding whether they would buy such material. Some told me that they received a great deal of teaching material for free on an ongoing basis from a wide variety of sources. Virtually none had been checked by teachers or had involved the provincial Ministries of Education. In most cases, teachers told me that this material was thrown in a drawer where it stayed. An Alberta teacher told me that, "If I spend some of my small discretionary fund of $100 dollars a school year to buy a product you know, I will certainly use it."

The company told me they would handle the marketing, distribution and sales for $149.95 a kit. We would provide all the material. I thought this was a great deal for them, but at that price, I didn't think many teachers, or for that matter schools, would buy it.

"Too expensive," I told the representative. "How about $ 49.95?"

"Ridiculous, we can't sell it for that."

"Then we don't have a deal," I said. She wouldn't budge. I thanked her and got up and left, knowing we had another 'big' job to get these kits into schools across the country.

My first stop was at the Dominion Command of the Royal Canadian Legion. I met with Dwayne Daly, the boss, and asked him if he would be willing to get Legion branches across the country to help. His first reaction was that if we were selling our material to schools the Legion couldn't be involved. It took some persuasive talk but I finally convinced him that it was much more likely to be used if there was a cost involved.

In the following months, Legion branches did come onboard. In many cases, local branch would buy kits from their own funds and give them to local schools.

George and I then began to attend Provincial annual conferences of Teachers' Associations and School Boards across Canada. These two/three-day gatherings created a great deal of interest about the kit amongst teachers. It also provided an opportunity to talk with thousands of teachers.

Other departments showed some interest. The DG Communications at Transport Canada asked me to send him a copy of the kit so he could look at, since obviously transportation was widely covered in the material. A few days later I met with him. He asked me the cost. I told him. "I'll buy 1,000 copies," he said. "$50,000 and we will get it into schools." He told me that he felt we were doing more to publicize the history of transportation and its involvement in WW II than his own Department.

About two hours later, we got a fax from his office with a contract to buy the kit. He obviously had the authority. Wow! What a great boost for the program.

I am not sure how many we sold but we continued to promote them until I left the program two years later.

With the WWII commemoration program over in mid 1995, we began to work on education products regarding WWI – the Great War.

A highlight involved putting together a group of 12 students representing each province and territory who would accompany six veterans who actually fought at Vimy Ridge in April 1917, on a pilgrimage back for the 80th anniversary of that battle.

We identified the students by enlisting the help of Encounters with Canada, described by the institution as Canada's largest youth forum. They state that every week of the school year more than 120 students from across Canada aged 14-17 come to Ottawa. Here they discover more about their country through each other. They learn about Canadian institutions such as Parliament, meet famous and accomplished Canadians, explore career options, develop leadership skills and, for a week, live a bilingual experience.

The Director of Encounters with Canada selected the students based on their performance and stated interest while they were in Ottawa.

In April 1997, the six WWI veterans, the students, some WWII veterans, Veterans Affairs 'minders,' George and I boarded an RCAF transport aircraft for our flight to France. We had been told that Governor General Romeo LeBlanc and his wife Diana would be on the flight so we were assured we would be treated very well on board. Shrimp cocktails and steak for dinner, continuous drinks on request and first-run movies for the whole flight. "Don't expect to get treated like this when you fly commercial," I told the students.

But they were happy, getting to know each other, telling jokes and laughing. That would all change within 24-hours of our arrival in Lille.

We would visit a number of WWI battle sites and cemeteries during our seven days in France including Passchendaele, Ypres, and Beaumont Hamel. They were all sobering, but perhaps the one that affected the students the most was Vimy Ridge. I had asked them to read Pierre Berton's book 'Vimy' before leaving home.

This would give them an idea of what happened. But nothing could prepare them for the emotion they felt as they walked through the tunnels where Canadian soldiers, some as young as 16, spent almost a year training for the battle; through the huge, very deep bomb craters; and, finally, visiting the row upon row of white crosses.

As they walked down the rows tears began to flow not only amongst the girls. One of the girls told Miles, a new friend from Winnipeg, himself only 16, that, "If the 12 of us had been here 80 years ago, probably only half of us would have come back."

Indeed, there were 15,000 Canadian infantry soldiers who overran the Germans beginning on April 9. But by the end of the battle 3,958 Canadians had been killed and more than 7,000 wounded. A historian travelling with us told the group that if you served in the Canadian infantry during the First World War, you could expect to be killed or wounded. In fact, according to the Canadian War Museum, during the 1914 – 1918 War, 61,000 Canadian soldiers were killed and more than 172,000 were wounded.

The Vimy Memorial unveiled in July 1936 by King Edward VIII bears the names of 11,285 Canadian soldiers who died fighting in France but have no known graves.

It was here that a moving memorial ceremony was held, watched by visiting dignitaries, thousands of French citizens and hordes of international media.

It was a grueling day for the veterans; two of them in wheelchairs and all of them aged 100 or more.

A standout for me was Tommy Spear. A spirited 100 year-old, he stood for the whole hour-long ceremony without flinching. He read the Act of Remembrance from memory. With a forceful voice, which might have been that of someone 40 years younger, he said:

"They shall grow not old as we who are left grow old. Age shall not weary them, nor the years condemn. At the going down of the sun, and in the morning, we will remember them."

Later, at a reception, the veterans were sitting quietly recovering from a difficult and emotional ceremony and listening to a small band playing. Suddenly Tommy grabbed one of the 16-year-old students and began to dance with her. "Tommy," I said rather amazed, "What are you doing?" With a twinkle in his eye he looked at me while twirling his young partner and said, "Why, Len, do you want all these young girls for yourself?"

What an inspirational man. We visited him a few times at his home in Calgary en route to our family in Sylvan Lake, Alberta. We learned that he had been retired since 1963, after a 50-year career with Canadian Pacific Rail. He rode 10 km every day on his stationary bike, kept a garden, drove his own car, played golf, shooting below his age, and curled. He also went to schools and gave talks about his experiences, particularly in the weeks leading up to memorial ceremonies on November 11. In 1999, the Province renewed his driver's license for two years at the age of 102.

At 100 he was invited to participate on the CBS Late Late Show and later appeared on the syndicated Donahue show along with several other centenarians to show what older people are capable of doing. He also was part of the Discovery Channel documentary '100 Something.' He wrote and published his autobiography in 1999 when he was 102.

He died on Sept 28, 2000, just 24 days short of his 104th birthday.

In a review of his book, Cliff Chadderton, President of the War Amps Society, wrote, "Tom Spear has been a constant inspiration to me. His take on life is simple and direct and should be communicated to every adult and child in the country."

This was great praise coming from Cliff Chadderton, who had been on the pilgrimage to Vimy as he had been on many other such trips. He himself was an incredible inspiration to many.

While in Vimy, he related to me how he had lost his leg. At the battle of Leopold Canal, in November 1944, he was in a trench; looked up and saw a German soldier, "Tossing a grenade on me.: The blast took off half of his right leg below the knee. But as he said, "He could have blown off my head."

That would have been a great loss to Canada and Canadians.

After returning to Canada and being fitted with what he called a rather, "Primitive chunk steel prosthetic," he joined War Amps. By 1965, he was the Executive Secretary and led the organization, retiring in 2009 as the Chief Executive Officer at the age of 90.

He was an amazing, tireless worker who felt that amputees could understand and help other amputees like no other person.

He made significant contributions to the welfare of amputees. He was recognized nationally and internationally as an influential developer of programs and services for war, civilian and child amputees.

But what he was most proud of was his work on behalf of children. He founded the internationally known Child Amputee Program (CHAMP), which assists thousands of children across the country with the cost of artificial limbs and education, and also provides counseling.

Throughout his career with War Amps he received many awards and honours including being appointed as a Companion of the Order of Canada in 1998.

When he died at the age of 94, in November 2013, the office of Prime Minister Stephen Harper issued a statement that read in part, "Canada has lost a great man, but his legacy will live on in the many people whose lives he has touched."

No doubt meeting individuals like Tommy Spear and Cliff Chadderton on this trip made a significant impact on our 12 students. In fact a few years later, I met Miles Morgan, who had recently graduated from the University of Winnipeg. He told me, "That trip changed my life. I am completely turned around in what I wanted to do with my life. I am off to Vimy before starting grad school and I am going to work as a guide there for the summer."

Back in Canada, we worked with the small company we had hired to make a 20-minute documentary, which would be suitable for use in schools. It contained a soliloquy from Melissa, a student from St Stephen, NB, who, when asked by a TV reporter what she had learned from this trip, replied from the heart, with so much emotion that tears began to stream down her face.

"I'm Canadian, I'm so proud to be Canadian. So many say our Nation was formed on this land. And it angers me so much when people don't remember. When people don't remember what people like these six men did, I think if I, at 17 years old, had left my home, my family, my job to go and fight and stand up for something that I thought was right, I would hope that 80 years later someone would remember what I did. We have forgotten how to say thank you. We have forgotten how to love our country, Canada. Canada is ours, it's my country, it's my life." She then turned to the 101-year old veteran on her right and kissed him on the cheek and said, "Thank you."

I looked around, the students were crying, the interviewer was crying and so were the cameraman and a number of the veterans who heard her answer. Indeed, when we put this segment into the documentary, it similarly moved many of those who viewed it.

This documentary plus another that we produced using a student to explain Canada's involvement in WWI, along with a teaching manual featuring various aspects of the war years, and two posters, made up an educational resource entitled 'Canada and the Great War 1914 – 1918 A Nation Born.'

All of these materials had been developed with the help of many educators at all levels across Canada. Much credit has to be given to Allan Bacon who had retired from teaching and his position with the Canadian Teachers' Federation and for two years worked with George and me under contract to help develop this material.

We had been invited to attend a number of national and provincial school board and teachers' annual conferences from St John's, Newfoundland, to Victoria, BC. In most cases we were given an opportunity to address interested teachers and set up a booth where we could display our materials.

The feedback from school administrators, school board officials and teachers across the country about both kits was most gratifying. We learned that not only did teachers like our material and use it in the classroom, but the students liked it as well.

Gail Saunders, a member of the instructional curriculum unit at the Saskatchewan Ministry of Education wrote: "Saskatchewan Education is very pleased to recommend the Canada Remembers Educational Kit, Canada's Coming of Age 1939 -1945 to all schools in the Province. This information and attractive kit is an excellent resource for Social Studies, History and English Language Arts courses, grade 9 -12."

Donna Cansfield, President of the Canadian School Board Association, stated in a letter to David Nicholson, the Deputy Minister of Veteran Affairs:

"On behalf of the Canadian School Board Association, I would like to extend our sincere congratulations for a job well done regarding Canada Remembers. The students of this country are richer in their knowledge on the contributions of our military as well as have a better understanding of the roles of the military in times of conflict and peace. Thank you for a terrific program."

Carole James, President of the BC School Trustees Association, wrote: "The demand for Canada Remembers by educators across the country is a testament to its effectiveness in filling an important gap in our collective memory as a nation. Our curriculum people in BC recognized the quality of your material, but it is the teachers who quickly identify the most effective classroom resources and the magnitude of their demand for your resource kit is remarkable."

By mid-1997, my extension to work on the Canada Remembers Education Program was almost over. I would be returning to my former position in the Privy Council Office.

As much as I had enjoyed working on the program for more than four years, I was exhausted. I knew that once I went back to PCO, it would be full speed ahead from the moment I stepped into my office. No time to rest and recuperate.

So, Shirlie and I sat down to discuss what I should do. I was 58, had been working for 40 years, 38 of which were with the military and government. I had a military pension. Shirlie had retired from her nursing position at the National Defence Medical Centre. She told me that she would like to have me around more, particularly when I wasn't so tired and we could spend more quality time together.

So we made the decision. I wrote to my boss at PCO and told her that I was submitting my resignation effective Dec 31, 1997.

Word apparently spread that I had resigned because suddenly I began getting calls from other federal departments asking if I would be interested in helping them with developing educational products. Dennis Wallace, ADM Veteran Services, made the first offer. He asked if I would take on a small contract for a few months to help George become more comfortable in his position as now head of the Canada Remembers Education program.

I talked to Shirlie and we decided there would be less pressure in this type of work. I wouldn't be working every day and my love for the program still ran deep. So, I accepted.

It would be the start of a whole new chapter in our lives for Shirlie and me, but now working together.

CHAPTER 19 - OUR OWN BUSINESS

About three months into 1998, we formed our own company, 'Leonard Dent and Associates, Education Consultants', and became federally incorporated. Economics played a major role in this move. Any money we earned would be taxed apart from our personal income and there would be some write-offs that could be claimed each year.

I accepted seven contracts that first year, some very small, using my knowledge in more of an advisory capacity on a specific project. Others would run for one to two years and the final one much longer. I didn't mean to take on that many, but I was new to this contract business and didn't want to turn down some of the very interesting projects that came along. Also, I didn't know if there would be any others.

It certainly wasn't for the money. Most of my offers were single source contracts and as such were usually $25,000 or less. From this, I had to pay for home office expenses and in most cases travel expenses including flights, meals and accommodation.

In the eight years that our company functioned, I never drew one cent, because any pay would have been added to my personal income. Rather, I paid a small salary to Shirlie. She took an accounting course and began to look after the books. It was a tough job. In fact, in order to make sure that we were functioning correctly, we hired an accounting firm who would go through her records annually and file our income tax for us. This led Shirlie to tell me one year that we were operating as a 'not-for-profit' business. In fact, in our last year, when were we down to one major contract, by design, I think the accounting firm made more than we did.

Nevertheless, we wanted to do this work because some of the projects were intriguing and most were designed to make Canadian youth more aware of our country's history and to be more empathetic to Canadians who have faced trials and tribulations over the past centuries.

Our contracts were primarily with Veterans Affairs, Canada Post, Heritage Canada, and Indian Affairs and Northern Development (DIAND). Although we were driven by our desire to help produce material to go to teachers and students, working with the bureaucracy in some departments could be frustrating. As an example, we would spend our own money to book flights and pay for hotel rooms, etc., and submit our claims. It could take up to six months to get the money back.

More importantly, sometimes projects were cancelled. In one case we had worked on a project for over a year, which was enthusiastically supported by teachers and school board authorities across Canada. Many educators spent hours reading, editing, and providing constructive comment to help develop a better product. They were all looking forward to it being used in the classroom.

A new department head quickly ruined that. When briefed by the project manager, he decided he didn't like it and immediately cancelled any further work. He could not be convinced by the departmental staff who argued for the benefit of this program to schools across the country, and what it would mean for the image of the department. Never mind the time, effort and money that had been poured into the project! And now wasted!

I had the difficult task of telling all my contacts that, "All their work was for naught." It was very frustrating and not great for my credibility, even though the program manager with whom I was working told me to tell them it was, "The department's fault." How could I expect educators to come onboard the next time I approached them to spend their valuable time on a project?

But there were many successes. And for me perhaps one of the most memorable was the work we did with the Department of Indian Affairs and Northern Development. DIAND wanted us to help them design some educational resources to complement those which they already had developed and sent to schools. They told me that our vast network would ease the difficulty of developing appropriate material and reaching the teachers they wanted to reach. We designed a proposal that included producing three resources, which would cover grades 1 to 10, ages 7 to 16.

Producing any teaching resource focusing on Aboriginal peoples was difficult given the number of Bands across Canada. Three groups of people are included as Aboriginal: First Nations, Inuit and Métis. These are three distinct peoples with unique histories, languages, cultural practices and spiritual beliefs. Reportedly, there are 600 recognized First Nation Governments or Bands and 2,300 Reserves where about 60% of 850,000 First Nation-status people live.

Our first project was to design a resource that would enhance students' awareness at the lower grade levels regarding Aboriginal communities, with an emphasis on First Nations and Inuit. The department wanted to provide an overview of some of the historical and contemporary contributions that Aboriginals have provided to Canada and to the world. The project manager told me that she thought a colouring book would be a good tool to accomplish this.

I was rather dubious, so contacted a number of my education friends across Canada, including those who were Aboriginals. They were unanimous that it had to be more than a colouring book.

Jon Bradley and some fellow professors at McGill became particularly involved in helping to conceptualize and write, not only this, but all three projects that we would design for DIAND.

The story would be focused on a young girl from the Odawa Nation who asks her grandfather to tell her more about her history and culture so that she could complete a classroom exercise telling her fellow students where she came from and the contributions her people have made to Canada.

We would involve 19 organizations and influential individuals across Canada including, as examples, the Aboriginal Educational Study Committee of the Elementary Teachers Federation of Ontario, the National

Association of Friendship, and several Aboriginal Education consultants across the country.

John Mazurek, a Professor at the Ontario Institute of Studies in Education (OISE) from the University of Toronto, offered to have his students review the draft product. He told his 85 'would-be' teachers that they were to go through the book and critique it, providing comments on why they would or would not use it in the classroom. It would be a marked exercise, he told them.

As a result, we received some most valuable comments, which we were able to use to improve the document. To help ease it through the DIAND approval process, we included a number of sketches that featured some of the contributions made by Aboriginals, which could be coloured.

Aimed at ages 7 – 12, the final document entitled 'Claire and her Grandfather', was 44 pages long and contained expected learning outcomes and related activities. It was made available to schools across Canada and soon became much in demand.

Our next project was to produce a resource that would increase the awareness of students aged 9 – 12 concerning the history, culture, life, and traditions of Inuit people, and in particular, those who live in Canada's northern Inuit community of Salluit.

Using the experience from our previous project, we asked Prof. Jon Bradley if he could put together a writing team, which he willingly did including finding project writers and advisors from the Inuit community.

'Through Mala's Eyes, Life in an Inuit Community' was the product of an extensive consultative process involving educators and experts in education, and Inuit culture and history from across Canada.

It was written as a first person narrative of a 12-year- old Inuk boy living in the Inuit community of Salluit, Nunivak, in Northern Quebec. Learning outcomes and teaching strategies were provided for each of the 13 chapters.

Because of the differences in provincial learning outcomes in their individual curricula, we recruited individuals in ministries, schools boards, teachers associations and universities, as well as Aboriginal educators in every province and territory, who dedicated many hours reviewing material and providing advice on the writing of the resource. Consequently, it became a resource that was welcomed Canada-wide and could be used particularly in the social studies, history and geography portions of provincial curricula. It was released in 2003.

Our final product, and perhaps the most challenging, was designed to enhance the understanding that non-Aboriginal students have regarding issues and realities facing First Nations and Inuit youth today.

Once again we relied heavily on Prof. Jon Bradley who put together a team of McGill professors and graduate students to write and edit this resource. I should add that virtually all of this work was volunteered. Teachers and students gave their time and expertise because of their love of education.

From the outset, because of the desire to have real experiences from real Aboriginal youth, it was readily evident that we needed to conduct interviews with a number of youth across the country. There was obviously some sensitivity involved in seeking the private feelings and experiences of these young people. So to try to protect their identities, we decided to interview three individuals from each of five communities across Canada and produce five narratives which would be anonymous. Aboriginal leaders selected the Nations and the youth.

Our next challenge was to decide on what questions to ask. On the train ride from Ottawa to Montreal, where I would meet at McGill with the team Prof Bradley had assembled, I wrote 32 questions that I thought would be a starting point to help us achieve our aim.

The team would spend considerable time over the next number of weeks carefully massaging, adding and subtracting questions. Consultations were also held with Aboriginal educators and leaders across Canada.

Finally we had a list of questions that satisfied everyone, or at least that all could live with.

The next step was to record the live interviews with the 15 youths across Canada. Interviews were conducted with youth representing Mi'kmaq in Nova Scotia; Mohawk in Quebec; Inuit in Nunavut; Cree in Saskatchewan; and Nisga'a in British Columbia.

The interviews were then synthesized to produce the five narratives, each drawn from the responses to the questions.

Most were very moving. I have never forgotten the comments of one girl in one of the stories, who said:

"When you go into a store, the people will watch you come up the aisle and try to pretend they are not watching you. It either has to do with the fact that we are young or we're Aboriginal or both. It makes me mad! It makes me uncomfortable to think that there are people who don't like me because I am Aboriginal. To help people understand better I would have someone come and live with me for a little while. I'm quite normal, and I think it helps if you know someone personally. If I could send a message to non-Aboriginal people it would be not to judge someone on how they look because you don't know them until you talk to them. We're not really that different. We want the same things and we go through a lot of the same things. Just because our skin colour is different, it doesn't mean that we are different on the inside."

An editorial team at McGill created selected activities to complement the narratives. A number of Aboriginal and non-Aboriginal experts and educators in First Nations and Inuit culture reviewed the document.

Before finalizing this written resource, it was reviewed by panels of Aboriginal and non-Aboriginal youth, and by Aboriginal and non-Aboriginal educators, to gauge the effectiveness of the material in terms of cultural accuracy, youth engagement, readability and potential for acquired awareness. Of course it was also sent to the many educators in each province with whom we had dealt on the previous projects for their input. Suggested comments gathered from all these reviews were incorporated into the final product which was titled: 'Five Voices of Aboriginal Youth in Canada – Ages 14 -16.'

My project manager at DIAND was somewhat skeptical as to whether this would be of interest to non-Aboriginal youth. When asked, she told me she had a 16-year old daughter. "Get her to read it," I suggested. A few days later she came back and told that she was rather amazed at the response from her daughter. "Mom," she said, "these kids sound just like us. They seem to have many of the same problems and fears that we do."

The resource was made available to schools in 2005 across the country and received wide acclaim throughout the country from educators and teachers.

These three products are still available from the Department of Indigenous and Aboriginal Affairs, more than 20 years later. It still gives us satisfaction to think that we played a part in getting these products into schools where they are used to encourage young people to be more tolerant and understanding of Aboriginal peoples.

But as we all know, there is still a long way to go!

Just after her 70th birthday in February 2005, Shirlie told me: "I am tired, I don't want to do this anymore. There is so much paper work."

We had been working hard. 'Five Voices' was now our only contract. "OK," I said without a second thought, "But let's work to the end of the year and finish this project."

So officially, on December 31, 2005 we wrapped up our business.

I was still on the Board of Governors for the Canadian Corps of Commissionaires in Ottawa. I still serve today, but in 2013, after 20 years of service, I was bumped up to be an honourary governor. I can still attend meetings but can't vote on any motion, which suits me fine.

In 2003, I received a letter from Chairman Bob Rae, the Chair of the Canadian Unity Council, telling me that I had been appointed to serve as a Governor with that organization. At that point I didn't know why I had been selected, or for that matter, what the Canadian Unity Council (CUC) was or did.

I learned that the CUC was, "A non-profit and non-partisan pressure group whose mission was to inform and to engage all Canadians in building and strengthening Canada."

It began in 1964 when a small group of Quebecers, alarmed by growing tensions between French and English-speaking Canadians, formed the Canada Committee. The Committee members worked hard to have Canadians better understand the roots of these tensions, to shed light on their significance and to find solutions. The name was changed to the Canadian Unity Council, which was considered a better name to reflect the evolving mission.

Over the next forty years, CUC went to great lengths to educate, inform and get citizens involved. It organized symposia and discussions in every part of Canada. It also operated a number of youth programs.

One in which I was involved was Encounters with Canada. The program began in 1982 and became Canada's largest and most successful youth program. Each week during the school year, 130 students aged 14 -17 travel to Ottawa from the 10 provinces and three territories. They stay at the Terry Fox Canadian Youth Centre for seven days. The program involves studying Canadian institutions such as the Senate and the Supreme Court along with a choice of one of the 11 themes offered each week in areas such as business, law, entrepreneurship and medicine.

The youth chosen to attend the program represent different economic, ethnic, racial and geographic regions and soon discover that their common values far outweigh their differences. It is a tremendous program; one that I had spoken to on occasion concerning the Canada Remembers program. As mentioned previously, it was also the program from which the students who became part of the pilgrimage to Vimy came from.

My connection to this program, and as I was told by one of the CUC Directors, my reputation for, "getting things done" was perhaps why I had been chosen to become a member of this auspicious group.

The number of CUC governors matched the number of Members of Parliament across the country. In 2003, there were 301 MPs, so there were 301 Governors, each one representing a Federal constituency. A list of candidates was submitted to a Board of Directors for consideration for each constituency and one chosen. I was indeed honoured to be selected.

Unfortunately, with all my other projects I didn't have time to get too deeply involved in any of the CUC programs. I was much like a backbencher in Parliament... part of the team but not a large participant.

In March 2006, the Federal Government decided to end the funding for the Council. After 40 years, the programs that were initiated by the CUC and that played such an instrumental part in promoting Canadian Unity, collapsed.

Almost immediately there was a massive national letter campaign, supporting Encounters with Canada. In May 2006, Heritage Minister Oda publicly announced that the program would be saved. The program now continues to run under the direction of the Historic Canada. A most important program for Canadians, Encounters with Canada, on its 30th anniversary in Sept 2012, boasted 90,000 student alumni. Now, after 35 years, it is still going strong.

By the beginning of 2006 I had finished working, although I did and do continue to volunteer in various areas, including in the community called Tweedsmuir on the Park in Kanata Lakes, Ottawa West, where we have lived for the past 15 years.

Wow! 48 years. Just over 48 years since I left Creemore, boarded a bus, and headed for Toronto to start my first full-time job.

But now I had the time to enjoy and spend more time with Shirlie. I had promised her, when I left the Government in 1997, that "God willing" over the next 10 -15 years, I would take her to all those places that I had been in my career and she couldn't go, or to places we wanted to go together.

As this is being written in 2018, we have completed 20 years of travel. We have visited close to 80 countries and been to seven continents. We are still planning and going. Every time I stop and think about our past I realize that we continue to be blessed.

And so, I will reflect and sum up my life to date.

CHAPTER 20 - LOOKING BACK

October 7, 2017 marked the 70th anniversary of my first stepping foot on Canadian soil at Pier 21 in Halifax, NS.

Looking back to that point, I could not have presumed to imagine what I would accomplish over the next 70 years.

My introduction to Canada had not been auspicious. We arrived to live on a poor farm run by poor farmers, my Dad's aunt, her husband and two sons. My parents and I were treated basically as slave labour, seven days a week. Basic lodging, basic food and no pay for my Dad, my Mom or me. Daily we were told how lucky we were to be living in this situation. They had no idea that when we lived in London, even though we were poor, we lived in a home, with hot and cold running water, electricity and inside toilets, none of which existed on this farm. And when Dad and Mom worked in London they got paid.

Nevertheless our situation got better. We stayed in Canada, although at one point Mom was so discouraged she wanted to go back to London. Dad eventually got a job in Toronto to try and save money to take us home. Three and one half years on the farm for Mom and me. Then he got a job at the nearby military base and we moved to the little town of Creemore. I finished Middle School in Creemore. At age 17, I graduated from Grade 13 at Collingwood District Collegiate, with a $500 scholarship to the University of Toronto. Mom and Dad couldn't afford to help me go to university. There were no student loans. So I got a job working at Canada Packers in Toronto.

One day I walked into an RCAF Recruiting Centre and my life changed forever.

I got my wings as a navigator, flew Search and Rescue, helped to save lives, find lost fishermen and hunters, got into public relations and eventually became Director of Information Services for the Canadian Forces, a job that took me all over the world. I met and worked with people at a level I couldn't believe possible.

Then I went to the Privy Council Office. I often sat at my computer drafting a note that sometimes went directly to the Prime Minister. Countless times I tried to figure out how this little boy in short pants that landed in Halifax so many years ago could have gotten to this chair.

Next was my move to Veterans Affairs to work in a Commemorative program for four years, a program that not only encouraged Canadians to say thanks to deserving Veterans but also attempted to educate Canadian youth about the exploits of these men and women, many of whom were teenagers, and yet sacrificed so much.

Trying to help Canadian youth develop, understand and take pride in what Canada and Canadians had accomplished during the two World Wars became a follow-on program and another challenge.

Finally, I was working in our own company for eight years trying to design and produce school products that would make young Canadians from coast to coast to coast more aware of recent history, and trying to encourage them to have more understanding of and empathy for less advantaged people living in this wonderful country.

In 2005 we retired!

None of what I accomplished would have been possible without the right partner. Shirlie has always been the right partner. She has supported me for the past 56 years.

In fact I often tell her that our relationship reminds me of the two horses that we had on the farm when Mom, Dad and I first came to Canada. Prince was a big, large boned, rather ugly horse. Beauty was a small, skittish, pretty mare that had apparently been beaten severely by her former owner. Prince and Beauty would be harnessed side by side and hitched to the hay wagon. You could see Beauty straining to do her best to keep up. Prince was doing much of the pulling but was slowing the pace so Beauty could keep up. But the job always got done!

So it has been with Shirlie and me. She has always pulled her weight and whatever we have accomplished has been because we pulled our weight together.

There were many times during my career when I was away for weeks and months at a time and in one case for a year. Shirlie had to be mother and father to two growing children, look after all the problems of running and looking after a home, while trying to also continue her career as a nurse. At our 50th wedding anniversary, in my address to the assembled guests, I made it clear that I was wearing all these medals but Shirlie deserved them.

I have always said that a military career either makes a marriage or breaks a marriage. In our case, all the trials and tribulations made ours a very strong marriage.

I often wonder, even now, how could I have been so blessed. A daughter, Susan, who is a world-renowned Research Oncologist, supported by a wonderful husband, Steve, who supports her 100 percent and behind the scenes has been father and mother to two daughters, when she was not able to be home. Older daughter Erin, now in her 20s, has a son, our sixth great-grandchild. Younger daughter Heather is at Queens University aspiring to be a veterinarian.

A son, David who, as a Nitrogen Supervisor, spent six years in Siberia teaching Russian oil men how to look after their wells, and then two years in Saudi Arabia overseeing nitrogen activities in the oil fields.

His two daughters, Stephanie, a Psychiatric Nurse, is married and has two beautiful daughters; and Vanessa, a hospital Administrator, is married and has a son.

David's partner Monica has two grandchildren. So, at the moment, we have four granddaughters and six great-grandchildren.

Blessed seems an inadequate word to describe the life I have lived.

But Shirlie and I have always been thankful for what we have had, even in the leanest of times when we were first married. We didn't wish to win the lottery. We tried to and continue trying to see the best in every situation and live every day to the fullest.

I have learned some lessons during the past 75+ years and have taken the liberty to list and explain the most important of them in the last chapter of this book.

Who knows, perhaps it might help someone to look at his or her life in a more positive manner. If just one person were to benefit, it will have been worth my effort.

Swearing David into the Canadian Forces in 1987. He served nine years before going back to school and joining the oil industry.

Our four grand daughters, Steve, Shirlie, Susan and I.

Celebrating 50 years of marriage.

Susan, me, Shirlie and David.

CHAPTER 21 - LESSONS LEARNED

Looking back on my 75+ years, I have been truly blessed. I have had an incredible wife for more than 56 years who, more importantly, is my best friend, buddy and pal. We have two wonderful, successful children and four talented, beautiful granddaughters, and now six great-grandchildren.

Over the years, I have learned a number of lessons, which I have then tried to follow. The 12 most important of these are listed below.

1. Be a shepherd... not a sheep.

I learned early in my life that you will not always be part of the in-crowd by doing this. I started wearing a button-downed shirt and tie to school when I was 15, in Grade 10, going to Collingwood District Collegiate Institute. Most of the boys, particularly those who came straight from their farm chores, laughed at me and thought I was crazy. But strangely enough some of their girlfriends thought it was 'kind of neat' and so, gradually, others started to appear in school wearing a tie.

Son David came to me after he had graduated from High School and told me that it wasn't easy being a shepherd. I knew he wanted to please me and had tried as much as possible to do this when working his way through school. I replied, "I know Dave, but remember anybody can be a sheep; it is much harder to be a shepherd."

So I have always tried to do what I thought was right even if it meant it could get me in trouble with my bosses, and in one case I believe cost me a promotion. But I have never had a problem shaving because I could always look at myself in the mirror!

2. Be the best you can be at what you can do.

In retrospect, this was probably the most important lesson I learned from my father. While, with some training, he probably could have earned a good living as an artist, circumstances were such that he became a Cleaner in Camp Borden, a job he did proudly for 23 years. Not everyone is capable of being an astronaut, scientist, engineer, doctor, teacher or nurse. What he taught me was that whatever you feel comfortable doing, do it to the best of your ability. I am not sure, but I believe that dad was probably the best Cleaner they had in all of Camp Borden. He took great pride in this work. His gleaming bathroom sinks and spotless classrooms drew praise from his superiors, who on his annual report cited his dedication, dependability and attention to detail.

I know that while I lived at home, he came home from work every afternoon, satisfied and proud, feeling that he had done a good days work.

3. Determine an achievable aim for yourself, regardless of what you are doing.

I attended the Canadian Forces Staff College at the age of 40. I learned so much during that year of training, but perhaps the most valuable and useful was the importance of determining the aim for anything that you wanted to do. We were taught that, "If you can get the aim right, the rest is easy." Setting the aim helps you to be satisfied with what you accomplish, and provides less chance of disappointment.

It isn't always easy to determine the aim. It often requires considerable thought, which I believe it is why many people do not bother trying to figure out the aim. Once, when I was Director of Information, a NFB producer and director came to me at DND headquarters looking for the help of the Canadian Forces to make a film about WWI war aces. They were so enthusiastic, had a budget of $2 million and were ready to start shooting. They just needed some help from the military with pilots, hangar space and some expertise. Once they had told me all this, I asked them what was the aim of making the film. "Well, that should be obvious," the producer said, "It's about planes flying in the First World War."

"But what do you hope to accomplish?" I asked. Neither could come up with an appropriate answer. I told them that I couldn't go to my superiors and ask for the help they were looking for unless they could tell them what the aim was for making the film.

They left my office rather disgruntled. I never heard from them again. But they did make the film and at a cost, I was told, of $4 million. I saw the final product as part of a group in a private viewing. I am not sure if this production ever hit the movie theatres.

I found that setting and focusing on an achievable aim could bring you much more satisfaction. For the three or four years before Shirlie's sister Mona died in 2017 at the age of 91, we would always drive the 1,350 km from Ottawa to Prince Edward Island to see her. Our aim was simply to spend as much time as possible with her during the four or five days we were on the island. We would eat all our meals in her apartment, drink wine, tell stories, hug each other, laugh and occasionally cry as we reminisced about our families and friends. These visits were all about her. We did not go out to any restaurants, visit the beaches, play the wonderful golf courses, visit old friends, or take in any theatre. But when we left, we felt complete. We had achieved our aim and had no regrets.

Ever since completing Staff College, I have used this technique both in my professional life and in our personal lives. I think it has resulted in us living much happier lives both as individuals and as a couple.

4. Dwell on your accomplishments or successes, not your perceived failures.

All too often I have worked or dealt with people who have concentrated on what they haven't been able to accomplish or what they considered to be their failures. One officer who worked for me was terribly unhappy because he hadn't been promoted to the level he thought he should have been. Twenty years before he had been a direct entry into the RCAF, had a high school education, and now served as a Major. He had a good wife, two great kids, a nice home and a salary that allowed him to live comfortably. Yet, he chose to concentrate on the fact that he hadn't been promoted. This made him miserable and impacted on those around him. He likely would have been a happier person if he could have focused on what he had been able to achieve. He would also have been a much more positive example for those who worked for him.

5. Be positive towards life and others. It is likely to rub off.

During my life I have noted that those who have a positive outlook on life normally lead a much happier life, and often a longer life. In addition, if they are in a leadership role, they can have a positive impact on those working for them. Nobody wants to work for someone who is miserable and always finding fault with his subordinates or superiors. I have worked for both types of individuals. It is much more fulfilling and constructive when you have a boss who can take on any challenge with a 'can-do' attitude, and sets the example with positive encouragement to his subordinates to get things done. I have also seen cases, particularly in the military, where when bosses were domineering and negative, these traits were taken home by subordinates who used the same methods on their wives and children.

6. Treat people the way you would like to be treated.

I think it is fair to say that most people want to be treated fairly and with respect. I saw lots of examples of this happening and not happening in the military. The military is a hierarchy. Those who are senior have an opportunity to treat people well, listen to their input before making a decision, or on the other hand, simply tell them what to do and expect them to obey, even if it might not be the best course of action or even the wrong decision.

When I was a young officer, I saw brand new Lieutenants, perhaps full of their own new importance, giving not well thought out orders to senior non- commissioned officers who, in some cases, had more years in the military than these officers had on earth. From observation, I learned quickly this was not the way to treat an experienced NCO. Their input could be invaluable to the success of whatever one was trying to accomplish. One thought that has guided me for years is, "Be nice to the people on the way up because you never know whom you might meet on the way down." Perhaps someday you will be in trouble and you could really need the help of that person that you have treated so poorly.

7. When you see what you want, go after it.

Often people find it difficult to make decisions which can either result in them not getting what they want or the delay costing them much more.

We started looking at buying a small condo in Florida in 1988. We set an aim to buy a small turnkey condo that required little outside maintenance, and was within the amount we wanted to pay and could afford.

For the next two years we researched many communities between Ft Myers and Naples. In one two-week period, while in Ft Myers taking a break from work, I visited 22 different developments. We finally decided on one that fit all our objectives and would achieve our aim... a medium priced, comfortable condo in a well-kept community, on a golf course with all the amenities where we could spend a few months each winter after we retired.

A few months later, while holidaying at our Time Share on Captiva Island, in January 1991, we saw a 'for sale' newspaper ad for a condo in our preferred community, where we had stayed several times with a friend. We called the agent and asked to see the home the next day. She was reluctant having shown it to 10 couples on that Saturday and wanted to take Sunday off. We convinced her to be there at 10 am on Sunday. She told us later that she thought it would be a waste of her time and would just mess up her day off. We showed up exactly at 10 am. We walked around the home, which was decorated nicely and completely equipped. The owner had spent 18 months in the home and had died suddenly a few weeks earlier.

At 10:10 am I looked at Ms Potts, the agent, and said, "How do we buy this condo?" She said," What?" I repeated my question. She said rather incredulously, "You want to buy this house?" "That's what I have been trying to communicate," I said. "Well, I guess if you give me a cheque for $1,000 that would be a contract."

"Write her out a cheque," I said to Shirlie, who I knew would support this decision.

At 10:30 we left and drove back to Captiva, arriving at noon. A few minutes later, the phone rang. It was Ms Potts. She told me she had just had a call from one of the couples that had toured the condo on Saturday morning. They had stayed up all night discussing whether to buy it or not. They told her that after hours of talking they realized that this was their dream house. "But it's sold," I told her. "I told them that," she said. "and they said, I was authorized to offer you a cheque for $5,000 US if you will tear up your cheque." "Too late," I said. "Sorry," and hung up.

Ever since Staff College, we have followed a policy of setting our aim, doing our research and being prepared to take something when it becomes available. This approach we have applied to almost all our decisions, including buying appliances to going on major vacations, to buying homes. We have always been happy with our decisions.

8. Share your talents and expertise to help others.

Everyone has talents and expertise, and some of those are not shared by all. Some can, as an example, be plumbers, computer-whizzes, designers, managers, planners, gardeners, bankers, lawyers or cleaners. But each has something that they can do to help others. We live in an active adult-style community of 133 homes where the majority are over 55, and most are retired. There are many widows amongst the approximately 200 residents, some of whom need help. It is gratifying to see how the men and women of this community share their talents and know-how to help anyone who needs help and who also step in to organize and run the multitude of activities undertaken on a daily basis.

In my case, I am not mechanically minded; I have told many of my friends that I cannot drive a nail in straight. Yet, I have some organizational abilities and communication skills that have helped me during my career. So, for more than 50 years I have volunteered with organizations at the local, regional, national and international level including, as an example, United Way, Children's Hospitals, Church Boards, Boy Scouts, Canadian Clubs, Community Associations, and the Corps of Commissionaires. These ongoing commitments have often taken me away from having time with my family, but Shirlie and I, and our children have been very blessed in our lifetime. We always agreed that helping others including, in some cases, those not as fortunate, was a way of giving back. And the appreciation that you receive from those being helped is often more rewarding than anything anyone could pay you.

9. Do what you think is right, not what will think will make you popular or get you promoted.

My theory is that in any job, or as you go through your life, you should stick to your principles and not change them because it might be less troublesome for you, or perhaps to your advantage to go along with the crowd.

I have seen many examples where advisors to senior officers and even to the Minister of National Defence have agreed with what that senior person has said even though they might not think it was the best or correct way to proceed. They just didn't want to disagree with the Boss.

But I always believed in telling my superiors what I thought they needed to know, not necessarily what they wanted to hear, regardless of what angst it might cause me. After all, as far as I was concerned, that was my job.

In one memorable case while at DND, I received a call from the ADM Policy who told me that the Minister was very upset with a story in the Toronto Globe and Mail and wanted me to call the Editor and make it known to him. I told him that I thought this was the wrong thing to do and I had another suggestion. He said, "You don't want to do what the Minister wants to do?" "You know I am a loyal officer," I said, "but I believe that the power of the press belongs to he who owns one, and in this case we, and particularly the Minister, would look foolish if we did what he wants to do." He told me he would get back to me.

A short time later, the Deputy Minister called and I went through the same conversation. "OK," he said, "I will call the Minister. He is on vacation at the cottage."

About thirty minutes later he called and said, "The Minister says to do it your way, but tell Len he bloody well better be right." I was fine with that. After all, it was my job to provide my advice based on my knowledge and experience. And, in this case, it worked out well.

I found during my career that when you provide honest advice your credibility goes up and you become more relied upon, even if you may not be on everyone's Christmas card list.

10. Be happy with the hand you are dealt; don't be envious of others.

Some of us are short, some tall, some good looking with a full head of hair, others maybe not so much. Some appear to be rich and drive fancy cars and live in big houses. Some have important jobs and others work at what are considered to be menial tasks.

Yet, I have learned not to envy anyone. Scratch the surface of some of those people who are handsome, rich, have high-level positions, live in big homes and drive fancy cars, and you might find they are not someone with whom you would want to change places.

Marital issues, kid problems, alcoholism; sometimes a combination of all three and more, impact on the happiness of these families that some would envy.

Best bet, in my opinion, is to try and be the best at what you do, look after your family and be happy with what you have. Don't dwell on what you think others have or what you feel you do not. I grew up very poor in Creemore as a teenager although I didn't know I was poor until years later when, on a return visit, someone in the village told me our family had been poor. Mom fed me good meals, I played sports, had friends in the village and at school. I didn't envy anyone and still do not today. In fact, every day I thank God for all the blessings that have been bestowed upon us.

11. Be tolerant. Don't expect everyone to do what you would do or do it the way you would do it.

As we get older, and wiser (?), we sometimes think that age and experience gives us the right to be critical, particularly of people who are younger than us, and who do things differently. It is hard for some of us who were born before there was television in our living rooms to try and deal with the incredibly rapid advance of technology today. We think perhaps that the manner which others in newer generations are doing things, particularly our children and grandchildren, will mean that they will not be able to have the same good lifestyle that we have led. But no doubt our parents and grandparents probably thought the same about us as we grew up.

There is little doubt that the advances being made today are astronomically faster than those of the 20th century. This appears to raise the expectation level and put more stress on most. But we had to learn from our mistakes. That should also go for our descendants.

12. Live every day to the fullest.

Each of us should try and make the most of every day we have. Too many people say that, someday they will take the kids to a ballgame, go fishing with a son, start that project that they promised to do months ago, or take that trip they have promised their spouse they would take for years.

Nobody knows just how long we have on this life journey. For some, it is 20 years, for others 95. Regardless, none of us want to look back in our final days and say we wished we had done things differently. Make plans, look forward to what you are going to do tomorrow and then relish in what you accomplished that day.

Be grateful for what you have; enjoy what you have. After all, as far as I know,

LIFE IS NOT A DRESS REHEARSAL